SO-AIF-767

CHALIAPIN

Chaliapin in the part of Boris in Mussorgsky's opera Boris Godunov;
portrait by A. Golovin, 1912 (Russian Museum, Leningrad).

CHALIAPIN

An Autobiography
as told to
MAXIM GORKY

With supplementary correspondence
and notes, translated from the Russian,
compiled and edited by
NINA FROUD and JAMES HANLEY

STEIN AND DAY/*Publishers*/New York

All rights reserved
© Nina Froud and James Hanley, 1967
Library of Congress Catalog Card No. 67–25616
Printed in Great Britain

Stein and Day/*Publishers*/7 East 48 Street, New York, N.Y. 10017

FOR TAMARA
WITH LOVE

Translator's Note

It is some fifteen years since I first contemplated the present book, as a consequence of which I made a number of trips to Russia, realizing that its background would never be right without examination of the material at the source, and I thoroughly explored the many archives that were made available to me. It was during my study of the correspondence of many of Chaliapin's contemporaries that I accidentally stumbled upon a reference to a manuscript about the singer written by Maxim Gorky. Two further years of burrowing in the archives eventually placed the Gorky manuscript in my hands; the first paragraph I read yielded up the hitherto elusive picture of their early life together, and it was depicted with all of Gorky's force, mastery and wrath. By this time I assumed a guardian angel to be working on my behalf, for here was the only possible opening to a book on Chaliapin, miraculously in my hands.

The resulting twelve years have been spent by James Hanley and myself, unravelling further mysteries, putting the pieces together, and finding even greater treasures, diaries, letters, and contemporary newspaper reports, out of which grew the pattern and volume of the present book. It was not astonishing that the supplementary material, and especially the letters, had not been available in the West, since much of it had been tucked away in the archives of various Soviet Institutions. But that a piece of writing by Maxim Gorky could be completely unknown seemed greatly puzzling to me, considering that it had been serialized in the Russian journal *Letopis* in 1917. We discovered that the explanation had its fantastic side, though it made a curious kind of sense, if one takes into consideration the strange ways of publishers.

How did Gorky come to write the book? It emerges from the examined correspondence, some of which is reproduced in this book, that it came to Gorky's notice that Chaliapin, then in the South of France, was being pressed to write his autobiography by a local French journalist, of no great importance, who would presumably ghost the work. Certainly the life of such a celebrity would have been of great public interest, and perhaps a very lucrative one as well.

Gorky was appalled by this news, visualising as he did the hotchpotch that would result from such a project, since the reporter lacked any knowledge of the Russian language, or of Russia itself. Gorky's letters to the singer concerning this are very explicit indeed, since none was closer to Chaliapin, and knew him more intimately. Indeed, he had begun writing his autobiography years earlier in the Crimea, and to Gorky there had seemed to be only two possibilities. Either Chaliapin would do it himself (writing as it came), or better still, he thought, the singer would come and stay with him in Capri, and Gorky himself would write it. The second procedure was adopted and Chaliapin arrived in Capri, and talked, and talked, and talked, whilst Gorky's secretary took down endless notes. These she later, and not without difficulty, transcribed, and Gorky took them, and all the oral material Chaliapin had supplied, as a basis, and wrote the life.

Though Gorky himself was an exile, he yet enjoyed a retainer from the journal *Letopis*, and was thus obliged to submit whatever he wrote to that journal. The manuscript being finished, Chaliapin took away the top copy, and it was agreed that Gorky would send his copy to *Letopis*, and allow a strictly limited extract from it to be published. But not surprisingly, the editor of *Letopis* found the material so exciting that he disregarded Gorky's specific instructions, and printed the lot. After all, Gorky was in Italy, and Chaliapin in Monte Carlo, too far away for any effective protest to be made. The editor also imagined he had covered himself by crediting the author with increased payment pro rata. Neither Gorky nor Chaliapin had been informed of this, and the first news of it broke disastrously, when an American publisher, to whom the singer was in the process of selling the book, rejected it as soon as he heard of its appearance in *Letopis*. The fact that this highly literary magazine could only be read by a handful of people inside Russia made no difference. The American publisher took the understandable view that he was paying the highest price for the manuscript, and was fully entitled to the world rights in it, as he had been led to expect. Thus, the cream having been skimmed, the "property" had lost its allure.

Our own contention is that the copyright situation being what it was at that time, the American publisher was probably also apprehensive about the possibility of a pirated edition. It was this incident that was responsible for the first serious rift between Gorky and Chaliapin, and the acrimonious correspondence that followed it temporarily marred the relationship. To save the situation, Chaliapin promised the American publisher a brand new version of his autobiography and he is said to have gone back to his French reporter. To what extent was the manuscript new? Obviously it had to cover the same ground, so the same episodes would be recounted. But that it had now lost the touch of Gorky's hand was painfully obvious, and a marvellous, fascinating story had been rendered unreadable (I have tried to read it, and I know). But whoever it was that helped in the editing of the "new" version, made up for his lack of knowledge of the Russian background by inventing *couleur locale* with a vengeance.

No one would disagree about the advisability of leaving certain untranslatable Russian words, like *vodka*, *troika*, even *sputnik*, in Russian. But the book with which I struggled, and it was never a penance to read about Chaliapin, was generously sprinkled with bogus Russianisms, in italics, leaving Russian words for which perfectly adequate translations exist in every language, like "bed", "chair", "little fathers" and "little mothers" haunting the pages, presumably to immerse the reader in the true "Russian" spirit. Not surprisingly the foreign editions based on this "original" met with little success.

Some ten years ago we were told that the publisher who brought out the volume, of the original 2,000 copies printed, still had some eight hundred in stock. This sounded to us like fatherly advice, to save us wasting our time on the proposed book. We were not held back by this, and it is for the reader ultimately to decide whether our time was wasted.

In June of 1966 I was in Moscow, and was fortunate enough to be received by Irina Fyodorovna Chaliapin, the singer's daughter. I found her flat in Kutuzovsky Prospect to be a veritable museum, filled with innumerable portraits of her father, his own drawings, as well as many personal belongings of the great singer, all carefully and lovingly preserved by his daughter. She spoke first of the great part which painters and sculptors had played in her father's life, and of his special approach to the art of make-up.

V. A. Serov, outwardly a dour and reserved man, but in reality a gay and witty person, was able, in his conversations no less than in his drawings, to produce whole images, with the briefest gestures and intonations.

Korovin, on the other hand, was a voluble, lively and temperamental person and raconteur, and this quality of his shows in his colourful, luminous paintings. If one were to make a special study of the Chaliapin make-up technique (and he invariably did his own), one sees at once that he took his clear-cut lines from Serov, and the picturesqueness from Korovin. Chaliapin had a rare quality for rendering the picturesque, not only in the regal roles of *Boris*, or Holofernes in A. N. Serov's *Judith*, but also in the rags of the miller in *Russalka*, and the peasant coat of Susanin. Undoubtedly, and I quote Irina, "as my father used to say, painting played a very important role in his life and work".

Chaliapin's contemporaries have all stressed the brilliance, the intense life he gave to his roles, and each pose or gesture cried out to be put on canvas. It is little wonder then that painters like Korovin, Golovin, and others, liked painting him. He was painted in costume, and in every conceivable attire; he was to remain their most fascinating subject, and not only because he was a celebrity. Serov painted him as a young man full of vigour and strength, in an almost nonchalant pose, the features radiating energy and determination, and always the characteristic forelock above the intelligent brow.

Repin was another of his friends, whose studio in Finland Chaliapin loved to visit, there to pose, and to listen fascinated to the artist's stories. For Chaliapin, Repin remained the living link with a vanished century, so full of distant and hallowed shadows. Repin was to tell him of Pauline Viardot's much talked of silver samovar, of her house in Paris, where Turgenev, Flaubert, Maupassant, and the then youthful Zola, were frequent guests. Repin described for him how Viardot sang, what Lizst looked like on the concert platform, described Dostoievsky's features, and even gave an imitation of the manner in which he walked.

Chaliapin would recline on a vast sofa, posing for Repin, forever fascinated by the painter's aged and work-worn hands, so bringing to mind the wonderful "Barge Haulers", for, being a Volga man, the singer had seen and remembered the Volga boatmen. Unfortunately this portrait no longer survives, for Repin was dissatisfied with it, and destroyed it, painting another subject over it. Only a photograph remains showing the artist at the easel and the singer posing.

I am particularly indebted to the Bakhrushin Museum (the Central Theatre Museum), the most beautiful museum building I have ever seen, with an atmosphere all its own, which magically re-creates for us the mastery and greatness of Chaliapin. There are many visual reminders of his artistic triumphs, and the unique voice, so fortunately preserved for us by records, thrills with its subtlety and variation of psychological intonations, and continues, and will continue, to yield us an aesthetic pleasure.

The director of the museum, a charming woman of great erudition, showed me a bouquet of flowers on the piano in the Chaliapin Pavilion, a homage from the singer's admirers. She told me that many people, some of them old ladies, came regularly to "visit" the singer, to hear him singing—the tapes are always there to be switched on—and to bring him flowers. Even when these "regulars" go away on holiday they leave instructions for flowers to be delivered to Chaliapin.

He constantly strove for perfection. Of him Rachmaninov has said: "A limitless phenomenal talent, in whatever he cared to approach. Music was his natural element, and he made it his business to know every note played by the orchestra. He knew not only his own role, but every part in the work concerned, and his study of them was deep and earnest."

Nature had been generous in its endowments. Chaliapin played the piano, violin and cello, and in 1917 even appeared as a conductor at the Mariinsky Theatre. Nor was he lacking in literary or linguistic ability. He wrote both lyrical and humorous verse, and in a later autobiographical work entitled *Mask and Soul*, wrote many articles, essays and poems. He translated the text of Boito's *Mefistofele* into Russian, and his roles in Russian works into Italian and French. And this from a man with only four years education in an elementary school, and not a single formal singing lesson.

Chaliapin was an outstandingly natural actor. Stanislavsky always considered him the master of the spoken word and frequently let it be known that he took the singer as a model for his "method". The famous actress, Savina, recalls an incident that took place in a painter's studio, which illustrates the singer's rare talent for improvisation. In the crowded studio, host and guests were carrying on one of those interminable Russian arguments about the meaning of Art, but Chaliapin took no part in this noisy and endless discussion. He quietly left the room. Suddenly the door burst

open and he stood on the threshold looking deathly pale, and wildly dishevelled, announcing with trembling lips, "Fire!" Panic followed, the studio was
filled with shrieks, and everyone made for the door. Some tried to jump
out of the window. In a flash the mask of fear and despair vanished from
the singer's face. Smoothing down his hair he announced with a laugh,
"That, gentlemen, is what I call Art!" Those present were convinced they
actually saw flames under the door.

In his memoirs, devoted to the literary and theatrical figures of the time,
the actor Nicolai Khodotov, of the Alexandrinsky Theatre, gave an illumin-
ating picture of the young Chaliapin, in which he describes how Dalsky,
rudely, though expressively, initiated the singer into the very mystery of evil,
vividly describing how Mephistopheles should emerge from the darkness.
This actor, wholly intent on submerging his life in debauchery, even to the
point of neglecting his own talents, was so impressed by his pupil, so carried
away by his own enthusiasm, that he was to instil many valuable lessons into
Chaliapin's ear.

The singer was at that time appearing at the Panayev Theatre, situated
on the banks of the Neva. It no longer exists. A dark, gloomy place, it held
no great attraction for the public. But Chaliapin had attracted attention,
and drew the public there. Even *The Artist*, a somewhat august journal, said
that Chaliapin was a "pleasant basso cantante", following his appearance in
The Tales of Hoffmann.

In his memoirs, Khodotov relates an anecdote of how the singer came
to give his first St. Petersburg concert, a charity performance in aid of
poor students, in which Dalsky was to have taken the leading part, and
as was the custom in those days a young student called for him in a hired
carriage. But Dalsky did not feel like going out, and suggested that the
young Chaliapin should take his place. This caused some commotion since
the inhabitants of the Palais Royal had to pool their resources to equip
Chaliapin, even down to a frock-coat. Remembering the singer's great
height, it could have been no easy matter. But he managed, and went to
the concert, which was a great success, and the student who accompanied
him on that occasion was later to become the great actor of the Moscow
Arts Theatre, Vasily Kachalov.

People now began to take notice of Chaliapin, and he was much talked
about. The Mariinksy Theatre accepted him, but it meant little, and was
no grand beginning, since, though he was accepted, he was given no work
at all. This outraged the famous bass, Koryakin, who, to help Chaliapin,
pretended to be ill, thus enabling the young singer to appear in Dargomyzhsky's opera, *Russalka*. Following the production, a well known critic wrote:

"Last night, and perhaps for the first time, Dargomyzhsky's exquisite
work revealed what talent is called for in the vocal rendering of the part
of the Miller, and it heralds something new and wonderful for the Russian
Theatre."

In his youthful dreams the singer had assumed that the life of the artist
was free and easy. Thus, it was inevitable that following the setbacks,

Chaliapin was to be assailed by doubts. Even at the height of his fame, these gnawing doubts would creep in. With him striving for perfection was a real passion.

He did not remain long with the Mariinsky Theatre, a bare year, and then left. The administration, mostly civil servants, let him go lightly, but one has to assume that his goodbye to St. Petersburg was one of no regrets. The stale, red-tape-ridden atmosphere of the Imperial Theatres had begun to have its effect, and out of this stifling frustration came many a bitter comment.

"I am no longer proud of the fact that I am considered an artist of the Imperial Theatres," he said. "Something has gone from my very soul. I feel empty. I have been walking along a beautiful wide road, and suddenly arrived at the cross-roads, and do not know which way to turn.

"Civil servants in uniform, carrying ignorance and indifference in their very persons. How dull and stupid. They know little or nothing about the demands of art, and will never know its power. Idiots! Lording it over artists."

He was to sing at the Mamontov Private Opera in Petersburg, in 1898, and this gave the famous critic Stassov an opportunity to be scathing at the expense of the whole Imperial Theatre administration. He wrote:

"The Mariinsky Theatre appears to have decided that it can do without Chaliapin. It seems that we just don't know what to do with our super-abundance of talents. This promising singer has had to go to a privately run theatre in Moscow. No-one detained Chaliapin, no-one wanted him. What's the use of him?"

These experiences did the singer nothing but good. Now he had the advantages of meeting many musicians, painters, actors, and was able to attend many of the celebrated Andreyev "Fridays", to which flooded the most gifted in the capital. Andreyev was the founder of the folk instrument orchestras. Of this experience the singer has written:

"This was my new world, and I responded with a leap, I drowned in the atmosphere, I watched, I listened intently, and I learned."

Khodotov is rich in stories of Chaliapin, one of which describes the singer arriving in Istanbul to the astonishment of the Turks who did nothing but gape at this giant in his long coat and Russian shirt, and the high boots. They took him for a Cossack. Later he was to cause a sensation in the baths, where he tried out his voice. This full-throated exercise caused much agitation among the Arab and Turkish clients.

In another story he describes how Chaliapin came on stage and noticed a fellow artist and friend sitting in the front row, with a venerable old gentleman beside him, who, before the singer had uttered a single note, was jumping up and down and wildly applauding. "Applauded even before he heard me!" said Chaliapin, when his friend arrived in his dressing-room. "And what was the venerable gentleman whispering to you?" he asked, to which the friend replied, "He is a famous surgeon, and the moment you appeared he gasped out at me, 'My God what a magnificent skeleton.'"

Even at fifty Chaliapin retained an incredible lightness in his movements; the control of his great frame seemed only one of the many gifts he had. He had a high bass baritone full of beauty, an almost endless variety of nuance, and a nobility of timbre. The voice could be powerful and commanding, humble and submissive, one moment full of youthful vigour, and the next creaking with senility, whatever the part demanded. His gift of diction was strikingly natural, never a word lost, sung loud or soft. He had great expressiveness, an iron control over rhythm, and not least a complete freedom of delivery that flowed out of the music itself.

Chaliapin was to live another twenty-nine years after his initial appearance in Massenet's *Don Quixote*, but the role was virtually his last creation. Yet he continued to search, to hope, to dream of new roles. When Taneyev's opera, *Oedipus Rex*, was announced to the press, and he learned that the chief role had been scored for a bass, he at once asked the composer to come and see him. However, nothing came of this, and the opportunity to create this tragic role was lost to him.

In 1915 it was reported that Chaliapin and Gorky were together in Finland, working on the libretto of a four-act opera. This was a dream close to Chaliapin's heart, for in 1913 he had written to Gorky saying he was sending him material on Stepan Razin, and wished Gorky to do the libretto. But the libretto for the four-act opera, for which Glazunov was to do the music, likewise failed, and again the dream faded. Gorky himself had long been thinking of an opera based on his own epic, *Vasily Buslayev*, in which venture Chekhov had been encouraging, and Chaliapin was highly excited at the thought of the role of Vasily which he was to portray.

It came to naught, so that finally it was the chivalrous Don Quixote that he came to, for always he had been carried away by noble dreams, and uplifting illusions, to such an extent that he was eventually to fall for the colourless libretto and the superficial, sentimental music of Massenet. If *Don Quixote* lived at all, it did so only by the genius of Chaliapin. Of his performance in this role, the Russian writer, Lev Nikulin, has written:

"In the aria of the first act the voice was clear, even festive, and this clarity of tone, lucid as was the singer's gaze and smile, illuminated for us the thought and meaning of its creator. The outward appearance of Chaliapin was a miracle of art. The audience saw the sharpened features, the haggard, emaciated face, the bitter smile, the burning glow of the dream. The great body, imprisoned in the ridiculous armour, was astonishingly right. It was an inspired conception of the tragic hero. Only a glance was required of us to mirror a noble and unhappy dreamer, misunderstood, irrevocably, finally. Chaliapin knew the secret that for centuries had captured the hearts of readers. The element of tragedy was never lost in this portrayal, especially in those moments when the dream was to clash with pathetic reality, the personification of grief and disillusionment, the collapse of everything loved. When, defeated, he drags after him his huge body, we realize he has taken leave of everything on earth."

Both Chaliapin and Gorky were destined to be linked together, inescapably,

13

right to the end. As children, only a street's length separated them, and neither could have been aware of how parallel their lives were to run, the one to become Russia's finest singer, the other her greatest writer of the period. Strangely, too, their very sense of mission seemed identical. And if we examine the facts, so well described by Chaliapin, it is immediately apparent that they were bound to be the sort of friends they were. Later, Gorky was to put these facts into literary shape, in his own remarkable and unmistakable style. Their childhood and youth were similar. As Chaliapin remarked:

"When I was a small boy in Kazan, apprenticed to the cobbler Andreyev, who lived on the corner of Prolomnaya Street, Gorky was an apprentice on the opposite corner of the Great Prolomnaya, serving in a baker's shop. I cannot recall the baker's name, though I remember that Dokuchayev's Tea Shop was just above it."

I have seen a photograph of this street. It was here that Gorky drew on the material for his first book, *Twenty-Six Men and a Girl*.

At sixteen Chaliapin was working his way from Astrakhan to the Nizhni-Novgorod Fair, and did a spell as a stevedore in the Samara port. Gorky too, was there, working as a manual labourer, wearing trousers made from flour sacks. In the Caucasus their paths were once more to cross, Chaliapin working as a clerk at the railway station, and Gorky as fitter and greaser in the workshop. He recalls an episode, so characteristic of their background: "We were neighbours in Tiflis, though by this time I was a singer, doing my first season on the Golovinsky Prospect. Close at hand was Gorky, a prisoner in the Metekh Castle." There is a well-known story of how, attending an audition together held by the Serebryakov choir, Gorky was accepted and Chaliapin rejected, as the latter's voice was just breaking at that time.

Gorky loved Chaliapin, both as man and artist, and he described their first meeting.

"This man Chaliapin is a genius, if you will forgive an understatement. Endowed with a natural intelligence, he is, in the social sense, a babe, although he is far too intelligent for a singer. Being so, it makes it easy for him to perform miracles. *What* a Mephistopheles, what a Prince Galitsky! He excels in concert work. I asked him to sing in aid of our People's Theatre, and he did, singing amongst other ballads: *The Two Grenadiers*, *The Prisoner's Song*, and *The Song of the Flea*. My friend, it was incredible. I have experienced nothing like it. Absolutely magnificent and original. I would go and hear him even if he sang but a single line, 'God have mercy on us,' for a whole evening. I swear to you that he could sing this phrase in such a way that God himself would be bound to hear him, and further still, either show us mercy or reduce us all to pulp. It would depend on Chaliapin."

We have spoken of Chaliapin's many gifts, and when we think of his productions of *Khovanshchina*, of *Boris Godunov*, *The Power of the Enemy*, and other works, we think of them in terms of an exceptional artistic ensemble, an organic unity of music, drama, and artistic design.

But not the least of his gifts was as a painter. He created many original drawings, some of which are kept in the leading art galleries and museums in the Soviet Union, including the Tretyakov Gallery, Bakhrushin Museum, the Leningrad Theatrical Museum, the Russian Museum, and others. He was equally successful in his efforts as a sculptor. He experimented with pottery and ceramics; the Bakhrushin Museum has a number of his plates, and his daughter, Irina, counts her father's gift to her children of cups with self-portraits amongst her most treasured possessions. This incredible many-sidedness of talent and artistic interests brought him into close contact with many distinguished men of Russian Art and Letters, and he counted among his friends, Gorky, Chekhov, Bunin, Andreyev, Kuprin, Grechaninov, Skitalets, and Rachmaninov. And amongst painters who influenced him were Repin, Polenov, Levitan, Vasnetzov, Serov, Korovin, Golovin, Ostroukhov. Many have immortalised him in their work.

Chaliapin's talent was so great and his art so influenced all walks of artistic life at the end of the nineteenth and beginning of the twentieth century, both at home and abroad, that it will never cease to attract the attention of musicians, artists, and writers, for he touched their worlds at almost every point.

I will close these notes with three Chaliapin stories from his accompanist, Ivor Newton, whose reminiscences have recently been published,[1] and who has kindly allowed me to quote. Of a recording session in London with Chaliapin, he writes:

"I arrived punctually, braced myself to meet the unaccountable, remembering all I had heard of his temperamental outbursts, and his capacity for hardly governable rage. Everyone present, as we awaited his arrival, even the recording engineers, appeared highly nervous of the terrifying morning in prospect, and perhaps the terrifying afternoon. Chaliapin had asked for a small orchestra with balalaikas to provide local colour with the piano for a Russian song, *Down the Petersky*.

"When he eventually arrived, beautifully dressed, and sunnily charming, he bowed, apologised for being late, and explained that his tailor had detained him. His courtesy was overwhelming, and he bowed to the only lady present as though she were a duchess. He settled down to work, and all went well until they reached *Down the Petersky*. It was difficult to get the balalaikas to play as the singer wanted them, and the more the music was discussed, the less satisfactory the performance became. Eventually Chaliapin decided to take control. 'May I take your baton?' he asked the conductor with the utmost politeness, and from that moment things went right. The band played as though inspired. The largest balalaika was in the hands of the only woman present, who was dressed severely in black, and, as the charitable put it, of a certain age. Her playing still caused him some concern, and, in the mood of extreme graciousness which still reigned, he asked her permission to demonstrate how he wished a certain glissando to be played. She then played it perfectly, and he thanked her, and threw her a kiss, and for a

---

[1] *At the Piano* by Ivor Newton, Hamish Hamilton, London, 1966. The above extracts are quoted with the kind permission of the author and publishers.

moment she became positively beautiful. I then began to realize the complete validity of the Chaliapin legend as I had known it."

Commenting on Chaliapin's sense of humour, Ivor Newton writes: "At times he was capable of wildly high-spirited nonsense," and recalls an occasion following a concert in a Scottish town, when the Lord Provost came backstage to pay his respects. The singer immediately noticed the dour, severe, almost puritanical look. "With a wave of his hand he presented me to the visiting dignitary. 'Sir,' he said, with great dignity, 'may I present my accompanist, Mr. Ivor Newton, a friend of sixty years' standing.' That, I could not help hoping was self-evident nonsense. He continued: 'In the world of music he is an aristocrat,' and then added with a conspiratorial whisper, 'and he is a rare judge of women.'

"As a singer and actor, Chaliapin was pre-eminent. Simply by virtue of his own performances, he set up a new standard of acting on the operatic stage. A born, instinctive actor, he was never less than natural, and he acted, not for effect, but because it was his nature to do so. Whatever he sang, he was able to colour his voice marvellously to suit his needs. Quiet songs, like *In Questa Tomba* appealed to him, and it sometimes seems that no-one has really sung a love song since Chaliapin died. His telling *mezza voce*, unusual in a bass voice, was always effective, but especially so in love songs, and he seemed to revel in his soft, high notes. One of his favourite concert items was an aria from *Aleko*, which Rachmaninov wrote when he was only twenty-one. It ends with a postlude of about twenty bars. Chaliapin would never permit this to be cut, and not a sound would come from the audience until I had finished playing. If applause ever kills the closing bars of a song, it is because the singer, by relaxing after his final notes, suggests to them that everything important has been done. Chaliapin knew this well enough, and could stand silent and motionless without relaxing a fraction of his control over his listeners until I finally released the pedal.

"When he first went to America, after the revolution, he did not take the precaution of learning English, and his Russian-born manager, Sol Hurok, had been long enough in America to forget most of his own language, but not long enough to perfect his English. Hurok arranged for a large press conference for the great singer, and asked an eager audience for questions.

"'May we ask Mr. Chaliapin how the revolution has affected the Arts in Russia?' asked one journalist.

"The question was translated, and Chaliapin thought quietly for a moment or two. Then, with all the dramatic power at his command, he rose and began speaking in Russian. He began quietly, but this quietness was that of a master of histrionic effect. What he told his audience, he explained to me later, was that Art in Russia stood like a knight in impregnable and indestructible armour. As he elaborated his ideas, he introduced into the oration every shade of tone in his magnificent voice, used every facial expression, and every masterly gesture of the eloquent hands. Climaxes

16

were followed by tense, dramatic silences, until with a cry of triumph he flung himself back in his chair.

"The journalists had remained spellbound, and turned eagerly to the manager, who hesitantly stood up for some moments, in deepest thought, and then delivered his translation: 'Mr. Chaliapin says it is much the same'."

Nina Froud

Acknowledgments

Through the years of assiduous work in preparing this book on Chaliapin based entirely on Russian sources, we have received aid and encouragement from many Soviet institutions.

We wish to express our deepest thanks to the following for their invaluable help and co-operation:

To the Iskusstvo State Publishing House, Moscow, especially for generously supplying us with the photographic material, printed for this first English edition and contributed by the family archives of I. F. Chaliapin, the State Central Theatrical Museum named after A. A. Bakhrushin, the Bolshoy Theatre Museum, the Leningrad Theatrical Museum, the Central Cine-Photo-Phono Archive, the Museum of the Leningrad Kirov Theatre of Opera and Ballet, the Gorky Museum, the State Russian Museum, the Tretyakov Gallery, the Brodsky Museum, Leningrad, and a number of private collections.

Chaliapin's letters to his children are published in English for the first time in the present edition by courtesy of Irina Feodorovna Chaliapin and the Iskusstvo Publishing House. The Chaliapin-Gorky correspondence was originally published in Russian in a volume of Gorky Readings printed by the U.S.S.R. Academy of Sciences in 1954. Chaliapin's obituary note on Gorky is taken from the same source.

Other material has been contributed by the Department of Manuscripts of the State Central Archives of Literature and Art, Moscow, the State Theatrical Museum, the State Lenin Library, Moscow, the Leningrad Public Library named after Saltykov-Shchedrin, the Gorky archives, the Museum of Literature, the Tretyakov Gallery, the Bolshoy Theatre Museum, the U.S.S.R. Academy of Sciences Institute of Russian Literature, Leningrad, from the Chaliapin family archives, and other private sources.

We also wish to thank Ivor Newton for his kind permission to quote an extract from his autobiography *At the Piano*, published by Hamish Hamilton Ltd. in 1966.

Last but not least, our thanks are due to the Association of Film Makers of the U.S.S.R. for facilitating the fearsome task of research.

Nina Froud
James Hanley

Contents

List of Plates

Introduction

In the summer of 1913, there arrived in London an opera company from Russia, of which company Feodor Ivanovich Chaliapin was the principal bass. The first presentation of Modest Mussorgsky's *Boris Godunov* could only be described as a great artistic explosion. Nothing like it had been seen in London, nor has the capital seen another season like it in the half century since. For opera-goers it was a memorable and incredible experience, the credit for which must surely go to the late Sir Thomas Beecham, who in his lifetime had done so much for the cause of music, and particularly opera. This man of genius and imagination squandered fortunes, large and small, in those crusading years, and the fading away of his British National Opera Company, after much struggle, indicates the pathetic nature of the response. He was surrounded by philistines. Some day, perhaps, a tributary tome will do him justice, for he changed the whole climate of music for this country, and his valiant efforts are a part of musical history.[1]

The focal point of this wonderful explosion was Chaliapin himself who headed the company. He was a man of the people, and it was something he never forgot. He was to become the greatest bass singer in history, and the finest operatic artist of all time. He is yet without an equal, and others who sing Boris, and Farlaf, Konchak and Dositheus, stand in his shadow. From the very moment he appeared over the horizon, the case was altered. He revolutionised opera, and it has never been the same since. He was not only a splendid singer, but a superb actor, and he has handed down to other artists the secret and art of make-up, and the magic of it. He transformed what he touched.

To-day there are no Russian seasons. The production of Russian works is itself of so fugitive a nature that one has to assume the enterprise to be more a matter of whim than actual consideration and calculation. The few productions England has had of the Mussorgsky work tend, almost obstinately, to lack the grand manner, to give out the feeling of "spectacle". They are exact, but passionless, unimaginative, badly produced, and with poor sets, uninspiring but safe, and sometimes, as in the hallucination scene,

---

[1] Perhaps his only Russian equivalent, in the purely philanthropic sense, was the railway magnate, Savva Mamontov, a source of hope, and indeed achievement for many Russian artists, and not least Chaliapin himself. Mamontov was utterly devoted to the Arts, and not only built theatres, but ushered in and supported a whole school of painters, of which Golovin and Serov are perhaps the most outstanding.

made noticeable only by the skeletal surrounds. Whether, in a recent production of *Boris Godunov*, Czar Boris noticed two very venerable Russian bishops blessing themselves in markedly different ways would seem to be more a matter for the producer than the usurper himself. And the absence of the great Polish scenes does not help, nor does the sheer poverty of the English language libretto.

There would seem to be no English Hofmannsthals about these days, though a recent announcement about a new arrangement of the libretto has a remedial sound about it, and might be encouraging. A Russian work, to be whole, total, requires its native language, and one is fully aware of the obstacles this presents. But there are Russian companies waiting to be invited to Covent Garden. The loyalty shown to language in the presentation of other works is too obvious to remain unnoticeable. One bows to the language in *Otello*, in *Don Carlos*, in *Falstaff*, to take Verdi alone, but quite often this is topped by much trifle, and Covent Garden can claim its due portion of Italian sugar. Chaliapin, who noticed many things, noticed this.

The tall, striking, and handsome figure, the subject of this book, was born on February 11, 1873, in the poorer quarters of Kazan. Of the humblest parentage, he was to experience nothing of the comforts and delights, the security, assurance, and educational advantages that we know to-day, and accept as the best formative elements in a normal childhood. His own was extremely harsh, and often without hope. He described it in person to Maxim Gorky, without rancour or bitterness, beautifully, and with a gaiety and humour made exceptional by the very fact of its origins. The very first miracle for this child was the one of actual survival, and perhaps there was one splendid day in his youth when he realized it. Chaliapin adored his parents, especially his mother, as he did his own children, and the many letters in this book remain the proof of it. And little did he know the world figure he was to become, nor the countless occasions on which he would circle the globe.

Chaliapin loved his country with a passionate devotion; he never forgot it. A Russian, at no matter what point of the compass he may be standing, is never really far from home. Gorky himself might have said that it was one of the virtues of being Russian. His relationship with Maxim Gorky dates almost from childhood, and they were to the heart close for a lifetime. The Russia of their day beggars description, for when it was dark it was very dark indeed, and even daylight itself seemed without eyes. They shared the horrors as well as the dreams, the hopelessness as well as the hope, the gnawing frustration, the utter meaninglessness of life, engendered only by the harshest tyranny ever known, in a Czar-ridden, police-ridden country. For them, as for others, life was one long continuous battle. Poverty was everywhere about, and there seemed to be no horizon, in any direction. The contrast between those who had, and those who had not, between those who waited and those who were attended to at once, is giant in its divisions. And always there was the corruption, the drunkenness, the terrible indifference, and not least perhaps the most appalling inertia. These very forces converged and fought each other for a place on the map. An insensate race, in which many were to be crushed. Chaliapin and Gorky were the living witnesses of it all.

This vast country boasted its own Acherontian monsters, and the earnest and the innocent were kicked into the gutter.

The struggle was endless, for survival, for a hope, for any hope. Both men lived in the gutter, and climbed out of it, by greatness of heart, by a sturdy belief, but perhaps most of all by the gift of their own natural endowments.

If Chaliapin had not sung, he would have acted in straight theatre, and if he had not done that, then he would have written, or sculpted or painted. However, the important thing was to survive, to hold on to it, and to carry it with one through every long, yawning, meaningless, bitter, Russian day. That he and Gorky did so is the measure of their achievement. They were not only great artists; they were a real *purpose* in the life of their country. Always they were aware of the great need for change, and they said so, privately and publicly. Because of their very origins they were always to remain suspect. To be suspect in their day was also a singular distinction.

The horizon advanced and receded, and advanced again. The sounds of revolution came early to their ears, and it was something to remember. The very climate seethed with the great needs; the desperation reverberated from one end of the land to the other. At the age of sixteen Gorky was already in prison, and Chaliapin had made his first attempt to kill himself. Gorky himself was to try later, but fortunately for us both of them failed.

Even before World War I, we find the singer discussing with Gorky the possibilities of his joining the Social-Democratic Party. Later Chaliapin was to write:

"If I did not join the Socialists it was only because he, Gorky, looked at me most severely, and then said in the friendliest of tones, 'You are not fitted for this. I beg you to remember, once and for all, never join *any* party. Be what you are, an artist. That will be quite sufficient.' " That wise counsel reveals not only a depth and closeness of friendship, but it also obliterates the many acres of words, written and spoken, profound and trivial, that have exhausted themselves on the problem of the artist in society, and his commitment to it. It is a dilemma, and it will remain a dilemma. The artist will always require a freedom, always be the floating doubter in the mind of society. His real home lies on its fringe. Society looks into the mirror, and so does the artist, and they will always see different things, and even the very levels of the air may seem different to both. But the battle of words will still continue. From Maxim Gorky, Chaliapin received the only answer that was necessary.

He was far too engrossed in his art, and in the pursuit of its surprises and revelations. From the age of five the child was already winged for his journey. He was possessed, he was driven, and driven again towards this vision of theatre, the living centre and witness of human curiosity, with its limitless possibilities. His spontaneous, passionate, and unrestrained nature was never, and could not be confined to any one fixed area. He was always moving, always exploring, always giving out, searching for new frontiers in his quest for perfection.

The Russian people were hungry, down-trodden, with each day as bloody and exacting as the next. There was something for Chaliapin to do, and this was a duty. He could sing to these people, he could lift the heart. It was his true commitment, for then, for always. And it was this great concern for theatre, for the realization of its best fruits, and of what had been entrusted to him (he had been voted into the Arts council of the Mariinsky Theatre) that was to lead him eventually into the private sanctum of Lenin himself. Things *had* changed, and the very violence of it was unbalancing, a kind of delirium set in with a vengeance upon the fanged days, and in all the uncertainty that surrounded them, the singer's first thoughts were for the theatre, and for what he might be able to save from the holocaust. Many things might be swept away, but the theatre must remain, and all the things that belonged to it must be saved. There were people who didn't care, and there were people ceasing to care. Only Chaliapin thought of the scenery and the costumes which were threatened by destruction. Immediate action was necessary. Lives were being washed away, but so, too, were the things that could lift life up and brighten it, illuminate it. It was in furtherance of this very necessary decision that the singer called on Lenin, and the following is his description of the visit:

"I walked into the most simply furnished room. There was a big desk piled with papers, and an arm-chair. A very austere, sober room. Out of a small door in the corner there glided a man with Tartar features, wide cheek bones, very little hair, and a small beard. Lenin. I noticed that he had some difficulty in pronouncing his 'r's'. We exchanged greetings. He kindly offered me a chair, and asked me the purpose of my visit. I began to talk, somewhat long-windedly, I must admit, and explained to him my excessively simple problem. I had scarcely uttered the first few words when Vladimir Ilyich Lenin said briefly, 'Don't worry, don't *worry*. I understand everything, perfectly'.

"I soon realized that I was talking to a man used to grasping meaning from the fewest words, and that there was no reason for me to spell it out for him. He won me over immediately, and I thought to myself, 'That's what I call a leader'. He continued: 'Go back to Petrograd, and don't say a word to anyone. I will use my influence, if I have any, and see to it that your entirely understandable apprehensions are taken into account, and that things will go in your favour'.

"I thanked him, and took my leave. And it would seem that he *did have influence*, for the decor and the costumes remained where they were, and no-one made any further attempt to interfere with them. I was happy." That was the big commitment.

Nor was Chaliapin devoid of a political outlook. His whole attitude to the stupidity of war is nowhere more apparent than in his letter to the authorities, in which he refused to take part in the opera, *A Life for the Czar.*

There were the occasions when his sensitiveness reached almost Gogolian proportions. He was always seeking to justify himself, and even in his talks with the soldiers he was excusing his own absence from the trenches.

"These people just don't *know* what they're fighting for." He did for the people that which he knew best how to do. He sang. Out of his own private funds he financed and opened two hospitals, and when in 1914 the Germans, during their offensive, bombed Warsaw, he rushed to the Polish capital to give concerts for the victims, and he recalls the capacity attendances, in spite of the falling bombs. He sang in aid of the victims of famine, for workers, for students, for other artists, and everywhere he was much heartened by the responses. The last concert he ever gave for the needy was to help out the funds of the South Wales miners.

As success grew, so too did the climate of spite and envy, and he was very often the unwilling target of the press. He was hated for his origins, as much as he was hated for his success, and perhaps the famous "kneeling incident" (see Chaliapin-Gorky letters) was the most sensational. It had every kind of unpleasant and unhealthy repercussion. The singer felt trapped. The conservative press became almost rapturous concerning it, interpreting the occasion as a "touching expression of his patriotic feelings", whilst the Liberal press spared itself nothing in the matter of epithets, and described the incident as proof of Chaliapin's "servile, lick-spittle tendencies". But the uproar raised by the newspapers only served to obscure the heart of the matter, for the demonstration organized by the choir was in no sense an expression of patriotic fervour, but rather a pathetic attempt on its part to draw the attention of the Czar to the petition they had put forward for better living conditions. Chaliapin's offence was magnified out of all proportion, so much so that in some Liberal circles there were even protests about the proposed publication of his autobiography in the pages of *Letopis*.

It was in reply to this that Gorky himself sat down and wrote an introduction to Chaliapin's book, on the singer's behalf. The so-called genuflecting ceremony had become so exaggerated that it actually affected the sober judgement of several Soviet critics, although the latter had at their disposal Gorky's own archives. These included letters to his wife, to Chaliapin, to Burenin, and others, in which the writer's assessment of the incident is clearly written down.

I quote from Gorky's hand-written manuscript which reads as follows:
"I deem it necessary to warn the readers that the autobiography was written, and is being published by me, and not necessarily in the interests of publicity. After a quarter of a century's work in Russian and European theatres, I require no publicity. I have written down and published a true account of my life, and it is nowhere a justification. I would like to inspire in its readers a somewhat different attitude towards ordinary people, and when I say ordinary, I mean those 'from below'. I would wish to instil in the reader a greater respect for those who struggle in the pit of life. I think that only attention and respect for those we call neighbours can hope to create conditions in which men can, with the minimum of wasted energy,

bring into life the maximum of beauty, goodness and understanding. That is my sincere desire.

"I know that I shall not be believed when I say that l am not as black as I am painted. It is true to say that there has been the occasion when I complained, or indulged in the use of the abrupt word, and for this I am sorry. What can I do? I am a man, and just as capable of feeling pain as any other man. I wrote these, perhaps boring, pages, so that those reading them, in moments of doubt, in difficult and depressing times, mistrusting their own strength, would spare a thought for one Russian, who, with great effort, managed to crawl out of the dirty pit, and who, having surfaced, feels that he has done some good to the cause of Russian Art throughout the world. This, I hope, will not be denied me. Forget that this man's name is Chaliapin, and instead, think of the hundreds of others, who by nature are no less gifted than Chaliapin and Gorky and Surikov, and others, but who did not have the strength to fight life's obstacles, and who indeed are daily perishing, crushed by life. On this I will end.

"Much in my book is left unsaid, and about some things I have been intentionally silent. Nor was this prompted by any desire on my part to hide myself away, for, after all, I was not in the process of making a confession. No. I have merely told of the forces, the intense pressures from outside causes, to which I have been subject by circumstance and contingency, pressures which, up to now, I am not in a position to eliminate of my own free will. I would like to be believed when I say that there is not the slightest necessity for me to indulge in any kind of hypocrisy, nor to hide faults or weaknesses, or to justify myself in any way, and generally to give the appearance of being better than I am."

It was unfortunate that the singer himself made no endeavour to reduce the great volume of noise which the occasion had aroused. He lost his nerve, and quite understandably so, faced as he was by all manner of base and monstrous accusations. Gorky advised him to "explain everything to the public", but unfortunately the singer's immediate entourage, which included Burenin, persuaded him against taking any such course. In a letter addressed to Gorky on September 23, 1911, Burenin said that he had taken no steps on Chaliapin's behalf, for the time being, and that he would advise him against writing any such letters to the press. He told Gorky that he had seen Vladimir Stassov (famous Russian critic) and that they had talked the matter over, and they were both of them agreed as to the attitude to be taken towards the newspapers. And that was that. The result of all this was complete silence on Chaliapin's part, and he was to pay for it in due course. He was terribly concerned about this "stain" on his character. But, having allowed the right occasion to go by, he could only go on hoping, and did so, even to the extent of provoking demonstrations against himself, if out of them the opportunity arose to explain the whole thing. That opportunity was never to come. The tone throughout is sad, the statement inevitable.

This translation of Maxim Gorky's "autobiography" of the great singer is based on the full, final, and authoritative edition of the work published by Iskusstvo State Publishing House of Moscow, volume 1 of which appeared in 1957, and volume 2 the following year. It was issued to commemorate the eightieth anniversary of Chaliapin's birth, and the twentieth anniversary of his death. The publishers stressed that the anniversaries were not the only reason for the issue of the work, but that, and I quote:

"In the world of singing, in the sphere of vocal art, in opera, there is no other name in the world that can rival Chaliapin's, for the spell it cast, for popularity, for sheer talent, and with every new generation interest continues to increase in the life and work of this great artist, and the number of his 'fans' continually grows."

In a commentary to the text, Iskusstvo point out that the present work is based on the original holograph manuscript kept in the archives of M. Gorky, in the Institute of World Literature, named after the writer. The introduction to the book states that not only is it the first volume publication, but that many sections of the work are being issued for the first time, in any form. I quote:

"The present text of Chaliapin's autobiography is published for the first time in the Russian language, based on Gorky's original manuscript, corrected and edited by the great writer himself. The manuscript has been prepared for publication by V. V. Grigorenko, scientific associate of the Gorky archives."

The world of theatre and opera owes great debts to this remarkable artist. His story is also the story of Russia at the most exciting, and certainly the most significant period in her history.

James Hanley

CHALIAPIN

AN AUTOBIOGRAPHY

as told to Maxim Gorky

I

I am sitting on the *polati*[1] in the hut of the miller, Tikhon Karpovich, in the village of Ometova, near Kazan, the other side of Sukonnaya Sloboda. My mother sits there, together with the miller's wife, Kirillovna, and a few women neighbours. They spin in the semi-dark room, its only light being that of the wooden spill. It stands in an iron holder, and I watch the burned pieces fall with a hiss into the waiting bucket of water. Shadows climb the walls, and the wind sighs in the chimney. I hear the falling rain. I listen to the women's stories as they spin, and even the most terrible of them is narrated with a strange calm. One of the young widows who are nightly visited by their husbands' ghosts. They come as fiery serpents, fall as showers of sparks into the chimney, then suddenly appear as sparrows in the stove, and quickly become the dear departed mourned by their wives. The widows kiss and caress, but dare not embrace, dare not touch the backs of their beloved ones. As Kirillovna explains:

"That, my dear," she says, "is because the departed one has no back, and where it should be lies only a green fire. To touch it is to be burned up completely."

A fiery serpent used to visit a neighbouring village so often that eventually one of the widows pined away. The village told her to go to the forest, collect some twigs, and bring them back. With them she must make the sign of the cross upon the doors and windows, and all the cracks of the hut. She took this advice. That night the serpent returned, and finding itself unable to get into the hut, turned itself into a fiery steed, and smashed the doors in half by a single mighty kick.

The women spun, and I went on listening to their stories. I was five years old.

My mother could tell quite terrifying stories, one of which I vividly remember. It was the story of Satanial. The Lord had an archangel in heaven, whose name was Satanial, and he was head of the Heavenly hosts. He became proud and persuaded the other angels and Heavenly officials to rise up in revolt against God. God discovered this and threw him down, after which he sought out the one who must replace him. There was a creature there, Mikh by name, shaggy and hairy, the hairs growing out of head, ears and nose. This Mikh was kind, and also guileless, for once he had stolen a piece of land from God. God admonished him and demanded

[1] Planking fixed between ceiling and top of Russian stove, used as a sleeping place.

its return, upon which Mikh began taking the land from his ears and nose, but refusing to reveal what lay in his mouth. Whereupon God issued the command "Spit", and Mikh spat, and mountains rose up. God sent for him and said:

"Although you are not clever, I will take you as head of the Heavenly forces and as arch-strategist. You will start no trouble here, and henceforth you will be called, not Mikh, but Satan."

I was greatly moved by such stories. They terrified and thrilled me, I would say to myself, "What wonderful stories abound in the world. Everything so terrifying, and yet so simple. How kind God is."

The stories finished, the women would then sing to the humming accompaniment of their spindles; sad songs of the soft white snow, of a maiden's grief. There was even one about the spill that would not brightly burn. And it never did. The melancholy words of these songs filled my soul with dreams. I imagined myself flying over the earth on a fiery steed, speeding over the vast expanse of snow-fields. I imagined God in the early morning opening up a golden cage, to release the bird of fire that soared skywards, high up to the limitless sun.

"It's time Ivan was home."

Through such dreams I would hear my mother's voice. Ivan was my father. It was generally midnight when he arrived home from work. He was up early in the morning, would drink his tea, and then depart for the office. This word "office" used to frighten me. For some odd reason it reminded me of the Court of Judges. Later, I discovered that the office where he worked belonged to the District Council. He had to arrive there promptly at nine o'clock, which meant a walk of some six versts[1]. He would return home at four, rest, have tea, then return to work until midnight. He was once absent from home for two days and nights, but on the third he turned up drunk, to be met by my mother's reproaches and tears.

"How shall we manage now?" she asked him.

It was horrible and painful to me to have to listen to his shouting and swearing at my mother. It could be heard for the length of the street.

"Leave me alone. Go to hell. Give me a chance to live. I'm sick of the lot of you. All I do is work, work, work."

I understood. His month's pay had been spent on drink, though he was not alone, since many other employees did the same thing. I also realized that our lives depended on his wages. It enabled my mother to buy the potatoes and cucumbers from which she made such delicious soups, not forgetting the hemp oil, and even the *pel'meni*, a dish I loved, and for which I always waited so impatiently. I was soon to learn the great importance of "the twentieth of the month".

I realized how dependent I was on my father, and from that time on became more considerate even though his words hurt and frightened me. The "twentieth" of the month became a horrible omen, for though at first it passed off without quarrels, and I would watch mother sit quietly in a

[1] A verst is 3,500 feet.

38

corner and cry, it gradually grew worse, and one day I actually had to witness his beating her. I remember shrieking and rushing to her aid. Not that my puny fists were of any use, since all I got for my pains were several blows on the head. I could do nothing but scream. Once she was beaten unconscious so that I feared her dead. I found her lying on a wooden chest, her torn garments trailing, her eyes closed, scarcely breathing. I yelled with despair. Later she came to, saw me, patted my head, and took me on her lap.

"Never mind. Don't cry."

The beatings over, life would become normal again. Father renewed his punctuality at the office, and mother resumed her spinning, her mending, and washing. Always she sang at her work. There was something thoughtful and sad in her singing, and it engraved itself on my heart. She must have been a very healthy young woman, though she did sometimes complain. "I never dreamed of a day when my back would ache," she said, "but now it is hard for me to scrub floors, and do the washing and mending. Once I could tackle anything."

She was often beaten, cruelly, brutally. By the time I had reached my ninth birthday my father was drunk almost daily. And now began the period of continuous beatings, even though at this time she was pregnant, carrying my brother Vassily. My mother was the one living person in whom I had faith, and my heart ached for her sufferings. She was always there to listen to my own few simple words. I lived for her with my very soul. She was to teach me the lessons that were made of iron, and those that were beautiful. An obedience to her, and to my father. To realize that life was harsh, that one must work, and work, and work, without respite. For the poor there was no way out. I hear the words in my ear. "Obey him, accept his advice, and his orders. Your father is clever." For her he was to remain the indisputable law-giver.

Thanks to her hard work and utter devotion, our house was always clean. The sacred lamp never failed to burn before the ikon. How often I watched her, her grey eyes gazing so humbly towards the light.

She was a small woman, her features were soft, and the light brown hair always so beautifully combed. Her very person was modest and inconspicuous. As to my father: all I can say of him is that he was strange. A tall man, sunken-chested, wearing a great beard. His hair, too, was soft, and always tidy, nor have I ever seen such beautiful hair on any man. How often I would stroke it, in pure affection. He usually wore a home-made shirt and a soft collar, and preferred ribbons to neckties, though when the fancy shirt became popular he resorted to a cord. He always wore a coat, and high boots, whilst the coarsest rags about his feet took the place of socks.

When sober he was a silent man, and often spoke in a whisper, and then only when required to. He could be kind to me, and he could call me by the most abusive names whenever he became irritated. I got the message by his grinding of his teeth, then walking away, and getting drunk again. It required only two or three glasses to turn my father into a totally different person. He became bitter, nagging, and even unpleasant to look at. I have always found drunken men repulsive, especially my father. He shamed me in front of my friends, street boys like myself, whose own fathers were also drunkards. I never understood why people drank, and I remember drinking vodka for the first time. I found it bitter, smelly. I could understand people drinking kvas, and even enjoying it, but not that other poison. I decided that people drank to summon up courage, and especially to precipitate quarrels. It was a kind of law. All drunkards were the same. In this condition my father became a nuisance to everybody, for he seemed able to find the simplest reason for disliking people, polite one moment, and insulting the next.

I have seen the most benevolently inclined person approach him, saying courteously, "And what can I do for you?" to be met by the wholly un-expected reply. "Why have you such pig-like eyes?" my father would ask. Or, "Aren't you ashamed of having such an ugly mug?" And always some-body would be passing by, telling father that he was crazy, and for that matter, scarcely human.

Such episodes took place on a date in the month that I had begun to hate, "the twentieth". People lost themselves in wild debauchery, poisoned them-selves with vodka, seemed to lose their human countenance. Senseless brawling, fighting, weeping, and much rolling about in the mud. Life became hellish, disgusting, nightmarish. My father would spend the whole day in bed, drinking kvas with ice. "More kvas, more kvas." In those twenty-four hours he would say nothing else, and he was a sight to see. Tortured features, the eyes demented. I was forever astonished at the amount he consumed, and would boast to my friends that father could drink like a horse. Nobody seemed surprised.

He seldom beat me when sober, but when he did, there seemed no reason for it. I remember once playing with a paper kite, a splendid affair with rattles, which I had made myself. It got caught in a birch tree and I climbed up for it, and retrieved it. As I came down a branch suddenly broke and I fell. First I hit the roof, and then the fence, and finally the earth, and with such a resounding thump that something seemed to crack. I lay there holding the kite, dreading some broken bones. I regretted my smashed kite, but the next day had forgotten all about it.

Father ordered me to get ready to go to the baths. This was something I loved. Going to the baths in the country is a wonderful thing, especially in the autumn when the air is translucent and fresh. I loved the delicious smell of the mushroom mould, and the birch twitches used in the baths. How thriftily people carried them under their arms. On such dark evenings, dimly lit by kerosene lamps, it was a pleasant sight to see these well washed people walking along the street, and the steam rising from them. I thought of them returning home to tea and jam, the always happy conclusion to my own bath.

At this time my parents had gone to live at Sukonnaya Sloboda.

Father was in a very good mood when we arrived at the baths. We both undressed. He prodded me, saying, "And what's this?"

I looked down at myself to find I was covered with bluish-yellow bruises. I was striped like a zebra.

"I fell and hurt myself yesterday," I replied.

He pointed at the stripes. "From where did you fall?"

I told him the truth, and the next moment I was being thrashed with the birch.

"Then don't climb trees in future," was all he said.

It wasn't so much the pain as the shame of having to stand before the assembled people. I felt offended, degraded, but the people were delighted. It was a source of amusement to them, and they shrieked with laughter, though without malice. They even encouraged father to continue the beating. "Go on. Give it him, give it to the devil. Don't spare him." I was rarely upset, for me beatings had become the order of things. In Sukonnaya Sloboda everybody got beaten some time or other, children and adults, day and night. But this was different. Standing surrounded by naked people, and for their amusement. It hurt me deeply.

It was only when I reached my twelfth year that I began to protest against the drunken scenes created by my father. He answered my first protest with a huge stick. Thinking he might kill me I ran into the street, dressed in the thinnest vest and underpants, and in spite of the cold, it was twenty-seven degrees below freezing point, I ran the length of two blocks, and found shelter in a friend's house. When I returned home the next day father was out. Mother approved of my running away, but I was greatly scolded for going barefooted through the snow. I only just managed to prevent her beating me.

Whenever my father got drunk he started to sing in a high-pitched voice, almost like a woman, a striking contrast to both his figure and character. I recall a song he sang because of its incredibly nonsensical words:

Sicksaniekma.

Chetvertakma.

Tazanitma.

Suleymatma.

Ussum ta.

Bishtinikma!

Dygin. Dygin.

I never dared ask the meaning of the extraordinary fractured, Tartar-sounding words.

On the subject of God he was always reticent. He seldom attended church, though when he did he prayed most devoutly. With great concentration he would look towards the altar and make the sign of the cross, bowing at intervals. I felt he was repeating all the prayers he had ever known, and they were few. He never spoke to me in church, though I received many a cuff for my undue interest in his beard.

"Don't fidget," he'd say, on which I would receive a tap on the skull, and at once became submissive before the Lord. When later I went to work with him in the District Office, I noticed how fond he was of drawing a grave upon his folder, underneath which I'd read: "Here there is no suffering, and no sorrow, no lamentation, only eternal life."

In spite of the constant quarrelling of my parents I still enjoyed life. I had many friends in the village. We boys were rarely unoccupied. We cart-wheeled in the streets, climbed roofs and trees, went kite flying, roamed the vegetable gardens, stealing cucumbers, scattering the ripe poppy seeds. We played on the threshing floor of the mill. Everything interested, life was revealing her little secrets to us. It taught me to love and understand all living things.

I made hideaways in the garden, built myself imaginary homes there, without parents, alone, free in the world. I dreamed of having my own farm and cattle. Vague, child-like dreams, and life was sometimes a fairy-tale to me.

I suppose my greatest source of pure joy came from the splendid festivals that were held twice a year. The girls dressed themselves up in brightly-coloured costumes, gay sarafans, wore ribbons in their hair, powdered and rouged their faces. The men wore their own special clothes. They encircled the girls, danced, and sang the most wonderful songs. The ceremonial gait, the gay faces, the lively tunes and colourful dresses invoked for me a new, strange, and beautiful life, so removed from those fights and squabbles, the drinking and debauchery.

I remember one occasion when father and I went off to the baths. It was near the end of autumn, and the ground was glazed with frost. Father fell and hurt his ankle. Somehow we managed to get home. Mother was in despair. "What will we do now?" she kept asking. The next morning she was sent off to explain his absence from the office, and instructed to tell them to come and see for themselves. "I'm really ill," said father, "and those devils might sack me." This was a dread omen. For father to be sacked would be terrible, and I imagined us going begging. It seemed bad enough already, living as we were in a tiny village hut at a rental of a rouble and a half per month. I shall never forget the terror in my mother's eyes, nor indeed her voice when she pronounced the terrible words, "They'll sack you."

Village doctors were important, and they were often very frightening people. Mother called one. He pummelled father's foot, and rubbed it with a murderous-smelling substance, and later cauterized it. Father remained bedridden for quite a time. It was this disaster that forced us to leave the village and get nearer to his place of work. So back to town we went, moving into the shack in which I myself had been born in the year 1873.

I must say I disliked intensely the noisy, dirty town. We lived in a single room, my parents, myself, and a younger brother and sister. I must have been about seven years old. Mother went out charring, and I would be left alone with the little ones, locked up in that room from morning till night. If ever a fire had started we should have been burnt alive. Later I learned to remove part of the window, and we children managed to crawl out into the street, always remembering to return home at the right time. The window frame was replaced, and nobody was any the wiser. It was frightening to be locked up in that room, for the darkness was complete when evening came. It was this that made me remember Kirillovna's stories. I was always expecting to see an ogre or a witch at the window. In spite of the heat of the place we stole under the blanket and lay quite still, stifled, silent, and those who coughed were counselled at once. "Ssh! Don't breathe."

But everything changed the moment we heard the light noise under the door that told us mother had come home. With what confidence, and absence of hurry did she open that door.

This led into a semi-dark corridor, which was really the back entrance to a General's flat. I once met his wife in the corridor. She spoke kindly to me, asked me if I could read, and I had to reply, "No."

"Then come to my house, and my son will teach you," she said.

Thus began my first reading lessons. Her son was sixteen years old, and when I got there it seemed to me he might have been anxiously awaiting my arrival, such was the impression left on me. I learned to read fairly quickly, much to the delight of the General's wife. Eventually I found myself reading to her in the evenings. At this point I must mention something that may seem wholly inexplicable. Whenever I finished reading a page, I found myself in a quandary, for I did not know which way the page should be turned, to the left or the right. Most patiently did that good lady explain its mystery. What a difficult art it seemed to me then. Oddly enough this peculiarity never left me, until finally the woman got angry about it, and called me an idiot. I burst into tears, and doubt very much if I have ever cried so bitterly since. She was moved by this. "That's enough reading," she said. I never returned to her.

Then I managed to get hold of a very tattered copy of a fairy-tale book, and made my first great discovery in the character of Bova Korolevich, a prince who with one single blow could dispose of an army 100,000 strong.

"There's a man," I thought, "that's who I'd like to be." This book was to give me my first thirst for adventure. I was now devouring every piece of print that came my way. In between I indulged in chasing the local poultry with a broom for which I received the usual beatings. But I loved reading. I recall picking up a prayer-book, and discovering the following on its inside page: "Let us pray for Ieraksa, Ivan, Evdokiya, Feodor, Nikolai."

Ivan and Evdokiya were my parents, I was Feodor, Nikolai and Evdokiya my brother and sister, but who was Ieraksa? The very sound of this name terrified me. I imagined its owner to be a highwayman, a sorcerer, an enormous creature. My curiosity grew, so I asked my father.

"Papa! Who is Ieraksa?"

His reply was immediate and concise. I have never forgotten it.

"Until I was eighteen," he began, "I worked in the village on the land, then later went into the town, where I did many different jobs, water carrier, labourer in a candle factory, a night watchman, then as clerk for a District police officer, Chirikov, in the village of Klyuchishchi. In the church there was a sexton by the name of Ieraksa, and it was he who taught me to read. I shall never forget the kindness he showed me. Nor must you ever forget, Feodor, the kindnesses that are shown you. The names of those who will be kind will be few, and very easy for you to remember."

The winter brought us visitors, great bearded men wearing bast sandals and peasants' coats. Their persons conveyed to me the smell of rye bread, a special Vyatka smell, and this perhaps because Vyatka people eat much oatmeal. These visitors were my uncle Dorimedont, and his sons. Immediately I would be sent off to buy vodka. They spent much time tea drinking, and talking, about country life, harvests, taxes, with special mention of those whose cattle had been driven away, or those who had lost a samovar owing to their failure to pay the tax. "Life is hard." This often repeated phrase came to have a monotonous ring about it. I'd think how fortunate father was living in a town, and no cattle or samovar to worry about.

Once I was quite startled by the look of alarm on my parents' faces, and by hearing the word "Prosecutor". The word sounded to me as terrifying as "Ieraksa".

"Mother, what is a prosecutor?"

"A prosecutor is greater than a governor."

Governors I already knew something about, having heard father discuss a particular one as he stood at the gate with some neighbours. "Skaryatin was the governor," I heard him say. "When he arrived he made the whole village lie on their faces in the street, and then lashed them with a whip."

Having heard which, and being told that a prosecutor was even greater than a governor, I expected the worst when he arrived. I saw the people lie down, heard the crack of the whip. And I felt I would suffer with them. My childish mind need never have been so burdened. The matter was a little simpler than that. It happened that mother's youngest sister had been abducted by somebody, and sold into a brothel, and my parents having discovered this, decided to seek the help of the prosecutor. After a while, my Aunt Anna came to stay with us. She was very beautiful, had the gayest laugh, and was forever singing. In this way did I learn that in life not everything is dreadful.

We looked out on a yard often occupied by stone-masons and carpenters, and sometimes I would bring them paper to make cigarettes with. They filled the paper with shag, and twisted it into a cigarette known as "dog's foot". I was once given one and told to smoke it. "It clears the chest," they said. I was quite sick after the first puff.

Holiday time saw these men getting drunk, with the usual brawling, in which my father would join. This I did not like, since for me, my father was different from these men. After all, he did wear a necktie, was well dressed, unlike this common lot.

The houseowner had a daughter who played the piano, and often I stood and listened. To me the music was divine. The landlord's name was Lisitzin. I thought at first the girl was merely turning the handle of some barrel organ, and that the music was "happening" all by itself inside the box. Then I found that she actually *made* music with her fingers and my admiration knew no bounds. I longed to play, too. Soon after something happened, and it was my first fairy-tale come true.

A lottery had been organized in the yard, and my mother purchased a twenty-five kopeck ticket for me. I won an antique harpsichord. I went wild with excitement, it seemed unbelievable. But there it was, and I very soon convinced myself that I would learn to play. Alas, it was locked up in the cupboard. In spite of all my pleadings I was not allowed to touch it. If I went anywhere near the cupboard, the warning came: "Don't touch. You'll break it." Oddly enough when I became ill, I no longer slept on the floor but on this very musical instrument. The times when I longed to lift that lid, and peep inside. To be allowed to sleep on it, but never to play it! Later it was sold for thirty roubles.

I saw my first clown when I was eight. His name was Yashka. It was in a booth at the Easter Fair. At that time Yashka was famed throughout the Volga region as clown and entertainer. I can see him now. An elderly, stocky man, rough faced, and black moustached. To me this moustache seemed made of iron. Yashka knew the man in the street, and how well he had mastered the heavy, coarse humour and wit which to this very day delights us. The weighty jokes, his daring gibes at the public, his thundering, raucous voice, enchanted and at the same time depressed me. To me he was a fearless leader and tamer of men. I imagined everybody to be afraid of him, even the police and the hated prosecutor. I would stare at him open-mouthed, delighted, straining to remember the best of his wit. He fascinated me. I stood until my limbs became numb, and my eyes blurred by the feast of coloured costumes of the street artists. My whole spirit leapt to Yashka. And how I dreamed. This was happiness.

These artists abounded with life, forever clowning, laughing, and cracking jokes. I would watch them move from booth to stage, steam rising from them as from a samovar. It never occurred to me that it was perspiration due to their hard work, the painful straining of their muscles. If they did not strike the first spark in me, they did awaken my soul, and thereafter I simply longed for the life of the artist. To Yashka, who gave of himself so unsparingly, do I owe my first real interest in the theatre, that "great spectacle" that was to be for me the reverse of reality. Later I was to discover that he had been a cobbler, and that he first started entertaining with his wife, son, and the apprentices. They were his first troupe. This knowledge only increased my admiration. After all, not everybody can emerge from the depths of a basement and reach the heights of a booth. For days I stood mute before that booth, lost in wonder. When Lent came I was heartbroken. Easter was over, and the village square was once again its dreary self, silent, empty. Nothing remained save the few wooden ribs of the booth. No people treading the already trodden snow, no wild scatterings of the husks of sunflower seeds, or the gay wrappings from cheap sweets. The holiday ended like a dream. Yesterday the place was alive and swarming with life, today like a cemetery.

For long afterwards I was to be haunted by the most fantastic dreams. I saw long corridors with rounded windows, through which I beheld the most beautiful fairy-tale towns, towering mountains, enormous temples, and nothing like it had ever before been seen in the town of Kazan. And things even *more* beautiful, buried in dreams.

There was to be another move, and this time into the village of Tatarskaya Sloboda. We went into a small room over a forge. Through the cracks in the floor one could hear the bright, rhythmic tattoo of hammer on anvil. The yard was inhabited by wheelwrights and coachbuilders, and, dearest of all to me, there was a furrier there. I spent the summer time sleeping in these carriages, smelling so richly of morocco leather, lacquer, and turpentine. The furrier was black-haired and black-eyed, and of an almost oriental appearance. He gave me work to do: I spread furs upon the roof, and sometimes dried and beat them with thin, flexible rods. For this I received five kopecks, to me a fortune. It seemed only natural that I should spend it at the swimming baths, and in the "Gentlemen's Enclosure" I would swim about until I was as blue as a roach from the cold. My brother and sister were too small to accompany me. He was lively, and clever, but my sister was a quiet and thoughtful child. I would buy halva with my earnings, and we would regale ourselves. How we loved sinking our teeth into the hard, stone-like mass of sweet. Sometimes it cemented our jaws, sticky as cobbler's wax, but later the mouth was filled with a milky sweetness, flavoured with chalk.

I remember the young blacksmith for whom I would blow the bellows. He sang quite well, and did *not* drink vodka. A change indeed. I can no longer recall his name, but I loved him much, and I think he loved me, too. Whenever he sang, my mother, sitting at the window, would join in. The blending of the voices delighted me to such an extent that I had a try myself, with the help of the blacksmith's encouragement. "Go on, Feodor, *sing*, it will lighten the heart. A song is like a bird, let it out, let it soar."

How true. Lying on my back in a field, and having sung, the song lingered, soared into the air.

I rarely went to church, though one Saturday evening, playing near the church of St. Varlaam, I suddenly went inside. A service was in progress, and the harmonious singing reached my ears as I crossed the threshold. Slowly I worked my way towards the choir of men and boys. I noticed the boys holding sheets of ruled paper. I had already heard of the mysterious things called notes, but these strange black marks on the paper seemed impossible to fathom. For the first time I was witnessing something beyond my comprehension. These boys were singing from one side of the paper only. It took me time to work this out. It was my first experience of choir singing, and I was deeply impressed.

Once more there was a shift of home, and this time back to Sukonnaya Sloboda, again into the two small rooms of a basement. That first night I actually heard singing over my head, and discovered that the choirmaster lived above us. They were having their practice. I was filled with a desire to join this choir, and sought the master, and having found him, asked if I could join. He looked at me in silence, took down a violin from the wall, and then said quietly: "Follow the violin."

I followed it with great pains, and sang a few notes.

"You've got a voice, and a good ear. All right. I'll write down something for you. Then you must go home and learn it."

He wrote down a scale, explained to me the mystery of sharps and flats, and the various keys. I was passionately interested. Soon, to mother's delight, I had mastered this great science. Father was quite indifferent, though he expressed the hope that by it I might be able to earn some money to help keep the family. Which is exactly what happened, and after only three months I found myself earning one rouble and fifty kopecks a month.

The choirmaster's name was Shcherbinin, and to me he was an extraordinary man. His black hair was always beautifully brushed. The spectacles he wore gave him a look of serenity, and even a certain nobility, and this in spite of his having been disfigured by smallpox. He wore a very loose, black dressing-gown, sleeveless, a kind of cloak. But upon his head he wore a "highwayman's cap". He was a man of few words. In spite of a noble bearing, he seemed no different from the other inhabitants of Sukonnaya Sloboda and drank his fill. He, too, worked as a clerk in the District Court, and for him also "the twentieth" was a fatal date. The apathy, the very misery, haunted me. These people, to the accompaniment of a deluge of oaths, wreaked great havoc on the town. The first time I saw my choirmaster drunk, my heart ached for him.

One evening some shop assistants were having a celebration in the house of their master, Chernoyarov, and our choirmaster was asked to supply a few choirboys. I was chosen, and spent the next few weeks in hard and concentrated study, and after our practice the assistants would treat us to biscuits and cakes, and most wonderful of all, as much sugar as we wanted in our tea. This was a luxury, even in the inns where we boys sometimes went between church services. One could drink tea "v'prikusku", that is, biting off a small piece of lump sugar, holding it in the teeth, and allowing the tea to filter through. I remember we were allowed five lumps to each glass of tea. They were nice, kind people. The evening of the celebration arrived, and so did some very important-looking ladies and gentlemen, and a few merchants. I remember we sang a trio for them, "A Hymn to Christmas". In this happy atmosphere did the heart lighten. But it did not last long, for shortly after the choir itself was disbanded. It depressed poor Shcherbinin and he began to drink even more heavily. When most drunk he would call me into his room, take down the violin, and together we indulged in long music sessions. There were times when I could have cried from the very joy of it, treasuring the wonderful experience, whereas the poor choirmaster immediately repaired to the pub, after which I would again be invited to his room. I cannot recall anything of significance that he ever said to me, either about myself or my musical exertions. Still, I realized that he liked me, and that was something, and I was always happy to return his compliments. Shcherbinin was a lonely, morose person, one of those rare

Russians who suffered in silence, too proud ever to discuss or complain about his fate. One evening he called me to him.

"Let's go," he said.

"Where?" I asked.

"To sing a Mass."

"But *where*, with whom?"

"Just us two," he replied.

So off we went, crossing the gullies, scrambling through the brickyards, until we finally reached the church of St. Barbara the Martyr, where we sang the Mass for two voices, descant and bass, and the next day sang for the morning service. After which it was a perfect round of church-going until Shcherbinin gave it up to become master of the Bishop's choir in the Monastery of the Assumption. I accompanied him as assistant singer. My pay was now six roubles a month, real wealth to me, and in addition to this we covered weddings, funerals, and church services. All my earnings I handed over to my parents, though sometimes I would hold back what I came to call "Yashka's money", that yielded me a few sweets. I was in heaven. What a magnificent occupation singing was. I enjoyed it, I loved it. And to be paid for it all, to be able to go and enjoy Yashka's talents. That was the real reward for me.

Like all choirboys, I sang from house to house at Christmas time, and the people enjoyed it. Sometimes we earned as much as six roubles a day, which meant enough money for the holidays.

By the following Easter I was determined to write my own trio. I took the violin and some music paper and composed a trio on the words "Christ is risen from the dead". How I came to learn the violin I will explain later.

The melody itself came easily, and without much difficulty I started to develop the second voice, which, as I then understood things, had to be major or minor, third to the first. But it was only when I began composing for the third voice, forming the harmony, that I experienced my real disappointment, for the whole thing now sounded false. At that time I didn't even know that such a thing as a quinta existed. However, I began to patch the thing up as best I could, worked over it again, and this time the first voice and the bass did harmonize, but the second voice eluded me, and I felt defeated. Again I tried, and finally mastered it, not without relief, and not without some pride. Indeed I could add that this first opus of mine really appealed to the public, thus enabling me to earn even more money "for Yashka". It was all written down in purple ink, and I kept this memento of my first efforts as a composer. Later it was lost, together with many of my father's letters, and a very old copy of Beranger's Poems, in the Kurochkin translation. That much-battered tome I actually found in a lavatory. One poem I well remember.

> "With ruddy cheeks,
> And careless clothes,
> Of wine he reeks,
> As gay he goes."

1. Chaliapin, 1893.

2. *D. A. Usatov, singer (tenor) of the Bolshoy Theatre Opera; Chaliapin's only singing teacher.*

For what length of time was the hero of that poem to remain my ideal, my attractive man, and yet be so unlike the people amongst whom I lived.

> "The cops stand by
> With ball and chain,
> He thumbs his nose,
> And laughs again."

But in Sukonnaya Sloboda there was never any question of adopting a humorous attitude to the police.

I was now attending Vedernikova's Private School for Elementary Studies, and still kept up my study of singing. The school was a mixed one, and before long I was having a romance with one of the girls, Tanya by name. I was a naturally quick scholar, studying came easy to me, though I could also be neglectful and often preferred skating to lessons. I sometimes lost my school books, sometimes sold them to get sweets, but I was never behind in my lessons.

Tanya was two years my senior. She sometimes helped me in difficulties, whispering the correct answers. This aroused in me a feeling of affection, and during a school break I was seized with a passionate desire to kiss her, which I did. It frightened her somewhat, and, looking both ways, she whispered, "What on earth are you doing? Suppose the teacher saw us. Wait. When we go to play in the yard, we'll hide somewhere, and then you can kiss me."

I was quite unaware that kissing was prohibited. It certainly wasn't a school subject. And now I longed to get closer and closer to Tanya, and I took every opportunity of meeting her. This passion was innocence and simplicity itself, a few kisses, childish caresses, which the heart so much desires. We were found out, and both of us expelled from the school. The reason for it never reached the ears of my parents, and I was relieved. It would only have meant one more thrashing.

This incident between Tanya and myself deeply touched my very spirit, and I knew that hidden kisses were sweetest. It awakened in me my first curiosity about women, and brought about a change of attitude towards my mother. Until this time she had always accompanied me to the baths. Now I refused to go with her, fearing that I might become ashamed.

Some time later I was attending the Fourth Parish school, but not for long, owing to an extraordinary incident. Coming from school one day a huge fellow darted out of a gate and struck me a dreadful blow on the head with a heavy stick. He fled and I lay there bleeding. After a while, I continued on my way, all the time wondering why he had hit me. I rubbed some snow on the wound, and made no mention of the incident, either at home or at school. I had frustrated another thrashing, another reprimand. Suddenly the wound was festering under my hair. It was my own disobedience at school that finally revealed everything. Our teacher had a habit of taking a tuft of hair from the back of the neck between his finger and thumb. This was called "pinching the grouse". He heaved me up from my bench and I yelled. Moreover, the wound opened, and bled even more profusely. I ran home and refused to return. The inevitable thrashing followed, father described me as "the cussed brute", and he made a decision. There seemed no hope for me. So I was at once apprenticed to a cobbler, Tomkov, who happened to be my godfather.

I had often visited his house with my mother, and was always fascinated by the great cabinet in the room in which he kept his lasts and skins, and I was attracted by the smell of the leather. It was a new adventure for me. I was very fond of the cobbler's wife, who often gave me nuts and peppermint cakes. Years later I was to return to Kazan as an artist, and meeting and talking to her again recalled for me those nuts and cakes, and not least her beautiful speaking voice. However, I did not start my apprenticeship with Tomkov without the usual fatherly enjoinings.

"When you know how to sew boots," said my father, "you'll be a man, earn good money, and be a help to us." I began my apprenticeship willingly enough, entirely convinced that it was preferable to the multiplication table. Mother made me two bibbed aprons. I remember it was particularly frosty when I set off with her for Tomkov's shop. Though barefooted, I wore my new apron and, as befits a real cobbler, tucked my hands into the bibs. And as I walked I wondered how the Kazan people were now regarding me. Yet I treasured the secret thought that the whole of Kazan was saying, "Ah! Yet another new Master among us." Mother glanced at me and sighed. She bought five cucumbers at the market, I stuck four in my bib and one in my mouth, and marched on, showing a vast green tongue to the world.

Tomkov was tall, sedate, curly haired, and wore a white shirt stuffed into sateen trousers. He greeted me kindly. "Just look around for today. Tomorrow you can start work."

My sudden obsession about work resulted in a bad night, but in spite of this I was up and about by six a.m. I still felt sleepy when I got up. I was given a glass of tea, and some bread, after which work began. My first task was to learn how to wax the thread. I threw myself into the work with some enthusiasm, but the results did not come as easily as I expected. For a while the other workers had maintained a respectable silence, but suddenly they were swearing at me. "You great clumsy idiot."

The first lesson learned, the next was how to insert a bristle into the thread from both ends. This was more difficult, and not helped much by my growing even more sleepy. I was lucky in having Tomkov as godfather, since the other workers had to consider him. Still, fate never intended me to be a cobbler. I caught a cold and fell ill. I can remember lying on the hot stove, quite unable to get warm. Tomkov gave me an apple. I took only one bite, and flung it away. The taste was foul. Then I was back home. I can remember too, and it is still like a dream, suddenly accompanying my father to the cemetery. He carried a coffin slung on a towel over his shoulder. In it lay my brother Nikolai. I remember myself going to hospital, and finding my sister in the next bed. I experienced a feeling of intense burning in the soles of my feet, as if they had been set on fire. A black-looking man began spraying them with an atomizer. Mother was sat on my sister's bed, and I heard her say, "*What* is that you say? How can you cut a person's throat?" My head seemed full of mist, everything shimmered in front of me, and yet in some queer way I seemed aware that somebody was going to cut my sister's throat. I wasn't surprised. This was no hospital, but a bandits' lair. And that seemed how it had to be. If her throat was cut, then it had to be so. But mother fought hard against this, and my sister died. Now it seemed to be my turn. But I was lucky, since I slowly recovered, shedding my skin like a snake. After which there came a painful and enormous appetite. There never seemed to be enough food about. I recall a student arriving, enquiring as to what I would like.

"Well? We have cutlets, pearl-barley soup, chicken. Choose what you want."

I chose the chicken, and what a tiny morsel of it floated in that soup.

"Where's the chicken?" I asked.

"In the soup."

I stared at the man. And he stared back. "You didn't think you were going to get a whole chicken?"

"I did."

"That never happens here," he replied, and it seemed final enough.

"What a pity," I thought to myself.

Soon after I left hospital I was back at cobbling again, but this time I had a new master, a complete stranger. My father had decided that Tomkov spoiled me, added to which, in his opinion, he never really taught me anything.

I was soon to discover that my new master, Andreyev, treated his apprentices with an iron hand. I knew the elementary facts of cobbling, and was now instructed to learn to scrub floors, light samovars, and accompany the master's wife to the market, from which I carried her heavy baskets, and this was what I called hard labour. I hate to have to return to this subject, but I must record that I was mercilessly beaten by this new master, and often his wife helped. The only surprise to me was that nobody succeeded in maiming me. It wasn't due to any lack of effort on their part, but more to the toughness of my own bones. Nevertheless I can say I got on passably well in the new establishment, even to the extent of taking some odd jobs during the holidays. My one pleasure lay in delivering the goods to the customers, and I always took the longest route. This ensured me the longest period out of doors, to say nothing of a feeling of real freedom. Sometimes I got a tip, and since I suffered from undernourishment, it was generally spent on the purchase of white bread to have with my tea.

"Be very careful," the cobblers used to say, "You might overeat."

It's true that Andreyev supplied us with food, but there was never enough of it for anybody. There was one great drawback, and that was when the watery soup was served at table from a common bowl. First the liquid was drunk, and then came the signal from the headworker, a tap on the edge, and one made an immediate dive for the meat. How quick one had to be, yet if the headworker noticed me wolfing my food, he would take a mean swipe with his spoon, and a man who is handy with it can raise a big lump on the forehead even with a wooden spoon for a weapon!

Autumn came. It wasn't too bad, though the long evenings produced a thriftiness in our employer, which meant us sitting for long hours in the darkness. The nearer we came to Christmas the more the work increased, and we often laboured beyond midnight. Considering we had to start work at five in the morning, we were generally exhausted when the new day began. Over twenty hours a day did seem rather much, if one remembers the remuneration doled out to us. I was skin and bone myself, and was often afflicted by the thought of my bones growing thinner and thinner.

However, I never allowed the arduous work to conflict with my choir singing, to which I had become more devoted than ever. Invariably I turned up for a morning mass, though weddings and funerals were right out of the picture. Often I wished to sing at an evening mass, but sheer physical exhaustion prevented it. Sometimes I found it impossible to remain standing on my feet.

How glad I was when spring arrived, and to know that one could walk barefooted through the streets again. Alas, when this beautiful season arrived I was again ill, and was forced to tell my father that I could no longer work. The illness was nothing definite, but curiously hard swellings had appeared on the soles of my feet. The skin hardened to such an extent that it began to worry me. Though it didn't hurt, I took advantage of the circumstances and showed them to him. Imagine my horror when he rushed me off to the clinic.

"What on earth is going to happen now?" I asked myself.

I dreaded the doctor, who might know that my feet didn't hurt, and the inevitable consequence, just one *more* beating from my father, and the forced return to the workshop. I foresaw another beating *there*. Indeed I had now begun to hate this workshop.

Science saved me from torture. Examining my feet the doctor thought they would be of interest to his students. After prescribing an ointment for me, he forbade me to walk. I can recall that walk to the chemist's with my father. I limped even worse, but only out of gratitude and respect to science. The moment he left me I ran off home and joyfully explained to mother that though ill, it didn't really matter very much. All she was required to do was to apply the ointment. But I became impatient at this, I was longing to get back to the streets again, and to enjoy the companionship of my friends. This however was not to be. The fact that at Vedernikova's school I had learnt to write well worked against me, and ruined my happiness.

"Enough of loafing," father cried. "You have a beautiful handwriting, so from now on you will sit down at this table and copy two or three pages for me. It's time to think about your joining me at the office."

And it had to be. I found this copying work painfully boring, even though the words were occasionally incomprehensible yet beautiful. My heart lay out in the street where so many of my friends were playing cops and robbers.

And here I find I have omitted something. Following my recovery from scarlet fever, and before I went to work for Andreyev, my father had apprenticed me to a turner, and that day I could really spell toil with a capital T. I was badly fed by the master, and the carrying of the heavy planks undermined my strength. I was terribly thin at this time, and only ten years old. I remember going back with one of these heavy 5–6 inch planks and falling exhausted to the ground. I started to cry. A passer-by asked me what was wrong. As soon as I explained the matter, he picked up the plank, and bade me follow behind him to the master.

To my utter amazement this man began upbraiding my employer, and even threatened to take him to court. The master listened in complete silence, but the moment the man left I was savagely beaten. "So you go about complaining, do you?" he cried, as the blows fell.

But I hadn't complained at all. I had only said to the passer-by that the wood was heavy, and that I was afraid of being late for my work. Having thrashed me the master threatened to sack me if the occasion were ever repeated. This taught me to control myself.

Just a few days later he was again cursing me, and, more unfortunate still, caught me making faces at him through the mirror. He said nothing at the time, but just before breakfast the following morning when I was savagely hungry, he said in a quiet voice: "Collect your things and get out. Go to hell. I will not have the likes of you here."

I realized why he was sacking me, but how on earth was I to explain this to my father? I collected my few clothes, picked up my little box, and left. Afterwards came the questions.

"What is wrong?" demanded my father.

"The master sacked me."

"Why?"

"I don't know."

My father beat me, and then went off to see the turner. On his return he maintained his silence, and beat me again.

The end of this episode saw me moving off to the Sixth Town School. How happy I was to discover that the teacher, Bashmakov, was a lover of choir singing, and even had a violin. I had coveted this instrument for a long time, and had often begged my father to buy me one. It seemed such a simple matter to learn to play it. But even the money I was secretly saving would not have been sufficient to purchase it. Nor could I dare disclose to my father that he was not receiving all the money that I earned. Finally he did buy me one, in the flea market, for only two roubles.

My first lesson produced nothing but screeching from the instrument, upon which father swore he would break it on my head. In spite of this threat I managed to master the first few steps, but could go no further. Choirmasters themselves were often self-taught men, knowing little more about the violin than I did myself. Yet these lessons did help me to write my first trio.

I was now in my eleventh year, and had several good friends, all of whom, alas, died very young. The leader of our group. Zhenya Birilov, became an officer and later died of syphilis, whilst Ivan Mikhailov became a hopeless alcoholic; Stepan Orininsky, a veterinary student, was murdered, whilst Ivan Dobrov, a village deacon, fell from a sledge in a drunken stupor, and froze to death. Birilov was the son of a retired army captain, and though his family wasn't rich, it was comfortably enough off. I remember having dinner with him on one occasion, and how well I cleaned my plate after the dessert. When I saw that my friend had left a portion on his plate, I assumed such behaviour to be the sign of nobility. Birilov was the most intellectual of our circle, and he educated us. I remember how, before I met him, I used to wander the streets during feast days, watching the illuminations, being drawn into the noisy crowds. We often filled our mouths with kerosene and blew flames into the air. It was my friend Birilov who finally persuaded me against wandering the streets in my bare feet. He taught us to wear boots, those who had them.

And from the deacon Dobrov I learned another lesson: that the Latin alphabet, unlike the Russian, carried the letters any old how. I was moved by the music of this language, especially so on one occasion when Dobrov declaimed Cicero's speech against Catiline. I was unable to understand how the mixed-up alphabet of such a language could yet be so beautiful. And why Catiline, and not simply Katerine? In one's twelfth year the world abounds in amazing things.

There was another friend, Petrov, the oldest of us all, who worked in a lawyer's office, and was a literary man. Friendly with a librarian, he often obtained books from him, which I and my friends read assiduously. How often I heard them talking of Lermontov, Puskhin, Gogol. I understood little of what they said, and was far too shy to ask them, indeed far too ashamed to demand an explanation. Not wishing to lag behind I joined the library, too, and began to read. I read *The Government Inspector*, and *The Wedding*, and the first part of *Dead Souls*. I found these books interesting, clever, but their real significance was lost on me. I can remember Dobrov, with whom I used to sleep on the stove in the winter months, devouring a writer by the name of Mayne Reid. We read *The Rifle Rangers*, and *The Scalp Hunters*. At that age I found such books more appealing than Gogol, and the rest, and I was tireless in my search for new titles. In this way I waded through whole acres of novels and stories, lived with villains and highwaymen, and in my dreams watched entranced as men in cloaks and wide-brimmed hats awaited their victims in the darkened streets.

I had read much about Paris. When I eventually arrived in that city I felt I had lived there all my life.

2

I was twelve years old when I went to the theatre for the first time, and it was the happiest accident. There happened to be singing with me in the church choir a young man, Pankratyev by name, who, although seventeen, still sang descant. He later became the archdeacon of the Monastery of Kazan. During one of the services he asked me if I would like to go to the theatre, as he happened to have a spare twenty-five kopeck ticket. I knew the place he spoke of, an enormous building with bay windows that were rarely clean, but if you peered through them your eye met all kinds of junk. It seemed hardly the sort of place to provide something of interest to me.

"What are they doing?" I asked him.

"*A Russian Wedding*," he said. "A matinee."

A wedding. I had sung so often at weddings that the ceremony itself no longer aroused my curiosity. A French wedding would have been of greater interest. Still I bought the ticket, rather unwillingly I must admit. So for the first time I actually found myself in "the gods". Some holiday was on and consequently the place was packed. I recall having to stand, holding on to the ceiling with my hands. I stared down with amazement into the enormous well of the theatre, its seating arranged in a semi-circle, and in its darkest depth there were rows of chairs already fully occupied. The theatre was gas-lit. The smell from these lamps has remained with me for life. The orchestra was playing, then suddenly the curtain shuddered and rose. I stood rooted to the spot, I was bewitched. Before my eyes a vaguely familiar fairy tale was coming to life. In a magnificently decorated room, splendidly dressed people strolled about, talking to each other in a beautiful manner. I understood not a word of what they were saying. But the spectacle itself had shaken me to the core, and still unblinkingly, thinking of nothing at all, I went on staring at these miracles.

When the curtain descended I still stood, motionless, lost in a dream, my dream of living theatre, for which I wait to this very day. The sea of people around me shouted and pushed, receded and advanced, but I did not move. I felt sad when the performance was over, and one after another the lights began to go out. Somehow I could not believe it was finished. I remained numb, and when I finally reached the street I swayed. It had been a revelation, and far more interesting than anything that ever came out of Yashka's booth. In that moment even the daylight seemed strange to me, as did the bronze monument to Derzhavin still catching the rays of the setting sun. I went back to the theatre and bought a ticket for the evening performance.

That evening they were giving *Medea*, the title role of which was played by Palchikova, with Strelsky playing Jason. On this occasion I had a more comfortable seat, and so was able to watch the performance leaning on the barrier. And once more I was drawn in, drawn away, lost, never once taking my eyes off the stage, which this time was lighted by a moon borrowed from the sky, where Medea was suffering, fleeing with the children, whilst the handsome Jason dashed hither and thither. Until the interval I sat and stared with open mouth, and suddenly noticed that I was drooling. I looked carefully round, wondering if my neighbours had noticed this. Perhaps they hadn't.

"You must keep your mouth shut," I said to myself, yet the moment the curtain rose again my lips parted quite involuntarily. I covered my mouth with my hand.

The theatre almost drove me out of my mind. I felt drunk with it. Returning home along the deserted streets, the lamp-posts seemed to be winking at one another. It was a living dream. I would suddenly stop dead in my tracks, recall the magnificent speeches of the cast, then begin declaiming, imitating the mimicry and gesture of each actor.

"I'm a Queen, and I am also a woman, a mother," I enunciated into the still night, much to the astonishment of sleepy watchmen. Sometimes a gloomy passer-by would exclaim, "What's wrong with you?" He probably thought I was drunk.

The moment I got home I told mother everything. This desire to convey my experience to her became torture to me, but I felt I must transmit to her some tiny part of my own intense happiness. I told of Medea and Jason, and of Katherine in *The Thunderstorm*, and not least, about the incredible beauty of the people in the theatre. I quoted their exquisite speeches, yet all the time I felt that it did not greatly interest her, and might even seem incomprehensible to her. "Yes, yes," she'd say, thinking of something else. Yet most of all did I want to talk to her about love, the shining pivot around which the whole of this exalted life of the theatre revolved. But I could not explain it simply and clearly, and it remained an awkward subject to talk about. Nor could I understand why, in the theatre, love was spoken of as something beautiful, uplifting, pure, whilst in Sukonnaya Sloboda love was a dirty, sordid occupation that aroused nothing save a malicious ribaldry. On the stage it inspired the noblest deeds, but in the streets nothing but brawls. Were there two kinds of love, one to be considered as the highest attainable happiness, and the other debauchery and sin? Such were my thoughts at the tender age of twelve, and I didn't spend too much time pondering on such contradictions.

My desire to open up this new world to my mother was without success. I could not do it. In the end I myself couldn't understand the simplest thing. Why was Jason Jason, and not simply Jacob? Why was Medea not Maria? Who *were* these people? Where was it all taking place? And what was the Golden Fleece, Colchis?

Play-bill announcing the pro-
...ction of Gogol's Government-
...spector, at the Russian Comic
...era, March 2, 1891, in which
...aliapin made his first appearance
...the stage, as one of the policemen
...Derzhimorda). His name is listed
second from the bottom.

РУССКАЯ КОМИЧЕСКАЯ ОПЕРА И ОПЕРЕТТА.
въ субботу, 2 Марта 1891 г.,
ВЪ БЕНЕФИСЪ А. Н. ВАСИЛЬЕВА,
представлено будетъ:

РЕВИЗОРЪ

Комедія въ 5-ти актахъ соч. Н. В. Гоголя,

...тонъ Антоновичъ Сквоз-
...ъ-Дмухановскій, городничій Г. Пеняевъ.
...на Андревна, жена его - Г-жа Станиславская.
...рія Антоновна, дочь его- Г-жа Рѣпникова.
...ка Лукичъ Хлоповъ, смо-
...тритель училищъ - - Г. Нѣмовъ.
...ена его - - - - - Г-жа Ларская.
...мосъ Ѳедоровичъ Ляпкинъ-
...Тяпкинъ, судья - - - Г. Васильевъ.
...темій Филипповичъ Земляни-
...ка, попечитель богоугодныхъ
...заведеній - - - - - Г. Бородинъ.
...анъ Кузмичъ Шпекинъ,
...почтмейстеръ - - - - Г. Дунаевъ.
...ръ Ивановичъ ⎫ городскіе Г. Мѣшалкинъ.
...ръ Ивановичъ ⎭
...Бобчинскій ⎫ помѣщики Г. Брагинъ.
...анъ Александровичъ Хлес-
...таковъ - - - - - С. Я. С.-Самарскій.
...ипъ, слуга его - - - Г. Жилинъ.
...стіанъ Ивановичъ Гибнеръ
...ѣздный лѣкарь - - - Г. Нейбергъ.
...епанъ Ильичъ Уховертовъ,
...частный приставъ - - Г. Смирновъ.
...ступовъ ⎫ полицейскіе Г. Афанасьевъ
...ежиморда ⎭ Г. Шаляпинъ.

...ght 4. Chaliapin as Bertram in
...eyerbeer's opera Robert le Diable
...anayev Theatre, St. Petersburg),
1894.

5. *Chaliapin's sketch for his make-up for the part of Ivan the Terrible, made by him in 1914, for the production of* The Maid of Pskov.

6. *Chaliapin as Ivan the Terrible in Rimsky-Korsakov's opera* The Maid of Pskov (*Russian Private Opera, Moscow*), *1897.*

7. *Chaliapin as Ivan the Terrible in Rimsky-Korsakov's opera* The Maid of Pskov
(Bolshoy Theatre, Moscow), 1911.

8. *Chaliapin as Ivan the Terrible, sculpture by Kavaleridze (Bolshoy Theatre Museum).*

"Yes, yes," mother would say. "Still, I don't think you should go to the theatre. You'll lose your interest in work. As it is your father complains, says you do nothing, and I am always covering up for you. It's quite true, you know. You are a loafer."

It *was* true. I didn't do anything, and my studies were being neglected. In the end father refused to allow me to go to the theatre. "Suit you better to get a job as a night watchman, instead of this trailing round theatres. Get a job, and you'll always have a piece of bread to eat. But refuse to learn a trade, and you may find yourself rotting in gaol. Look how workers live. They have enough to eat, they're clothed, they've even got boots."

Yes, indeed. I had seen the workers all right, lots and lots of them, mostly in tatters, bare-footed, hungry, and generally drunk. But I did not accept my father's reproof. "I *am* working," I replied. "I'm copying documents. Just look at the pile I've done."

He remained adamant. "Just wait till you finish school, my lad. *I'll* harness you. Remember that."

In spite of this threat the theatre continued to draw me, irresistibly, and more and more frequently I concealed the money I earned by singing. Though I knew this to be wrong, it seemed impossible for me not to go to the theatre. What I really wanted was a companion, someone with whom I could exchange impressions. So I began taking friends with me, paying for their tickets, perhaps my friend Mikhailov more often than the others. He, too, was an enthusiast, so that when the intervals came we got into hot discussions, appraising, criticizing the acting, searching for the play's meaning.

As if this were not enough, the opera arrived. Immediately the price of tickets rose to thirty kopecks. Another shock for me, but a delightful one. As a choir singer I wasn't surprised by the fact that people could sing, or that sometimes words did not seem to make sense. For instance, I understood little of the actual words of the marriage service. No, the astounding thing was this discovery of people's ability to sing about everything, instead of talking about it, as happened in the streets and houses of Kazan. Here were extraordinary people, in extraordinary costumes, singing when they asked questions, and when they answered them, when they thought, and when they were angry. They even sang when they were dying, and they did so standing up and sitting down, in choirs, duets, in every possible way. This then was the appeal. If only people everywhere sang like this, in the streets, the bath-houses, the workshops. For instance the master sings to me: "Feodor, hand me the wa——ax-ed thread."

And I sing back to him, "Here you—ou—ou are."

Or perhaps the policeman taking somebody by the scruff of the neck proclaims in the loudest voice, "I'll take you to—o—o the police sta—tion," and the poor victim replies in a squealing tenor, "Have mer—cy—have mercy, po—ol—iceman."

As I dreamt about these things, my ordinary life was transformed into an opera, and when father, said "Feodor, bring me some kvas," I would reply, singing descant on the highest notes, "I'm bringing it." "What on earth are you yelling about?" he'd growl. Or else I'd sing, "Father, get up, get up, it is ti—me to drink te—a." He would glare at me with bulging eyes, then remark to my mother, "Hear that? All this theatre business. Where is it going to end?"

The theatre had become as necessary to me as bread, and the part of the spectator having a seat in the gods no longer sufficed. I wanted to penetrate and explore back-stage, to find out where the moon came from, where people vanished! And from what did they so quickly build towns, from where did the costumes come, and most important of all, where did all this wonderful life go? I tried to find my way into this wonderland on several occasions, but always some ferocious man was there to keep me out. Only once did I manage to satisfy my craving. I opened a little door and found myself on a dark stairway, buried under all kinds of junk, broken window-panes, pieces of décor. So this was it, the road to the miracles. Exploring further I found myself beneath the stage itself, a devilish forest of ropes, bars and machines, all of which moved, shuddered, and squealed. In all this chaos people rushed about with hammers, shouting at each other. Creeping amongst them I finally found the stage, and climbed up. I was *there*. The dream had come true. I was surrounded by Redskins, Spaniards, and some dishevelled people, standing there, notebooks in hands. Though, like the carpenters, these Redskins and Spaniards spoke perfectly good Russian, it never detracted from their charm, and I scrutinized those painted faces with great fascination. There were some firemen amongst them wearing great brass helmets, and above my head some men resembling Yashka were doing acrobatics. All this made a terrific effect on me, it was wholly enchanting, never, never to be forgotten.

Shortly after this I found myself taking part in a production as an extra. My face was painted black with burnt cork, and I was given a dark costume. For this I was promised five kopecks. I submitted without fear, and with the greatest delight. How I shouted "hurrah", and with what frenzy, in honour of Vasco da Gama. I was in heaven, and the very feeling of it only lessened a little when I came to remove that burnt cork from my features. I remember on the way home stopping to rub my face with snow. Yet when I arrived home, I still looked like a chimney sweep. My parents took the affair very seriously, and an explanation was demanded. I did explain, but father wasn't satisfied, and there followed a walloping with my father crying out, "Go and get yourself a job as a night watchman."

The times I had asked him his reason for wishing me to be a night watchman. It obsessed him.

Of the artists of that period I remember particularly the bass Ilyashevich, in the part of Mephistopheles. I had heard countless stories about the devil, and to me he was a half-real being, a force that moved amongst the people. He was the enemy, one who enjoyed making life even more difficult. For me the interpretation of this role by Ilyashevich was frightfully convincing. To me he was terrifying, though at the same time vaguely recognizable. He was two men. When he rushed about the stage like a red flame proclaiming "People are perishing for metal", and when backstage he spoke ordinary words in a simple human voice. The mere sight of his eyes filled me with fear. With a fearful brilliance they gave out flashing red sparks. I began to think of this as the natural phenomenon of an artist's eyes. Later, and rather sadly, I was to discover this to be merely silver paper stuck to the eyelids.

Once, as I was passing his dressing-room, he called out to me, "Hey, little boy, here's twenty kopecks. Go and buy me some grapes." I rushed from the theatre and into the square where Tartars were selling fruit from the barrows. When I was rewarded with five grapes from the bunch I reached a blissful height, and decided to give them to my mother. Lovingly I carried them with me throughout the entire performance, fearing to crush them. Unfortunately childish curiosity overcame filial affection, and I ate them. Never before had I tasted such fruit.

The tenor Zakrzhevsky was the idol of the public, and to the young, particularly girl students, especially so. They adored him. Young people literally carried him on their shoulders. They pulled his carriage. I remember with what awe I stood outside his dressing-room door, staring at the plate affixed to it. *Julian Feodorovich Zakrzhevsky.* I experienced a fluttering of the heart, thinking, "Suppose the door were to open *now*, and I were to see this universally adored man." I was to meet him a few years later. He was a sick man, living in poverty, entirely forgotten. I had the melancholy honour of trying to help him a little, and remember seeing in his eyes tears of outrage and gratitude, wrath and helplessness. It was a difficult meeting. Such is the fate of an artist. He had ceased to be the public's toy. The voice had gone, the man is no more, forgotten, like the wooden soldier previously much loved, but now neglected by the child who has got bored with it. I thought to myself: "If one wishes to avoid undeserved degradation, then one must strike whilst the iron is hot. One must work, tirelessly, unsparingly."

At the age of thirteen I had finished with school, and to the amazement of my parents had even been commended, though to be honest I did fool the teachers a bit. We had to write an essay, something about our personal lives, for the school-leaving exam.

I persuaded myself that I could do such a story, but thought it even better if it could be copied straight out of a book. So I cribbed one about a little boy who went into the forest with his grandfather to cut wood, and saw a snake on the way. The story told of how they killed the snake, and about the feelings of the boy, what the grandfather said, and the position of the sun at that time. I handed up my effort with some trepidation, and was astounded when I received the highest marks. All honour and glory to learning and the kindness it bestowed on me. I hadn't forgotten that story of my sore feet and the doctor. And my success was soon to be repeated. I read two poems, Koltzov's *Steppe*, and Lermontov's *Borodino*, indulging in theatrical declamation and other histrionics. In *Borodino* I asked "Uncle" the questions, and replied to myself in a real Uncle's voice. Though I conquered the hearts of my teachers, I must confess that my schoolfellows treated the affair with ridicule, though I was quick to note with what interest they listened. They saw something false and disgraceful in my rendering.

"Well now," announced my father, "you're literate. Time to get out to work. Time to finish with all this hanging about in theatres, reading books, singing songs."

He'd call me to him whenever he was drunk, rap me on the forehead with his knuckles, and repeat over and over again, "Get yourself a job as a night watchman." The night watchman's job never arrived, since shortly after he got me a job in Pechenkin's pawnshop.

"At first you'll work without pay," father said, "then you'll take what they give you."

So from nine until four I spent my time behind the counter at Pechenkin's. I watched the sad-looking people come in, bringing spoons, fur coats, rings, coats, icons. The man would value the article, but always paid out a lower sum, and this often led to bargaining and quarrelling. Always there was somebody weeping, begging for a little more money, pleading a mother's illness, a son's death. And there I sat writing out receipts, and still dreaming about the theatre.

I worked for two months without pay, and was finally paid a salary of eight roubles a month. I loathed the work, even though I took pride in my earning power, and my ability to help mother. I performed my duties well, and was considered a good worker.

That summer, in the Panayev Gardens, an operetta was performed on an open stage, and naturally I was a frequent visitor. I was passionately interested in the artists, and at the same time afraid of them, and always I watched from a distance. "What amazing people they are," I'd say to myself. "There stands a man only lately a king, and here he is dressed like everybody else, drinking beer, and eating salted rusks." On or off stage these people excited my interest, these Kings, Achilleses, Calchases, and Lambertucci, these gypsy barons and governors, all drew me like a powerful magnet. And they were so gay and amusing, always with a joke on their lips. I thought how easy their life was compared with my own, sitting in a pawnshop, listening to the groans and pleadings of people, and it was not confined to Pechenkin's. In Sukonnaya Sloboda it was little better.

I wasn't to remain long at that pawnshop. The terrible drawing power of the theatre dictated everything, and it certainly killed my enthusiasm for my job. Father was furious with me, and almost at once I was packed off to an industrial school in the town of Arsk. Little did I know what a choice my father had made. There was no theatre in Arsk, and I can say that of all the towns on God's earth Arsk was the dullest.

For the first time I was leaving my parents' home, going alone to some unknown place with the local postman, a Jew named Holtzmann, a delightful person. It was a wonderfully dry autumn, with the golden trees stood sentinel-like on the road, and spiders' webs, "Mermaid's Spinning", floating about in the blue, translucent air. I imagined myself moving into beautiful country, even glad to be putting Sukonnaya Sloboda behind me, where life had seemed to get harder and harder for me. Once in Arsk I decided to choose carpentry as my trade. One of the things that pleased me was the senior pupils being allowed to make little boxes for themselves. I was soon to find the work tedious, besides which the teacher beat his pupils, me more frequently than others, with any instrument or material that lay handy, including set-squares and boards. We were banged on the head with jack-planes, butted in the stomach with other tools, far more painful than a tanning at school. In addition to carpentry I was also learning to bind books, and I did this both quickly and rather well. This was not the only work. We were required to help in the vegetable garden, cutting and shredding cabbage, and pickling cucumbers. The whole thing was rather dull. Nor did I like my companions overmuch. There remained just one pleasure, and that was the Saturday night visit to the baths. We steamed ourselves until we looked red and raw, then flung ourselves naked into the snow. Snow was early and abundant that year. Some said it was a bad sign, but we thought it was great fun.

On St Nicholas's day I found myself sitting on a bench outside the gates, thinking and dreaming of Kazan, and the theatre there. As I sat there, contemplating, staring around at this dull, insignificant, meaningless, and empty town, I felt the few kopecks in my pocket, and there and then made the decision. I would return to Kazan. I cared nothing about the consequences, I simply got up and left, but I had barely covered a dozen versts when two horsemen caught up with me, one the school watchman, the other a senior pupil. They took me back, and I received a thrashing that was to discourage me from a repetition of the process. I gave in, and reconciled myself to the fact that I could not get away before the spring.

Suddenly, right out of the blue, there came a letter from my father. Mother was dangerously ill, and there was nobody to look after her and I was to return home at once. I left with a convoy of sledges journeying in that direction. It was a dreadfully cold journey, and I was frozen stiff. It was a delight to arrive at the inn and drink scalding tea and eat black bread.

I found mother very seriously ill, and I felt she would die. We took her to the clinic, and there Professor Vinogradov cured her. To the end of her days she mentioned his name with reverence.

Following my return home father got me work as a copying clerk in the District Office. Now we were going to work together. We copied vast reports with miles of figures, and often, having to work late into the night, we slept on the office tables. The secretary was a man named Dudkin, a charming young man, who had replaced the former secretary, one Pifiev by name. Father told me that this Pifiev kept a whip at home, and with it he taught his wife how to live. Dudkin thought well of my father, who was considered a good worker, even when in some drunken stupor he would try and pick a quarrel. When he behaved insolently, Dudkin kept silence, and just puffed and blinked.

It was now that I began to dream of love, if only prematurely. I had read enough bad novels, and seen something of the theatrical life. Nor was I the only one; my friends were much occupied by these same sweet dreams. We all imagined ourselves to be in love with Olya Borisenko, the beautiful schoolgirl who was indifferent to us, and who walked her demure way, looking at the world as though it did not exist. How eagerly we longed for Easter, and the chance to exchange a kiss with her. I remember an incident outside the church where some Tartars were plying their trade with cotton goods, fancy work, soap, and some astonishing perfumes. We bought some scent, and without waiting for the midnight service to end, rushed out to the portico where each of us rubbed the perfume on his teeth, the tip of the tongue, and the lips. If the scent burnt, the fragrance itself was magnificent. Suddenly out strode Olya. We went up to her in single file, as if queuing for the theatre, exclaiming, "Christ is risen," and carefully pecked at the lady of our hearts, though she remained as indifferent as ever.

Zhenya Birilov for some reason, christened her with the silly name of Dulcinea of Toboso. "Of Tobolsk, you mean," I tried to remonstrate. For this Dulcinea, and as befits a true cavalier, I fought a duel with swords. This duel was more playful than earnest, we having become saturated with Dumas and Poncon du Terraille. A young grammar school boy became friendly with us. He would steal rifles from his father and sell them, and with the proceeds he treated us to beer in the alehouses. We liked him well enough, but only as the provider of the ale. The time was to arrive when he permitted himself the insolence of showing disrespect to our lady. Nothing of a serious nature, but when one is in love jealousy is never far away. To be able to say just a few words to Olya was a happiness conceded to us, and somehow I always seemed to have less time than my friends. I was the youngest of them all, the least good-looking, nevertheless I told the grammar school boy to go to the devil. He wanted to beat me up there and then, but I had the backing of my friends. He hotly agreed that a duel was essential.

I was chosen as duellist since, imitating Mephistopheles, Faust and Valentine, I could bend a stick like a sword, apart from making all kinds of heroic pirouettes and lunges. It was decided that I should run him through. So Zhenya brought the rapiers from home, where they always hung as decorations. The tips of them not appearing sharp enough we took them down to a grinder and asked for them to be sharpened. I can remember the black blade of my own weapon, and its bright silver tip.

We chose the Osokin Woods, my friends acted as seconds, and remained scrupulously honourable. The duel began and, having twice crossed, we now struck where we fancied. My opponent got me in the forehead, I found his shoulder. He was evidently hurt since he dropped his weapon, though its tip remained sticking in my head. I pulled it clear, and out followed the blood. It flooded my eyes, and was already streaming down my opponent's arm. We terminated the duel, our wounds were bandaged, and we shook hands. Seconds later we were stealing apples from somebody's garden. I returned home that evening with a feeling of elation, though a sound thrashing soon reduced it. A real blow to my pride. Did Olya know of this duel, I asked myself. Somebody must have told her, yet there seemed no change in her attitude towards either me or my fate. Love that lived in the theatre, that tormented the people of Sukonnaya Sloboda, still disturbed my vivid imagination. Everybody was seeking love, everybody suffering from it, the single and the married, the civil servants and the seamstresses, the workers and peasants. There were aspects of it frighteningly incomprehensible to me. I thought of the way the village girls spoke of love in a sad and touching manner. Why? Men and boys indulged in lewd stories about it. They visited the brothels in Peski, crudeness and mockery hung on their lips. I knew what a brothel was, but never reconciled it with say *The Lady of the Camellias*.

I thought of the weddings at which I'd sung, the brides looking like white doves, and, most often, weeping. Village girls always cried on their wedding day, and sang songs cursing a married life. They bore children in suffering, yet they all longed to get married. To learn the essence and meaning of life? Perhaps.

The little I knew concerning sexual relationships was contradictory to the utmost degree. It was clear to me that in everyday life a woman was simply a domestic animal, and the harder she worked, the better and more valuable she was. At the same time I knew that wherever woman walked, she brought the light, and that life with her was more pure, more beautiful.

I used to go to little evening parties in the workshops. There they were, workers and apprentices, foul-mouthed drunkards all, and us boys being made to tidy up. Having bought biscuits, sweets, and liqueurs, they invited in the seamstresses, match-box makers, and housemaids. There would be dancing and games, the favourite one being forfeits. Some desperate young man would choose a girl and parade arm in arm with her, whilst the rest sang. To witness the joyous embarrassment of a cobbler was incredible, and so with tailor or carpenter, when clumsily and shyly he kissed the girl of his choice, her face shining from the very blush of that big moment. Perhaps today this kind of thing appears ridiculous, but to me it was wonderful, and in some strange way it ennobled the hard and squalid life of the peasants. I felt woman to be the joy of life, its great mistress, but always there remained the manifestations that were degrading to her. I remember a particular ritual that struck me in an unpleasant way. The sister of a boy I knew got married to a postal worker "for love". I attended the wedding, watched the celebrations. All was interesting, and gay. That night the young couple went to sleep in the attic, and I and my friend in the hayloft.

I was woken in the morning by shrieks and howlings, and looking into the yard below beheld a sight not soon forgotten. Drunken, half-dressed, dishevelled women were leaping about there, performing a wild dance, raising skirts higher and yet higher. Some sang in high-pitched voices, others assaulted the walls of the house with pan lids. One waved a white rag in the air, stained with blood. It all seemed mad and frightening to me.

The drunken men roared with laughter, embracing the women, all leaping about like mosquitoes over a puddle. And there on the steps of the house stood the young married couple. Before this degrading scene they themselves looked blissful. Nor have I ever forgotten the happiness that shone in their eyes that morning. My friend was older and more experienced, and I asked him what was going on.

"They're celebrating of course. *Can't* you hear? Can't you see that the sheet is stained with blood? That means that my sister was an honest girl. The red flowers have blossomed." In a mixture of astonishment and embarrassment, I asked, "Has she now become dishonest?"

And at great length did my friend explain what constituted a girl's honour, and I felt uncomfortable and ashamed, though I listened with avid curiosity. In all he said, in all I had witnessed, I detected something wrong, a mockery of women and love. I suppose the only remaining bright spot was the shining happiness in the couple's faces. It seemed to me that no matter how much filth people might try and make around this subject of love, it was still a happiness. That may not have been the moment of my singular thought, but looking back I am glad that it came to me early, whilst still a boy. I think I owe this idea, with all its consequences, to the fact that I knew a woman too early.

I happened to know a laundry-woman, a habitual drunkard. One of her daughters, once a housemaid, had married a general, so that the mother was able to live comfortably on the money her daughter sent her. She even subscribed to the magazine *Niva*, from which I read stories to her, and the captions from the illustrations. There was one other daughter, a very beautiful girl, but unfortunately mentally afflicted. She had had a love affair with a young officer, and gone off with him, and had lost her reason when he abandoned her. Though I was extremely sorry for her, she inspired in me a feeling of terror.

She was always so silent, except for a rather frightening laugh, a kind of giggle that to me seemed evil. Her beautiful blue eyes stared fixedly at you, at everything. I was never able to look at her for long, and often dreaded her doing some harm to herself. "Why is she so unhappy?" I would ask myself. "She's so beautiful. If only she could have married that officer, as my friend's sister had married the postman." The dead stare, that silence, never left me.

Around Christmas time her mother took me to see some friends of hers. They were dancing a quadrille, eating and drinking, playing forfeits. A fat girl took a fancy to me. She would lead me behind a stove, and with a special kind of kiss made my head go round. I was unpleasantly disturbed. It was late when we left, and the drunken laundry-woman suggested that I stay the night at her place, since Sukonnaya Sloboda was too far away. I agreed, and she made my bed on a big chest in her daughter's room. I was then thirteen years old. Unheeding my presence, the mother undressed her daughter in front of me, and then put her to bed right opposite the chest on which I was lying. She then turned out the light and left us. I was unable to

64

sleep. The kisses of that fat girl had excited me. It was now that I recalled the stories I had heard about love, I remembered the books I'd read, the beautiful speeches of lovers in the theatre, and not least the happy face of my friend's sister, as she stood in front of that dervish-like crowd. I thought to myself, "Suppose I can take the place of that young officer, perhaps this beautiful girl will then be cured." I got up and crossed quietly to her bed, took her head in my hands, and turned her towards me. In that darkness it seemed to me that she looked at me with a far more comprehending eye, and it certainly increased my courage. She remained silent, unresisting, and seemed scarcely breathing. When I came to, I saw that her eyes remained fixed on the ceiling, as dead as ever.

Probably not all of this episode is true, perhaps in reality I had behaved in a rougher manner. I feel that the thoughts and the excuses were later invented by me. But what can I do about that? No man living but stands in need of some justification, in his own eyes. I might well have kept this story back from my readers, but I just had to say that whatever I did from that time on, I did for a woman, to deserve her attention and love.

I have seen both the Mediterranean and the Atlantic oceans, yet to this day it is with the deepest affection that I recall that quiet, dark, Kaban lake. It drew me so forcibly on summer evenings. How often I would climb the biggest willow tree, and, like a bird, rest there till daylight. There I dreamed, staring across that lake, and the very stillness and peace put my thoughts in order. Certainly they diverted my attention from the vile life of Sukonnaya Sloboda. Sometimes in that restful peace and silence, and from the direction of Peski, where the "sporting houses" are situated, a sad, even, on rare occasions, sober voice would be heard singing a song that was fashionable at the time, about a young girl who stood beneath the moon in a field of silver

"And vowed to heaven to keep her purity,
Until the grave. . . ."

I would listen attentively to the watchman sounding his wooden clapper. A long staccato rattle indicated a fire, and if I heard it I was down that tree in a flash, rushing off to it, guided by its glow. The unhurried casual rattle signified that all was well, and that thieves could get on with their business quite undisturbed. I must confess I adored fires, they were so dramatic, and I can recall a great blaze when Shamov's five-storey mill was burnt to the ground. It played like a red cat with a mouse, flaming sheets of iron flew into the air like great red birds, even the windows of the governor's house appeared bloodshot. The chief of the fire brigade, a little fellow utterly soaked in his own sweat, ran about screaming, "Pump away, pump away there, you devils," and clouted anyone within reach. But the spectators didn't want to pump, and shied clear of the over-zealous chief. Some gave the simplest answer.

"Serves them right. Let it burn."

"It's all insured, anyhow."

"Probably set fire to it themselves."

All seemed glad that it was a rich man's property, and nobody spared a thought for the tragedy of much work reduced to ashes. It was sad watching a fire, but it was also very exciting.

One of the pastimes I really loved was going into the woods to gather mushrooms. I remember rising early one morning and going off with some friends, wearing bast sandals, and carrying baskets. Suddenly someone announced that there would be an eclipse of the sun. We had heard of this phenomenon, but had never taken it seriously, putting it down to rumours invented by students. But when the black rim appeared on the sun's edge, the people in Sukonnaya Sloboda got worried, thinking there must be something in it after all. The sky was cloudless, the morning bright, yet suddenly everything was enveloped by this grey shadow. Someone advised us to watch the event through pieces of glass, held over a flame until they were smoky with soot. I did, and there before my eyes was the fading sun. I held on to the glass, watched the sun get blacker and blacker, yet I stood there, still unbelieving. The earth grew dull. The sudden alteration of the whole landscape tugged at my heart. I heard the lowing of cows, and somehow even this seemed different. Everyone remained silent, staring up at the sky. Their eyes seemed to have lost their own light, even their faces had turned grey. A frightened cat rushed across the yard, a bewildered cockerel flapped madly at our feet. And for a second or two there was no sun at all, only a black disc the size of a frying-pan, with pale little rays emerging like red needles. I was frightened to tears. But in a second the golden sickle of the sun was through. The grey shadow decreased, the brightness returned. I think the first to rejoice was the cockerel, and slowly, one after the other, the people were normal again, and so was the place. I heard somebody shouting, "I'll give it to you. I'll give it to you."

We went on our way to gather the mushrooms. We travelled ten versts from the town, along the Arsk fields, beyond the madhouse where once I saw a patient whom I have never forgotten. I had come with the choir to sing a requiem for a patient who had just died. We arrived early, and went into the garden to pass the time. There I saw a pale, tired-looking man in an old faded dressing-gown, slippers and underpants. He paraded silently up and down the path. We decided he was crazy. Then suddenly he was standing by us, talking quite sensibly, enquiring why we had come, where I sang, and in what church, even down to the names of the composers. His speech was so sane that at first I mistook him for the doctor. Then he pointed to a log, exclaiming, "Let's roll it."

"Where? *Why?*"

"To beat Christ with," he replied, with deadly earnest.

"How?" we asked. "What Christ?"

"Christ the god who stopped me from living in the world."

The attendants came up and led him away.

I was staggered by this incident. In spite of his mad fantasies, he had not forgotten the habits of the sane, to beat and fight.

It was almost evening when we reached the forest. Having gathered our mushrooms, we struck camp on the river bank, dug up potatoes from a near-by field, got a fire going, and made ourselves some soup. After this we lay around the fire above the river, surrounded by the great dark wall of forest, and in this setting we told each other terrifying stories, one of which I particularly remember.

Some students, sitting in an alehouse, were boasting that they were unafraid of anything. One said he would go into a cemetery at night and dig up a grave.

"But you mustn't dig graves," he was warned. "You can be sent to Siberia for that." But he insisted.

"Would you like me to go and lie down in a newly dug one?" he asked.

A wager was made, and it was decided that he should enter one of the cemetery tombs, and bring back something, a handful of earth, some plaster, anything at all. He agreed and departed. His friends decided to play a trick on him, and followed behind. Hiding amongst the graves they lay in wait. They watched him approach a newly dug grave, and prepare to enter it. At this moment they decided to intone with sepulchral voices. Our friend was quite undismayed, and called forth: "Never mind, dear departed ones, don't you worry, and don't try to frighten me. I'm not scared." He lay in the grave for a while, got out, and went to the tomb. His friends flung clods of earth after him. He laughed and ran from them, suddenly cried out and fell. When they reached him he was dead. It turned out later that a hoop lay in his path, and he had accidentally trodden on it. It hit him in the legs, and that was enough to make anybody die of fright. I found this episode both pleasant and scarifying. It reminded me so much of Kirillovna's stories, as told to village friends.

Now it was my turn to collect wood from the forest. But I was frightened and asked somebody to accompany me. I was laughed at and told to go alone, which I did eventually. I got the wood and was glad to get back. Yet that night I could not sleep a wink.

In the morning we again went mushroom gathering, and by afternoon had returned with full baskets. But on the way back we had stopped to rest, and I fell asleep. When I woke it was to find myself alone. It was quite dark, the forest loomed all about me, and it seemed to me as though somebody was moving silently through the trees, lying in wait for me. I hurried away and never once looked back, indeed I was hardly aware of my feet under me. The forest seemed to pursue me, and always the trees were barring my path. I could feel somebody grabbing me by the heels, breathing coldly down my neck, and then as luck would have it, I had to pass by a cemetery. I imagined the dead watching me from over the fence; there they were moving around, shaking the crosses, standing in white shrouds under the birch trees. I tried my best to ignore them, sang and talked to myself, though it did not lessen the horrors. I knew that I shouldn't be frightened of the dead, who, I thought, were better in many ways than the living, neither drinking nor swearing, nor fighting. Knowing this, I yet remained sceptical. I don't know where I found the strength to get home that night, I felt my heart must burst. After this, nothing could persuade me to go mushroom-gathering again in a distant forest.

I had a young friend, Kamensky by name. He was seventeen and, like myself, very theatre-minded. He performed small parts on the open stage in the Panayev Gardens. One day he came to me in great excitement. "There's a marvellous opportunity for you to get into the theatre. Though our producer is very strict, he is kind to the young. Go and ask him."

"I shan't be able to act," I said.

"Never mind. *Try.* Perhaps you'll get a small part, saying two or three words."

I hurried off to see the producer, and was immediately offered a part in the play *Gendarme Roget.* The play abounded in thieves and tramps, they played all kinds of tricks, and the gendarme tries to catch them, but does not succeed. The part of this clumsy policeman was given to me. Out of sheer joy, and a consciousness of the responsibility being placed on me, I drowned in a kind of sacred and constant trepidation. I was due for rehearsal at eleven o'clock the following morning. This was rather complicated, since I was supposed to be at work in the office. Something had to be done about it. When I got to the office I approached the book-keeper, an agonizing look on my face, and begged to be allowed to go home. "I've a terrible headache." A dark-eyed man wearing spectacles, he looked at me in silence for a moment or two, then, as if wishing to crush by a single glance, replied, "Go." The word itself had the prick of a pin. So off I went, unhurrying, holding my forehead, knowing that he did not believe a word I said, yet going through the motions of rubbing my "aching" head. To make certain that nobody saw the direction I was taking, I bent down and huddled my way past the office windows.

How gay were those Panayev Gardens. The birds twittered in the paths, actresses walked like queens, laughing, and exchanging jokes. Some of them I had already met, and even copied their parts for them. I felt rather proud about that. I was absurdly shy, in fact painfully so, yet at rehearsals, amongst the people I knew, and with the curtain lowered, I managed to work, to master my part and, as much as was possible, learned how to move. Then came the long-awaited evening. I was the first to arrive, and went straight to the dressing-room. I put on a green calico uniform coat, with revers and cuffs, pulled on trousers of white frieze, ceremonially referred to as "doeskins". Over my boots I put leggings of oilcloth. Then I painted my face. In spite of much effort I wasn't very pleased with myself. My heart beat madly, my legs refused to obey me. The performance began.

What I felt that evening is practically incommunicable. I recall a whole series of excruciating sensations. My heart appeared to break clear of its moorings, fell away from me. I remember a door opening, and being pushed on to the stage. I fully realized that I had to walk, speak, live, yet I seemed wholly incapable of it. My feet appeared anchored to those floor boards, my arms remained glued to my sides, I could utter not a word, move not a finger. Then from backstage I was conscious of hissing voices. "Go on. Speak. The devil take you. Hit him somebody."

Everything swam before my eyes, and guffaws issued from some enormous throat, in many voices. The stage began to sway, I felt I was vanishing, dying. When the curtain ran down I was still standing there, stiff, still, turned to stone. The producer—a tall, thin man—began beating me. He was mad with rage, and started to tear off my uniform. My oilcloth leggings fell clear, and finally, wearing only my underpants, I was chased into the garden. A second later my own clothes followed me. I went into a deserted part of the gardens and hurriedly dressed. Having got over the fence I allowed my feet to take me anywhere they would. I wept.

Later, I was to find myself in Arkhangelskaya Sloboda, and for two whole days and nights, without food, hid myself in a barn. I was afraid to appear in the street. I felt that the whole town, right down to the village women hanging up their washing, knew that I had disgraced myself, and had been beaten. I finally decided to return home, but half way there I realized I had been absent from work for two days. Naturally I was at once asked where I'd been. I lied, of course, whereupon mother exclaimed sadly, "They'll probably sack you now. The watchman's been here enquiring about you."

The next day I reported at the office, and asked Stepan, the watchman, what my chances were.

"You've been replaced," he said.

I sat with him under the stairs for a little while, and then went home.

Matters had not much improved there either. Father was now constantly drunk, and looking at my mother I could see her daily losing her strength. Yet she continued to do her work. I remained in the church choir, but this brought in little, besides which my voice was breaking. I was past fifteen. Somebody advised me to send in a petition asking for work as a copying clerk at the Law Court. This I did, and was accepted. So there I was, sitting in a stuffy, smoke-filled room, copying the court's decisions. Oddly enough, they were mostly concerned with sexual relations with animals and, of course, rape. Here, the employees went about not in civilian jackets and coats, as at the District Office, but in uniforms with bright shiny buttons. Everything around was orderly, austere, inspiring in one the greatest respect. But I had a feeling that I would not long serve in the temple of Themis. In this court, and for the first time in my life, I tasted that pleasurable beverage, coffee. The commissionaires would supply it to me with cream at five kopecks a glass. As my pay was only fifteen roubles, I couldn't afford its daily luxury. But I often worked late doing the work of others, and this enabled me to enjoy lots of coffee. Even those with better salaries did not indulge as I did.

The head clerk appeared to be a very important person. He was a handsome creature, grey-haired, and wore a goatee beard. His hair was always brushed neatly back from his forehead, and he wore gold-rimmed pince-nez. His eyes were shaded by thick brows, and he spoke in a magnificent voice that resembled the actor Kiselevsky's. And in another sense he reminded me of the Marquis in the Dumas novels. If I have described the gentleman in detail, it is because I am unable to understand, even to this day, how one of such splendid appearance could throw me out of the Chamber so rudely.

I often had to take home papers for copying and remember an occasion, when, after being paid, I went off shopping for various provisions, tea, sugar, and so on. I then bought myself some books from a second-hand dealer. It was only when I was on my way home that I realized I had lost a bundle containing decisions of the Court. I was horrified, rushed madly about the shops, enquiring of passers-by. But they never turned up. The remainder of that day was one of suspended horror, ending up with a sleepless night. Next morning I reported the loss to the commissionaires. They appeared appalled by the news, gravely shook their heads. "Oh! That's bad." I confided in a friend, Zaitzev, and he replied with a singular "Oh". From the look I got from him I felt that even if I didn't go to Siberia, I would end up in some gaol. I kept clear of the Chamber, and remained below with the Commissionaires. How wide and impressive was that staircase. It seemed to invite mortals to pass under the sword of the blind goddess. Suddenly I heard the voice of the head clerk, that beautiful velvety voice, exclaiming, "Where's that anathema, that——." He swore obscenely, and spared neither his tongue nor his throat. Bent double, I crept from under the staircase. There above me towered the clerk, mighty as Zeus. His spectacles flashed fire, the black ribbon holding them trembled, whilst the skirts of his frock coat flew like the wings of a cockerel. He rushed about like a maniac, stamping his feet, releasing floods of abuse. About that whole episode there was something Roman, Olympian, picturesque, grandiose.

"Out," he roared, then swung round on the commissionaires. "Why are you standing there like that? Hit the devil. Pitch him out. Don't force me to come down or I'll murder him. Out of here now, spawn of the devil."

It occurred to me that it was the only thing to do, and I dashed into the street. How all this was going to end I hardly knew, though I felt less frightened, indeed a little better in the open air. This "Marquis" head clerk shocked me, so magnificent, yet swearing like any common Sukonnaya Sloboda trooper. At home I found my father, mother, and small brother awaiting me. Life had to go on, work had to be done.

Mother often made pies and sold them by the piece in the street, but this was not enough to live on. Nor could I now sing in the choir, my voice having gone. I spent days without food, roaming the streets in search of work, but there was nothing to be found. I would go off to the banks of the Volga, to the wharves, and spend hours watching the brisk, unceasing work of many hundreds of people. Ships came sailing in looking like enormous swans, and the stevedores sang the popular song of the workers, "Dubinushka". On the deep hot sand of these banks, the Tartars would set up their stalls, selling soap from Kazan, Morocco slippers, Bokhara cloth, whilst the Russians sold bread, sausage, all the usual foodstuffs. Everything looked bright and festive, and I, like a creature condemned to roam about pining for work, suffered intensely whenever my thoughts returned to my mother. I felt that I must leave this town, get far away from it. It had served no purpose, brought me nothing but ill-luck. And desire became actual decision. Following this, I discussed and even managed to persuade my parents into going to Astrakhan. We sold everything we had, and took a fourth-class ticket on a boat going down the Volga.

This great river entranced me. There was something inexpressible about this queen of the waters. I don't think I slept for a single night, so afraid was I that I might miss something, perhaps some miracle that *had* to be seen. I was happy in a moment when an elderly gentleman began talking to me about the Caucasus. Snow peaks reaching to the sky. And the heat! People wore sheepskin hats in the summer-time. There was so much that was strange, fairy-tale-like in his descriptions. It reached to my heart. I felt the immensity of this land, the very riot of places to be seen.

Astrakhan welcomed us rather unkindly. I had visualized this place as very special, for its very name promised wonders. But the confrontation was a shock. To my eyes it seemed even worse than Kazan. That enthusiastic trip down the Volga, that excitement, was suddenly dimmed and intent receded. It seemed the same old story all over again. The horizon I had conjured up seemed very far away. My heart sank.

3

Having left my father and brother on the jetty, mother and I set off in search of a place to live. The sandy streets were hot as ovens, the stone houses exuded their own heat, and everywhere one beheld the glistening fish scales. The very air gave forth the smell of smoked roach. We eventually found a hovel of two rooms, and took it for a rent of two roubles. It crouched in the corner of a dirty yard, in which hummed millions of flies. The other inhabitants consisted of dockers and droshki drivers. The yard itself was full of old carts, sacks, boards, every kind of junk. After the spaciousness and magnificence of the Volga the squalor seemed degrading.

The following day father and I set off to seek work. We visited shops, offices, factories, yards, in fact any place at all that revealed an open door. We were met kindly enough, people were genial, some even suggested that we send in our applications for work. This we did very promptly, and applications went flying in all directions. Not a single reply has ever been received to this day. We were entirely without money, indeed it looked like a starvation period for us all. How much that period taught me, how amazed I was by the sheer steadfastness of my mother, her never ceasing resistence to poverty. We have in Russia a special breed of women, who all their lives struggle against privation and desperate need, without complaint, and often without hope. How stoically they stood up against the blows of fate. They had the courage of martyrs. And my mother was such a person. She would not accept defeat, and started up again baking and selling fish pies, fruit pies, her own special gifts were always to hand. How often I have longed to eat them myself, but she guarded her treasure as a miser his gold, not only from me, but from the hordes of flies. But even this effort would not feed a family. She began washing up on boats, from which she would bring back left-over scraps of food, even the tiniest bones that had meat adhering. It didn't happen very often, and we starved.

There was an occasion when father went searching for something in a field, and suddenly fell to the ground. "I can't go any farther," he said. And I knew that this was weakness from lack of food. I sat beside him for a long time, torn by a limitless despair. What were we to do? Somehow I managed to get him back to the town, and into the house. And there I left him, and went off to a chapel, to pray, the bitter tears streaming down my face. Oh, my friends, if you but knew the degradations of hunger. Yes, if you but looked, how differently you would treat men.

9. *Chaliapin, 1898.*

10. Chaliapin with his father, Ivan Yakovlevich Chaliapin, and brother Vassily, 1898.

11. Chaliapin and Iola Tornaghi, the Italian ballerina and the singer's first wife, 1897.

12. *Chaliapin's children by his first marriage to Iola Tornaghi: Feodor, Irina, Boris (the distinguished painter), Lidya and Tatyana, 1909.*

Fortunately my voice now came to my aid. I had become, all of a sudden, a baritone. The church paid me a rouble and a half for helping out at an evening mass.

There was a pleasure garden in Astrakhan called Arcadia. Off I went and enquired whether they would take me into the choir. A small, clean-shaven man wearing a tussore silk coat was pointed out to me. "That's Impresario Cherkasov."

"How old are you?" he asked.

"Seventeen," I replied, though I was a year younger.

He looked thoughtfully at me for a moment and then said, "All right." I smiled my thanks.

"If you want to sing, then come and sing. You'll be given costumes, but I shan't pay you anything. My affairs are going badly, and I have no money."

I was glad to accept even those terms. It would never feed us, but it would serve to brighten up a miserable existence. I was then introduced to the choir-mistress. She handed me a score for the chorus from *Carmen*. That evening, dressed as a soldier, I was living in Spain.

It was hot, and the lights blazed. People in the brightest costumes sang and danced. I did also, but with a sinking feeling in my stomach. I went home that night, boasting to my father about my work in the theatre. He lost his temper completely, stamped his feet, then struck me some heavy blows, grabbed the score from my hands, and tore it to shreds. "And is that why we were dragged all the way here? So that we might die of hunger?" He followed this with a shout. "I know you. All you ever care about is theatre, theatre, theatre. Damn it. Curse the theatre." Now what was I to do?

And how could I return to the Arcadia without the score? I never returned there. I was furious with my father, and in an instant decided to leave. I set off almost at once for Nizhni-Novgorod Fair. In the Panayev Gardens in Kazan I had often heard story-tellers and couplet singers, and I had picked up much, including their patter. On occasion I had myself put on an act, and been praised by listeners. It was this that finally made up my mind for me. I would try my luck as a story-teller. I borrowed my fare from a choirmaster, two roubles, knowing very well that I would never be able to repay it. By this time my parents had realized that I could never be driven away from the theatre. So they let me go. Once again I found myself aboard ship, this time on a tug towing barges. At holiday time the crew would sing and dance, as did the passengers who happened to be aboard. As I could sing, the sailors accepted me, and the crowd itself grew fond of me. With them I ate and drank.

The boat sailed on, unhurriedly, yet business-like, stopping from time to time to load and unload cargo, delivered her barges, took on fresh tows, new crews, even new women, and new accordions. My journey was pleasurable as far as Saratov, a real artistic outing. We did nothing but sing and dance. I had enough to eat, and I was happy. We remained in Saratov for a whole day. I went off into the town, to discover a lovely garden on the river bank. And there over the entrance was the magic sign "OCHKIN'S GARDENS, OPEN STAGE". Suppose I tried there? I suited the action to the word, and spoke to the first man I met. Where was the boss?

"What do you want him for?"

" I want to perform. On the open stage."

"Wait here."

A gentleman appeared, wearing a white shirt, bright tie, and a smoking-jacket. He gave me an indifferent look. "What is it?" he asked.

"Do you need a story-teller?"

"A story-teller." He repeated this, and became reflective. My heart fluttered with fear and anxiety, for I now recalled the fiasco of the Panayev Gardens. Suppose the same thing happened here. However, the elegant gentleman, having reflected enough, calmly informed me that he did not require a story-teller. He said this with a great confidence, and departed. In a sense I was grateful for the refusal. I went for a walk round the town. "But this won't do," I kept telling myself. "No. It just won't. And supposing you were to get a job at the Nizhni-Novgorod Fair. Would you have enough courage to go through with it?" The thing didn't appear so easy as it once did in Astrakhan. I went back to the ship.

She had taken on a fresh tow, there were new sailors, new women, new songs. I felt depressed. My money had gone on food, and the new crew did not seem half so friendly as the old one. When we arrived at Samara, I enquired of some stevedores if I could work with them. The answer was swift enough. "Why not? Go on. Work." They were loading flour. On that first day I was worn out carrying those one and a half hundredweight sacks. My neck was very painful, and my back ached. For carrying 200 sacks the dockers received four roubles. I was paid twenty kopecks a day, for which I carried eighty sacks. The following day I could barely walk, and they laughed at me. "Never mind, you'll soon get used to breaking your bones. Softie." They mocked without wanting to hurt my feelings. We shipped water melons as well as flour, and after leaving port the work was easier. At each jetty we came to, a man with a corkscrew beard made us unload the melons. Boards would be flung across, and the melons thrown from hand to hand, chain-gang style, and always to the accompaniment of much joking, and not a few obscenities. If a man missed with his melon he was immediately struck by the one with the corkscrew beard. Each place has its own special laws. I received twenty kopecks for the unloading, and two water melons. This was wonderful. To me it meant five kopecks worth of bread, which I could eat with a melon. My stomach swelled almost immediately. I felt like a rich merchant.

It was on this journey that I was to meet the people of the Volga for the first time, and I was provided with excellent opportunities of observing them. A mixed lot, but all were kind, gay, and good-humoured. Of a sudden we had arrived at Kazan. Oh, the joy I felt, actually seeing my native town again, even though it had rarely been kind to me. Once again there came to my nostrils that strong smell of oil, a smell unnoticed anywhere else, except Astrakhan. In Kazan it was thicker, more pungent. It smelt sweet enough to me. "The smoke of my Fatherland."

Leaving my luggage aboard I went straight off to see a friend of mine who used to loan me the library books, and who read poetry. He was delighted to see me, and that evening I met more friends at the inn. There I played billiards, and for the very first time got drunk. It was worth it, celebrating such a joyous occasion. Later we tumbled into the street, and immediately began a tussle with the night watchman. He was utterly routed, until he gained the help of other watchmen, whereupon we were arrested and flung into the police-station. Younger than my friends, I appeared to be the most obstreperous. I became insolent to the inspector, swore, and behaved in a rather disgusting manner. It had its dire consequences, for this gentleman called two policemen who beat us up thoroughly, and then threw us into the street. I recall this episode with little pleasure, though my conscience will not allow me to leave it out. I spent the night with my friend. His mother was asked to rouse me in good time. A God-fearing woman, she got up at five o'clock every morning to go to church. Of course I overslept, even though she did call me. When I finally reached the quay my boat had departed, and with it my few belongings that were most precious to me. That Beranger volume, that precious Trio I had composed, so I decided to remain with my friend in Kazan. He had no objection to this, but his good mother did, and she now began to poison my very existence. Daily she dropped the most transparent hints, commented upon the great inability of some people to earn their daily bread. She felt the earth should swallow up such people. I did manage to find myself a job. This was in the Ecclesiastical Consistory, copying papers at the rate of eight kopecks the page. They dealt mainly with divorce cases, so that I became aware of the incredible and staggering filth which the Consistory officials so carefully fostered. They were all of them confirmed drunkards, the worst I've seen in my whole life. They drank themselves into fits, the wildest of hallucinations, and inspired in me nothing but pure terror. Only one amongst them, the secretary, looked human, sometimes almost too human. He had a uniform coat, and used very strong scent. His soft, insinuating voice was accompanied by cat-like movements.

Surely such a person must draw the very soul out of me, and subtly enough not to be noticed. He was the arch-questioner when it came to partners seeking a divorce. I can remember his conversation with a priest, whose wife was complaining about his inadequacy for married life. Cunningly, smoothly, this secretary drew the answers, and the squeaky voice of the priest got thinner and thinner. I felt he would die from exhaustion. It was terrifying to listen to.

Usually I copied out about four pages a day, though on the advice of a drunkard I would put down twice that number in my report. This enabled me to count on at least eighteen roubles, though when the pay envelope arrived, I found in it only the eight roubles I had honestly earned.

75

Fortunately my cheating efforts were never reported. What generous people. I was now seventeen years of age.

There was an operetta in progress in the Panayev Gardens, and I was its nightly visitor. One day a chorister said to me, "Semyonov-Samarsky is getting a choir together for Ufa, why not go along and ask him to take you on?"

I knew Semyonov-Samarsky as an artist and adored him. A fine-looking man, he went about in a top hat, carried a cane, and wore gloves. But on the stage he was like a fish in water, most happy in his own element. And how expressively he sang his part in *The Beggar Student*: "And I only kissed her on the shoulder. . . ."

Women melted before him, as wax before fire. I decided to take my courage in both hands; I went to him, removed my cap.

"What can I do for you?" Then a pause. "Oh, I see. Come to my hotel tomorrow," he said.

When I did make an appearance I was refused entry by the porter. I pleaded with this man, and was near to tears. Finally he relented, and sent a boy off to Semyonov-Samarsky's room to ask whether he would receive a lanky, somewhat under-fed tramp. A moment or two later the boy returned with the news that I could go up and see Semyonov-Samarsky.

He was standing there in a dressing-gown, his face covered with powder, so that he reminded me of a miller who has just finished his day's work, and hasn't had time to wash. There was a young man seated opposite him, obviously Caucasian, and a lady half reclining on a sofa. I was always very shy, especially in front of women, and now my heart missed a beat. I felt I could say nothing in her presence. But Semyonov-Samarsky put me at ease immediately by his kindly enquiry.

"Well," he said, "what do you know?"

The fact of being addressed in the second person plural didn't surprise me, since a gentleman could not do otherwise, nevertheless the question frightened me. I knew nothing. I decided to lie. "I know *Traviata* and *Carmen*," I said and, without waiting for his reply, I proceeded to list all the operas I could think of. It made not the slightest impression on him.

"How old are you?"

Shamelessly inventing, I replied, "Nineteen."

"What is your voice?"

"First Bass."

The kindness in his voice encouraged me, and I lost my shyness.

"It's like this," he said, "I can't really pay you the same salary as choristers with a repertoire."

"Oh, I don't want that. I'll do it without pay," I blurted out to him.

This seemed to amaze the entire gathering. They stared at me in complete silence. I went on to explain that I had no money at all. "None," I said, "so perhaps you could give me something. . . ."

"Fifteen roubles a month," said Semyonov-Samarsky.

"I require just enough to live on, that is, without starving. If I can live in Ufa on ten roubles, then give me ten. If I need sixteen or seventeen——" The young man laughed, and exclaimed, "Go on, give him the twenty."

"Sign then," said Semyonov-Samarsky, handing me a paper. I trembled with happiness as I signed my first-ever theatrical contract. "In two days I will give you your ticket for Ufa, and an advance," he said.

An advance. I didn't even know what that was, though I liked the sound of the word. There must be something good behind it. I left, accompanied by another chorister named Neuberg, who had just signed a contract for double my salary. He was a former chorister from Serebryakov's opera, into which I had tried to gain admittance at the age of fifteen. Neuberg turned out to be a wonderful friend.

At home, in Petrov's house, I summoned all my friends and with the greatest pride flourished my contract. The way was open at last. I could now serve in the temples of Thalia and Melpomene. My ambitions were met with the greatest scepticism, and it hurt me very much. Still, I had my first triumph, and I lost no time in reminding them of their early mockeries, as I once declaimed to them in the street: "You wait, in three years I'll be singing in *The Demon*", as indeed I was, though his real name was Mephistopheles. Two days later I received my advance of six roubles, and a second class ticket to Ufa. It was September, and the weather rather cold and grey. I had only a jacket, though Petrov's mother had obliged me with an old shawl to wrap about my shoulders. I was in such splendid spirits that the weather did not upset me, besides, I was actually travelling second class for the first time in my life.

When our boat reached the Belaya river, it started going aground at least twice daily, and the captain without any ceremony at all, calmly informed second and third class passengers that they must get off the boat and walk. It was desperately cold, and I did cartwheels and other acrobatics in order to get warm. I was met with some jeering from peasants stood near a haystack on the opposite side. They guffawed. "Just look at the gent squeezing his guts out. Look at the antics. A very skinny tree indeed."

"Some gentleman indeed," I thought.

One night, after returning to the ship, I came out on deck, and leaning on the rail looked back down the river. Looking up at the stars, I thought of my parents. I had heard nothing from them for such a long time, and all I knew was that they had departed for Samara. It was a depressing thought. Later I began to sing. "Oh, you dark, dark night," I sang, crying as I did so. Suddenly a voice rang in my ears.

"Who is that singing?"

"It's me," I answered timidly. Perhaps singing was not permitted on passenger boats?

"Who are you?"

"Chaliapin."

A Caucasian gentleman appeared. His name was Penyayev. He was a nice man, who, noticing my tears, said in a friendly manner, "You've a good voice. Why are you sitting alone? Come and join us. We've a funny merchant aboard."

"Won't he throw me out?"

"He's too drunk to throw anybody out," he replied.

So there, in a first-class cabin, I saw the red-faced merchant seated at table. He had drunk too much, and was in a distinctly lyrical mood. The table was loaded with vodka, caviare, fish, bread, and many other good things. He stared with glazed eyes at these delicacies, and at the same time spread a puddle of wine with his fingers. He was obviously quite bored. Penyayev introduced me, the merchant raised his fat lids, stuck four fingers into my face, and said, "Smell." I sniffed. "What's it smell of?"

They smelt of wine and herring. "Fish," I said.

"Damn fool. Smells of stockings, and you say fish. You should be able to distinguish such things at once." He poured me out a glass of vodka. "Drink! And who may you be?" he asked. I told him.

"Aha! One of them, eh? Never mind. I like it. What do you do?"

"Sing."

"Oh! Can you do tricks?"

"No."

"A pity. Then sing," he said.

I started to sing. He listened, and after a time began to cry, he sniffed, his shoulders shook. With his permission I then called in Neuberg, and we sang together. The merchant was much moved by this. It was my first performance before a "serious" audience.

Early the next morning we arrived in Ufa. The town itself was five versts away. It was raining, and the amount of mud was incredible. I gathered together my precious "things", which consisted of a single multi-coloured necktie. Neuberg and I reached the town. We must have looked the oddest pair, since he was short and fat, I, long and skinny. We found the hotel where Semyonov-Samarsky was staying, though on first sight of us, the servant informed us that he did not admit such dirty people. We removed our boots, and went off bare-footed to see the impresario. As in Kazan, he greeted us in his dressing-gown, with a powdered face, and laughingly offered us tea.

Later in the day we installed ourselves in the room of a house owned by a theatre musician, at a rental of fourteen roubles apiece. This provided us with morning tea, dinner, and supper. I rushed off at once to Semyonov-Samarsky. "I've managed to get myself fixed up at fourteen roubles a month, so I shan't require the other six. I came to you for the pleasure of serving in the theatre, not for money."

"You're a funny one," he exclaimed.

The rehearsals soon began. There were seventeen men and twenty women in the choir. We practised with a violin played by the chorus-master, a decent, good-natured man, but a terrible drunkard. To my horror I heard that Semyonov-Samarsky had taken on too many choristers, and he would be sacking some. I felt certain I would be one of them, so I mentioned this to the chorus-master. "No, not you," he replied. "You haven't a bad voice, and you appear talented."

Not merely a stone, but the whole Ural range off my chest.

We opened up with *The Singer From Palermo*. I was the most excited of all. How wonderful to see my name on the bills. "Second basses, Afanasyev and Chaliapin." The costumes were in two categories, Spanish and peasant. The peasants' consisted of woollen tights, down-at-heel shoes, shorts, and a jacket made of a material known as the "devil's skin", piped with braid, with a white collar worn over it. The Spanish ones were in a deep plush, with a bolero, and a short cape. Cardboard hats covered in plush and satin completed the outfit. I put on my Spanish costume, made myself small moustaches, darkened my eyebrows, tinted my lips and applied as much powder and rouge as would transform me into a respectable Spaniard. I was incredibly thin, and now for the first time I found myself wearing tights. I felt awkward and ashamed. The chorus was called out, and I stood in the front row affecting a Spanish pose, with one foot forward, hand on hip, and elbow turned out. Proudly I threw back my head. The pose proved beyond my strength. My legs trembled violently, I seemed unable to control them. Ignominiously I hid behind the rest of the chorus. The curtain rose.

My initial moments were a mixture of fear and happiness. Here was one more dream. The public applauded, and shouted approval. My own excitement was almost uncontainable. Before my eyes the footlights indulged in fiery dances, the black cavern of the auditorium shook from the shouts, and the air itself was alive with waving hands.

Just one month later I was standing on stage with perfect ease. I remember being given my first small part, in which I would walk to the centre of the stage, and loudly announce to the hero of the operetta: "A man from below would like to see you."

I found both the troupe and the stage hands extremely helpful. I loved the theatre so much that every job in it seemed a delight. I filled the lamps, cleaned the windows, swept the stage, climbed into the flies, put up the sets. Semyonov-Samarsky was very pleased with me.

At Christmas time we put on the opera *Halka*. Halka's father was down to be sung by a very tall man with a rough-hewn, horse-like face, and indeed a jaw like one. To me he was an unsympathetic character, forever tale-bearing, lying, and generally unpleasant. He sang flat at rehearsal, often went off the beat, and finally announced that his contract only obliged him to sing in operetta. This put the whole troupe into a ridiculous situation, and there was nobody to replace him. Right out of the blue I was sent for.

"Chaliapin, d'you think you could sing that part?"

I was rather scared. It was a big part, an important one. I felt I ought to refuse it, and then I heard myself saying, "But you *can*."

"There you are then. Here's the score. Learn it by tomorrow."

It seemed unbelievable to me. I rushed back to my room and spent most of the night practising, much to the annoyance of my room-mate. The next day I sang the whole score at rehearsal. Yet I was still scared, for I had made some mistakes. All the same I had gone right through with it. Afterwards came the appraisal, the slaps on the shoulders from my fellow artists. What pleased me was that there wasn't a sign of envy in any of them. I suppose that was the one single season in my life where I did not feel that envy was directed against me. I had not even credited its existence in theatre at that time.

I floated on air until the next performance, felt inches higher, and on the great day found myself putting on make-up hours before the performance began. I found it somewhat difficult to look like a mature father of a grown-up daughter. I put on false nose, eyebrows, and moustache, and used a vast amount of paint in order to look old. But the biggest problem was yet to come. How was I to overcome my excessive thinness. I tried a padded jacket, but with dreadful results. My stomach stuck out as if I were suffering from dropsy, whilst legs and arms looked like matchsticks. It so depressed me that for an instant I was on the point of rushing back to Kazan. I recalled the occasion of my rough rejection from the Panoyev Gardens. This halted me, besides it was far too late to run away from my responsibilities. Suddenly someone was behind me, and with friendly words.

"Don't be afraid. Cheer up. All will be well."

And when I turned round, there was the impresario himself. Thus encouraged, I went out on stage. To the right of me were two armchairs and a table, and to the left, the same. My colleagues walked across stage talking cheerfully, pretending to be Poles, and I envied them their self-possession. Then I sat down, protruding my stomach as much as I could. The curtain went up, the lights danced, a yellow mist blinded me. I sat as though I were stitched to that chair, and I heard nothing. Only after Dzemba had sung his lines did I myself begin, like an automaton, and with the shakiest of voices:

"I lift my goblet to friendship," to which the chorus replied, "To happiness."

I rose from the chair, and was swaying as I went towards the prompter's box, I felt as if I was approaching the scaffold. During the rehearsals the conductor had said, "Watch me when you sing." Staring at him like a bull, and carefully watching his baton, I began my aria in a mazurka tempo.

> "Oh, my friends, what happiness!
> I am confused
> And unable to express my gratitude
> For your sympathy!"

These exclamations the hero obviously addressed to his guests, but there I stood with my back to them, and not only paid no attention, but completely forgot the existence of anyone on stage except myself, a very miserable man. With my eye firmly on the conductor, I sang, made futile attempts at gestures. Fortunately for me, my voice sounded unforced. When the applause ended, I could hardly realize it was for me, until I heard the conductor whispering, "Take a bow, you idiot, take a bow."

This I did, excessively, and in all directions, as I made a slow retreat to my armchair. One of the choristers, Sakharov by name, who was a manufacturer of rubber stamps, moved my chair a little to one side, for a reason known only to himself. The next minute I found myself sitting on the floor. The theatre rocked with laughter, and applause broke out again. I was quite stricken by this, but somehow managed to stuff myself back into the chair. I sat there, silent, weeping, angry at my own clumsiness, and angrier still with the public. My friends tried to reassure me in the interval, but it was of little avail. I finished the opera without enthusiasm, mechanically, and wholly convinced that my operatic future was hopeless. But the performance over, Semyonov-Samarsky addressed some kind words to me, and no mention was made of the awkward incident. I was calmed by this gesture, and at the next three performances sang the aria with great success.

But whenever I retreated to that armchair my right hand was always ready behind me.

I was next given the role of Fernando in *Il Trovatore*, and received a rise of five roubles from the impresario. I refused this, explaining my utter happiness in just being allowed to act. Semyonov-Samarsky was persuasive. "Another five roubles will not come amiss," he said.

My confidence returned when I came to sing the Fernando part. Penyayev was most kind to me. At the time he was having an affair with an extremely jealous and quarrelsome lady, and he himself, though good-natured, was yet extremely volatile. They acted some kind of drama almost daily, separated weekly, took different flats, were again united, all of which meant routine processions of suitcases, hat boxes, and other articles from one house to another.

By the time winter arrived I was still walking about in my jacket and shawl. I couldn't yet afford a coat, and of underwear there was none. I spent my money mostly on treats for my friends. My boots were in a sorry state.

There came the occasion when Penyayev made it up with his lady, and, feeling generous of spirit, gave me a coat. Though it was on the short side, I managed. Now there happened to be a girl in the chorus whom I took to be a "lady". She dressed well, and looked the actress all over, always used wonderful scent, and had her own maid. Once, as she was stuffing costumes into a bundle, the maid said, "Why loaf about backstage. Help me carry this bundle home, Mr. Actor."

I was willing to serve her at once, feeling most chivalrous, quite apart from being flattered at being addressed as an actor. The weather was very cold, the distance grew, but away we went. I scarcely noticed the snow that piled itself into my boots, so absorbed was I in the maid's conversation about marriage and women. Her one stout resolve was that she would never marry, not even an actor. When we arrived at the house, she regretted having to refuse me entrance, even for a cup of tea, explaining that it was late, and that for me to cross the threshold through the front door would be to cast doubts upon her modesty. But tea was a terrific enticement, and the maid herself even more.

"You have a room of your own?" I asked.

"Yes."

"Is there a back entrance?"

"Yes, but the gates are closed."

"I'll climb the fence."

"If you can, then do."

And I did. So as not to make a noise, I removed my wet boots and left them at the bottom of the staircase. The tea arrived, and I thoroughly enjoyed it, it certainly warmed me up. The maid then invited me to stay the night. Everything was going splendidly until about three in the morning, and then there was a sudden ring on the bell.

"It's the master," she exclaimed.

I knew the master. He was very rich, he had one eye, always wore blue-tinted pincenez, and inevitably sat in the front row at the theatre. I heard him enter, heard the maid addressing him, whilst I lay waiting for her in a soft, warm bed. At that moment an enormous St. Bernard dog appeared in the room, sniffed at me, and began a fierce growling. I lay very still, dreading my discovery. Then hurried steps, the door itself flung open, and the master himself asking: "Why is he growling?"

The maid kicked the dog, and said sweetly: "Go on, Sultan, go on." The dog moved away. The maid explained. "I don't know, sir. Probably he's seeing things."

I heaved a sigh of relief the moment the master left the room, lost in admiration for the maid's presence of mind. When the dawn came I returned to my room in quite frozen boots, vowing that never again would I become the victim of charming ladies.

Meanwhile things at the theatre were progressing wonderfully. Company and chorus got on well together. Quite often after a performance was over we remained up till four or five in the morning, rehearsing for the next production. In return for this devotion the administration occasionally treated us to beer, bread, and sausage. Life positively glowed. Shortly after Easter I was addressed by Semyonov-Samarsky: "Chaliapin, you've been a very useful member of this company, and I would like to thank you. I am therefore offering you a benefit performance."

I almost fell down from the sheer surprise of it. "How do you mean, a benefit performance?"

"Like this," said Samarsky. "You choose your own opera, and then some Sunday morning we'll put it on, and you'll get a share of the takings."

Before that season had come to an end I had developed a courage almost bordering on impertinence. For quite some time I had dreamed of singing the part of the stranger in *Askold's Tomb*, a part which Semyonov-Samarsky generally reserved for himself. I made my suggestion to him.

"I would like to sing in *Askold's Tomb*."

"Which part?"

"The stranger."

"Really? Do you know the part?"

"Not perfectly, but I'll learn it."

"Then go ahead."

The following Sunday I put on a black beard, a tunic with a red cummerbund, and walked on stage carrying an oar in my hand. My part began with prose, and the moment I heard myself I realized at once that my Central Volga accent was wrong. I was stressing every "O". It very near ruined my performance, so great was my embarrassment. Nevertheless, the aria, "In the olden days our forefathers lived" was greeted with terrific applause. The words were full of o's, and the audience was smiling. From that moment onwards I was determined to learn to speak correctly. The performance over, Semyonov-Samarsky handed me fifty roubles in an envelope, a gift from the public, and a silver watch on a steel chain, in addition to which my share of the takings "from the top" came to thirty roubles. I was rich. Never had I had such a pile of money, and a watch to boot. Then, alas, the season was over.

Members of the company started moving off their separate ways. I was presented by the conductor with a kind of jockey cap with a button on top, and a long peak to it. I bought myself a dark brown camel-hair coat, a leather jacket with a half-belt, of the kind worn by engine-drivers, boots, gloves, and a walking stick. Arrayed in this magnificence I went off for a walk in the streets of Ufa. Each time I met a citizen I thought worthy of my attention, I would ceremoniously take out my silver watch to look at the time. I did want everybody to see that I had a watch. I was so happy, and on top of all this Semyonov-Samarsky sent for me.

"I'm taking a few artists with me to Zlatoust," he said. "We want to give a recital there, a few extracts from operettas. D'you know any ballads?"

I was overjoyed, and enumerated all the songs I knew.

"Excellent," he said, and added with a twinkle, "Tanya Repnikova is coming with the troupe."

This absolutely sealed my happiness. An actress in our company, she was about thirty, with light brown hair and a pair of magnificent blue eyes. The face was beautifully oval. I was attracted to her, but dared not show my feelings. She treated me kindly and simply, like an elder sister. I went to see her immediately, and offered to help her pack, adding that I would be glad to look after her on the journey. On the train I waited until she had retired, then went down the corridor to the platform. This was my first railway journey. It was so interesting to see the land and trees flowing past, the sparks from the engine jetting into the air as golden threads. Though snowing, it was quite warm. The roofs of village houses seemed swollen under this snow, churches and haystacks appeared moving, floating in the fields. And there I remained till morning, admiring it all, and thinking about Tanya, and of the happiness of loving a woman.

We reached Zlatoust later that morning. I installed Tanya in an hotel, and immediately booked a room next to hers. Suddenly I heard a man's voice in her room, joyous exclamations, and much laughter. When she invited me in, and I was introduced to the gentleman, I was torn with jealousy. But his qualities were immediately enhanced when I discovered he was her husband, an actor, a comedian. Since at this time I desired to know every actress and actor, it was an honour to make his acquaintance.

The recital took place in the Arsenal. It had been decided to put on a single act of *Bluebeard*, and then Semyonov-Samarsky discovered that he'd forgotten the wigs and hair, so there was nothing with which to build up the character. I cut off a good handful of my hair, dyed it blue, and promptly handed it to the impresario. Semyonov-Samarsky was much touched by this gesture, though he little knew that I would have cut off my very ear for him.

"But Chaliapin," he said, "you can't appear at this concert in a leather jacket, and looking like an engine-driver, to say nothing of that bald patch on your head. Here! Take my tail-coat and go and have your hair waved." This I did, and for the first time in my life stood before the public in a tail-coat. They appeared very amused, and once or twice I heard mocking laughter. The coat did not fit, naturally enough. I was tall. I imagined myself looking like a stork, but nothing dismayed me. I sang, and I got my reward. The public liked my *Russlan* aria, and Kozlov's song. I was really excited, for I knew that I had sung well.

During the interval a man in military uniform, very fat, and breathing with difficulty, approached me. His moustache was enormous, he perspired freely, and was completely bald. He exclaimed with some astonishment, "I expected you to sing descant."

"How old did you imagine I was?" I enquired.

"About fifteen."

I felt hurt. "Why, I'm nearly twenty."

"Really. Well then, that's what I call a voice. If only we could get a chap like you."

"For what? Where?"

"The police," he said. "I'm an inspector."

It amused me at the time.

Semyonov-Samarsky gave me fifteen roubles for an evening's concert, and now I really began to think they were spoiling me. We then returned to Ufa. Suddenly I was feeling lonely and miserable. I felt I was living in a cemetery. The theatre was empty, the actors had flown, the town was dead. I went off and got lodgings with a washer-woman, in a big house perched on a cliff above the Belaya river. This house, with the many additions built on to it, and shooting off in all directions, was packed like caviare in a tin with hordes of people. Theatrical carpenters, stagehands, restaurant waiters, and quite a number of people who looked to be seeking oblivion in drink. This was a rude awakening for me, who hitherto had been living an almost ethereal existence in the glowing theatre. Life was made easier by the fact that I was very well looked after by the washer-woman's daughter, a soldier's wife, an attractive woman in spite of her disfigurement by small-pox. How she fed me, and how I remember the cutlets swimming in butter. Far too rich, but I ate them, not wishing to offend her.

One week passed, two weeks, and my money was beginning to dwindle. It was necessary to look for work of some kind. Then one day an extraordinary thing happened. Into the filthy yard came a most elegant carriage, and out of it stepped a beautifully dressed gentleman. The horse looked well fed, a beautiful creature. When the gentleman enquired for me I was astounded. He turned out to be a lawyer named Ryndzyunsky, whom I remembered seeing in the theatre. Having exchanged greetings he informed me that he had come "on business".

I hardly dared invite him into my miserable room, so we remained standing in the yard, I like a lamp-post. I listened to him explaining that the local arts circle was planning to organize a concert. Would I take part? I was overjoyed, flattered, and agreed at once. I started rehearsing immediately, but two days before the event caught a cold, and lost my voice. It was a terrible dilemma for me. What was I to do? I gargled and gargled with salt, swallowed raw eggs, but nothing seemed to help. Then an idea occurred to me and I rushed off to the inn and bought a half-bottle of rum for 30 kopecks, dropped several eggs into it, crushed some sugar in a rag, and began to roast it in a metal spoon over a candle. Having concocted this potion of overpowering smell and taste I started to drink it, singing a little after each dose. I was convinced my voice was right, and that it would be perfect by evening.

The lawyer sent me a frock coat. I dressed, stuffed the bottle into my pocket, and went off. I hadn't got far down the street when I felt drunk, but in spite of this duly presented myself at the hall, and on the staircase greeted Ryndzyunsky with great familiarity.

"Ah, Mr. Ryndzyunsky. How do you do? As you see, I have arrived."

He stared in apprehension. "What is the matter with you?"

"Nothing," I said. "Why?"

"Are you not well?"

"I'm perfectly all right," I said.

Yet there was something in his question that brooked no good. He became very severe. "You are not well at all. Go home to bed immediately."

It was then that I pulled out the accursed bottle, and said, "I'm perfectly all right, really. Perhaps it's this wretched eggflip."

He forced me to go. I left that theatre with an aching heart. For two whole days I lay in bed, not daring to show my face. And how sadly I glanced up at that frock coat. I plucked up enough courage to parcel it and return it to its owner. The next time I met him he greeted me pleasantly.

"A fine eggflip you invented, young man. No home-made medicines next time. You'll poison yourself. Be here tomorrow for the rehearsal."

I returned home on wings, and two days later I sang Mephistopheles with great success. The public, including the chairman of the local council, all praised my voice, saying that I had talent, and that I should certainly study. There and then someone offered to collect money and send me to St. Petersburg and Moscow to study. Later they changed their minds, saying it would be best for me to remain in Ufa, and get a job with the town council. I could take part in amateur concerts, and I would be found a post that would earn me twenty to thirty roubles. But I was to continue singing, and in the meantime my friends would collect money on my behalf.

Clerking as such didn't appeal to me very much, yet it was so tempting to be given the opportunity to study. So again I found myself copying papers, always boring, and often enough their content completely escaping me. My presence aroused some hostility in the other employees and I felt I was distrusted. It was hard to bear, since I was always sociable and gregarious by nature. This kind of thing was new to me. I had never before met with such unfriendly treatment. Whenever I appeared on the scene everybody stopped talking at once. I even thought they suspected me as one sent in by the boss to spy on them. Finally I could no longer bear it, and spoke to one of them.

"Look here, what is all this? Why this attitude towards me? What have I done? You surely don't think I was sent in here to spy on you. Allow me to tell you that I abominate council offices, clerks, pens, inks, and miserable piles of statistics. I sit here as one of you only because the council has promised to help me get to the Conservatoire to study. That, and nothing more."

The poor fellow was quite contrite, immediately invited me to his home and, perhaps as a token of particular faith in me, played for me a polka on his guitar. He then confided in me.

"Yes, we really thought you were a spy."

How those chiefs could compromise their employees. "The chairman of the council actually shook hands with you," said this poor clerk, "and he never shakes hands with me."

All the same life was quietening down, becoming boring. A crippled clerk shared my lodgings at the laundrywoman's. I always remember with what endearing simplicity he would beg me to sing to him before going to bed. This I did, and often sang the poor fellow to sleep. I remember that clerk, he is the reminder of many thousands of frightened men, afraid of life, lonely dwellers in their own deserts. Life for such people was hard, and it saddened me.

Even my landlady's daughter was unhappy, and often hysterical. Gloomy when sober, she became gayer the moment she was drunk, dancing and singing, and uttering obscenities that no censor would ever pass. I once had an affair with her, and recall being confronted later by a maniacal village yokel waving a cart shaft at me, smashing doors, windows, and declaring death to all actors by strangulation. I, unfortunately, was the only actor in the house. Realizing his ferocious jealousy I fled my room, and not a moment too soon, for the maniac soon followed, laying about him and wrecking everything in his path. We returned with a policeman. There was the yokel stretched out on the floor, his stomach bared to the world. This the policeman promptly aimed a kick at, but the man did not move. The policeman then removed his belt, exclaiming, "The swine's pretending," and began letting him have it with the buckle end. The man got up and quietly left the house, the policeman fixed his belt, and said, "And now, how about a tip?"

After which episode I had a great respect for the police, though an endless sympathy for all rebels. I decided to change my lodgings, and took a room in the house of a clerk. He, too, played the guitar, in fact almost everybody in Ufa appeared to play this instrument. I would sit watching him strumming away, his eyes lifted to the heavens, unblinking, he might have been a wooden doll. He was married with two children, and their lives flowed along, drably yet peacefully. It was a strange atmosphere. Sometimes as I looked at them they gave me the impression of people falling asleep against their wills, and I with them, the victims of some hidden force. He taught me a strange ballad. The words haunted me:

"The poet hymns the fragrant rose,
Its crimson petals fair to see,
But mine is but a peasant's trade,
And poet's fame is not for me."

When I sang this melancholy song, he would make strange, impulsive gestures, disappear behind the door, flick away tears with his fingers and generally behave in a highly nervous manner.

Singing moved him very much, especially when drunk, and like so many others it was on that fated twentieth of the month.

"How lucky indeed you are to be able to sing," he once remarked. "When I was young I drank my voice away."

The life here was beginning to stifle me. I felt that nothing would ever come of the council's promises. And the arts society appeared to have run into all kinds of trouble. Moreover it was now May. By the greatest good fortune a Ukrainian company turned up at the Summer Garden Theatre, and immediately I went off to have a talk with one of the choristers there. They looked a jolly lot, with their bright embroidered shirts. Their language wasn't quite comprehensible to me. I had heard many Ukrainian words, but had never credited them with an independent language. I even imagined that kind of speech to be an affectation. Now here they were actually doing productions in that language. Glad I was to see them. My spirit soared. How different these people were from the dull, grey, Ufa people. And it was pleasant to me to hear the new and beautiful songs.

It didn't take me long to inform them that I was an actor of sorts, and that I had even had a benefit performance given in my honour. It raised much doubt in them, there was a lot of "umm-ing" and "ah-ing". Even my mention of the Conservatoire failed to convince them. Then one day I sang in a pub. They came up to me at once. "Why not come and sing with us."

"But what about the Conservatoire," I said.

"To hell with it. This is our Conservatoire, just going from town to town. It's a good life."

I was fired by the idea, and went to see their manager. The moment I sang he said, "All right. Join the company. We'll pay you forty roubles."

What a magnificent salary, I thought. I was on the point of joining them, when I suddenly remembered that poor clerk and his guitar, his young wife who had looked after me like a mother. I even remembered the pretty schoolmistress who, whenever I sang, walked into the yard carrying a book. I didn't know this teacher, had never heard her voice, but of one thing I was quite determined, I was not going to leave her in Ufa. Suddenly, right out of the blue came the town council's confirmation that they were at last going to send me to study.

The company gave a few more concerts before leaving for Zlatoust, from where it intended going on to Samara. I woke up on the morning of their departure with somewhat mixed feelings; this terrible longing for the theatre, and a sudden black depression that refused to explain itself. I didn't want to remain in Ufa, yet I had no money with which to go elsewhere. I borrowed fifteen roubles from the council that day, out of which I bought myself a quarter pound of tobacco, and much earlier than usual, I retired to sleep in the hayloft. I knew I dared not tell the poor clerk I was leaving. I was overwhelmed with tenderness for his little family. Before retiring I embraced them both, impulsively, warmly. I felt sorry for them, and not just because of their kindness to me. I remained in the hayloft an hour or so, then collecting my tobacco and cigarette cartridges, left all my belongings behind me, and stole away like a thief in the night. I was on shipboard by seven that morning, and once again wondering about repayments. This time to the Ufa council. Would I ever be able to do it? Soon I was back in Kazan.

There I learned that the Lyubimov Operette was at the Panayev Gardens, and went at once and applied for work, and saw one more man, in one more dressing-gown. He was seated at table eating a salad. It was the first time I had ever seen a man eating grass, liberally sprinkled with oil and vinegar. Lyubimov turned out to be a sombre humorist. "So you'd like to sing in the chorus. Please do. Sing whenever you like as much as you like, but I'll pay nothing. Nothing," after announcing which he stuffed his mouth with grass and chewed. I stood waiting, hoping.

"Haven't even the money for my own company," he said.

I wasted no time, and took a boat for Samara, hoping I might find the Ukrainian company there. My parents were then living in Samara. I had written to them several times, giving them all my news, saying how splendidly things were going for me, and that I was rich. Their own replies were simple enough.

"Things are pretty bad, but on the whole, bearable, thank God."

"I can't appear before them in all this finery," I thought. I was wearing a dark blue cheviot jacket next my skin, my chest and neck covered by a guttapercha dickey with a collar. As soon as I reached Samara I went off in search of the Ukrainians. The manager met me with mockery in his eyes.

"We don't want you now," he said.

I must have turned pale at this news, for he quickly added, "I don't know

13. Chaliapin as the Varangian Guest in Rimsky-Korsakov's opera Sadko *(Russian Private Opera, Moscow),*
1898.

14. Chaliapin as Ivan Susanin in Glinka's opera of the same name, also known as A Life for the Czar *(Mariinsky Theatre, St. Petersburg), 1900.*

15. Chaliapin as the Brahmin Priest, Nilakantha, in Delibes' opera Lakmé *(Bolshoy Theatre, Moscow),*
1901.

16. *Chaliapin as Biron, in A. N. Koreshchenko's opera* The Ice
Palace *(Bolshoy Theatre, Moscow), 1900.*

17. *Chaliapin as Farlaf in Glinka's opera* Russlan and Ludmilla
(Bolshoy Theatre, Moscow), 1901.

what to do with my own people." Then a moment's pause, and he concluded with, "I'll take you for twenty-five roubles a month."

I signed the contract there and then, and literally ran to my parents' home.

They were out when I arrived. I found my brother playing in the filthy, cramped little yard. He took me into a tiny, miserable room. It was clear to me that my family were living in the direst poverty. But how could I help them? At that moment my father came in. He had aged considerably, and looked worn and thin. He showed no joy at seeing me, and listened indifferently to the story of my life and plans.

"Things are bad with us," he said. "No work."

He did not look at me. Through the window I saw my mother entering the yard. She was carrying a canvas sack on her shoulder. She embraced me joyously, then suddenly, blushing with shame, she went into a corner and hid her bundle.

"You see," said father. "Your mother now goes begging."

I have never forgotten that dreadful homecoming.

4

The whole thing was dreadful. I felt so impotent, incapable of helping. I spent two days with them, and then left with the Ukrainian company for Buzuluk. Enormous pigs roamed the streets of this town, even in the public gardens, not to say many sheep and chickens. We were only a short time there, and then went on to Ural'sk where we were to appear before the Cesarevich, the heir to the throne. Having time to spare we called in at Orenburg, and from there went off in carts on an excursion to the Steppes.

It was very hot that summer, we were tormented by thirst, and with both sides of the road lined with melon fields we choristers soon took advantage of the situation, consuming many a juicy gift from heaven. Mostly we travelled at night in order to avoid the unbearable heat. One night we were held up by a crowd of horsemen, who surrounded us with shrill shouts, and much rifle firing. It was difficult to make out whether or not they were just plain robbers. The manager of our company ordered us to take up arms. We rushed off to get rifles and swords from among the stage props and took cover behind the carts. There was a frightful commotion, with women screaming. Luckily it was dark. We could see these horsemen, and the flashes of fire. I am no coward, but I certainly thought my last day had come.

But the morning came, beautiful and clear, and the sun was rising. The fields were so peaceful, it seemed absurd that men should be fighting one another. We sent off some of our men bearing white rags to parley with the enemy. It turned out that the Cossacks were demanding twenty kopecks per head from us for stealing the melons. We were soon on our way, and eventually reached Ural'sk, a town that must remain notorious for its sheer abundance of filth, and an utter lack of greenery of any kind. The theatre, a brick building, lay in the town square, and it smelt revoltingly of dead rats. We played one concert in that mausoleum for rats.

The Cesarevich arrived the following day, when we were sent to the Ataman, in whose house he was lunching. There we sang songs on an open stage. We gave of our best, and I myself had taken the role of leader.

The performance took place in an enormous yard in which were planted some very sickly-looking trees. Under the spare, dusty foliage a large white marquee had been erected. There were row upon row of tables, at which sat the splendidly dressed ladies and gentlemen. It was odd to behold such magnificence in this hastily thrown together town. Two young girls presented the Cesarevich with a bouquet, and immediately a fat man in a

Cossack coat burst into tears. After three hours of singing we received a present of two roubles each, and the impresario was given a ring set with red and green stones. The inhabitants, mostly old believers, were in a festive mood, though I must confess it manifested itself in a rather dreary fashion.

We choristers were occupying rooms over a public-house, the windows of which faced on to the public square. One of us had the bright idea of celebrating in our own fashion, so we had a whip round and bought vodka, sausage, bread and biscuits, and invited in the Cossack women who were trading in the market. We spent the whole evening singing and dancing, finally ending up with a kind of Roman orgy. I remember waking up the next morning among the recumbent bodies of men and women. As always, when I felt myself transgressing, I thought with shame of Tanya Repnikova, and wondered what she would think of such conduct.

From Ural'sk we proceeded to Samara, Astrakhan, Petrovsk, Temir-khan-Shur, and Uzun-Ada. It was a most interesting life. I was filled with new impressions, and, too, it had for me a certain quality of vagabondage. By this time I was speaking and singing Ukrainian freely. The fast-moving life captivated me, though I must confess there were occasions when I was filled with an incredible longing.

In Kizil-Arvat I was astonished at the sight of the huge molten ironworks, from which the metal poured out in great streams like thick, red oil. I had never seen its like before. It was even more astonishing to see a steel-worker, his sleeve rolled up to the shoulder, suddenly plunge his arm into the molten mass. I found the heat stifling, and soon forgot it when the man suddenly pulled out his arm, quite unharmed. He stood there laughing. Later, an actor named Ivanenko explained the trick to me.

Ivanenko was a splendid actor, but, like so many good-natured Russian people, he drank voraciously. I was often held spellbound by his acting. I tried to be useful to him in many ways, but his drunkenness I really detested. "The stage is not Sukonnaya Sloboda," I thought to myself. But then so many of the artists drank. I had a great friend, Kolya Kuznetzov, who came from my home town, Kazan. He was a very clean and tidy person, and always had his own sheets. He even managed to keep his clothes fresh and unstained. I dwell upon what may appear to be trifles, small details, small people, because for me they hold a great significance. They were my education, and we learn from trifles. The things that are taught us by Shake-speare and Tolstoy only touch the surface of our minds. It is the trifles of life that penetrate to the heart, like dust into velvet, sometimes poisoning it, sometimes ennobling it. Which is just why I feel like talking about good little people. The big ones may tell their own story. It is these others, living their quiet, unknown lives, who fade away without a sign, remembered by nobody, and denied the great gesture. Yet these people loved, and beauty was accessible to them. They, too, longed for the good life.

On the way from Ashkhabad to Chardzhui I had an experience that was both ridiculous and disgusting. It depends of course on the way you look at things. I was sitting in the third-class compartment of a train, eating garlic sausage and bread, when Derkach, the boss of the company, a monstrously fat man, came in. "Throw that hellish sausage out of the window. It stinks."

"Why should I throw it away? I'd rather eat it."

He was furious. "How dare you eat that stinking mess in front of me?"

The only reply I could give was that first-class passengers should affect not to notice the habits of third-class passengers, but this only made him more furious. The train had just pulled into the station, and in a sudden rage, he pushed me out of the train. There I was on the platform, surrounded by foreign-looking people wearing their long robes and turbans, a black-bearded assembly that looked not too kindly at me. The train went off, and, as I hadn't a cent, I decided to follow it on foot. It was getting dark, and as I hurried along I glanced from side to side, all the time wiping the perspiration from my face. Lizards darted about the rails as I walked. I had been told that tigers and many unpleasant insects abounded here. Far away I could see the enormous sun setting over the sandy hillocks of the Steppes. It looked like molten iron spreading across the sky. I became more apprehensive; a miserable sort of Crusoe before he happened upon man Friday. When I reached the station I took the first train to Chardzhui, and rejoined the company.

Derkach pretended not to notice, nothing might have happened between us. I dreaded being abandoned in this part of the country, with its hair worms, poisonous spiders, scorpions, tarantulas, fevers, and not least those dark-robed and very silent men with the strange look in their eyes and the teeth of cannibals.

I remember Samarkand with its astonishing mosques, and the white-robed boys moving about there. It suggested a sort of dreamland, a heavenly backwater. Swaying on their haunches, the white-robed recited from the Koran in sing-song fashion. And how silently these people went along the narrow streets, moving like shadows past the low, white-walled houses, and always somewhere about, the cry of the camel, the bray of a donkey. And in what sleepy fashion the Muezzins sang. Sometimes as one walked these streets a Sart would sidle up to you, and in broken Russian, and with the utmost persuasion, offer you a little girl, whose age was communicated to you by finger signs.

"Ten years. You want? Very good. Eleven years. Yes?"

We had covered a good deal of Asia before we finally returned to Baku. Posters on the walls informed me that Madame Lassalle's opera company was appearing at the Tagiyev Theatre. There, among the listed artists, I discovered Semyonov-Samarsky and his wife, Stanislavskaya-Durand. I called on the impresario immediately, and was warmly greeted. He offered to try and get me work with the French company. I certainly had not had too easy a time with Derkach and his company, and was glad of the opportunity of saying goodbye to it. I made a point of mentioning this to Derkach's wife, a comical old woman both on and off stage. She lost her temper with me.

"God! We wanted to make a man out of you, and what's the outcome? The outcome's a pig."

Such scenes were not rare, and I had long felt that the company had been indifferent to me. Consequently I was surprised by Madame Derkach's outburst. I was even more surprised when her husband refused to hand me my passport. Upon my insistence, he replied in a rather sinister manner: "All right. Let's go to the police then. I'll hand over your passport in their presence."

To this I agreed, and we went off. He kept threatening me on the journey, again and again. "We'll see what'll happen when we get to the station."

By this time I was really frightened, for I knew only too well how people were treated by the police. Nor were matters improved when we got there, for the first sound I heard was that of screaming, and somebody pleading for mercy. To the police beating was a passion. I was convinced by this horrible scene, and changed my mind at once. I said I didn't want the passport, and that I would remain with the company, and we returned to the theatre good friends. The manager was delighted. But I wasn't destined to remain, for some days later a telegram reached me as I was playing in *Natalka-Poltavka*. The few words seemed like stones.

"Mother is dead. Send money. Father."

But I had no money, and I was in debt. I sat in a dark corner, mourning this cruel loss, and I immediately resolved on action. I went up to the boss and asked him for an advance. I was playing important parts for him, yet other choristers were earning twice as much as I. The boss shoved two roubles at me. I asked for more.

"Two's enough," he said. "Somebody's always dying somewhere."

On hearing this I exploded, and I never returned to the company. They left Baku. I remained in the town, without a passport, and later joined the French Operette chorus. Though French in name, there were only four Frenchmen in it, the remainder being Jews and Russians. Nor was their company doing very well. Baku itself was never very particular about foreign languages and the gibberish we sang with such good feelings, "Colorado, Niagara, Charpentier, eau-de-vie," was good-humouredly accepted as the purest French. I received no salary, and the manager strongly objected to my going about in a sheepskin jacket. He gave me a chit to take to a shop where I acquired a thickly padded woollen coat. Shortly after this the company went broke, and I was left in the street again, on my uppers. This was the time to draw in the belt, and I lived on tea and bread. Worse still, the winter was approaching, and an endless rain had already begun. The cold wind was blowing. Nor could I sleep any longer on park benches. With two friends, I managed to get into a wooden booth that had housed the circus, which was now closed down for the season. We slept in the gallery, my sheepskin jacket serving as blanket for all three of us. One night my friends vanished, and I had that sheepskin jacket all to myself. Though I was a little warmer by night, life was no less difficult, and then I got myself involved in an affair that might well have resulted in my being sent far beyond the Urals at government expense, and not in a singing capacity.

I cannot clearly recall how I came to fall in with the young man who introduced himself as a former dramatic actor. He certainly had a greater confidence than myself, and though without money, managed to live in hotels. This way of life was recommended to me in such a convincing way that I decided to try it. We took a room together and remained one day. The landlord demanded payment, and we promised to pay, remained another day, then vanished to try yet another hotel. One day my friend went out, and when the landlord angrily stormed into the room he told me he would not let me out of his sight, and that I would get no food until he had been paid. I endured captivity for two days and nights, without food, and then decided to escape. There was a small balcony leading into the yard, but unfortunately it was always full of people, day and night. I had noticed that the cornice beneath the window linked up to a wall, and although the wall reached to the second floor, and was practically roof height, I decided to chance it, for if there was one thing I could no longer stand, it was hunger.

I got out as night fell, climbed the wall, and dropped down. But what I imagined to be a manure heap turned out to be a pile of scrap iron. I found myself in the deserted yard, and was soon in the street, where I at once vanished into one of those thieves' dens, an experience not entirely new to me. I used to sing in them, and they fed me. I had an idea that there were a few escaped convicts in their company. Nameless creatures, they were generally recognized only by nicknames. One who particularly interested me went by the name of Klyk[1]. A black-bearded, curly-haired man, he had had his teeth knocked out, and underneath his low forehead I beheld grey eyes of a most magnetic quality. He never combed his hair, and it fell over his forehead like a haystack. His voice had a masterful ring about it, and one realized at once that he commanded a universal respect. I was dead sure he was a convict. But his worst features were always redeemed by his kindness, and I was always addressed as "singer". Often he begged me to sing to him.

"Go on. Sing. Please. I beg of you."

I sang, and he sobbed. I was touched by this response, and I grew attached to him.

One day he suggested to some of the men, including myself, that we should go to the circus in the evening, and there cut the throat of a fat merchant who often paraded about in patched clothes. Klyk was sure that untold wealth was concealed under the patches. The suggestion was immediately approved, and Klyk at once issued his instructions. They certainly meant business. I myself was to remain on the corner, and watch for the police. I dare not refuse, if only because of the kindness he had shown me, besides which I was quite certain that I might be beaten up for doing so. And on the day planned for the murder I kept clear of the thieves' den, purely for my own safety. But having parted from them, I had lost my only chance of

[1] Klyk—Russian for "tusk".

94

obtaining food and drink. I had already offered my services to the cathedral choir, and had been rejected. I could not blame them, for I looked such a sight. Dirty, unkempt, I probably looked both drunkard and thief. I decided I would go away and seek work among the stevedores. I was successful in this, and received some thirty kopecks a day. It helped me, but not very much.

It was during this period that the terrible cholera epidemic broke out. Everywhere people were being seized by convulsions, and the streets were full of dead bodies. The soldiers had been ordered out, and they, covered in pitch as a protective measure, had to go about collecting the dead. Death strutted through the town like the governor himself. Stevedores fled in fear, so once more I found myself alone. I was without work, and without bread, living on the boiled salt water that everyone in the town was drinking. Chaos reigned in Baku. Even the authorities fled, and those that remained died daily in their hundreds. Life ceased. Only the railway station seemed busy, but I could find no work there. Yet fortune smiled on me in this blackest period, for I found a knotted handkerchief in the street, and inside it eighty kopecks. I rushed off at once to a Tartar shop to buy some lyali-kebab. Having eaten, I returned to the station, where I offered what was left of my money to the train driver and begged him to take me to Tiflis. A kind person he was indeed, for he carried me there for thirty kopecks, and I travelled all the way on the brake platform of a goods truck. Suddenly, without realizing it, I had walked into hope, for I discovered that Semyonov-Samarsky, the impresario, and an officer named Klyucharev, were getting together an opera company for Batum. Vanderik, Flyata-Vanderik, Walter, Lutsenko, and Kruglov, were amongst the company. It was here that I met my friend Neuberg, and in addition the two comrades who had abandoned me in Baku.

It was now Lent, and as it was forbidden to sing opera in Russian, the company assumed an Italian name, though there were only two Italians in it, a chorister named Ponte, and the orchestra's flautist. I was soon given the part of Oroveso in *Norma*, for which I had to use the Russian lettering in copying out my part. I tried to imagine how musical my Italian must have sounded. Later we left for Kutais. It was here that I sang successfully the part of the Cardinal in Halévy's *La Juive*, and Valentin in *Faust*. Alas, one of the artists, and may his bones rot in hell, eloped with Klyucharev's wife, and the opera collapsed. I returned to Tiflis with three of the choristers, Neuberg among them, and there all four of us lodged together. We had with us a singer named Sessin, and he had one incredible talent, his ability to find a fiancée in any new town. This became useful for us, since, in his own ingenious fashion, he was able to keep us supplied with things like meat-balls, fruit, bread, and even a little money. In Tiflis he ran into difficulties, for his affairs with a new fiancée did not go at all well, and he suddenly disappeared. He was greatly missed. Meanwhile my other friends had managed to obtain work.

But I, less clever at adapting myself to circumstances, remained alone and, as usual, hungry. The landlady turned out to be kind, and did not press unduly for my rent. So many failures had produced an apathy in me, and I did nothing but sleep, sometimes for two whole days at a stretch. By now I was quite used to doing without food, even for as long as four days at a stretch. All the same it was no joke.

I continued to search for work, and by this time my clothes were in tatters. I was minus underwear and had been for some time. Oddly enough, I did manage to find a hat. I must have looked a sight. I remember walking into a timberyard, where the workmen jeered and chanted loudly, "Gentleman". However, it is difficult to starve in Tiflis, for there is always some cooking going on in the streets. My nostrils were being continuously tempted by the most delicious odours. Yet I often despaired, and on one occasion thought of begging, but dared not. Finally, unable to bear these conditions any longer, I decided on suicide. I walked into a gunshop, asked to be shown a pistol, thinking that as soon as I got my hands on it, I would pull the trigger. I was determined to kill myself, even though at the same time I longed to live. I reached the doorway of the shop, then suddenly heard a familiar voice. I swung round, to find myself face to face with Ponte.

"What's wrong with you?" he asked anxiously. "Why are you looking like that?"

I dared not tell him, and was quite unable to reply. I broke down and cried. I hadn't eaten for four days, and I was glad to be taken along to his place.

It was simply wonderful. His wife gave me some macaroni, of which I ate an incredible amount. My greed must have astonished her. I was greatly helped by this meeting with Ponte and his wife. Their macaroni, their very warmth, strengthened me.

On the following day an announcement caught my eye, a poster informing me that an amateur performance was to take place. I went off to enquire, and was confronted by an eccentrically-dressed man, who had the appearance of a circus artist. He took a fancy to me, and asked me many questions. He turned out to be the actor, Okhotin. He led me to a far alley in the garden, and asked me to sing. Having heard me, he announced that he would give me a Russian national costume, in which I would appear on an open-air stage.

The gardens were small, and rather cramped, and there was no great rush on the part of the public to visit them. However, I appeared twice a week, and received two roubles for each performance. It was whilst I was there that I met some people working on the Trans-Caucasian railway. They would now and again treat me, and for such hospitality I responded with some anecdotes. After I had given them some idea of my very complicated life, and having heard that I had had clerical experience, they suggested that I should apply to the railway accountant's office for a job. I acted on their advice, and was immediately successful. I took a job as a clerk at thirty roubles a month. This was most fortunate for me, and extremely useful, since by this time I was no longer living alone. I had met a chorus-girl, Maria Schultz, a very beautiful girl, whose one great misfortune was drink. It was during my starvation days that she suggested I should go and live with her. I was greatly attached to Maria, even though her features were now disfigured by much drinking. In addition, her behaviour was coarse and unpleasant. Still, she was a human creature, and she had a heart of gold. I can remember explaining to her how inconvenient it would be if we both lived in the one room. She replied with the utmost simplicity. "And what is the inconvenience? When you undress I'll turn away, and when I do, you'll turn away."

This seemed convincing enough, so I moved into her tiny hovel. She slept on a bed near the wall, and I on a heap of rags against the other wall. In less than a week we were no longer turning our backs on each other. She had a little money saved up, but we soon ate our way through it. Then she started pawning her things, her clothes, the bedsheets. We finally ended up in a dark, windowless basement, and the only light came from a fanlight over the door. It was agonizing and degrading to me to be living on this girl's money, and I was greatly relieved when at last I got work. Now I felt I could live like an ordinary family man. I would return from work to find Maria busy cooking bortsch on a kerosene stove, and singing away as she stood over the pot.

We had even managed to acquire a few household utensils. She kept the basement clean and tidy. Yet it was horrible to return home nightly and find her drunk. I begged her to give it up, and she replied that she would willingly do so. Alas there was no will-power, and my efforts were quite useless. She would hide the vodka under the bed, and the moment I was asleep took to the bottle again. Thus it was that we two continued to live. It was in some ways a sweet life, bound in affection, and yet I could not have wished the same to my worst enemy.

I greatly missed the theatre. Then one day one of the members of the choir turned up, and offered the suggestion of organizing a concert in Kodzhory, a small resort some forty versts from Tiflis. I readily agreed to this, and eight of us took two days off from work, and made for Kodzhory on foot. Our choirmaster, Karl Wendt, was a splendid person, but like almost everybody else, an incurable alcoholic. The concert did not take place owing to the fact that the public was totally indifferent to us. Nor did it help much when the heavens started to spout rain, an almost pre-historic deluge that was followed by a hurricane. We were surrounded by the elements of disaster. I have seen much rain in my life, but nothing approaching that at Kodzhory. Great torrents tore down the mountains, and earth always following after them, trees fell and vanished, and the wind never stopped howling. It was in these conditions that we made our way back to Tiflis. We dreaded being late for work, I most of all. Worse still, we appeared to be making no progress, and often enough we were down on all fours, if only to prevent the wind and water sweeping us into the abyss below. Somehow we managed to get back.

By midday diphtheria was diagnosed and now I was terrified that I would lose my voice. I was already racked by anxieties, not least on behalf of Maria, who would be worrying about me. I did manage to send her a note from the railway sickbay. She came, of course, but was refused entrance. How dull was that hospital period. I seemed to have been forgotten by everybody. I lay on the bed in a kind of prison garb, and waited for the doctor. When hungry I was given a very watery soup. Yet I felt well enough, and pleaded to be allowed to return home. But no, the watchman would not hear of it, and, declaring that the doctor would arrive in a week's time, made up his mind that I was to stay there. This news finished me. I decided that the hospital, and everybody in it, could go to the devil. Creeping into my closet, I got my clothes, quickly changed, climbed through the window, and ran home. But I was not allowed to return to work the next day, since the authorities had now been informed of my absence. Almost with tears in my eyes I pleaded with the railway people that I was perfectly well. In the end they did send for the doctor who pronounced me fit.

Shortly after this I received a letter from Semyonov-Samarsky, in which he said he could get me work with the Petrovsky Opera, in Kazan, singing second lead at one hundred roubles, adding that he would send me an advance for my fare. I leapt into life, and sent the telegram right away. "Awaiting your advance." His letter came a few days later, enclosing with it twenty-five roubles. The same day I left my job, and told Maria that I was going away. I hated leaving this girl, and was intensely sorry for her, but the theatre had to come first. I remember buying a tin of cocoa, and we shared this, and sang songs to each other.

A curious thing happened to me at about this period. For some time my colleagues had been telling me I had a good voice, and strongly advised me to take lessons from a local professor of singing, a former artist of the Imperial Theatre. His name was Usatov. The very day of my departure from Tiflis I summoned up my courage and went to see him. What had I to lose? When I was ushered into the singer's apartment I was surrounded by pug dogs, followed by a short, round man, whose moustache was waxed to points that would have outdone any operatic villain. The clean-shaven cheeks were almost bluish. He was not long in coming to the point.

"What can I do for you?" he demanded, somewhat coldly.

I explained.

"Ah," he said. "Right then. Let's go and shout a bit." He beckoned me into his studio, where he immediately sat down at the grand piano, and then asked me to sing a few arpeggios. My voice sounded well.

"Yes. Do you sing opera at all?"

Thinking that I had a baritone's voice, I offered to sing him Valentin's aria. I began, and taking a high note, began to hold it fermato. The professor stopped playing, and painfully prodded me in the ribs, so that I stopped abruptly in the middle of a note. There was a momentary silence. Usatov sat there staring at the keys, I looking at him, and imagining it was all very bad. Unable to bear it any longer I asked quietly, "May I have singing lessons?"

He looked at me directly, and replied, "You *must*."

I felt cheered up at once, and then told him of my plans. I explained that I was on my way to Kazan to sing opera there, for which I would earn a hundred roubles a month, and that I would be there for five months. I would earn five hundred roubles. I had decided to save four hundred of them for singing lessons, and to live on the balance. His reply came quickly enough.

"Drop all that. You won't save a kopeck. I don't suppose they'll even pay you. I know how these things are done. Remain in Tiflis and I'll teach you, and I won't take any money from you."

I was flabbergasted. This was an occasion, and the first time ever that I had been so treated, with such understanding, kindness, and imagination. He then said: "Your chief is a friend of mine. I'll write and ask him to give you back your job."

I was inspired by this turn of events, and rushed off to my chief with Usatov's letter. The post had been filled. I felt crushed by this news and returned to Usatov.

"Never mind," he said, "I'll address a letter to someone else," and he did so there and then, and sent me off to the owner of a chemist's shop, an oriental-looking man. Having read the letter, he asked me if I knew any foreign languages, and I replied that I could speak Ukrainian.

"Useless," he said. "Tell me, can you speak Latin?"

"No," I said.

"A pity," said the chemist. "All the same I'll give you ten roubles a month, and here is two months' advance."

"What shall I have to do?"

The advance pleased me no end, though his whole manner left me intrigued.

"Nothing at all," he replied. "Just study singing and receive from us ten roubles per month for doing it."

I could have shouted for sheer joy. Surely this was a fairy-tale.

Counting the advance I had received from Kazan, my fortune now totalled forty-five roubles. Usatov ordered me to find a better room, and to hire a piano. But were I to return this advance, I would be unable to do so, so I wrote to Kazan, told them I was suddenly taken ill, and could not come.

This was wrong, of course. Still, I could console myself with the thought that many people in the world did far worse things, and often enough for ignoble reasons.

Things at home were far from good, and Maria was drinking more and more heavily. There was nothing that I could do to help her. She became very cantankerous when intoxicated, and it often placed me in awkward situations, such as the occasion when she quarrelled with the wife of the policeman who lived in our yard. She in her turn gave as good as she got, and ended up by calling Maria the most atrocious name. This so angered me that I found myself quarrelling with the woman myself. That evening her husband came in threatening me with every kind of disaster, and even began beating me, though having had some experience of the Kazan police, I was not long in worsting him.

The house where we lived was crammed full of people, a very odd collection indeed, and their main interest centred on any affair that was not their own. I remember a very wild-looking person dressed in a white overall, most of the time drunk, who took a positive pleasure in persecuting me. He had an enormous dog, a ferocious beast, and he would urge it to attack me. If I happened to be crossing the yard he immediately began shouting: "Go on, Hector, go on. Get that devil. Bite him."

And forward the dog would come, quietly, most purposefully. I would press myself against the wall, and look pleadingly at dog and master. I suppose he thought it his bit of fun, but I took a very different view of the matter. I became really afraid of this man. I remember a day I was going off for an appointment with my teacher, and as I left the room I heard a thunderous voice behind me, calling out: "They ought to have made a damned deacon out of you, spawn of the devil. Trash like you always prevent people from having any peace." I disappeared into that basement in double quick time. I was beginning to find life unbearable amongst these people, and Maria improved nothing. She was never sober, never out of the pawnshop. Once as I was passing a pothouse I saw her there, senselessly, pathetically drunk, and dancing, whilst an equally drunken crowd stood by and watched her, the few pothouse regulars roaring with laughter, and for good measure pinching the drunken women from time to time. I led her away and took her home. How furious she became, even telling me that if a man accepted a woman's caresses, he should pay for them. I was informed in the rudest manner that I was nothing but a tramp, and could go to hell. The quarrel never resolved itself, and Maria went off to Baku. It hurt me deeply. She was the only human being who had ever shared my joys and sorrows. Not that I loved her very much, or indeed that she loved me in any deep way, but we did give a warmth to each other, a meaning to our lives, bound by our common situation. Woman for me has always been a force, and has awakened my best instincts. It was the end of a union.

During my lessons with Usatov I met others of his pupils, people from various walks of life, where officers mixed with civil servants, and even society ladies. Particularly do I recall Iosif Komarovsky, later assistant-producer at the Bolshoy Theatre, and the bass, Starichenko, a most conceited man whose egotism seemed without limit. And there was Pavel Agnivtsev, who went insane. I loved his wonderful voice.

In the house itself everything was new and strange to me. The furniture, the parquet floors, the pictures and, not least, the tea and sandwiches so beautifully prepared by his wife. I was also surprised by the familiarity with which the pupils conducted themselves with Usatov. They laughed, joked, and behaved like free people, equal human beings. Such relationships were foreign to me; I had never experienced them. They appealed to me very much, yet I felt I dare not adopt such familiarity. Besides I was still shabbily dressed, and because of an extreme shortage of clothing, not always very clean. I went to the baths frequently enough, yet still could not keep myself really clean. My one shirt I washed almost daily in the Kura river, after which it would be subjected to some roasting over a kerosene lamp, in order to remove any vermin. One day Usatov exclaimed during a lesson, "Chaliapin, you smell awful. You must indeed forgive me for saying so, but you must know these things. My wife will supply you with some underwear and socks. Do put yourself in order."

I was embarrassed to the point of tears. I still did not understand that if we do people a good turn, we need not necessarily choose our method of doing it. However, I turned up at the next lesson well washed and shaven. Usatov invited me to dinner.

I thanked him but declined it. I felt that to eat with him and his family and friends would be something of an ordeal. I had seen how they dined. They had a maid serving at table, who offered one various dishes and plates, and there were napkins on the table, not to mention masses of cutlery. I did not know what to cut with which knife. However, the Usatovs pressed me. The meal was a torture, for many of the dishes presented to me I had never seen before, nor did I even know the technique of disposal. I can remember a hard-boiled egg floating in a greenish liquid. I pressed it with a spoon, and it jumped off the plate on to the table-cloth. I transferred it back to my plate with my fingers. This operation was watched in complete silence, and I felt the disapproval behind it. However, after a series of these agonizing lessons, I learned to eat without embarrassing my neighbours by such tactics as helping myself to salt with my fingers, or picking a bit of meat out of my teeth with a finger nail.

Usatov intrigued me, I so much admired him. He had an aristocratic way of saying everything, but with such endearing simplicity that it left a kind of mist before my eyes. He would suddenly advise me:

"Chaliapin, you should not sniff at table."

But I did not possess a handkerchief, and how can one avoid sniffing when the food is both hot and delicious? Or he would instruct me. "If you continue to eat with your knife, you'll slit your mouth to the ears."

He made me sit up straight at table, and warned me not to eat fish with a knife. Assiduously did he apply himself to my social education.

I was doing well under him, and once he made me study an aria from *Fenella*, and one of Bakhmetyev's ballads. After I learned it he sent me off to the Music Lovers' Circle. This Circle used to organize students' and amateur performances, existing as it did quite independently from the Tiflis Art Circle.

It was at one of these concerts that I met a young lady in pince-nez, behind which lay a pair of black eyes. I remember a diaphanous dress she wore as she sang "My Gondola". To me there was something near divine about her beauty, and her small, flexible voice entranced me. I applauded her performance and left the hall in a state bordering on exaltation. I recall her stretching out her hand to a gentleman in the wings and the promptness with which he kissed it. I thought to myself, "What lucky people there are in this world." A few days later Usatov informed me that if I continued to sing in the circle they might offer me a small stipend. I said I would. He even gave me his frock-coat. This of course did not fit, since I was long and thin, he short and fat. However, I managed to adjust it to my skeleton.

The day of my debut arrived. I appeared on stage, and rendered the Bakhmetyev ballad, "My Beard". The audience laughed, but were kindly disposed. I was quite certain that my frock-coat remained the centre of their amusement, but they were just laughing at me, perhaps because I sang so touchingly about a beard, and I a very beardless youth. I know I looked almost boyish on that stage. The applause was considerable, and when I bowed I suddenly recognized the young girl of the pince-nez and the black eyes. "I'll sing for her," I told myself. She had touched my heart. For an encore I gave them "All ages are subject to love". I imagined her applauding more vigorously than the rest. When the concert ended I was introduced to her by the accompanist. I followed her across a desert of highly polished floor, my legs threatening to give way under me at any moment. Though extremely nervous, I was also happy. She shook hands warmly, and paid me any number of compliments. My answers were awkwardly put, and I cursed myself for my clumsiness. If she had asked me to accompany her home, even from Tiflis to Archangel, I would have done so. And I would have kept vigil below her window had I known where she lived. I was in love, with all my youthful ardour.

There was an Italian named Farina who came up to me after one of these circle performances and offered me fifteen roubles a month if I would help him all I could. I agreed at once, and was soon taking part in all their activities. I sang and acted in productions like *Poverty is Not a Vice* and *The Forest*, and played Peter in *Natalka-Poltavka*. I also cleaned the lamps, looked after the props, put up the sets, all with great enthusiasm. Meanwhile, my lessons with Usatov continued.

He was a very strict teacher, and stood on no ceremony with his pupils. If I did anything wrong his snuff box came out at once and, digging the snuff out with his baton, he sniffed in a noisy manner. He had definite signs of showing his displeasure. If he heard a pupil's voice weakening he immediately began thumping his chest, exclaiming loudly, "Press down, you fool, press down." It took some time for me to realize that this indicated to the pupil that he must concentrate the sound.

But now, carried away as I was by this young girl, and by my work at the Circle, my studies began to suffer, and I often failed to take in the real meaning of a lesson. If I forgot something in the score, I would leave it open on the piano, and glance at it out of the corner of my eye. Once Usatov noticed this and positioned himself between me and the score. I immediately stopped singing. His reply to this was to hit me with a stick. "Not working, not working, you lazy good for nothing," he exclaimed as the stick fell. I had quite a few wallopings from Usatov.

Years later we recalled such episodes and we laughed about them. He was a very good man. He coached me for the third act of *Russalka*, for a Circle concert, and the serenade from *Faust*. I still looked quite ridiculous in his clothes, and I was as long and thin as ever. Still, the public liked my singing, and that was all that mattered to me. It was particularly gratifying after I had sung The Miller's aria. To this very day I can remember the great hush that came over the hall, and seconds later the thunderous applause. They stood up and shouted. The following day a review in the paper, *Kavkaz*, compared me with Petrov, the great bass. This notice was signed by Korganov, whom I knew to be not only a sapper officer, but a great connoisseur of music. He had recently written a book on Beethoven. Reading his notice I knew that the incredible had happened for me, something of which I had never dared to dream. I knew I had sung The Miller well, but felt that the notice had exaggerated the greatness of my gifts. I was frightened, and even embarrassed. So much would be expected of me now. Even Usatov himself praised me. Laughing, he slapped me on the back. "Well, lazy bones, that's the style." I was far too shy to tell him I had already read the Korganov notice.

I continued to meet the young girl, whose name was Olga. Her father was a lawyer. He seemed quite indifferent about her, as though he didn't care a damn what happened. She lived with her mother in a very beautiful apartment. The mother was a simple woman, and looked at life in the most realistic way. I noticed, however, that she favoured the rich Armenians who cast eyes on her daughter. There was something a little odd about Olga's mother, and something repulsive into the bargain.

Olga, who had studied at the Conservatoire in St. Petersburg, was able to give me very interesting and picturesque accounts of that city. I could imagine how beautiful it was. An interesting and delightful girl, though with a rather proud and haughty way of looking at some people, almost as if in contempt. I began to visit her frequently, much to her mother's dislike. I would sing, and she'd accompany me. I certainly loved her much more than she loved me, and I felt an inability on her part to express her real feelings about me. Later our relationship was to assume a more definite form, and she then told me she had had an affair with the composer of her favourite song, "My Gondola", who, she said, was now living in America. Perhaps it was this fact that held back her feelings for me, but now, since she had told me about it, I thought she might come closer. Nothing happened, added to which her mother's preference for those rich Armenians angered me. I became extremely jealous, I became a bundle of nerves. I remember on one occasion I thought she accompanied me badly on purpose, to upset my singing. I stopped abruptly and exclaimed, "I no longer wish to work with you." She flung a box of chocolates at me and left the room. I was flabbergasted at her conduct. It seemed so strange to me, especially in a girl of such fine upbringing, of such delicacy of nature. Moreover, she was far better educated than I was, but here she was flinging things at me as if I were one of the dogs. I remained in the room for a while, pondering upon this sudden change, and then went home. I sensed that something irreparable had happened. My ardour weakened, and there was a sudden hole in my happiness. I felt as if I had been struck with a whip. I found it impossible to sleep, and my bed swayed like a ship in the ocean. Unable to bear the torment any longer I went off to see her. In fact I met her on the street. She came up to me, reached out her hands, and giving me the sweetest smile begged me not to take her tantrums too seriously. We made it up. And then something quite stupid occurred.

Driving together in a phaeton we met her mother, who until now was wholly unaware of our relations. We were both of us very alarmed, and rushed away and hid in a shop, bought a few things, and then returned to her house. The door being locked, we knew her mother had not returned. I put on the samovar and we sat there waiting. I told Olga of my burning desire to be on the stage, but that I was finding it most difficult to study on other people's money. I begged her not to leave me, and if I had to go away, to come with me.

Suddenly, perhaps too suddenly, her mother was standing before us. We had not heard her come in. She was outraged at this conduct, picked up a chair, and started to lay about us both. Olga told me to flee. I did. And all the way home I laughed like an idiot. There was something funny about the affair. When I reached my room, it was to suffer the most severe nervous shock. Olga had got right into me, I would have done anything for her, but now I felt that her mother had tainted it with a kind of sordidness, and once again I was positively hating those Armenians, and the mother's rank materialism. I felt unutterably sad about the girl. I even assumed that following this scene Olga would want to leave her mother. I at once sent her a letter, begging her to come to me, that I was waiting longingly, that we could live together on thirty-five roubles a month, which was my total salary in those days. There was no reply, and I assumed that mother and daughter

18. Chaliapin, 1900.

19. The composer César Cui, with actors of the Bolshoy Theatre, 1901. Chaliapin is on the extreme left.

20. A typical "Wednesday" group. Left to right: poet and writer S. G. Skitalets; writer, dramatist and theatre critic L. N. Andreyev; Maxim Gorky; N. D. Teleshov, writer, organiser of the "Wednesday" literary circle and, in the last period of his life, director of the Moscow Art Theatre Museum; F. I. Chaliapin; poet and writer Ivan Bunin, translator of the "Wednesday" circle, fellow of the Russian Academy and winner of the Pushkin Prize for his excellent translation of Longfellow's works; and E. N. Chirikov, poet and dramatist.

21. Gorky and Chaliapin, 1903.

22. *An address to Chaliapin from the regulars of the "gods" of the Bolshoy Theatre,*
dated January 16, 1907.

had made it up. To my amazement this was so. Before the week was out I was again visiting her. But something *had* happened, and my romantic ardour became clouded with suspicions.

The summer was drawing to a close, and there were rumours of Lyubimov and Forcatti's Opera coming to the State Theatre. At that time I did not know a single opera in its entirety, and I discussed this matter with Usatov. I asked him if I should try to get on the stage. His answer came quickly enough, "Why not. Let's try."

I stood looking at him, carefully listening to everything he said.

"You can sing, and you can carry on with your lessons here. But you'll have to learn several operas. *Russalka* and *Faust* will be your bread and butter. Do remember that. You must also study *A Life for the Czar*."

I got to work with great energy and studied these three operas throughout. Then one day Lyubimov called on Usatov to hear both Agnivtsev and myself. He liked this singer, and offered him 250 roubles per month, but he didn't like me, although I sang through the third act of *Russalka* for him. For this I had been praised most of all, yet it did not satisfy Lyubimov. It was depressing news for me, and the stage seemed further and further away, my future dangling uncertainly. It was then suggested to him that he should call again and hear me. He did, and this time he liked my singing.

"I'll pay you 150 roubles a month, Chaliapin," he said. I would gladly have taken half that amount. My spirits soared skywards. I signed the contract, and then began regular rehearsals. I remember the conductor Truffi remarking to somebody, "Thissa boy has a gooda voice." Was I pleased to hear it!

We began the season with *Aïda*, and everything went swimmingly until Amneris got her dress caught up in a piece of scenery, and was unable to free herself. I, the High Priest of Egypt, helped by lifting her train. The following day the notice contained a strict rebuke, saying that it was unthinkable for the High Priest to handle Amneris's train.

Quite unexpectedly I found myself carrying the whole of the bass repertoire, then suddenly I had all the leading roles in the opera. The experience of *Pagliacci*, done in Tiflis, I had found of great help. The part of Tonio suited the range of my voice, and I had also acted it well. *Pagliacci* was frequently produced, and always a success. I was now preparing my roles at a lightning speed, and sometimes I would be assigned a role with only hours to spare. This put me on my mettle. Working under this sort of pressure might have proved detrimental to me, had I not received such earlier training as I had.

Now when I walked on stage I was no longer lost, and uncertain. I knew exactly where I was going, and I loved my profession far too much ever to treat it in a light-hearted fashion. What I learned and loved were the direct results of long and intense night study. Each part, any part, shook me, took entire possession of me.

Meanwhile, my lessons with Usatov continued. Sometimes he praised me, and that was pleasing, then again he could be severe with me. I always listened to him, and always had an affection for this man who raised me out of the gutter. He was so generous with his time, his energy, his immense knowledge. As a teacher of singing he had a tendency to the mechanical, but he really knew music, and loved it. Often he would gather the pupils together in order to run through and analyse some particular work. He would explain its qualities, its defects, always improving our taste, furthering our education.

There came the day when the Circle produced the Inn scene from *Boris Godunov*. I played the Commissary. Then, when Varlaam began his irksome and seemingly nonsensical song, against the great orchestral chords, and the False Dmitri talked to the Innkeeper's wife, I suddenly felt something quite extraordinary happening to me. In this strange music there was something dear to me, very close to my heart. I felt that all the trials and tribulations of my own life had been accompanied by this music. It had always lived with me, in my very soul. And more important still the fact that it was something that I knew.

Thus do I now formulate it, but then I felt a simple kind of reverence, that merged on happiness, on sheer joy. This strange work contained within it the song of the world, and the song of the soul, a moving, wordless song.

With the season now drawing to its end, it was arranged that one of the remaining days should be devoted to me as a benefit performance, in recognition of the fact that I had rendered to the company even more service than had been expected, as the manager put it. So when the big evening arrived I put on two operas, *Pagliacci*, and the whole of *Faust*. My powers of endurance were colossal. I could sing the twenty-four hours round, and I was as hardy as a camel. How often this passion for singing, for pursuing my own road, got me flung out of lodging after lodging.

On the evening of my benefit performance, the commandant from Tiflis, General Ernst, died. He had always looked like a skeleton to me, a real bag of bones, a strange creature. Many funny stories were told of him. There was one in which he happened to be driving along the road on a rainy day, and saw a military clerk in galoshes and white gloves. "Stop," he commanded. "Take off those galoshes." The clerk removed them, then stood to attention in the mud. "Wipe your galoshes with your hands," he was told. The clerk wiped them with his gloves. "Now put them on again, and go and put yourself under arrest for two days." It was said of him that the moment he began scolding his wife she would sit down at the piano and play the National Anthem, whereupon the husband immediately stood to attention. He was certainly something of a character. If he attended the theatre he invariably took a box just under the orchestral pit, and always near to the brass section. On one occasion he noticed there was a pause for these instruments. They stopped for a while, then carried on. General Ernst summoned the director of the theatre. "Why aren't those instruments playing?" he asked.

"They're observing pauses," he was told.

"Do they get paid for them?" he asked.

"They get paid like everybody else," said the director.

"Then please inform them forthwith that in future they will play without pauses. I will not abide idleness."

I was to meet this gentleman face to face, just after I had sung the part of Gremin. Ernst had already made enquiries about me. "Who is that young man?" Given the answer, he commented, "H'm. That's very strange. I thought he was a general's son. He plays the part very well." Later he visited me backstage, praised my singing, but said my costume was incomplete. I had neither orders nor decorations.

"Also," said the general, "your gloves are disgusting. When next you have to sing General Gremin, I shall supply you with gloves and decorations."

He was as good as his word. He arrived at the theatre for my next performance, and ordered me to put on my costume, during which time he kept prodding me in the stomach, chest and shoulders. He then issued commands. "Right turn. Left turn. Forward march." I did my best for the General. Taking out a star and cross wrapped in a handkerchief, he pinned them on my chest. "I say, Chaliapin, you mustn't forget to return these to me."

"But certainly, Your Excellency."

"There was another one here," explained the general, "yes, another bass. Lent him my orders. What did he do? Pawned them, got drunk. Never saw them again."

This eccentric old man died on the eve of my benefit performance. I was rather upset by this, and feared the performance would be cancelled, but it wasn't, and turned out to be a great success. The hall was packed to the doors. I was presented with a gold watch, a silver goblet, and three hundred roubles, as my share of the takings. Usatov even erased his name from a sash that had been presented to him, and awarded it to me, together with a laurel wreath. I felt immensely proud of the honour.

The season was now ending, and I had to think about the future. Naturally I felt drawn towards Moscow, the very centre of artistic life. Usatov approved of this, and gave me a number of letters of introduction to the directors of the Imperial Theatres, and the conductor Altani, and the producer Bartsal. So in the middle of May, Agnivtsev and I set out for the post station. Olga and her mother came to see me off. And again I was pleading with Olga to come away with me, but all to no avail. Moreover, our relationship had deteriorated, and was replaced by a curiosity that one expects people to adopt towards a circus acrobat. "I wonder if he'll break his neck tomorrow?" I was still very much in love with her, and I felt hurt by her treatment of me. Then almost before I quite realized it I was driving through the very street in which she lived, bound for the Georgian Military Highway. Passing her house, my heart contracted.

6

For the first time in my life I was travelling along the Georgian Highway.
I had heard so much about its scenic beauty, but alas, I saw little or nothing
of it, since for most of the journey I cried, and nothing my friend could do
appeased or consoled. This break with Olga had been dreadful, and I still
felt it. It wasn't until we had got beyond Ananur that I started to look about
me. There was a majestic beauty about the Caucasus, and it was this that
eventually consoled me.

On reaching Vladikavkaz we decided to give a concert. We hired a hall,
had some tickets printed, not one of which could we sell, and the whole effort
turned out to be a failure, though this in no way discouraged us. Agnivtsev
suggested that we go on to Stavropol where he had a relative, an officer in the
army, who, he said, might be able to help us. The atmosphere lifted a little
when we met the relative, who greeted us warmly, and started the prelimin-
aries for the concert, after which Agnivtsev and I went off in search of an accompanist. We had been given the address of one of Anton Rubenstein's pupils.
She lived in a tiny house with a glazed terrace, and when we arrived there we
began talking to a woman with her skirt tucked up high and a filthy rag in her
hand, who explained to us that the pianist was at present indisposed. Still, she
would inform the lady of our presence. She asked us into the house, and
then disappeared from sight. We sat down. We were somewhat astonished to hear groans and sighs coming from the other side of the wall.
Suddenly a woman came in, her face blue, the pupils of her eyes painfully
dilated.

"Yes," she announced, "I am indeed Rubenstein's pupil, but I cannot
accompany now, or indeed play at all at present." Then she went out. A
moment later we heard her shout, "Get the midwife." We then left the
house, a little bewildered by the reception. The woman with the tucked
up skirts calmly informed us that the lady was going to have a baby, a
commendable occupation no doubt, but to us it seemed quite out of place
at that moment. We went off in search of another accompanist. It seemed
that all the musicians in Stavropol were women. Our next introduction was
to a young blonde girl, with very fluffy hair, and obviously of a quite
cheerful disposition. Whatever we said, she pealed with laughter.

"So you'd like me to accompany you?" Another peal of laughter. "But
I have played for Levin," she said, "you do understand. Levin himself."

Never having heard of the gentleman, we were somewhat taken aback. However, we pleaded for her help, and her reply was emphatic.

"No, I'm afraid I could not accompany unknown artists. Still, I could give you a note to a girl. . . ." and I noted the emphasis on "girl".

We were grateful enough for the note, and went off looking for the "girl". We reached the outskirts of the town, landed in a deserted street, passed a long fence behind which we discerned a field overgrown with weeds, and finally reached a ramshackle dwelling. What I thought to be a bundle of felt lying on the step leading to the door, turned out to be a dog. There was washing on a clothes line. We spent some time knocking on the locked gates. Then a woman peered out at us rather suspiciously, and having thoroughly examined her visitors, condescended to let us into the yard. Having got a detailed account of us, she called out to somebody, and a rather decrepit old lady suddenly appeared on the steps. Her head trembled on her shoulders. Agnivtsev, as befitted a former officer, very smartly clicked his heels, and enquired whether M'lle So-and-So lived there.

"Why do you want her?"

"We have a letter for her."

Agnivtsev was now convinced he was talking to the accompanist's grandmother, and handed over the epistle from the blonde young lady. She started to open it.

"I beg your pardon, madam," said Agnivtsev, "but the letter is addressed to a M'lle . . ."

"I am she," announced the old lady.

We now understood the reason for the blonde's laughter. Having read the letter, the old lady informed us that she hadn't played the piano for thirty years. This left us in a desperate situation.

"You see, I haven't studied very much. I only played for myself, and I'd be of no use to you."

We begged her to show us an example of her art. The result was appalling. She played atrociously, could scarcely sight read, and had not the slightest idea of movement or rhythm. I was sufficiently musical to slow down the tempo when she went wrong. Agnivtsev paid her no attention at all, he just sang. The poor dear was still trying to find her way through the score. If there was disappointment in this, there was also humour. In one way and another we managed, and eventually the concert took place, and not without success. The Police Inspector was particularly delighted. So the next day, having bought ourselves third-class tickets, we set off for Moscow. On the way I was invited to play a game called "Three Aces", by three rascals, and I came off badly, losing around 250 roubles. I never mentioned the disaster to Agnivtsev. Suddenly, wonderfully, there was Moscow.

It quite overwhelmed us provincials. The brightness, the noise, the intense activity. As soon as I found a room I rushed off to have a look at the Bolshoy Theatre. Its columns and its four horsemen on the pediment made a grandiose impression on me. I felt like some insignificant insect, very, very small in front of this temple. The next day I called upon the administration of the Imperial Theatre. Commissionaires moved grandiloquently about in their gold-braided uniforms, upon which were embroidered the double-headed eagles. They appeared very bored. People dashed up and down the corridors with pieces of paper in their hands, every one of whom looked frightfully important. Somehow or other, it didn't look like a theatre. One of the commissionaires took my letter, turned it over uncertainly in his hands, and then addressed me in a languid manner.

"Who's this Usatov? Where's he from? Wait a minute."

I sat down on the bench-cum-chest, the typical piece of furniture associated with government offices. They generally contained dusters, candles, and boot brushes. I sat there for an hour, for two hours. Finally the commissionaire was sought, and I asked him if he would remind Mr. Pchelnikov of my presence. He was very unwilling to do so, and only when we reached the point of altercation did he agree to go and remind the gentleman. I waited another half hour. When he returned it was to inform me that I could not be seen, that this was summer-time, that the Imperial Theatre was closed. Most impressive, I thought, if not very courteous.

Now it happened that both Altani and Avramenko lived in Pushkino, so I went off to see them. I was kindly received, but they told me that the season had closed, and that auditions would not commence until Lent. And so for me too, did Lent arrive. I had no money. Agnivtsev and I registered at Rassokhina's Theatrical Agency. I handed in my photographs, theatre bills, and newspaper notices. Rassokhina then expressed a wish to hear me sing, and having done so, she said she liked my voice. "Excellent," she said. "We'll find you a theatre."

My companion and I used to eat in a pub for about thirty kopecks, and I was still reluctant to tell my friend of the near fortune I had lost on the train. Eventually I found myself making excuses for not accompanying him. But I found it very dull sitting alone in a room, without food, so after two days of this privation, I made my confession to Agnivtsev. He cursed me soundly, and then offered to pay for my meals, and I was to settle with him later. He was a dear and kind person, but he could be irritating, and often pedantic. If he spent seven kopecks, he immediately wrote down that I owed him three and a half. Perfectly correct, of course, but how boring.

"Why don't you put down that I owe you four kopecks?" I asked.

With the utmost seriousness he would reply, "Because the half of seven is three and a half. And the half of five is two and a half."

To escape the boredom of these mathematics I would go off for walks into the Vorobyev hills, from which I could feast my eyes on the grandeur of Moscow, which, like much else in the world, looked more beautiful in the distance than close at hand. Quietly sat there, isolated, I would think of my life, of Tiflis, in which I had spent so many happy hours, of Olga, to whom I now wrote long letters, and whose replies got less and less frequent. I had no luck in love.

A whole month passed by. Then at the beginning of July I received a note from Rassokhina, inviting me to come to her office. There I found seated an enormous man with a long white beard and curly hair. To me he looked like a mighty warrior. He was certainly impressive, but rather severe. A real Moscow impresario, Lentovsky by name. I had heard the name before, and was suddenly awed as he looked me up and down. He turned to Rassokhina and said, "He might do." Rassokhina then asked me to sing, and I did an aria from *Don Carlos*. Lentovsky listened for a while, then said, "All right, that'll do. What else do you know?"

I told him.

"Have you ever sung *The Tales of Hoffman*?"

"No," I said.

"You'll sing 'Doctor Miracle'. Take the part with you, and learn it. Here's one hundred roubles, and you're to come to St. Petersburg to sing at The Arcadia."

All this was most impressive, the laconism of the impresario, the thick eyebrows and weighty fobs, but not least that hundred roubles.

"So that's how Moscow does its stuff," I thought to myself. I signed that contract without even looking at it, and overjoyed, rushed back to my room. Shortly after this I signed a contract for a winter season in Kazan, to sing for Unkovsky, but I was told that he required a guarantee that I would definitely come, and that it would be necessary for me to sign a promissory note for 600 roubles. I signed it, and went off to St. Petersburg, having taken my leave of Agnivtsev. The preceding weeks had been most unfortunate for him. He had had trouble with his voice, he lost his baritone and began singing in a tenor voice. He had had a hard life, what with its failures and disappointments. He had to take some sort of administrative job in Siberia, where he became insane and died.

I had always imagined St. Petersburg as standing on a hill, very clean, white, and surrounded by greenery. Could it have been otherwise in the place where the Czars lived? But my first view brought disappointment, factory chimneys, and clouds of smoke from the roof-tops. Yet I found a beauty there, too, it was original, though a little morose. But it made an impression on me.

I had also imagined the sheer luxuriousness of The Arcadia, but it turned out to be something like the Panayev Gardens in Kazan. Many concerts were given there, and at that time a magnificent chansonette singer named Paula Cortez was appearing on the open stage. I went daily to hear this talented woman. I did not understand a word she sang, but I loved her voice, intonations, gestures. Her "little" songs penetrated deeper than the ear.

Lentovsky turned up a fortnight later, and sporadic rehearsals began, followed by equally haphazard performances. It turned out later that the man really sponsoring these concerts was not Lentovsky at all, but a barman, and the pair of them indulged not only in quarrels, but in fisticuffs. The famous "impresario" was often so busy walloping the barman that the operas were not properly attended to.

Later I played Doctor Miracle for him, but *Tales of Hoffman* was a failure. The public, for reasons of its own, would not come to The Arcadia gardens. I was supposed to be receiving 300 roubles a month, but in fact received nothing at all, apart from the hundred Lentovsky advanced me in Moscow. I often had to turn to the impresario for a couple of roubles, and was rewarded in kopecks. And by this time I was getting pretty sick of starvation diets. It was quite unseemly to be starving in the capital city. The season ended in fiasco. I had to go to Kazan under contract, but had no money. I was then asked to join an opera company which intended performing in the Panayev Theatre. I was forced to explain that I already had a contract with the Kazan people. "Nonsense. What's a contract? Rubbish."

Very odd conduct indeed. It certainly wasn't "rubbish" to me, but a genuine contract, and I was in honour bound to fulfil it, quite apart from the fact that I had signed that promissory note for some six hundred roubles. It was something to ponder on. Yet I disliked the idea of leaving St. Petersburg. I loved its wide streets, the electric lights, the Neva, the theatres, the whole tone of life there. As the city pulled hard at me, so too, did Kazan get more and more distant. Finally I went along to the Panayev Theatre, where all the members of the opera company were meeting, together with the conductor, Truffi, whom I had already met. There and then I declared that I was ready to join them, and was heartily welcomed. So there I was, with good friends, signing all kinds of papers, getting money from heaven knows where, rehearsing, the lot, when of a sudden it was announced that all theatres would close for six weeks owing to the death of the Emperor, Alexander the Third. Frantic negotiations were then begun, and in the end we were allowed to carry on with our concerts.

They were very successful, and I was lucky enough to attract the public's attention, not to mention the famous personalities of the musical world, many of whom came to see me backstage. They all seemed to like my rendering of Bertram in *Robert le Diable*. V. V. Andreyev then told me that the Mariinsky Theatre was interested in me, and a little while later I was asked to go there for an audition before Napravnik. I must mention here that once, when I sang the Invocation from *Faust*, the public, to my astonishment demanded an encore. This equally surprised my co-actors, because none of them had ever paid any great attention to this aria. Andreyev advised me to sing this when I appeared before Napravnik.

I found Napravnik a cold, morose, and uncommunicative man, and it was difficult to know what he did or did not like. He uttered not a single word after I had sung the aria. I wasn't kept waiting long for news that there was a plan to give me an audition on the stage at the Mariinsky, in the presence of its director. I knew they needed a bass, as the famous Melnikov was just then ending his career. I had never dreamed of replacing such a man, and was somewhat alarmed to learn that I was down to do Russlan's aria, one of Melnikov's star parts. The audition took place, but my rendering of this aria did not satisfy the examiners. I followed this with the aria and recitative from the fourth act of *A Life for the Czar*. I sang it, not as it was usually sung, but in my own way, as I do today. It impressed the directors, and I can remember Figner coming to me with tears in his eyes to shake my hand. The following day I was offered a contract, and so was accepted into the company of the Imperial Theatres.

Was I glad? I can hardly remember. There seemed to be so many other things to be happy about. I continued singing at the Panayev Theatre, and made more and more friends, and especially with Andreyev, whose famous Friday evenings were always attended by painters, singers, and musicians. Here indeed was the new world, and my soul imbibed its riches. Here they painted and sang, recited, talked and argued about music, whilst I looked on, listened, and lapped it all up. The evenings generally ended up with a visit to Leiner's restaurant, the haunt of artists, where we would sit talking and singing until daylight. It was there that I met Mamont Dalsky, then young and highly successful.

I often sang at students' concerts, and charity affairs. I remember an occasion when the student, V. I. Kachalov, one of the organizers, came in a carriage to fetch me. I was greatly flattered. Until then I had only seen titled ladies and archbishops in carriages, and there was I, actually riding in one myself.

[Nikolai Khodotov, an artist at the Alexandrinsky Theatre, and closely connected with literary circles, has recorded the following account of the Dalsky-Chaliapin relationship in general, and of the above episode in particular:

Dalsky took Chaliapin under his wing, and rudely, but expressively taught him how to act. There is a photograph of them together, and it reveals the admiration that Chaliapin had for this man. He stands there, handsome and still slim, wearing a Cherkess coat with a dagger at his waist, and Chaliapin lanky, and still very young, looking at the other with profound affection.

Khodotov's account of how Chaliapin came to give his first concert in St. Petersburg, goes like this:

Dalsky was invited, and promised, to take part in a concert and, as was the custom in those days, a young student called for him in a hired carriage. Dalsky was not in the mood that evening, he said he did not feel like going and suggested that Chaliapin, then still totally unknown, should go instead. Reluctantly, the student agreed—he had no choice. This started a great commotion: the inhabitants of Palais Royal had to pool their resources to equip Chaliapin, who had no formal clothes. To dress Chaliapin, remembering his great height, was no easy matter. Finally, this was managed, after a fashion, and he went to the concert. The result was a resounding Chaliapinesque success. The student who accompanied Chaliapin on that historic occasion was none other than Vasily Kachalov, the future great actor of the Moscow Arts Theatre.]

How young I was then and how naïve. Kachalov was talking to me in the carriage, and I replied rather vaguely, continuing to stare out of the window, thinking of my childhood, of Kazan, and of nights that I spent sleeping in carriages such as this, when I worked for a furrier. The smell of the leather brought back these memories. When finally I appeared on the stage of that noblemen's assembly, I was at once struck by the magnificence of the auditorium, the great columns, the mass of spectators. I was a mixture of fear and joy, but I sang with enthusiasm. *The Two Grenadiers* was particularly successful, and a positive tumult arose in the auditorium. The public would not let me go. I had to repeat each item two or three times. But I was so moved, so elated, that I was ready to sing until morning.

What congratulations my friends showered upon me. I was told that this performance would be of great service to me in the State Theatre. My state was one of sheer exultation. I gave more and more students' concerts. And there was one strange evening, when Dalsky and I were both invited to sing at a particular concert, but no carriage arrived for us. As they were not coming for us, we decided to go to them. But where? We had no idea at all. We found ourselves calling at hall after hall, enquiring of managements whether it was that particular hall we were invited to. Nobody was expecting us, said the management, but if we would like to take part. . . . And take part we did, after which we proceeded to the next hall, and again we were not expected, and the same routine followed. In the end we visited four halls, sang in each, and never found the hall at which we were due.

What a country bumpkin I really was. And with what great skill and tact did V. V. Andreyev endeavour to educate me. He finally persuaded me to get rid of my "choirboy" hair. He taught me to dress decently, and generally acted as a father to me. This was highly necessary since sooner or later I was bound to be involved in a mishap. For instance, I recall being invited to a very elegant household for tea, for which I dressed up in Usatov's frock-coat, and polished up my high blacked boots. Thus attired, I bravely entered the drawing-room. I was unpardonably shy, and there sitting right next to me were some very gay and mischievous young girls. I was suddenly aware of somebody pressing my foot under the table, and recalling what friends had told me of this manoeuvre, choked myself with tea, agitated about which of the girls was doing it. I was dying to look under the table, but dared not. Unable to endure it any longer I declared to everybody that I had to go, jumped up, and began bowing in all directions. To my astonishment I noticed that only one boot was highly polished, the other had turned ginger and was quite wet. Then out from under the table emerged a huge dog, still licking its chops, its muzzle smeared with what looked like boot polish, though it was actually pitch. My disappointment knew no bounds, and I fled from the house, tearing down the street in boots of contrasting colours. As the final seal on my disappointment, Andreyev told me that frock-coats were not usually worn for tea, and certainly never high boots. I **was always learning.**

7

I now decided to make a careful study of the contract I had made with the State Theatre, and in doing so discovered therein a clause which stated that I was entitled to three appearances only, and if following them the public did not like me, the contract became null and void. This set me working at once. I had some visiting cards printed, in which I described myself as "artist of the Imperial Theatre". The title flattered me, and I became very proud of it. My début came in *Faust*. In those days I had dreamed of playing the part of Mephistopheles as I play it today, but the administration were strict and ordered that it be played in prescribed costume. The make-up, which I had invented for myself, caused a great stir, and no end of derision in the theatre. This perplexed me, indeed it cooled my enthusiasm, and consequently I did not sing very well. I was next given the part of Zuniga in *Carmen*. I sang this part with a comic touch, and it created a better impression.

Following on this I was asked by the producer whether I could sing the part of Russlan. He explained to me that my interpretation of this role would have great bearing on the final decision of the directorate. I had become infected with self-confidence, something peculiar to beginners. Had I not already tasted success in the Panayev Gardens and at charity concerts? Hadn't I received flowers from admirers, and heard my name pronounced in hushed whispers? This and the praise of friends, together with the newspaper notices, had turned my head. I began thinking of myself as an outstanding artist.

Knowing from experience that I could quickly learn a part, I told the producer that in three weeks I would learn, not one, but two roles in that opera. "Then learn them," he said. I immediately found an accompanist and swotted up the part. The day of the performance arrived, and it was conducted by Napravnik. Dressed as the legendary Russian hero, stuffed out with padding, and wearing a light brown beard, I made my appearance. Alas, from the very first note I realized I was not singing well. Indeed I felt the very reverse of the hero, more like the Russian hero associated with Christmas time, and dancing the quadrille and the lancers in rich merchants' houses. I began to lose confidence in myself, and more or less went to pieces. I made terrifying faces, there was much arm waving, but nothing helped. As for the conductor, he, from behind his rostrum, was also making terrifying faces and hissing "ssh" at me.

It was not rewarding in any sense. The newspapers wrote that a certain

Chaliapin, a young artist, sang the part of Russlan execrably. The critics put the blame on the administration for entrusting such a part to a musically uneducated milksop, especially so after the famous Melnikov. Other bitter truths were to follow. I can only thank God that this disgrace fell upon me early in my career. It was a real lesson, a real sobering up. Now I had to consider very seriously what abilities I possessed, and the cause which I hoped to serve. Overnight my conceit and self-confidence vanished.

New rehearsals were ordered, and I was once again allowed to do the part of Russlan. And this time my singing improved, though during it I must say I felt very like the crow does when suddenly facing the barrel of a gun. I was inwardly trembling, my heart pounded, and I had to fight for breath. All ended well, however, and the trial performance over, I was kept on, and given many parts. I went off to Pavlovsk for the summer, and took all the scores with me. I had with me a 'cellist friend, Wolf Israel, of the Mariinsky Theatre. I then started my visits to Taskin, an excellent musician and accompanist, and with his daily help I got deeper and deeper into the roles I was later to perform. I began to live more modestly, took long walks in the park, did some fishing, and meditated on the way to play this or that part. Friends and acquaintances all declared, "You must work. You have a splendid voice, but it requires schooling."

What exactly that enjoinder meant, I didn't fully know. I had supposed that the only requirement was the learning of my parts, and a diligency paid to my exercises. But they kept on repeating in my ears, "You must work." How exactly this was done nobody ventured to explain. Besides which, the season having begun, the chances of work were fugitive. They just would not let me sing. I sang Russlan and no more. Later, however, I did get the part of Count Robinson in that lovely old opera of Cimarosa, *Il Matrimonio Segreto*, and sang this several times, in addition to repeating my performance in *Carmen*. And nothing else. This worried me a great deal, and I found some consolation by singing at charity concerts.

But daily concerts require a clean shirt. My salary was 200 roubles a month. But during my service with the Panayev company I had signed all kinds of documents, and now it turned out that I was being sued for the debts of this company. I must confess that at that time I would have signed my own death warrant just to get work. The inevitable followed, for the moment I began work with the State Theatre, a veritable stream of demands and summonses began arriving from all quarters. Demands for 500 roubles, for 700, for 1,000, even for 5,000. I dared not go to court, quite apart from having a great fear of the judiciary. The result of this was that all court decisions were made in my absence, and consequently never in my favour. Half of my pay was deducted, so that I was only receiving some 100 roubles a month. It was very difficult to live on such a sum, and it would have taken me around sixteen years to pay off such debts. Fortunately M. F. Volkenstein came to my rescue. This lawyer took from me a power of attorney, and succeeded in winning the last two cases for me. Thus was I freed forever from the burden of working for "somebody else's uncle".

Still my affairs in the theatre continued to go from bad to worse. For instance, I was well aware that every time a member of the theatre council suggested a role to me, the majority of its members would immediately reject it. There were some Czechs around, who stated that if a singer named Chaliapin were given a part, it would end up in a complete fiasco. Perhaps this was deserved treatment, for I had sung the Russlan role badly, but I yet considered the general conduct somewhat unjust. I felt they should have helped when I was weak, and not hindered. All they did was frighten me and bother me very much.

I may have been awkward on stage, perhaps my very gestures were incompatible with the rhythm, but I was quite certain that I knew and felt my own Russian language better than any Czech, and more understandingly. Nor did Dalsky himself help to improve matters much with his habit of reading to me the weekly repertoire lists. He would hammer it in. "An artist worth his salt must have his name included in the programme at least twice a week. If he is not included, it simply means one thing. He just isn't in the theatre." Then he would follow this up by quotes from the billings.

"Look! Monday: *Hamlet*, with Dalsky. Wednesday: *Belugin's Wedding*, with Dalsky. Friday: *Innocent but Guilty*, again Dalsky. And now look at the operas. *Russalka*, sung by Koryakin, and not by Chaliapin. *Rogneda*, sung by Chernov, but not by Chaliapin."

I found these remarks very depressing, and I would throw up my hands, turn to my friends. "But what am I to do if they won't give me parts?" And the reply was unanimous.

"If they won't give you parts, then leave them."

All very well, but where on earth was I to go? In despair I would resort to Leiner's restaurant. And it was my frequent visits to this place that first created the legend about my drunkenness. And the longer the season the more difficult the whole thing became. The rehearsals I found very hard to bear. The whole world seemed to be teaching me, producer, prompter, choristers, carpenters, the lot. Andreyev took my failures seriously to heart, and to his everlasting credit did his best for me by trying to enlarge my circle of acquaintances, from whom I might learn.

Thus came my introduction to Filippov, whom I had already heard was an important person in the world of art. He was also a friend of Ostrovsky, and a great admirer of originality in any form. It was in his house that I sang many songs, and the trio, *The Golden Cloud Has Rested*, with Koryakin and one other whose name I cannot now remember. I do remember that when Koryakin pronounced the word "quietly", he did so so loudly that the glass rattled in the window-panes. Filippov was very kind to me. It was at one of his "evenings" that we were invited to hear a young boy, a virtuoso pianist. He was small, consumptive-looking, and seemingly insignificant. But the moment he began to play the world changed. I was astounded by such power, such force, such musicianship, such tenderness. I felt I was being initiated into some great mystery. The little boy was Joseph Hoffmann. The more I met such people, such wonderful talents, the more did I seem to get the measure of my own insignificance. What a deal I had to learn. But where? From whom? How?

In conversation with Dalsky I often confessed to him that the art I was endeavouring to serve was still not quite comprehensible to me, and that I was deeply dissatisfied. I told him, too, of my great regret that I could not appear in drama, for I felt that no kind of singing could express as much as the living word itself. He agreed with me. From that moment onwards I was tortured by one single idea, one single thought. "Could not opera and drama combine, and would there not be a great gain, a great stride forward, by a new road."

The thought followed me everywhere, would not let me go, it was like my own shadow. At the season's end I was informed that I would be singing the part of The Miller in *Russalka*. I was disturbed by this news, I had not forgotten my experience with the role before that Tiflis public. I felt it was not my part. When I explained this to the producer he called me an idiot, and ordered me to get ready for the production which would be in the morning, the second Sunday after Easter, "Forgiveness Sunday". In studying this role Dalsky suggested that I should read the introductory aria to him, which I did.

"I don't think you understand the character of the man. The Miller is no fidgety little man, but a sedate and prosperous moujik."

My error was at once apparent, for that is just how I had acted him in Tiflis. So that on that Sunday I acted the part with great success, indeed it was my one and only success that season. There was much applause, and I was handed a laurel wreath. Strangely, not one of my colleagues on stage appeared to notice my success. Nobody congratulated me, not a single kind or helpful word was spoken. As I walked backstage with the wreath in my hands, even the producer seemed to suggest that the whole thing had had nothing to do with him. Indeed, he turned his back on me and began to whistle, and that was the measure of his indifference.

These failures apart, I hated going to the theatre if only on account of the treatment that was meted out to artists by the administration. It has always been my contention that the artist is a free and independent man. Yet here, when the director came backstage, the artists immediately stood to attention, for all the world like soldiers, and enthusiastically shook the two fingers that the director condescended to offer them. I had always been associated with government offices, but to take this as far as the theatre seemed to me intolerable. I can remember an occasion when I was rudely ticked off because I did not go to the director's office on New Year's Day to sign the visitors book. It was degrading to me to have to express my respect to my chief through his doorkeeper. I was hardly aware that such ceremonies existed. There were other irritating trifles, enough to make me lose my pride in being an artist in the Imperial Theatre.

Of that period the only pleasurable recollection I have is that of meeting Rimsky-Korsakov, on the occasion of the rehearsal of *Christmas Eve*. It was with the greatest interest that I watched this silent, deeply reflective musician at work, his eyes hidden from view behind double spectacles. And it appeared to me that he was being treated no better than I. I can remember with what ruthlessness whole pages of his opera were struck out. I recall his actually wincing at the news, and of his protest, though I admit that this protest had its fair share of pigheadedness. It was explained to him that if the opera was too long it would only bore the public. Perhaps these people were right, perhaps their cutting of the beautiful music and the most interesting of productions was due to a lack of taste in audiences. It is true that they would often exclaim: "How very dull. Russian composers are always so boring."

There was an appalling lack of admiration for Russian opera, at least I thought so. I recall an occasion when I wished to sing the *Trepak* from Mussorgsky's *Songs and Dances of Death*, a work that had greatly appealed to me. At the rehearsal, held in the home of the actress organizing the concert, I met a well-known contemporary critic who was to be the official accompanist. He stared at me.

"What on earth are you going to sing *Trepak* for?"

"Because I like it," was my reply.

"But it's awful rubbish," he said, amicably enough.

"Nevertheless, I shall sing it," I replied.

"As you like then," he said, with a great shrug of his shoulders. "However, give me the music that I may look through it at home."

I gave him the score, though not with the intention of relying on his judgment, indeed I had already made up my mind to have another accompanist. Later I was told that my action had hurt him very much. When I came to sing the *Trepak*, it was soon apparent that the critic was right. The public did not like such work.

Some time later I returned to St. Petersburg with the Mamontov company. I sang in many concerts, but the critics had not lessened their hostility towards me. Perhaps hostility and criticism are related professions.

When I first caught sight of the Palais Royal I got the impression of some gaunt warehouse, though this was indeed the noted haunt of the St. Petersburg artists. It stood on the corner of Pushkin Street, behind the small square in which a statue of the poet stands. In my day the place was filthy. Perhaps the one good thing about it, the people apart, was the fact that the stairways were not too steep, and a great help, considering that I was housed on the top floor in a dirty little room. The curtains seemed to have been hanging there for ages, and time had eaten into them in a voracious manner, though it hadn't eaten into the dust and flies and fleas hidden somewhere in their folds.

In the dark corridors of this building one could meet drunken people of both sexes at almost any time, though strangely enough scandal was a rare thing. Dalsky was living in the same corridor as myself, and to his room there came a constant stream of musicians, actors, and not least admirers. He would hold forth on any subject with the greatest confidence, and not surprising, since he appeared to know everything in the world. I would listen to him with avid attention.

One of our frequent visitors was an old man by the name of Gulevich, a raconteur who was then living in a home for aged artists. He was a witty person, and at a moment's notice could make up the most wonderful stories. I remember one telling of what happened to the Popes after their decease. He arrived to see me during Holy Week, and informed me that the home would be having a celebration, but that he would come and spend the night with me. He turned up on Easter Saturday carrying a number of little bundles that intrigued me. I was delighted, thinking he had brought some food and drink, for at that time I didn't have a farthing in my possession. But these bundles contained only paper lanterns and candle stubs.

"There," said Gulevich, "I've been working on these for a whole week. Let's hang them all over your room and light them at midnight. We'll have *real* illumination."

"That's all very well," I said, "but we can't eat candles."

The remark upset him, and I was sorry afterwards. As luck would have it we were left quite alone, for even Dalsky had gone off with friends for the evening. Gulevich's eye then alighted on the icon in the corner, and immediately he got on to a chair and took it away and carried it into the corridor, saying, "When actors are sad, they do not wish Thee, too, to be sad." He then placed the icon in a window facing the street. At that moment there was a knock on the door, and there standing on the threshold was a man in livery with an invitation to a midnight feast from a titled lady, a well-known and very charming person, to whom I had been introduced by Andreyev. To answer this unexpected invitation I had to borrow a coat from one of the hotel attendants, my own having been pinched and pawned by a neighbour.

I arrived at the house to discover the dining-room already filled with guests, eating, and drinking, and chatting. Looking on at this I could not but remember poor old Gulevich, and I felt unhappy about him. So I went up to my hostess and explained that unfortunately I had to go back as I had an old man waiting on me, and would she be so kind as to give me something to take to him. She was perfectly charming, and simple and understanding, and immediately ordered a basket to be filled with food and drink; and she even gave me some money. Half an hour later I was back in my own room, where I found the old man sitting alone, pondering as he curled his moustaches, and looking somewhat melancholy as from time to time he spat on his fingers. He quickly unpacked the basket, and exclaimed excitedly that there was not only vodka there, but champagne also. Immediately he went out and returned with the icon, put it back in its place, and remarked: "We should be separated when miserable, but together when celebrating."

So we saw in that Easter in the most marvellous way. When I woke up the following morning there was poor Gulevich stretched out on the divan, groaning and convulsed with pain.

"What's the matter with you?" I asked, and then noticed that the bottle containing my gargle was empty. "What happened to my gargle?"

"Was that the gargle?" he asked.

23. Chaliapin, 1902.

24. *Portrait of Chaliapin by V. A. Serov, 1905.*

Above left 25. *Portrait of the painter K. A. Korovin by Chaliapin, signed and dated, September 14, 1906.*

Above 26. *Chaliapin, caricature self-portrait, 1908.*

Left 27. *Chaliapin, caricature self-portrait, sketched by him in the course of a conversation with the director of the Imperial Theatres soon after his first appearance in the opera* The Maid of Pskov, *December, 1911.*

28 & 29. Self-portraits by Chaliapin. The left-hand drawing is inscribed: "To Byleyev, in the Cubat Tavern, after Judith, November 14, 1908."

"I'm afraid it was," I replied.

"After last night I used it as a pick-me-up."

So much for the sad farces and the ridiculous episodes of my "home life" at the Palais Royal.

Much more serious at this time was my feeling of being an utter stranger in the theatre. I felt more and more isolated from the artists, since there was no apparent friendliness towards me, nor from anyone in the State Theatre. Something had gone from me, I felt quite empty. The road had looked so long, so splendid and full of adventure, but now there seemed nothing but cross-roads. It was bewildering. Which way was one to go? There was something I badly needed, but for the life of me I just could not put a name to it. And so the season came to an end. I took with me the scores I had to study for the next season, wondering where I might go for the summer, when Sokolov, a baritone I knew, suggested that we both go off to the Great Fair of Nizhni-Novgorod. He spoke enthusiastically of the group that was being assembled there, and pointed out its plans and aims. I decided to join them.

I had never travelled up the Volga beyond Kazan, and Nizhni-Novgorod quite bewitched me by its beauty, the walls and towers of the Kremlin, the great expanse of the river, the vastness of its meadows. Slowly my spirits rose, my happiness returned, but then a sight of the Volga always gave me a lift of the heart. I didn't waste a moment on arrival, but rushed off and found myself a room, rented it from an old lady, then went off to have a look at the theatre. It was a newly-built affair, and it was certainly clean. The rehearsals had just begun. I introduced myself and friendships were struck up immediately. And here I felt at home, since with the private companies the relations between artists were so much simpler, and perhaps even more important, they were sincere. Among these friends I found Kruglov, a man whom I worshipped, having remembered him from boyhood days back in Kazan. More pleasurable still was the discovery that the company was run by Savva Ivanovich Mamontov, of whom I had heard so many interesting things back in Tiflis from the conductor, Truffi. He was one of the great patrons of the arts, and deeply artistic by nature. As yet he had not arrived at the theatre. Madame Winter, who managed the company for him, gave a number of interesting and stimulating parties, to which the entire company would be asked. I always joined in with great enthusiasm, chatting and story-telling, recalling episodes from my early life, and by this time I had quite a number of them to relate. I was touched by the sympathetic interest it aroused in my colleagues, and this itself made me feel very much at home.

Arriving for dinner one evening I found a Mongolian-looking gentleman already seated, and in absorbed conversation with the young man beside him, who sported a kind of Henry IV beard, and whom I learned was Korovin. I can remember Mamontov looking at me for the first time, and somewhat gravely, but he did not speak to me. As usual I joined in the conversations, sharing jokes and laughter, and I noticed that Mamontov was amused by some of my reminiscences. I also met there the son of the famous artist Melnikov. Under Mamontov, Korovin, and Melnikov, the company had achieved a real brilliance.

Later the Italian Ballet arrived. I can remember this as though it were yesterday, and especially the incredible noise and bustle and general air of gaiety which the Italians brought into our theatre. Everything about them was different from anything I had ever seen. Their ebullience, their very gestures, intonations, and movements. What an astonishing crowd of volatile people. It was all quite new to me. They arrived straight from the station carrying their boxes and suitcases and trunks. No single one of them spoke Russian. They were like children. There and then I decided that my own temperament was well suited to such people and resolved to find rooms for them. This feat was carried out with a wealth of eloquent gestures. I was surrounded. They shouted and gesticulated, and at first it sounded to me like cursings, but it was nothing of the sort. We roamed the town searching for rooms, climbed up to attics, descended to basements, with the crowd following me shouting, "Caro, caro." They clutched their heads, giggled, laughed, and generally disapproved of everything. I, being a Russian, endeavoured as best I could to reconcile them to the inevitable. But in the end I managed to house them all.

Now I really was working, acting more and more, and Mamontov's backstage visits to me became more and more frequent. He neither praised nor criticized me, but he had certainly become more considerate, almost to the point of affection. And here I can say with the greatest pleasure that in Nizhni-Novgorod I had achieved a tumultuous success. Walking with me one day he asked me to give him some idea of my future plans. I told him I intended working in the Imperial Theatre, even though I was not happy there. He made no comment, but confined himself to his own affairs. He mentioned the exhibition that was going on, and threw out a number of hints about people not understanding him. Nor did I. Later he invited me to this exhibition.

I had been told that he had built some sort of railway, and naturally I expected to find railway engines and trucks, but I was very astonished when he led me into a big wooden building, on the walls of which hung two enormous paintings. One of these was painted in a somewhat queer style, a building up of hundreds of small, multi-coloured cubes. Extraordinarily colourful, but quite beyond my comprehension. Up to this time I had seen very little painting, beyond the kind that one might describe as careful and dainty, somewhat resembling the sugar of Italian opera. Staring at it, I could only think in terms of chaos in paint. But Mamontov contemplated it with obvious pleasure, and kept on repeating in my ear, "Devilish good, don't you think?"

"Why is it good?"

"The time will come when you'll understand," he said. "You're still a boy." He then proceeded to describe the other work.

Returning to town Mamontov kept complaining bitterly about the judges in the Art section, saying how unjust the committee had been to Vrubel who had painted these strange pictures. He referred to the judges as "house decorators".

I found these conversations stimulating, and I began spending my free time roaming round the exhibition, especially in the Vrubel Pavilion. By comparison with this painter's work, those chosen by the committee seemed lifeless and boring. Vrubel did have originality, and for this was sentenced to be housed in a separate building. The difference here was so painfully obvious, the kind of dynamic opposites as with the work of Mussorgsky and early Verdi.

Meanwhile the Mamontov season was progressing splendidly. The theatre was alive, humming with an inexhaustible energy. Just to realise that all this would soon be over depressed and saddened me. Soon I would have to resume the full rehearsals at the State Theatre, and to take part in performances that resembled nothing if not examinations. The thought of parting was all the more painful because Mamontov, Korovin, and Melnikov had become so dear and necessary to me. Walking through the Nizhni-Novgorod streets Mamontov invited me to come to Moscow and to remain with the Winter company. I was overjoyed by this invitation until I suddenly remembered that I would have to forfeit a sum of 3,600 roubles to the State Theatre if I did not honour my contract.

"I could give you 6,000 roubles a year, and a three-year contract," announced Mamontov. "Think it over." I said I would.

I must for a moment return to the Italian Ballet. There was among them a ballerina to whom I was enormously attracted. How beautifully she danced, far better I thought than all the ballerinas put together at the State Theatre. She always wore a sad expression, and it was soon obvious that she was not at home in Russia. I understood this well enough after my Baku, Tiflis, and Petersburg experiences. I made a point of going up to her at rehearsals and reciting all the Italian words I knew. "Allegro, andante, religioso, moderato," at which she smiled, but only for a moment, when again her face became shadowed by her sadness. A few days later I was dining with her and two of her friends. It was a beautiful moonlit night, and I so much wished to explain to these girls that to retire to bed on such a night was a sin, but unfortunately I did not know the Italian word for "sin". I expressed myself something like this: "Faust, Margarita—you understand—him, bam—bom—church—chiesa—Christ—not Margarita." They immediately burst out laughing. "Margarita peccata," they said. I concurred immediately. "Yes, yes, peccata."

After much effort we managed to compose a phrase. "La notte e cosi bella, que dormire e peccato." (The night is so beautiful it is a sin to go to bed.) These Russo-Italian conversations became a great source of amusement to the dancers, and no less to me. But shortly after this the girl who so powerfully attracted me, her name was Tornaghi, fell ill. I looked after her, brought her broths and wines, and finally persuaded her to come and live in the same house with me. This made looking after her much easier. She talked a lot to me, and I saw how greatly she missed Italy, the sun and flowers, if only because she talked so much about them. I sensed rather than understood the burden of her speech. I recall telling Mamontov that if only I could speak Italian I would marry her. A few days later I learned that he had given her a contract for Moscow.

And now the time had come for the hated return to Petersburg, to life in the Palais Royal, and the dreary routine of rehearsals. It turned out to be a misty, rainy autumn, and Petersburg, with its electric lights, lost its charm for me.

The first part given me for the new season was that of Vladimir in *Rogneda*. And throughout the rehearsals it was made plain to me by a series of mutterings that Melnikov used to sing this role splendidly, and how badly I was doing it. I was shown how he walked on stage, how he used his hands. Quite obviously Melnikov and I were as different from each other as chalk from cheese, and it would be an absurdity to imitate him. But my first real tussle was with the producer. On interpretative matters I would not agree with him.

Prince Vladimir, as I conceived his personality and character, could not make such gestures and movements as were now being forced on me. The part turned out to be rather pallid, and my only achievement was in polishing up the musical content. In this connection I suffered a great deal of unpleasantness with Napravnik, only to discover later that he was right, and what I had thought a pedantic attitude to the strictly rhythmical interpretation of the various parts was in effect the fruit of both knowledge and feeling. This great artist instilled into me the truth by which I live.

The Imperial season was three weeks old when Tornaghi arrived and begged me to join the Mamontov company in Moscow. It broke my heart to refuse her, but there was simply nothing that I could do. Yet the moment she left I was in a terrible fit of despondency. Within hours I was myself in Moscow, sitting with the artists in Madame Winter's box. I received a warm and loyal greeting. But I found the theatre dull, the attendance bad, and what I thought to be a very poor Mephistopheles prancing about the stage, and unable to pronounce at least sixteen letters of the alphabet.

The moment I saw Mamontov he was pressing again, and I could think of nothing now save this forfeit to the State Theatre if I broke away from them. Mamontov settled this at once by offering me 7,200 roubles a year, saying that he would split the forfeit to the Imperial Theatre, each paying 3,600 roubles. I agreed, and joined his company.

His very first production excited me. It was *A Life for the Czar*. Would I be able to justify the confidence of my colleagues, and the hopes of Mamontov himself? After the production the following notice appeared by the prominent theatre critic, Kruglikov.

"An interesting artist has appeared at the Solodovnikov Theatre. His interpretation of Susanin's part was new and original. The artist had enormous success, but unfortunately the attendance was very poor."

The public was affected by this notice, and the next performance had a much better attendance. I was then given the part of Mephistopheles in *Faust*. Thus came my real chance to talk with Mamontov. I told him that the role as formerly played by me was most unsatisfactory. I visualized an altogether different kind of costume for the role, and would much like to deviate from a long theatrical tradition. So we both went off to Avantso's shop and examined all the available representations of the character. I chose a Kaulbach engraving, and we ordered the costume. On the day of the performance I got to the theatre early enough to allow me plenty of time for experimenting with make-up for the chosen costume, and finally found something that harmonized with it.

When I made my appearance on stage I felt as though I had found a new self, a new freedom of movement, and at once I was conscious of strength and vigour. I was young then, supple, and my figure more suitable to the part than it is to-day. I acted and sang with heart and soul, and was filled with happiness. It all came out so naturally, and so freely. The success was enormous, and on the following day Kruglikov was writing:

"Yesterday's Mephistopheles, in Chaliapin's interpretation, wasn't quite perfect, but nevertheless of such interest that from now on I shall never miss a single production in which this artist appears."

The whole tone of the review was markedly serious and so different from the usual run of theatrical notices. Mamontov came to see me.

"Fedya, now you can do exactly what you like in the theatre. If you want costumes, say the word, and you shall have them. If you want a new opera, then we'll stage one for you."

I rejoiced. From this I got an entirely new outlook on things, and for the first time in my life I felt free, strong, and capable of overcoming all obstacles.

I have already said that opera as it then was did not really satisfy me. I could see that Dargomyzhsky in *Russalka*, by stressing the dramatic element in certain phrases, was obviously endeavouring to make a harmonic whole of opera and drama combined. I noticed, too, that both singers and producers in opera tended to emphasize the lyrical rather than the dramatic moments, thereby depriving the work of both spirit and force. Dalsky used to say to me, "What is opera? You can't act Shakespeare in opera." I did not believe this. Why on earth not?

I realized, however, how greatly the operas of Rimsky-Korsakov differed from those of Verdi, like *Traviata* and *Rigoletto*, and even from *Faust*. But I had to find my way through all this, to set myself precise criteria, and somehow I could not, and was left sitting between two stools as it were. But the thing haunted me. Now that I had virtually been given carte blanche by Mamontov, I started work, perfecting all the roles in my repertoire. I was not interfered with, there was no knuckle-rapping, nobody informed me that this or that was wrong, and nobody kept rubbing it in that Petrov or Melnikov did it this way. The chains fell away from me at once. It was a new life, a new day.

I began to widen the circle of my acquaintances among the painters.

V. D. Polenov came to see me backstage, and kindly made a sketch of a costume for Mephistopheles for me. I met Serov too, and Vrubel, Vasnetzov, Yakunchikova, and Arkhipov. I liked Serov, Korovin, and Vrubel best of all. These experiences greatly stimulated my interest in painting. At first these artists seemed like anybody else, and it was only when they began to talk, to expound, that I realized how different they were. The very phrases they used when discussing their work were to me fascinating, and moreover I was amazed at their ability to give clear pictures of the form and content of their work, with the minimum of words and gestures. Life was enriched by the friendship of these people. I would listen to them enthralled, the preciseness of exposition, the certainty of idea, the feeling of mission that emanated from them excited me. I liked Serov particularly, although he was popularly supposed to be rather a dry and severe person. But he had a great sense of humour.

I remember an occasion when we talked about the droshky drivers waiting on the rank near the monastery, and he astonished me by sitting in a chair and imitating one of them to the life, even down to the dialect and the call of "six roubles the ride". I might have been listening to a real cabby. Showing some sketches to Korovin one day, he remarked, "I wanted to paint a cloud of sparrows risen together in the air with a great whirring of wings, but it just didn't come off. It doesn't always, worse luck."

I learned much from such people. How to be more expressive, more plastic, more exploratory, both in my life and in the theatre.

The roles in my repertoire, once so stale, so uninteresting, now took on another dimension. I knew that Rimsky-Korsakov had an opera *The Maid of Pskov*, and now I offered to produce it and play the part of Ivan the Terrible. But immediately everybody in the theatre, including Mamontov himself, treated the idea with scepticism. However, he did not object to it and as it happened this choice turned out to be a felicitous one, both for the theatre and for me. I had stumbled on the very thing that would link those two elements, the lyrical and the dramatic.

When I really began studying the opera in more detail, I must admit to a certain scepticism arising in myself. Everything new has its price, and its pain, and now I was being concerned with a fact that was as plain as a fist, the fact of the public. I sensed at once that my idea would make little or no impression. There wasn't an aria, or duet, or a trio in the opera—nothing that tradition decreed. Nor did I have at that time the benefit of the wonderful teaching of Klyuchevsky, who helped me master the part of Boris Godunov. I was forced to fall back upon my painter friends, who helped me understand not only the epoch, but the very character of Ivan the Terrible. But imagine my horror when I came to produce it, and the bitterest disappointment when I realized that I could do nothing with this role. I knew that Ivan was a sanctimonious bigot, and therefore his words, "Shall I go in?" uttered by him on the threshold of Tokmakov's palace, and with which the drama opens, I myself uttered quietly, but in a venomous and hypocritical manner. And having thus begun, I carried on in the same tone. For me the stage was flooded with inconceivable tedium, flatness. I felt it, my colleagues felt it. And the second rehearsal was no better than the first. I remember tearing up the score, rushing to my dressing-room, and in sheer despair bursting into tears. Mamontov came along, patted me on the shoulder, and was kind and friendly with his advice.

"You must stop being hysterical, Fedya. Take yourself in hand. Pull your cast together, and make that first phrase a little stronger."

And at once I realized my mistake. Of course Ivan was a bigot and a hypocrite, but he was also *Terrible*. I rushed back to the stage and altered the whole tone of the role, and this time I felt it had improved a little. Yes, I had got it right. Everything came to life, in me, in my colleagues, whose whole approach had changed as had my own. And I still went on, pursuing, finding out, exploring.

To establish the face of Ivan I went along to the Tretyakov Gallery to look at the paintings of Schwartz and Repin, as well as Antokolsky's sculpture. I was unsatisfied. Then somebody showed me a portrait of Ivan the Terrible by the painter, Vasnetzov, in a private collection. To this day I believe that portrait remains unknown. It made a great impression on me. The features were shown in three-quarters, with one blazing eye looking to the side. By combining this, and adding to it what I had learned from Repin, Vasnetzov, and Schwartz, I managed to create quite a successful portrait, and I was now certain that Ivan had the right stature.

This opera was written in 1874 and produced in 1897. The public were ignorant of its existence to such an extent that, when I rode on to the stage on horseback, they expected me to sing, but the curtain came down without a note having been sung. In spite of the audience's bewilderment at having to look on at this silent picture, they yet applauded so vigorously that the curtain had to be raised several times.

The Maid of Pskov was a furore, and during that season was performed on no less than fifteen occasions, and always to a full house. Mamontov was delighted with it, even though he was an admirer of Italian opera. The most famous singers, people like Mazzini and Tamagno, sang for him. I had often heard people remark, "Yes, Mazzini is a magnificent singer, but one should listen to him with closed eyes."

I couldn't agree with that, I knew that he sang like an angel out of heaven and there was something ennobling in the performance he gave. He was, too, a superb actor. I have seen him in *La Favorita*, almost giving one the impression that he didn't want to act, and he seemed so negligently dressed, with his much worn tights and odd costume. He could behave on stage like some unruly boy until the last act, in which he dies of his wounds. A wonderful actor, an opinion shared by such an experienced dramatic actor as Dalsky, who was thrilled by Mazzini and always moved by him.

8

In the summer of 1898 I was invited to stay at T. C. Lyubatovich's country house in the Yaroslavl province. There, together with Sergei Rachmaninov, our conductor, I began the study of Boris Godunov. Rachmaninov had only just graduated from the Conservatoire. He was full of vitality and vivacity, and excellent company. He was a first-rate artist, a magnificent musician, and a pupil of Tchaikovsky. He it was who particularly encouraged me to study Mussorgsky, and Rimsky-Korsakov. He taught me something about the fundamentals of music and harmony, striving to complete my musical education.

Boris Godunov appealed to me to such an extent that, not content with learning my role, I sang the whole of the opera, all parts, male and female. Now I realized the usefulness of studying a "whole" opera, and consequently I began to study other works in their entirety, even operas I was already familiar with.

The more I delved into Mussorgsky, the more did I realize that one could act Shakespeare in opera. For me everything depended on the composer of the work. I was terribly moved when I made my first acquaintance with Mussorgsky's biography. Indeed I was awestruck, appalled. To have such a magnificent and original talent, and to have lived in squalor, poverty, and then to die of alcoholism in a filthy hospital. It was unbelievable. Many talented Russians had been similarly lost, before and since. Alas, Mussorgsky was not the last one to end his life as he did.

Apart from this thorough exploration of the Mussorgsky music, I began to look at him from the historical angle. To this end I began reading Pushkin and Karamzin. But this was not enough, I wished to go farther, and consequently I enlisted the aid of the famous historian, Klyuchevsky, who happened to be spending the summer in Yaroslavl Province.

The great scholar received me most warmly. He gave me tea, and then told me that he had enjoyed my interpretation of Ivan the Terrible. I then asked him if he would tell me something about Godunov. He suggested that we go for a walk into the woods. I shall not soon forget that incredible walk among the tall pines, over a pine-needle-filled sand.

The small old man beside me had a kind of pudding-basin haircut, a little white beard, rather narrow, but wise eyes that shone behind his glasses. Every few moments he would stop, and in an oily voice, and with a cunning smirk upon his face, enact the conversation that passed between Shuisky and Godunov, almost as though he had been an eye witness of the event, and followed this up by speaking of Varlaam and Misail as though he had known them personally. He described the personal charm of the Pretender. He talked much, and his descriptions were picturesque, and full of colour. I could actually see the people portrayed. How I wished he could sing, that we two might have enacted the whole thing together! This experience with Klyuchevsky left a deep impression on my mind.

As he spoke of Boris, the man stood out for me as a powerful figure, and one of great interest. Indeed I began to feel a sympathy for this Czar of power and intelligence, who, though he wished to do good for Russia, yet created serfdom. The old historian emphasised the solitude of Godunov, his quick-thinking mind, his effort to bring some kind of enlightenment to his country. Listening, it almost seemed as if Vassily Shuisky had come back to life, and was in that very moment confessing his mistake in destroying Godunov.

I spent the night with Klyuchevsky, and on the following day took my leave of this remarkable man, and how grateful I was for that lesson in history. I often went to him for advice.

The rehearsals for *Boris Godunov* began. At once I realized that my colleagues did not see things my way and that the existing school of opera did not meet the requirements of such a work. There seemed a deficiency, even in the performance of an opera like *The Maid of Pskov*. I myself, of course, was a product of the same school, a school of singing, and nothing more. This school taught how to hold the sound, how to broaden or reduce it, but what it did not teach us was the psychology of the character portrayed. Certainly nobody was ever instructed to make a study of the epoch in which a character had lived. The professors of this school were wont to use the most baffling terminology, often incomprehensible. They talked of "holding the voice in the 'masque' ", of "placing it on the diaphragm", or of, "pressing down". It may have been necessary, but it was not the essence of the matter. To me it seemed not enough to teach a man to sing a cavatina, serenade, or ballad; he must be taught to understand the meaning of the words he sings, the feelings they evoke. They are not just some other words.

Certainly the weaknesses of this school of opera became most apparent at the rehearsals, and I think of those in which the words are those of a poet, Pushkin, or Karamzin. It was just not possible to act if one did not get the expected response from the partner, especially if he was not in the mood of the scene. Shuisky was my main worry, even though this role was sung by Shkafer, a most intelligent artist. Yet hearing him, I couldn't help but wish that my little old historian could have been given the part.

The *décor*, the props, the orchestra and chorus of the Mamontov company were good, but now I felt that the greater resources of the Imperial Theatre stage would make an even better production of *Boris Godunov*.

The day of the performance arrived. Since the production of *The Maid of Pskov*, I had become perhaps the most popular artist in Moscow, and the public flocked to productions in which I took part. In the beginning *Boris* was greeted coolly, apathetically, and I was worried. But suddenly the hallucination scene electrified the audience, and the opera ended in triumph. It seemed strange to me that this opera had never before made such an impact, and yet this work is Shakespearean in its power and beauty. The performances that followed brought the public nearer to it, and now from the very first act they seemed to fall under its enchantment.

Prepare as I might, study and strive as I might, I never once walked on to the stage with the feeling of mastery. That was something that grew in the act itself; and the reward and the knowledge arose out of my performance. It was this living of the role that, with each production, I broadened and deepened the character. There was one exception. When I walked out as Ivan the Terrible for the first time, I was that man, and I knew it. It was this feeling of real achievement that sent me back again and again to other roles. In this lay real growth, real understanding.

In the summer of 1898, whilst staying in the country with Lyubatovich, I married the dancer Tornaghi in a little village church, and after the wedding we had a funny celebration, rather Turkish in character. We sat on the carpeted floor, and behaved like children. There was nothing at all of the conventional wedding reception. No richly decked table, no flowery speeches but lots of real wild flowers, and lots of wine. And at six o'clock the next morning I was rudely awakened by an infernal din. When I threw up the window there stood Mamontov himself, with many of my friends, conducting a concert with stove lids and other household utensils. It brought back memories of Sukonnaya Sloboda.

"What on earth are you sleeping for?" yelled Mamontov.

"People in the country don't go to sleep. Get up at once. Let's go off into the woods for mushrooms." The din was resumed.

This ear-splitting clamour was in the capable hands of conductor Rachmaninov.

When the new season opened we began it with Mussorgsky's *Khovanshchina*. The role of Dositheus was not fully clear to me, so once again I went off in search of my historian. He was not long in enlightening me, and gave me many interesting details concerning the Princes Khovansky, the Streltsy and the Princess Sofia. But I felt uncertain, a little afraid. Perhaps we might not be allowed to produce this work, considering that two scenes in it resembled church services, but we got permission, and were thankful for it.

Its first production was a success, though it never conveyed the same impression as did *Boris* or *The Maid of Pskov*. The audience listened attentively of course, but there was little enthusiasm, and I was disappointed. I felt that Moscow should have hailed it. I remember an incident during the third performance when I sang, "Sisters, hearken to the Lord's word." An offended man's voice cried out from the gallery: "What a disgrace. Enough about God."

For a moment or two I dreaded the worst. Surely this might mean the work being withdrawn, but fortunately the voice of the censor in the gallery did not reach the ears of the powers-that-be.

I could see that Mamontov was becoming more and more attracted to Russian music, and it had its happy consequences, for we put on *May Night*, *The Czar's Bride*, and *Sadko*, the latter work only recently completed by Rimsky-Korsakov. Mamontov took an active part in these productions, and invented quite a few novelties, which seeming absurd at first, later turned out to be just right.

His artistic sense never failed him. Thus, in *Sadko*, the *décor* for which had been done by Vrubel, and in which he had astonishingly produced the bed of the ocean, Mamontov now introduced the serpentine, a dance already almost done to death in practically every *café-chantant*. One would suppose there was no place for it in serious opera. But Mamontov proved everybody wrong. Splendid costumes were made for the ballerinas, and the dance on the ocean bed came off wonderfully. It was something entirely new, and conveyed the undulations of waves.

I took no part in this work, and it was only the weakness of the man singing the Varangian Guest that brought me into it. I remember how, as I was dressing for it, the painter Serov rushed in—all the painters were captivated by *Sadko*—and exclaimed: "You look splendid, but your arms are too feminine." So I made up my arms, underlining the muscles, and the artists approved of my efforts. Their praise meant more to me than any amount of public applause. I was highly pleased with the result.

The more I studied Boris Godunov, Ivan the Terrible, Dositheus, the Viking Merchant, and the Head-Man in *May Night*, the more convinced I became that acting equated with singing, and had to be so. In opera we must sing as we speak. I have noticed that artists who have imitated me have not quite understood. They didn't sing as they spoke, but quite the reverse.

It never came more clear to me than when the occasion arrived for me to sing and play the part of Salieri, a task I found more difficult than all previous ones. All the arias I had sung, all the monologues, had to a great degree been grounded in an old opera tradition, but Rimsky-Korsakov's Salieri was different. There had to be a new melodic recitative. Here was a new task, bristling with potential as well as difficulties, and I knew at once that all that was worth solving could be done by one man only, Rachmaninov. To him I went. Wonderful, magnificent Rachmaninov.

The composer of *Mozart and Salieri* had conveyed his musical movements in conventional terms, thus, "Allegro, Moderato, Andante," and so on, but I found it was not always possible to follow these instructions. Sometimes I would suggest to Rachmaninov that this or that movement should be changed, and almost immediately he knew where it was possible, and where it was not. So, without in any way distorting the conception of the work, we yet found a way to give definite shape to this tragic figure of Salieri.

The part of Mozart was sung by Shkafer, who always tackled his part with great feeling. I was thrilled by the idea that by producing this opera we could show to the public the merging of the dramatic element with the purely lyrical. I put my whole heart and soul into this work, but alas, the public remained cold and indifferent. It quite bewildered me. And now, once more, the painters gave me encouragement. This time it was Vrubel. He came backstage bubbling over with excitement. "That's magnificent," he said. "One listens to a whole act, and hears the reverberations of wonderful words, and there are no feathers or hats, or E flats."

I well knew that such men were not in the habit of showering one with empty compliments. They treated me as a serious artist, and when the occasion arose severely criticised me. But I trusted them, and I now saw that they were enchanted by Salieri. Their judgment was for me the supreme judgment. It is works like these that bring new life and meaning into opera. There are many people who maintain that Rimsky-Korsakov's work does not attain the height of Pushkin's text, yet I remain convinced that this is a new form of art which successfully unites music with psychological drama.

During the Lent season of 1898 Mamontov's company moved to the Conservatoire Theatre in Petersburg. It was not a very good theatre, either from the artists' or the public's point of view. Its accoustics were poor; there was hardly room enough to turn round on the stage. It was therefore apparent that Ivan the Terrible's entrance on horseback, or the first act of *Boris Godunov*, could not be satisfactorily carried out. In spite of this, however, the productions met with success. On one occasion, just after my scene with Tokmakov, I was seated in my dressing-room when I heard a thundering, excited voice behind the door.

"Show him to me, for goodness' sake. Where is he?"

The door was flung open, and there stood a giant of a man with a long white beard, with big features and the most youthful eyes.

"Well, my dear friend," he exclaimed. "You astound me. Astound me. How do you do? You see, I've even forgotten to greet you. Allow me to introduce myself. I live here in Petersburg, and I have been in Moscow, and abroad. I have heard Petrov and Melnikov, but I've never in my life heard anything so marvellous as this. Never. Thank you. Thank you." He spoke quickly, excitedly, loudly. Behind him stood another, a very dark man, with delicate aesthetic features.

"You see," the giant continued, "we thought it would be better if we both came. I felt that alone I could not really express myself, but together . . . He also has worked on Ivan the Terrible. This is Antokolsky, and I am Stassov."

I was quite dazed, and could only stare with admiration at the famous giant, and his companion. I was far too embarrassed to speak. "You're still so young," said Stassov. "How old are you? Fifteen? Where do you come from?"

I can't remember what I said to him. He was deeply moved, and embraced me with tears in his eyes. He then left. Antokolsky also praised my work. I was left alone, haloed in happiness.

The following day I went to see Stassov in the public library, where he greeted me in his usual exuberant manner.

"Come in. I'm delighted to see you. Thank you for coming. Do you know, I haven't slept the whole night, remembering your performance. This opera has been done before, but oh, so badly. What a magnificent piece of work it is! And isn't Rimsky-Korsakov talented? Just look what he can do. Though not everybody understands him. Do sit down. No, not there. Here, in this armchair."

Stassov untied a tape that extended across the chair, obviously to prevent anybody being seated in it, a thing that roused my curiosity.

"On this chair," said Stassov, "sat both Gogol and Turgenev," at which remark I hesitated. "Sit down, sit down," he exclaimed, "and never mind that you're still so young."

This man radiated warmth. From few people have I derived such happiness; he gave so generously of his nature. He discussed my artistic career, cursed the State Theatres, described them as cemeteries, and congratulated me on having left them, in spite of the forfeit.

"To hell with money, what is money? That will come. It's always like that; at first there's no money, and then it comes. Money is dross. What a wonderful person is Savva Mamontov. Look what he's doing now. What a change from a too large dose of Italian trifles!"

He went on to extol Rimsky-Korsakov, and Russian art in general, lamenting the fact that the authorities were so indifferent to it, showing such a lack of appreciation. He let himself go, shouted, waved his arms about, a creature of limitless energy and true Russian bonhomie.

Stassov became a daily visitor to our theatre. Often I would come out to take a bow, and see him towering above the audience like a belfry, beating his great hands. But if something displeased him he swore without restraint.

Very suddenly, right out of the blue, there appeared in the newspaper *Novoye Vremya*, a most damning review, in which the view was maintained that *The Maid of Pskov* was a bad opera, and Ivan the Terrible, as portrayed by Chaliapin, even worse. I read this article, which seemed to me to have both logic and conviction, but nevertheless I was disappointed. I realized the intelligence of the writer, but this in no way diminished the disappointment. I felt like a fly in October.

Later, when I went to see Stassov at the Imperial Public Library, he greeted me, exclaiming: "All right, I know. I know. I've read it. All rubbish. Pay no attention. He's just a camel. Whether you put oranges or lumps of hay before him, he'll turn up his nose. Don't worry. I'll reply to him."

The following day Stassov's article, "Night Blindness," was printed in *Novosti*, and in it he swept away the whole argument of the *Novoye Vremya* critic. From then on I relied on Stassov in any difficulties; if I wanted advice, I went to this real father. Sometimes I travelled from Moscow to see him, and he never failed me.

He was very attached to *Mozart and Salieri*, spoke of it with enthusiasm, and immediately followed this up by begging me to produce *The Stone Guest* by Dargomyzhsky. "It's a magnificent work, you must produce it."

I was soon buried in the score of this opera, and saw at once that superb artists would be required to play the roles of Laura and Don Juan. Any routine interpretation was out, and could only distort. Realizing Stassov's enthusiasm, and not wishing to disappoint him, I learned the whole of this work, and then offered to sing all the roles for him. This delighted him, and almost at once a party was arranged to take place at Rimsky-Korsakov's house, at which, in addition to the host and Stassov, there were also present the brothers Blumenfeld, César Cui, Vrubel and his wife. It was an electrifying evening. I sang through the whole of *The Stone Guest*, and followed this with Mussorgsky's satire, "The Swaggerer," "The Flea," and other songs. The evening went with a swing.

After dinner we performed Borodin's quartet, "Four Cavaliers' Serenade to a Lady". Rimsky-Korsakov sang second bass, I first, Blumenfeld first tenor, and Cui the second. There was something indescribably funny about the performance. Rimsky was well hidden behind his beard and his double spectacles, and he treated this musical joke seriously, unsmiling, though the remainder of the quartet could hardly conceal their amusement, especially with the phrase, "Oh, how I love you." It had the atmosphere of the burlesque. But the noisiest of all the visitors was, of course, our friend Stassov. Certainly it did not look like a gathering of celebrities whose names were household words to every cultured Russian. Rather did they resemble a bunch of students. These men seemed to me to be as young as I was, and I felt perfectly at home. It was an unforgettable occasion.

I talked with Stassov about *The Stone Guest*, and he seemed very disappointed that it could not be done, though he agreed that lacking the right supporting cast, there was nothing I could do.

"But if we do find the artists, then we'll put it on."

"You promise?"

I promised, but alas to this day I have not seen *The Stone Guest* put on the stage, and whenever I met Stassov he always reminded me of my promise. My giant friend died, however, without the happiness of ever seeing this opera performed.

I shall always remember him, a very remarkable man. Once during a season I was indisposed, and Stassov turned up at my place on the fourth floor. He was then seventy. I protested at his climbing that height, but he dismissed it, saying, "I had to come, I heard you were unwell. Besides it was on my way."

He lived on Peski, and I on Kolokolnaya, and this calling on me from his place was really like travelling from Kiev to Moscow, via Astrakhan. He remained with me quite a time, talking of his visits to Europe, to La Scala and the Escorial, and of his friends in England.

"You must go to England," he urged. "They are ignorant of Russian art. They are a wonderful people, the English, but they have not heard anything like *Boris Godunov* and *The Maid of Pskov*. You simply must show them your Ivan the Terrible. Yes, my friend, you must go to England."

"But for this one must know languages," I said.

"Languages nothing. Just sing in your own language. They will understand everything. There is no need for languages. Go to England."

Stassov was an exceptional man, a great lover of Russian art, and he had a profound faith in its power.

9

My success with the Mamontov company had now come to the notice of the Imperial administration, a new head of which had recently been appointed, a cavalry Colonel named Telyakovsky. It had caused some amusement in theatrical circles:

"The man who was in charge of horses will now be in charge of actors."

I met this man soon after his appointment, and he made an excellent impression on me, and all my sympathy went out to him. It was quite clear to me that he not only understood, but had real knowledge of the art he served so well. To this man did I entrust my dreams. Our conversation led to his offering me a contract with the State Theatre.

My contract with the Private Opera was on the point of expiring, and it pleased me much to know that I should again be working for the Imperial Theatre, since it provided the artist with far greater opportunities, and there was greater scope for the production of opera. Added to this satisfaction was the comment of Telyakovsky himself.

"Gradually," he said, "we shall come round to doing what you consider necessary."

I signed a contract with them for three years, with a sliding scale of salary, one of 9,000 roubles for the first year, 10,000 for the second, and 11,000 for the third year. There was a clause providing for a forfeit of 15,000 roubles in the event of any breach of contract.

As soon as the season of the Private Opera began I was feeling sorry indeed at my parting with Mamontov and his company. The result was that within hours of signing with the Imperial Theatre, I had definitely decided to remain with Mamontov and my friends. But it was soon explained to me by Telyakovsky that such things just couldn't be done without handing out the forfeit. It gave me food for thought. Forfeiting was one thing, but what happened if suddenly the authorities decided to banish me from Petersburg, or even forbade me to sing altogether, because of this sudden whim. I reflected that anything was possible, considering the Russian way of dealing with people.

All the same, I was soon asking my rich friends to lend me 15,000 roubles. All were charming, but offered the polite excuse that they had no money. Of a sudden they had all become poor, so with much regret I said goodbye to the Private Opera.

In the spring of 1897 I realized my long-cherished dream. I went abroad.

30. Chaliapin as Galitsky in Borodin's opera Prince Igor (*Bolshoy Theatre, Moscow*), *1910.*

31. Sketch by Chaliapin for his make-up as Don Basilio (The Barber of Seville),
November 15, 1912.

32. Chaliapin as Don Basilio in Rossini's opera The Barber of Seville (*Bolshoy Theatre, Moscow*), *1913.*

33. Chaliapin as Dositheus in Mussorgsky's opera Khovanshchina *(Bolshoy Theatre. Moscow), 1912. (There is a[l]so a remarkable self-portrait in this part, which Chaliapin made in his dressing room at the Mariinsky Theatre on Novemb[er] 30, 1911, using grease-paints. Art critics said they could "hear Mussorgsky's music in this most musical of his se[lf-]portraits.")*

34. A scene from Mussorgsky's opera Khovanshchina *(with libretto by the composer and Stassov), produced [by] Chaliapin at the Mariinsky Theatre, St. Petersburg, 1911.*

The moment I reached Warsaw I was struck by the astounding difference in everything. It is true that the cab drivers swore just as powerfully, and the police themselves seemed not a shade different from that of my country, but there was something new; the unmistakable stamp of another kind of life, with different customs and manners. And when I left that city the train went at such a terrific speed that I fully expected it to go off the rails at any moment. Indeed this fear was so real to me that periodically I made my appearance on the platform, ready to jump off in case of a crash. I found the journey of great interest.

For instance, the fields themselves seemed so different from Russian fields; things appeared to grow better than in our land, and one felt the love that these people bestowed upon it. I found it a thickly populated country. I admired the stone barns, the tiled roofs. Smoke poured forth from factory chimneys.

Vienna sailed by. It looked immense, and after that fascinating city came the kind of landscapes that hitherto I had only seen in paintings—mountains and bridges, fairytale castles. There seemed to be a kind of festive prosperity in the air itself.

For three days and nights I hardly slept. And finally I reached Paris. With every hour I felt the mounting excitement of dream, of pure fairytale. The night lights of this stupendous city, the glow in the sky—to me it was unforgettable. Here at last was Paris. I felt stunned amid such a multitude of people that milled about the precincts of the railway station. I joined in too, weaving my way among the dashing Frenchmen, and feeling such a carefree gaiety. I collected my belongings, caught a cab, and set off for the address which Melnikov had given me, 40 Rue de Copernic.

It was six o'clock in the morning. Looking at the big grey houses, the boulevards, the churches—indeed all that I saw on the way—gave me a feeling of having been there before. I certainly recalled the novels of my youth—my avid reading of Montespan, Gaboriau, Terrail.

I watched men in blue blouses and aprons pouring water on the streets, scrubbing the pavements like sailors scrubbing decks. How wonderful, I thought, to be able to get them to do the same for the Moscow streets, or better still Astrakhan. We reached the Rue de Copernic, and pulled up before a small, two-storied house. I rang the bell, and a white-aproned man appeared, and began talking to me in French. With the aid of mimicry I explained to him as best I could, combining the use of both hands and feet in the process, the uselessness of speaking to me in French, and stressed my desire to see the gentleman named Melnikov. At that moment a charming old lady arrived. She was beautifully clean, simply dressed, and her hair most beautifully done. I noticed that she wore a hairnet made of hair.

I did my best with her in Russian, asking the number of Melnikov's room. She understood at once, and pointed to a door, on which I immediately started to hammer.

"Wake up there," I shouted, "it's a disgrace to sleep in Paris." The door burst open.

I was overwhelmed with joy at being in this wonderful city, of being able to speak my own language. Suddenly I started singing, upon which I was hastily gagged by my friends, who pointed out that there were people still sleeping in the pension, and making a noise was strictly forbidden. After a wash, I dressed, then took some coffee, and wanted to go out at once, somewhere, anywhere. I was wildly excited at this new world, but my friends prevented my going, saying they would take me for a quiet walk after lunch. I accepted their decision and sat down. I studied the room. It looked very cosy, and well furnished. Everything was clean and beautiful. There was a fireplace, and above it a mirror in a gilt frame. There were many statuettes on the mantelpiece. I assumed that all this must cost quite a lot of money, but was quite staggered to be told that this room, with breakfast, lunch and dinner, including wines and coffee, cost only eleven francs per day. It scarcely seemed possible at the price.

"Then I suppose the food is rotten." But the meals were excellent—to my great delight.

Some ten of us sat down to lunch. My five Russian friends, an abbot, a very elderly gentleman, a singing teacher, a journalist, a young Greek, and last but not least, an incredibly beautiful Greek woman who rejoiced in the name of Kalliope. I drank a few glasses of wine, and wished to drink more but dared not, thinking it would embarrass the company, if not our hostess. But my friends informed me that I could drink as much wine as I liked. Indeed my hostess told me that it would delight her. I remember so well that kind and courteous lady.

Lunch over I went off to see the Eiffel Tower, climbing to the top, and was able to look down at the great expanse of the city for the first time. I was struck by the fact of there being so few Frenchmen there, and supposed that it was another case of familiarity breeding contempt. My friends stressed that this tower was nothing in particular, that Paris was full of far more beautiful things, as I later discovered after visiting in turn the Louvre, the parks, and the boulevards. I was intoxicated by the Louvre, such a vast house of treasure, and I returned to it again and again. I was soon in love with Paris, with Parisians, but most of all, perhaps, the abbot staying in our pension.

A delightfully benign old man, who drank much wine, yet never got drunk—how well he could take a joke against himself and his cloth, never losing his dignity, always sincere, always so beautifully simple! This sense of dignity I found did not belong to him alone, but even extended to servants and cabdrivers.

After a month in Paris I went off to Dieppe to see a woman who had taught singing to my friends. I had to learn the part of Holofernes in *Judith*. When I got there she told me there was no room available for me, and I had to be content with an attic, an old storeroom really, but quite clean. I was made very comfortable, and fortunately it was summer time. I could not refrain from commenting to this lady upon the excellence of French beds, even down to the servants', to which this good lady replied that this was because the French spent about a third of their lives in bed. She was precise, logical.

"To work well, monsieur," she said, "one must rest well."

I found a restaurant on the seashore that had an excellent orchestra, and there were some gay light-hearted singers there too. One thing caught my eye and was soon my downfall, the mechanical horses. The temptation was too much. I began by putting on five francs, and in no time had lost all my money. Mamontov replenished my purse, gave me a scolding, and forbade any further gambling.

My Paris visit ended all too quickly, but my farewell to it seemed even kinder than her reception of me. In the singing teacher's house where I stayed there was living a charming young girl pianist who was taking lessons. When I practised *Judith* she kindly accompanied me, and in spite of every insistence on my part, refused to take any payment. However, I was able to return her kindness in quite another way. She was very anxious to learn to cycle, and I spent some time coaching her in the squares of Dieppe. As with my first Frenchman, I couldn't converse very well, and again resorted to exclamation, gestures, and often, much laughter.

The time came for my return to Russia, and as I had to start at the crack of dawn, I retired to my attic early that evening. I woke up in the small hours to feel lips against my own, and on opening my eyes I was astonished to behold the young lady pianist. I am quite unable to describe the emotion I felt at her soft caresses. I wanted to cry, I felt so happy, so pleased with the world. We had never even discussed love, and certainly I had done no courting, and had not noticed any romantic inclinations on her part. I couldn't even ask her why she did it, but I felt in it something warmly human, a womanly tenderness. I never saw her again. Leaving Dieppe I felt sad, and yet in another way, happy also, as though I had been kissed by some new life.

I passed through Berlin on my way home, but like the rest of Germany it left no lasting impression upon me. But how quickly, and with what strange feelings, I was suddenly noticing how, the nearer I got to my home, the more faded and subdued the colours became; the sky was grey; people looked sadder, and lazier. Nostalgic I certainly was, as my mind switched back to the days of light, to France. I wondered if I would ever return. An unpleasant, nagging feeling began to gnaw at me, and I asked myself why it was that abroad people seemed to live better, fuller lives, happier, gayer lives.

It was like life split in two pieces. Abroad people were different, and treated each other with mutual trust and respect. Even waiters in the restaurants seemed to be more educated, and they did things for you with charm, like hosts to their guests. More important still, there was nothing servile or cowering in their behaviour.

How different Moscow, where the moment I arrived I was informed that my luggage had been mislaid. I tried hard enough to trace it, to gather some information about it, but none of the station staff could enlighten me, and all I heard was the boringly repeated phrase, "Come back tomorrow."

This not only irritated me, but also flooded me with shame, confronted as I was by such uncouthness. Here was I, back in my own land, returning to the railway station again and again, speaking my own language to them, which they all understood, yet all my countrymen could do was to make disagreeable faces, and flatly declare that they had no time to go searching for anybody's lost luggage. In France I could not speak a word of their language, but I was listened to with such patience, and people even tried to understand my extraordinary chatter. I expressed these rather naïve thoughts to a friend some time later, and was told that Russia simply could not compete with other countries. "How can we?" exclaimed my friend. "We've only just begun to live."

Is it necessary to live for six hundred years before you can learn to keep a town properly clean? Why should a young country exist in filth? I felt angry, irritated. It depressed me, and I was soon dreaming of another trip abroad. As if my depression and feeling of frustration were not enough, I heard suddenly that my friend Mamontov had been arrested, and was being kept in prison. This crushed me completely. It seemed so incredible, so utterly ridiculous. A man like Savva Mamontov was the last sort of person to be languishing in gaol. I knew him only as a man devoted to art. Later I heard that even in prison he was still working, sculpting a head of Ivan the Terrible, designing patterns for his ceramics, and inventing new methods of firing glazed tiles. It was painful, and it was also shameful that this good old man, one who counted Vrubel, Serov, Polenov, Korovin and Vasnetzov among his friends, a man who had always been surrounded by the finest and most talented people in Russia, should lie in prison. A sad homecoming.

The first production in which I appeared for the Imperial Theatre was *Faust*, and I was tumultuously received by the public and presented with a laurel wreath. This experience most convincingly showed me the resources behind Imperial undertakings. The orchestra and choir were superb, and the opportunity was there to create new *décor* and entirely new costumes. So much lay at one's disposal. I seemed to be realizing my early dreams. There was something to be said for the State Theatre. I felt that here one might create an entirely new school of opera singers.

I lost no time in conveying my feelings to Telyakovsky, who was at once agreeable, and promised me that we would make a start in the next season. But for the first season we had to do the best we could, and *Boris Godunov* was produced with the same old décor. I was advised to choose the costumes I considered necessary, and allowed to use my own discretion in the matter. Yet in spite of all this, of the great promise and the golden opportunities, there yet remained the burdening conviction that all the time one was working under men in uniform, men who had nothing in common with art, wholly unable to understand its cultural power, its ennobling influence. They were quite indifferent.

Besides, in private opera, I was accustomed to being a free man, and artistically my own master. I was therefore determined to draw a clear line of demarcation between these uniformed officials and the artists. The opportunity to put it into practice was not long in arriving. On one occasion I actually saw an official on stage shouting and ranting at the company. They might have been common soldiers, or even night watchmen. I spoke to this official in no uncertain terms, and asked him to leave the stage. I told him exactly where to go, and that he was to leave the artists alone. This astonished him; he was quite taken aback, and left us in peace.

I pointed out to my colleagues that we could, of course, respect these officials, men who appeared to think that disorder was sometimes necessary, but the stage was no place on which to demonstrate it. There, we were the masters, and if not, then we were nothing. Fortunately I was backed up by my fellow artists, some of whom described my action as heroic. They expressed their gratitude to me for my attempt to free them from the drill and yoke of the pen-pushers, the purveyors of red tape. In this way we artists began to get closer to each other, as an assertive and determined family. Officials now appeared only when strictly necessary. Telyakovsky used to say, "We are here to serve the artists."

It did not last long, however. We had very soon reverted to the old rhythm, the stale pattern. Reforms, whatever their nature, do not last long in Russia.

My fellow-artists now began explaining to the officials that I was right, but modified the contention by adding that perhaps I had started out somewhat ruthlessly. The opinion grew that I was tactless. The officials crawled back to power, and as we say, they understood that people were again ready to bring geese to the back door. Very soon I acquired the reputation of being presumptuous, insolent, a troublemaker, a capricious despot, an uncouth moujik. I will not deny that I can be rude at times, but only towards those who are first rude to me. "An eye for an eye and a tooth for a tooth," held hard. Not everyone is content to bare his back for the stick.

Unfortunately rumours of my impossible temper soon spread beyond the confines of the theatre, and became public property. There is always somebody handy and ready to tear another to shreds.

Also the legend about my drunkenness grew stronger. It was said that at home I became abusive, and hit people with such things as chairs, samovars, and even wooden chests. I recall an occasion when during the singing of Mephistopheles' *Serenade*, I was seated on the steps leading to Marguerite's house, and not in the usual standing position. It was said that I was too drunk to stand up. These things are trifles, of course, but so too is a mosquito, and a number of the latter plaguing you can make life very unenjoyable.

The truth was that ever since childhood I had been used to spending all my free time in pubs and restaurants, and naturally enough found pleasure in it, not because I enjoyed getting drunk, or deliberately drank to get drunk, but because from my youngest days I had seen these places as retreats where people were more interesting, gayer, and freer than at home. I did not arrange things that way.

When I was a choirboy I often dashed into an inn between services, but mainly because I would find a music-box there. There were always people of interest in those places, men having grave discussions about market prices —people like furriers, timber-merchants, and artisans of all sorts. It was not my fault if I had been educated in a public house instead of a public school. Besides I enjoyed seeing such people, even though after sundry drinks they had a habit of asking the barman where he hid the Clos de Vougeot. The resourceful barman generally replied that it was down the corridor, "second door to the left."

I found it amusing to sit in a restaurant after a performance—say, after doing Mephistopheles, or the Brahmin priest in *Lakmé*. And there was always some gentle soul at hand, who, seeing me in my ordinary dress and with a "naked" face, would exclaim: "But my goodness, isn't he young? How marvellous! Unbelievable."

I would find a diversion in listening to people discussing the protuberance or otherwise of my Adam's apple, and how this eventually affected the singing voice. In a public house there was always something to listen to, and more important, something to laugh at. Still, the time did arrive when such visits became much less pleasant.

I might be sitting alone at table with a bottle of wine, anchored in dreamland, only to be disturbed by some drunken sot who hailed me as follows: "Hello! Aren't you Chaliapin? If sho, I musht shay I'm very fond of you, and would like to embrace you." I would shy away from his embrace, and wet moustache, under the pretext that he was not a woman. With amazing alacrity, he would be off, informing the other patrons that Chaliapin loved kissing women—"he's a libertine".

From such episodes arose the legend concerning my debauchery. We Russians have a penchant for speaking ill of people, and have even invented the proverb: "A good reputation lies quietly, but a bad one will run fast."

I am not trying to say that I am irreproachable—indeed, it's probable that, like others, my faults exceed my virtues, but there are occasions when one feels good, at one with the world, and I wish to be generous of heart, but not to those who react like hedgehogs, looking hostile and suspicious, as they ask themselves: "What dirty trick is he going to play on us now?"

At such times I want to give people something to complain about, a little of their own miserable rations.

The gossip of the Russian public about personalities had the Sukonnaya Sloboda aspect. In human relationships a mutual uplift is redeeming, the good man raises the bad woman to his level, and vice versa. But the "public" —begging its pardon, though one should not apologise for telling the truth —is in no position at all to have an ennobling influence on any artist, who is far the more talented in any case. The "public"—and this time no pardon is asked—is always ready to drag its betters down to the gutter.

These are the conclusions of a rich experience. The public "loved me", but I had a dread of it. I was pleased that my work should please them, but there were other factors beyond their comprehension. The intimate life of the artist, and his professional existence, suffers and is made complicated by what I can only describe as Russian peculiarities, and are unknown to "the public". What a pity they had not known it, for they would have loved me less, and not been so ready to judge my shortcomings. I accept the judgment of friends, and I accept the judgment of enemies. But there is neither warmth nor friendliness in a public judgment.

By this time I was gaining a fluency in Italian, and was already dreaming of another journey abroad, thinking of a possible début in Paris or London, but at the moment it seemed impossible. Having been to France on several occasions I was embarrassed by the behaviour of my fellow countrymen. I have felt like a pigmy in that wonderful city of Paris, and can remember an incident on one of the boulevards, when a Russian gentleman, dressed like a merchant, climbed on a chair in a café, pulled a bottle of brandy from his pocket, and began waving it in the air, and shouting. The inevitable crowd gathered. The gentleman pushed the bottle into his hairy mouth and

swallowed the entire contents at one draught, probably in an effort to demonstrate the prowess of his stomach. The crowd ah-ed and oh-ed at this
astonishing achievement, but I felt unhappy that such incidents should be
the only ones for arousing the interests of other countries in Russia. Such performances were only too frequent.

In 1899 I went to the World Exhibition in Paris, an experience I had long
been looking forward to, because I knew that Andreyev, of my early days,
was there with his Balalaika Orchestra, and quite a number of other Russians,
and here Russia might be projected from angles other than that of consuming
spirits. In any case we cannot shake Europe with that; they know how to
drink, too. Anyway, I met Andreyev, and he lost no time in introducing me
into various musical circles. I began singing at their "five o'clocks", although
I had never been a salon singer. It was a new experience. The works of
Mussorgsky, Glinka, Schubert, and Schumann did not seem to me to fit
into the drawing-room, yet these recitals proved a great success. As a result
I was invited to an evening organised by the newspaper *Le Figaro*, and the
most popular song on that occasion was "The Two Grenadiers".

I had returned to my dear old landlady, Madame Chalmel, in the Rue de
Copernic. My strong desire to learn French overcame my shyness. I must
confess I wreaked havoc with their beautiful language, but the French were
always polite about it. It was not much help, and I got into some embarrassing situations. I remember an American girl who was staying in the same
pension and who, when she spoke French, always seemed to have a hot potato
in her mouth. Unfortunately she suffered from an even worse shyness than
my own, and I was often compelled to talk with her, as when I happened to
be seated by her at table. I blush when I remember how, wishing to say to
her, "You are shy," I said instead, "You are pregnant."

The poor young lady was shocked, went purple in the face, and having
uttered something mysteriously Franco–American, abruptly left me. I saw
how offended she was, but I had a perfectly clear conscience, and took the
situation calmly. But my friend Melnikov tackled me at once.

"What did you say to that girl?"

I told him, whereupon he burst out laughing, and explained my mistake
to me. I went cold from embarrassment. What a difficult language I found
it! But in the end I managed it.

This visit to Paris and my performances in the salons led to an unexpected,
and to me, most important event, for in the spring of the following year I
received a telegram from La Scala, Milan, inviting me to sing in Boito's
Mefistofele, and asking my terms. At first I treated it as a practical joke,
but my wife persuaded me to treat the matter seriously. I sent off a reply
to Milan, and asked them to repeat the text of their message. I still could
not believe this invitation to be serious. But it was no joke, and for a moment
the surprise threw me quite off-balance. I was afraid of it, since I could not
speak Italian, and certainly could not sing it, besides which I did not know
Boito's opera. I felt I dare not reply in the affirmative. For two whole days
I was in such an agitated state of mind that I could neither eat nor sleep.

Finally I found a score of the opera, and saw that it was easily within my range. Even this did not supply the confidence required, and I sent off a telegram asking for what I thought to be impossible terms, secretly hoping they would refuse them, and so let me out. But they actually agreed to them.

I vacillated between feelings of elation and apprehension. Without waiting for any score from Italy, I started studying the work from my own copy, and decided to go there for the summer. It happened that Rachmaninov was the first person to whom I would always turn in perplexity, and who so often shared my joys and fears. He at once expressed the wish to go to Italy, saying, "That's splendid. I shall study music, and in my spare time help you to work on the opera."

He shared with me an understanding of the importance of my first appearance in Italy. We were both sensible of the honour done a Russian singer in the land of singers.

We travelled to Varazze, a little resort on the way to San Remo. There we lived very modestly, gave up smoking, retired to bed early, and arose early. I found work under these conditions a delight, and was soon making rapid strides with the language, thanks to the friendliness of our hospitable and considerate hosts.

This wonderful country enchanted me with its magnificent scenery, and the gaiety of its people. When I went off to drink wine at the little trattoria, the landlord, upon learning that I was to appear in *Mefistofele* at La Scala, began treating me as his best friend. I found him encouraging, and we discussed La Scala and its famous productions. Proudly he informed me that he never visited Milan without attending at La Scala. Secretly I hoped that the innkeepers in Milan were equally fond of music. But before I could find this out I was on my way back to Russia to take part in the autumn season. Of that season there is little I can say, except that during it I was under considerable nervous strain, thinking only of the oncoming performance of Boito's opera at La Scala. As with my other operas I had thoroughly studied it, learning not only my own role but all the parts in the work.

For a long time I had cherished the idea of playing Mefistofele nude—an abstract figure that would have a special plasticity; a dressed-up devil is no real devil. I was seeking some special line, but always there was this notion of appearing nude upon the stage. Could it be done without shocking the public?

I had already acquainted my painter friends with the idea, and they approved of it; Golovin himself made a number of sketches for me, although he produced no actually naked Mefistofele. Having studied some of his sketches, I finally decided that I would play the part naked to the waist. It was nothing like the conception I had had in mind; in any case the central pivot of the opera is not the prologue, but the classic Sabbath in Brocken.

I found myself in a quandary. I visualized a kind of iron figure, something metallic and powerful. It was the construction of the spectacle that I found hampering, it being a series of separate scenes, quickly following upon one another, and broken up by short intervals. But in the face of necessity I had to resign myself to the traditional presentation, making only some changes of costume. It was far from satisfying. However, the costumes being completed, I set out for Milan.

On this return visit I seemed to see nothing at all of the country, my mind utterly absorbed by the theatre. I was warmly received by the director of La Scala, an engineer by profession. Rehearsals had already begun, and I had to be on stage the following day. I was so excited about this début that I had not slept for several nights, but I managed to appear on stage the following morning. I was staggered. The theatre looked so vast, so grandiose. When I saw the depth of the stage, I exclaimed aloud. Then somebody clapped their hands together to demonstrate the resonance to me, and the sound floated in a wide, deep wave, lightly, harmoniously. It was wonderful.

The conductor, a young man named Toscanini, spoke in a hoarse and colourless voice, informing me that the theatre had formerly been a church, Madonna della Scala. I was amused by this. In Russia the transformation of one temple into another would have been quite impossible. I examined everything I was shown with great interest, and I must confess that an involuntary tremor passed through me. How would I sing in this colossal theatre, in a strange tongue, before a strange people? The rehearsals began almost as a murmur, the artists, among whom I found Caruso, then a young man just starting his career, sang in a low voice. I followed this example, being tired and feeling that it would be wrong for me to use full voice when no one else did.

The conductor looked quite ferocious to me. A man of few words, unsmiling, he corrected the singers harshly, and spared nobody. Here was a man who really knew his job, and one who would brook no contradiction. I remember him turning to me in the middle of rehearsal, and asking in rasping tones if I intended to sing the opera as I was singing it then.

"No. Certainly not," I said, embarrassed. "Well," he replied, "I have not had the honour of going to Russia and hearing you there. Thus I don't know your voice. Please be good enough to sing as you intend to do at the performance."

I saw that he was right, and I sang in full voice. Often he would interrupt the other singers, offering advice, but he never said a word to me. I didn't know how to take this, and it left me with a feeling of uncertainty.

Again the next day there was a rehearsal in the foyer, a beautiful room, the walls of which were hung with old paintings and portraits. The very atmosphere commanded a respect, and I thought, "What artists this room has seen!"

The rehearsal began with the Prologue. I gave it full voice, and when I had finished Toscanini paused for a moment, his hands lying on the piano keys, inclined his head a little, and uttered one single word in a very hoarse voice.

"Bravo."

It was quite unexpected, and had the effect of a pistol shot. I hardly realized this praise was meant for me. Elated by this success, I sang with tremendous enthusiasm, but Toscanini never uttered another word. The rehearsal ended. I was then summoned to the office of the director, who greeted me kindly.

"I am delighted to tell you that the conductor likes you very much. We shall soon commence rehearsing on the stage with the chorus and orchestra. But first you will try your costumes."

"I have brought my own costumes," I said.

He appeared taken aback. "Oh! Then you have seen this opera before?"

"Never."

"Then what costumes have you got? You understand, we have a certain tradition, and I will have to see how you will be dressed."

"In the Prologue I wish to portray Mefistofele semi-nude."

"What?"

I sensed his alarm—could even hear him saying to himself: "Barbarian. He will cause a scandal."

"I don't think that would be possible," he said quietly.

I began explaining the kind of interpretation I wanted, and he listened, and grunted mistrustfully, twirling his moustaches.

At the rehearsals that followed, I realized I was the subject of speculation, if not alarm, among the other singers, the administration, and the director's secretary. They all watched closely. Having gained the friendship of the secretary, I was able to learn what it was all about. Everybody was afraid, really afraid, and the result was a Mefistofele dressed up in coat and trousers. I found it inhibiting. Toscanini, who produced, would come and watch me, order me to stand this way, that way, the other, sit like this, like that, walk that way, not this way. He would wind one of my legs round the other corkscrew-fashion, or make me fold my arms à la Napoleon. In fact what I was being instructed in was the technique of provincial tragedians, something with which I was already too well acquainted. If I asked him why he found this or that pose necessary, he replied with the utmost confidence: "Perche questo e una vera posa diabolica" (because it is a truly diabolic pose).

"Maestro," said I, "I have memorized all your instructions, so don't worry, but at the dress rehearsal kindly allow me to play the part as I see it." He gave me a piercing look, and said, "All right."

I found the Italians somewhat negligent about their make-up. There was no wig-maker in the theatre, and the wigs and beards they used seemed almost primitive to me, and to add to it all, these would be stuck on any old how. When I appeared on the stage in my costume, there was a sensation. The artists, the chorus, even the stagehands surrounded me, exclaiming enthusiastically like children, touching me, fingering my costume. Seeing that my muscles were emphasized by make-up, they were beside themselves with delight. The Italians are people who neither wish nor care to restrain the expression of their feelings. Naturally I was touched by this mass approval, delighted in the way it was expressed. Having finished the Prologue I went up to Toscanini and asked him his opinion of it. The result was surprising. For the first time he smiled, a child-like open smile, slapped me on the shoulder, and then croaked: "Let's not talk about it any more." We didn't.

Opening night approached. Milan became a hive of activity for various theatrical parasites. In no other country in the world are there so many people engaged in speculation. Nowhere on earth can one find such importunate and brazen claques. The unknown artist is forced as by a law to pay a contribution to the claque, the sum being dependent on the fee received by the artist. I, of course, was quite ignorant of this institution, never having heard of its existence.

Imagine my surprise when a group of people suddenly appeared, announcing that they had taken it upon themselves to "ensure my success", and requesting me to provide them with several dozen tickets, and the sum of 4,000[1] francs for their guaranteed applause on the opening night. I threw them out. This disgusting approach nevertheless gave me cause for anxiety, and a curious feeling, like cyanide in honey. And on the following day the same people returned for their answer.

"We are asking Signor Chaliapin for only 4,000 francs because we like him. Seeing him in the street, we thought he had a pleasant face. From anybody else we should ask much more."

I told them to go to hell, and they made their exit, warning me that Signor Chaliapin would have cause to regret this. I felt angry about this and stamped into the director's office.

"I have come to La Scala," I said, "with much the same feeling as a Christian approaches Communion. But these people disgust and depress me. I cannot sleep at night for thinking about it, dreading a failure. Perhaps I should return to Russia where such things do not happen."

This went right home, and he made great efforts to calm me, and promised me full protection from the claque. Unfortunately, however, the method of protection chosen by him was not a good one, and only left me feeling embarrassed.

Again the next day some people called, whilst I was still asleep. They were civilians sent to me from the police commissariat. They informed my mother-in-law that they were policemen, and had orders to arrest the representatives of the claque as soon as they arrived at my place. I was advised to send these men away, since Italians do not like appealing to the police for help. I dressed and went out to see them. I explained as best I could, suggesting that the matter might be amicably discussed over a glass of wine. I pointed out how unhappy I should be if anybody was arrested in my own house. The police appreciated the situation, and then explained.

"You are perfectly right, Signor Chaliapin, but unfortunately you cannot

[1] At that time, Italy, and other European countries, had adopted the French monetary system based on the gold franc of .29032 grammes.

cancel the order. We must carry out our instructions, even though we realize how unpleasant it is for you."

Again I rushed into the director's office, this time begging him to call off the police. He immediately did so. This made me feel better, though by this time the story had got around the whole town. When the day of the actual opening arrived I set out for the theatre with a heavy heart. I felt as if something had been taken out of me, and knew that in some way or other judgment would go against me. I resigned myself to failure.

I was greeted by two porters when I arrived. They had grown quite fond of me, and often hung about in the wings, looking after me almost like nurses. The kind treatment at the theatre was pleasant enough, but these porters simply excelled themselves.

"Don't worry, Signor," they said. "You will be a great success. We know. Oh yes, a great success. We have been here twenty years and seen many famous artists. If we say you will be a success, you will be a success."

Kind men, their words warmed me.

The performance began. I felt as nervous as I did when I made my first appearance in Ufa. As then, I hardly felt the stage beneath me, my feet seeming like cotton wool. The vast auditorium was packed with people, and this I saw as through a haze. I was wheeled into the cloud, stood in a hole screened with gauze, and began to sing. I sang without feeling anything, simply singing the words that I knew by heart, and giving as much voice as I could.

My heart fluttered. I seemed not to have enough breath, there was a mist before my eyes, everything appeared to float past me. The moment I finished, after which the chorus enters, there was a sudden loud crash. I thought a piece of scenery had fallen, or that the wheels on which I stood had broken. Instinctively I ducked, and only then did I realize that this great wave of noise was coming from the auditorium. Something quite unimaginable was going on out there. Those with experience of Italian opera houses will know what the quality of Italian praise or protest is like. The public literally went mad, interrupting the Prologue half way. Something happened to me, it was like something in me breaking up, I felt unable to stand. My knees knocked together, my heart filled with a mixture of feelings, both fear and joy.

The director appeared beside me. He was very pale, fluttering the skirts of his frock-coat, shouting at me, "Go on. Go on. Bow."

Suddenly I beheld one of my porters. He was dancing about wildly. "You see, Signor. What did I tell you? I know. Now you have them. Bravo," and he clapped and shouted in triumph, then still dancing returned to his place in the wings.

I remember standing at the footlights, seeing that enormous hall, filled with the white dots of faces, women's shoulders glittering with jewels, and thousands of hands, like the wings of birds, beating in the vast space. Never in my life have I witnessed such enthusiasm.

After this it was easier to sing, yet after the Prologue I felt flat, drained.

The opera was a great success. I kept on waiting for some form of demonstration from the claque I had offended, but there wasn't a single whistle, boo, or hiss. Later I was told that even claques loved art. It seemed they liked me, too.

The relations with the director, the other artists, and the stage hands, were wonderful. I had won their hearts. I was deeply touched by their congratulations.

In that country the staff of the opera houses, from the director down to the carpenter, is always profoundly interested in everything that happens on the stage. Stage hands gather in the wings, discussing the merits or defects of every artist, often surprisingly to the point in their judgment. One would have thought that with performances day in and day out such people would have become stale, and even bored by mere repetition, but it was never so. Their comments always interested me.

"He sang very well today. Much better than yesterday."

"Yes, indeed. A fine artist."

"I thought the aria in the fourth act was a little weak."

"No, not at all."

The arguments were endless, and they struck sparks of great interest from one another. If an artist's voice didn't sound right on a particular night, or there was a slip in the acting, these men remained silent. It was a form of commiseration with the artist. Since La Scala I have sung in England, France, Germany, America, and Monte Carlo, and whenever I discovered Italian stage hands in the theatres, I knew how well they knew their business; as for their knowledge of opera, it was stupendous.

On my free evenings I would attend the performances of other works like any member of the public, the administration kindly giving me a seat in the stalls, from which I could study the Italian public, not from the stage, but from its midst. I can remember as if it were yesterday the performance of Donizetti's opera, *The Love Potion* (Elisir d'Amore), so magnificently sung by Caruso, then a young man, full of vigour, and gaiety. An excellent comrade. He was Russian-like in his generosity, and never failed to respond to any appeal for help.

Caruso, already an Italian idol, sang superbly in his performance, and the audience, frenzied in its enthusiasm, demanded encore after encore.

"Bis, Caruso, Bis."

How struck I was by the Italian consideration for the artist. They treated opera and singing really seriously. They would hear the whole of a work, listening with great attention. During the intervals the most grave discussions went on in the foyer. Their knowledge of the history of opera quite dazzled me. I loved these people, and was often embarrassed by their attentions, almost everybody now raising his hat to me, clapping, crying "Bravo", loving me. How different from my native land where, receiving the applause of the public, you feel that it's doing you a favour, almost saying, "You see, we applaud you, mind you appreciate it!" The Russians are very fond of making love declarations in public, but there is little real love or respect behind it.

I have also seen the indignation of the Italian public, and it could be terrifying. For some time there had been rumours of a new opera being produced in La Scala, with Tamagno, and I was surprised that the composer was rarely referred to. As a musician he was not discussed, but it was very much in the news that he was a handsome young man, that he sang songs and was his own accompanist, that a princess had fallen in love with him, had left her prince, and turned the poor musician into a rich man. This was the man who was now so rich that he was backing the opera himself, and had already engaged Tamagno, and a well-known French singer for the female lead.

The public took a most lively interest in the production, so much so that on the opening night I could not get a ticket for love nor money, and saw the production only through the kindness of the well-known music-publisher, Ricordi, who had invited me to share a box with him and his mother, together with the composers Puccini and Mascagni. The orchestra played a very weak little overture, and rather hesitant applause sounded from the orchestra itself, but this was simply to announce the arrival of Toscanini who was conducting.

The curtain rose, and on the stage I beheld something that smacked of ancient Rome. Somebody clad in a toga was drearily singing, accompanied by even more dreary music. It seemed to me that the public was paying no attention to the stage, indifferent to it, singers, music, and all. They were far too busy talking to each other. In the box next to mine people discussed the best means of transport from Genoa to Marseilles, or where the food was better, and life gayer. The opera seemed very far away indeed.

Before I quite realized it the first act was over. There was no public reaction. Not a sound, not a single clap. They rose and went off into the foyer. Nobody appeared to have seen anything. Perhaps the opera had not even begun.

In the second act the French singer was quite busy. A contralto, she sang with a curious little wail in her voice, though it was resonant enough. I could see and hear people wincing, and many closed eyes. At that moment Tamagno appeared. The composer had given him an effective entrance phrase, and this evoked an immediate response.

Tamagno had an exceptional voice—*tenore di forza*—indeed I would say the voice of a century. He was tall and well-built, as handsome and fine an actor as he was a singer, and his diction was perfect. I have not heard any other singer who enunciated so well. The contralto followed with much singing, interrupted from time to time by the tenor, with short interpolations. They embraced and then neither she nor the orchestra was heard. Only Tamagno sang. And that was all that was required.

The opera ended in a storm of applause. Ricordi's old mother, miraculously rejuvenated, leaned out of the box, waving, and shouting "Bravo". Tamagno and the French singer, accompanied by a handsome man in a frock-coat, appeared at the footlights. I assumed the handsome man to be the composer, but the public simply refused to recognize him. Indeed many loud voices began chanting, "Who's that?"

It was a guess with them that the handsome gentleman was the producer, a friend of Tamagno's, the director's secretary, and even the manager of a cheese factory. Then a single voice shouted: "That's the composer."

A vast indifference. All the audience shouted for was the tenor, Tamagno.

With this pandemonium still going on, Tamagno had scarcely heard, nor had he understood that he was being asked to come out alone, and again came out with the handsome gentleman. He was greeted with such an unholy row that it went beyond my imagination. I had seen nothing like it. The most elegantly dressed people lost control of themselves, the entire audience went mad. There were cries of "Tamagno solo. Tamagno solo". The audience squealed, shrieked, shouted. I felt quite scared myself and wanted to get out. Ricordi's mother leaned perilously over the edge of her box, shouting in a most terrifying voice, almost as though somebody had insulted her.

"Out!" she cried. "Out, you swindler, mascalzone, ladro! Out!"

The final act was original in the highest degree, since the entire audience took part in it. I was sorry for the French contralto, whom they mimicked, howled at, maiowing, mooing, barking, imitating her singing. This was not all. In loud voices people in the auditorium discussed the best place to have dinner. Malice was quite undisguised when for the third time the composer of the opera was led out by Tamagno. The public really broke out and I watched the elegant, the noble, the splendidly accoutred officers actually sticking out their tongues at the unfortunate man. In my own box people were saying that the performance would never be over. And the acid remark that killed—"Perhaps it's the end that is original."

I wanted to laugh, to say to them as I waved my hand towards the audience, "But what can be more original than all this?"

I was answered immediately.

"It sometimes happens that several members of the public will pick up the conductor, stand and all, and carry him out to the foyer. . . ."

"Doesn't this hurt the conductor's feelings?"

"Not at all. Why? A friendly joke. It is then that the conductor knows the opera cannot continue. So why should his feelings be hurt?"

Why indeed?

But these goings-on really shook me, and I was afraid of what might happen at my own performance. I would not survive such an experience. But many fine artists had had to go through a similar ordeal. This was the typical Italian public.

Yet in Italy censure of the artist was never considered a disgrace. In reproving him, there was no personal attack. The censure lay somewhere within the framework of aesthetic evaluation. Beyond the theatre the artist was a person, belonged to himself, and was rarely berated.

The night of my own performance was drawing near. One of my two

35. Chaliapin with his children, in his country home in the village of Ratukhino.

36. Chaliapin with his son Boris, 1912.

37. Chaliapin's wife Iola Ignatyevna (née Tornaghi), with their children, 1910.

38. *Poster of the first concert given by Chaliapin after his return from abroad—in aid of the Famine Victims' Fund. April 21, 1911.*

39. *Programme of a concert given by Chaliapin in aid of the Famine Victims' Fund, written in his own hand, December 26, 1911.*

40. Chaliapin at a recording session in London, 1913.

41. Chaliapin listening to a play-back of his recordings in London.

friendly porters warned me that on the night the composer himself would appear at the first rehearsal. This was the first news I had of the composer's presence in the city. I awaited his arrival with some curiosity and interest.

I found him to be a rather elegant man about fifty years of age. Immaculately dressed, he had the appearance of a Polish magnate, the most exquisite manners, and an aristocratic simplicity in his approach to people. At the rehearsal I kept observing him, wondering what he was thinking of his work. But he was so calm, remote, that one could never have guessed. He remained only a short time, handed out some beautifully constructed compliments, and then left.

During a break in the rehearsals my favourite porter, Giovannino, who was a passionate admirer of Boito, told me how much he hated the public for not appreciating *Mefistofele*. He liked particularly the Prologue, Satan's conversation with God, the booming of the orchestral brass, and the Devil's concluding words.

Praising the opera, Giovannino felt certain that Boito would be far too nervous to attend on the opening night.

"But he was so calm and controlled at rehearsal," I said.

Giovannino laughed. "Do you expect him to show his feelings? Why, he is every bit as good an actor as you."

He did not come to the performance, but rang up to enquire how it was going. My porter already knew that the composer was delighted. "He'll come and thank you. You see. We've been planning this opera for a long time, but we never had the right Mefistofele. We have many wonderful singers, but for this part we require not only a singer, but an actor like you."

"Thank you, Giovannino," I replied.

"The worst thing about our singers," he said, "is that they eat far too much spaghetti, and it makes them fat." I must say that Giovannino himself fully showed up the merits of that delectable dish. "You cannot do otherwise in Italy," he continued. "It's such a splendid country. The people here eat a lot, and have excellent appetites. There is also much good wine, and it would never do for a man to drink wine and eat macaroni just to be thin. The only thin men in our country, Signor, are sick men."

Boito turned up for one performance only, and then remained entirely backstage. The performance over I was informed that he wished to see me as soon as possible at his home. I went off as soon as I was free. There was incense burning on the table in his study. He was a bachelor, and judging from the contents of his home, a great lover of beautiful things. He turned out to be a gay, jolly sort of person. I knew he was working on the opera, *Nero*, and I asked him about it. His reaction was odd. He made a terrifying face, took an enormous pistol out of his desk drawer, laid it on my knee, and in a tone half-comic, half-dismal, said, "Shoot me. Yes, do. Please, for indulging in such nonsense."

I realized he was a man who felt deeply about his work. I met him from time to time on later visits, but he never mentioned *Nero* again. I did once catch him running through the score, but he closed it quickly, saying,

"Only my secret music." He was full of interest in Russian theatre and music, and asked me many questions. He was very fond of Borodin. I knew he was doing a libretto for one of Verdi's operas, but I did not discuss it. In Italy he was considered a better poet than musician. His *Mefistofele* libretto was based on Goethe, Marlowe, and other sources.

After the first performance of the Boito work, I received a mysterious little note on a scrap of paper. It said, "Bravo, bravissimo, Signor Chaliapin." It contained many other compliments besides, though the signature of the writer was almost indecipherable, something like Amasini. But it was in fact Angelo Masini himself. I went off to see this idol of mine without a moment's hesitation. When I met him he was very simply dressed; indeed I thought he was an Italian working-man, with his shabby necktie, and his down-at-heel shoes.

He looked at me out of piercing blue eyes, and said how very glad he was to witness the success of a Russian artist in Italy; that he loved Russia only second to his own homeland, and most important of all, told me of the great experience he had had in singing in that country.

"They love me so much in your country," he said, "that whenever I arrive there I feel like a king. You can well imagine then how pleased I am with your success here. In applauding you, which I do from the heart, I am also thanking Russia in your person for a memorable experience."

I was touched by these words, and expressed my regret at not being aware of his presence in the theatre, otherwise I would have gone at once to his box.

"Box?" he laughed. "Why, I always sit up in the gods."

He was most attentive to me, not even the servant he had was allowed to do the waiting, even to helping me on with my coat, and seeing me to the door.

"I want to give myself the pleasure," he said, with the emphasis on "myself."

Only a fortnight later I was reading in *Novoye Vremya* a letter addressed to its editor by Masini, in which he spoke of my great success in Milan. A touching piece of courtesy.

I recall telling him of my agitation at the rehearsals and actual performance, and my great worry concerning the claque's attempt to exploit me. We were walking together in the city.

"You see," he said, pointing away to the Galleria Vittorio Emmanuele, "you shouldn't come here. This is the nest of all evil, and it can really prevent an artist from carrying out his sacred duty. There are very few real people here. This is mainly a promenade for dogs. *Cane*, a dog, also means a bad singer. When Italians express their disapproval, they use that word."

When the performance of the Boito work came to an end, I went off with friends to a restaurant, where we celebrated. People came up to my table, heaping congratulations on me, expressing their regret that the performances were over. I watched these people go. Only a few young people remained. I invited them to my table and ordered two dozen bottles of champagne. The waiters thought I had lost my sanity, but eventually understood. Among my guests was Gabriele D'Annunzio, then a young man, big-built, with a pointed beard, and very fair. He proposed a toast which must have been highly literary and abstruse, since I didn't understand a single word of it. I came to know him well as time went by, and, in fact, just before the war we decided to work together on an entirely new music drama. But nothing ever came of it.

I returned to Russia, via Paris. I was in excellent spirits; I had a sense of achievement, of having done something worth while, and not only for myself.

I I

The moment I returned home the old atmosphere came back—the innumerable pin-pricks, the cold ashes of trifles assumed their functions of extinguishing the fire in one's soul. My spirits immediately fell. An artist's work is one of nerves.

Again am I faced by the hard fact that my education was not conducted in drawing-rooms, and although I am well aware of how not to behave myself, I am not always able to remember it. I am unrestrained by nature, I can be abrupt, and I dislike half-truths, preferring the direct impact of homely ones. I am also sensitive, and I am strongly affected by atmosphere and environment. With gentlemen I can be a "gentleman", but with hooligans—begging your pardon—I can be a hooligan myself. I do unto others what is done to me.

I was very keen on staging Boito's opera as my benefit performance, and was hoping to include in it all that was not permissible in Italy. His opera was quite unknown in Russia, so that at rehearsals I was compelled to act as producer for my friends, explaining everything to them, even down to items about the ballet. The Brocken scene was particularly complicated, and required a deal of explanation. But I saw at once that my colleagues were not taking kindly to these instructions.

"What's he teaching us for?" they grumbled. "By what authority?"

I never gave my authority a thought. I didn't see myself in the role of teacher, but merely that of an adviser. Yet even in this role I had to do it in an apologetic manner. I saw no offence whatever in my advice. Naturally I lost my temper more than once. I remember telling our producer, Vassilevsky, that his actions very much reminded me of a "Turkish horse". The producer seemed in no way hurt by this, but the following day the newspapers were reporting that I had called the chorus girls cows. When I read this I tackled the girls at once. Had this ever occurred? No, they said, yet not a single one of them was prepared to deny the report in the newspapers, and it was quite impossible for me to deny it on my own behalf. There were many other incidents. The company walked about the stage with an offended air, and even decided to become less competent than they had been—not that this was saying much. But somehow the production went through. It didn't satisfy me, however, though the public received it well enough. But I could do nothing with *Mefistofele*. To this very day it doesn't satisfy me.

This awful apprehension of treading on other people's corns, on their exaggerated self-esteem! It certainly interferes with work, almost to the extent of denying a sense of living, of feeling free and a friend of the people.

The result of this performance was only to make my colleagues hostile towards me. Then rumours about my greed for money began to spread. Unfortunately this rumour gathered force because I, wishing to save the public from speculators, had organized the sale of tickets for the benefit performance in my own home. They labelled me a shopkeeper. This was most unjust, and it went deep. My natural gaiety dimmed, my carefree spirit sank, until finally I was suspecting everybody of hostility. Now I could realize that the story of Bova, the legendary hero, routing thousands of enemies with a broomstick, was but a fairytale. The result was that I found myself avoiding the acquaintance of theatrical people. Their verdict was that I was becoming conceited.

Am I endeavouring to find excuses for myself? No, I am simply narrating. Every man has the right to imagine that, somewhere unknown to him, there is a sincere and affectionate friend, and I am telling this story, as best I know how, to this friend. I have no reason for justifying myself, no cause to spare myself. My friend's judgment, however severe, I shall accept with gratitude. I am strong enough for that.

Outside the artistic world I had many friends among the merchants, among the rich people who were always eating salmon, sturgeon, caviare, drinking champagne, and seeing in this occupation the only meaning and happiness in life.

I can remember, for instance, seeing the New Year in at the Yar restaurant, amidst truly exotic splendour—mountains of fruit everywhere, tables groaning with salmon and caviare, and every brand of champagne. There, too, were all the man-like creatures dressed up in their frock-coats, some already drunk, though it was not yet midnight. After that hour they would all be drunk, all embracing each other and saying with typically Russian good humour: "I am fond of you, although you are a swindler."

And the reply would be: "The time is long past, my friend, for you to rot in gaol. Ah! Let us embrace."

They then kiss each other thrice. Very touching, and a little disgusting too perhaps. But the remarkable thing is that although they are all very drunk, hardly one of them misses the opportunity of saying something nasty or malicious to their friends, and it never affects their good humour.

It is now four o'clock in the morning. An exhausted waiter is dozing, leaning against the wall with a napkin lying in his hand like a flag of truce. A big man in a torn frock-coat is lying under the sofa, his feet stuck out, and one notices that his beautifully-made boots are soaked in wine. Two other prosperous-looking gentlemen sit at a nearby table. They keep throwing their arms about each other, weeping, slobbering, complaining of the bitterness of life, singing, and finally deciding that a decent man can only go and live in a gypsy camp. There is the inevitable pause for reflection. Then one of them says: "You wait. I'll show you another trick. Waiter! Champagne."

The waiter wakes up, brings the wine, and opens the bottle.

"Look at me," says the wet and sticky gentleman, about to perform the trick. His companion tries hard to focus, to look straight at the other, though this demands a deal of concentrated effort, if such be possible. The performer puts a full glass of champagne on his head, shakes his dome, meaning to catch the glass in his mouth, and gulp the wine. But alas, he fails. The wine pours down over his shoulders, chest, legs, and the glass shatters. "I didn't do it," says he, correctly. "I didn't manage it. Wait a minute. I'll try again."

But his friend has decided that it really isn't worth it, as he makes a hopeless gesture with his hand. Suddenly, and with tears in their eyes, they are both singing again.

All this is very funny, but it is also sad. These good-natured drunken people are very fond of me, but I can only think that something has snapped within their very souls, like a piece of string. They come and throw their arms about me, exclaiming: "You are ours!"

Once I had to reply forcibly to a too-persistent manifestation of affection. "Listen, you mug. I'm not yours. I'm my own. I'm God's."

Immediately they shouted that I was conceited. The next day it was all over the city. "Chaliapin despises Moscow." Of course I knew full well that there were occasions when the gentlemen would have loved to beat me up, just as successful people in Sukonnaya Sloboda used to be beaten up, just because they were successful. They would look at me, their fists clenched, and then hiss at me: "How much d'you earn, eh? Too big for your boots."

I was not averse to a fight myself, and when they saw this, they dared not attack me. In time I dropped these people.

The theatre held its own depression, like a lowering cloud. I was depressed by this horrible red-tape attitude to art. Even a single phrase might not be sung in a different way, it, too, was hallowed in tradition, just like the aria, the scene, the act, the opera. Any endeavour to breathe new life into work, if only to liven it up a bit, meant resorting to every kind of chicanery and hypocrisy. One trembled in fear, lest someone's hyper-sensitiveness was suddenly bruised by a cold draught of official air. To ask a conductor to take a phrase at a slower tempo was to be told that violins and 'cellos could not possibly drag the passage.

Perhaps the conductor was right. Unfortunately, I was not sufficiently educated musically to be able to argue with him. Behind this feeling of frustration and lack of imagination there yet remained the basic loyalty; one did know that the Imperial Orchestra was a miracle, that nothing was impossible for it. Every man in that orchestra was an artist in himself, a thorough musician. Candidates for it had to pass a very strict examination indeed. As for the conductors with whom I have sung, they have all—with the exception of Rachmaninov, and one or two Italians—been almost devoid of the sense of rhythm. It made me think often enough of a thin stick wobbling about inside a big boot.

I have many times been accused of being unwilling to create a school.

But here there is a fallacy. No one can be forced to study, nor do we seem to be too interested even in ordinary literacy. It is premature indeed to demand the introduction of compulsory theatrical education. And would a man, with an excessively distorted self-esteem, allow himself to be taught by Chaliapin, who has never even been inside a conservatoire?

No, he would not. I won't for a moment deny that they do study, but it hardly travels beyond the first blindness of the footlights, and the thunder of applause. Fruitfulness, maturity, lies somewhere beyond this frontier. Art was never a convenience, and I have seen it wither before now, long before the autumn.

People have said to me, "Open a theatre of your own." Fine indeed, and supposing I did. I would work hard, and I should expect others to do like-wise. But I have a feeling that, after the first season, I would be down in the books as an exploiter and slave driver. They, being the more educated, having what they'd call the cultural pull on me, would in all probability swamp me with their culture. It's almost inevitable. One of these smart-Alec producers might suddenly enquire of me: "What coloured stockings did the Spanish hidalgo wear at the Court of Carlos the Fifth?"

I'd be stuck for the answer.

Producers are an incredibly educated lot. I myself have heard one, indig-nantly and with languid melancholy, say to the props man: "What kind of candelabra are these? Did they have such things in those days? In *Boris Godunov* Pushkin definitely says. . . ."

Or the tenor playing the role of a prince would be strutting the stage looking, for all the world, like a barber, and I'd say to him: "I'm afraid, sir, that you'll have to cultivate a more regal manner. You approach your loved one as though you are about to give her a shave."

And he would snarl back at me: "Please don't teach me." I would get angry with him, and the result? He'd run away half-way through the performance. I would then have to appear before the curtain, bow to the public, and say with some embarrassment: "Ladies and gentlemen, owing to cholera, which has suddenly stricken our tenor, we are unable to continue the performance. I suggest that you please go home and amuse yourself there as best you can."

My audience, having first broken up all the seating, would proceed home, but on the following day the tenor would write a letter to all the important newspapers: "I am not suffering from cholera at all. This is a slander by the well-known scandal-monger, Chaliapin. I was forced to leave the stage from an innate sense of dignity, which, being outraged, by him, has caused me to lose my voice and my livelihood. As a result of this I am suing him for compensation to the extent of 600,000 roubles, and I invite all present at the performance as witnesses on my behalf."

So much for a theatre of one's own.

Of course, that is simply a joke, but allow me to say that in Russia life is never very far removed from such jokes. It invents anecdotes better than Gorbunov's, and satires more bitter than Shchedrin's.

But speaking quite seriously, I fail to see in the people of the theatre the great love for their cause. The cause is demanding, and lacking this love it dies.

We are well aware that there is no need for the artist to sweep the stage, or even put up sets and clean the lamps, as I did in my time in the full exuberance of my youth. Yet if one were to ask an artist with a name to do a walk-on part, he would feel highly insulted. He will, and how! He will write the inevitable letter to the editor of the most liberal paper, which will always take upon itself the burden of the oppressed, though it closes one eye conveniently enough, and is unable to see how the action of one single person can suppress a whole cause.

How wonderful it must be to be a sculptor, a composer, a painter, a writer. For them their theatre is their study, workshop, or studio. They are alone, the door is closed. Nobody sees them, nobody preventing them from creating what they wish. But in the theatre, try if you would to create a living character upon the stage and what happens? You are gazed upon by hundreds of people, among whom there will always be a number who are antagonistic, and determined to go in another direction. The atmosphere of the theatre is weighted by indifference; the artists might well be corpses.

Collective creativeness is only possible if all those engaged in it strive for some unity of purpose, and realize the vital necessity of achieving it. In its absence the true artist is simply working in the wilderness. And the desert is—alas!—not uninhabited.

It is quite possible that I behaved irritably at rehearsals; I may even have been despotic and rude. I have often offended people, great and small. Indeed, so much has been said about it that I am now prepared to believe it. I am not trying to justify myself. Shall I say that, though everybody is guilty, there is something in this atmosphere that is never wholly clear to me? The creator is not greater than the work he creates, and in its interest self-esteem must drown. It was never nice to shout at little men. I know that. But supposing he doesn't want to work, doesn't want to see, to accept— in brief doesn't want to give of himself—then in such cases I shout, and will continue to shout, for I believe only in the work that is warmed by love and charity, for out of these vessels comes the beauty and the value.

I shouted often enough when I was abroad, but people never considered me a despot, tyrant, or devil. Abroad is another country, another land in which the secret of devotion is known.

But enough of this, or else it will really look like airing a grievance; whereas all I am endeavouring to do is to learn how to express myself. There is so much I want to say, and often I cannot find the words. Perhaps people might have had a better opinion of me had I been downright dishonest, something that in other circles goes by the name of tact or diplomacy. The truth is I'm badly brought up, and have never been able to stomach hypocrisy. That is why I so often behave like the goose that turns up in the kitchen. "Please roast me, sirs." They're glad to oblige, of course, and without cutting my throat, plucking me alive, feather by feather.

12

My success in Italy had some exciting consequences. I received an invitation to sing at Monte Carlo in the theatre of Raoul Ginsburg, very well-known as an impresario in Europe, America, Asia, Africa, in the whole of the universe and probably beyond. I think of Monte Carlo as one of the prettiest places on earth, with an infernal reputation as a gambling den. For this tour it was necessary for me to learn several operas, both Italian and French. When I arrived there I found Ginsburg to be a little man with a big nose, and a pair of very scheming eyes. He received me with open arms and, twisting many Russian words out of shape, informed me of his delight in meeting me. How I remember that first encounter!

Wriggling and squirming below me, almost as though sitting over some sizzling cauldron, and delivering words at the rate of hundreds a minute, he told me how much he loved Russia, how he had served in the Russian army during the Turkish campaign, how he had been the first to enter Nikopol, and finally how he received a bayonet wound. To prove this latter fact, he quickly unbuttoned his trousers to show me the scar on his groin. Most diverting, I thought, and certainly unconventional.

"Here, Chaliapin, see! What a wound! It shows you how I love Russia. My heart is with the Russian people, and I fought for them like a lion. That is why I am so delighted to see you in my theatre at Monte Carlo. Yes. Alexander the Third is an intimate friend of mine, and it was I who took Nikopol."

"What for?" I asked.

"It was war. In war they always take things. One town, then another, and then the lot."

This hero looked no more than thirty-five years of age. At the time when he seized Nikopol he was probably ten years of age. Ginsburg turned out to be older than he looked. He must have been all of fourteen when he captured Nikopol! I found him a delightful person.

He bubbled over with life, and continued to surprise me. Apparently he had a castle of his own, a museum, a collection of paintings. He was rich and very interested in the theatre, not for material reasons but only out of sheer love of music. He himself intended to write an opera. This last statement shook me a little.

There happened to be a remarkable artist in Ginsburg's company, a singer named Renaud. I was told he had sung Mephistopheles in Berlioz' *Faust*,

I went to see him in the role. He was indeed magnificent, and after the performance I went round to see him, telling him how much I admired his interpretation. But the moment I got home I began working it all out, and realized that Renaud and I saw this character in very different ways, as different, say, as Berlioz and Boito.

My own first appearance was in this part. Ginsburg's was a tiny theatre with a small stage, and in the dressing-rooms hardly enough room to turn round. All the same I liked the elegance and intimacy of it, crowned of course by Ginsburg himself in his frock-coat, so inexhaustibly gay, and almost unjustifiably delighted.

"What a wonderful production tonight," he exclaimed, although the performance hadn't even begun.

I found here the same devotion as in Italy. One felt that live interest— an interest that at once doubles the strength of the artists.

The public acclaimed the Prologue. This was inspiring to me, and in the Brocken scene I think I reached one of the highlights of my career. But what a great help the theatre itself had been! The great distances between audiences and artists in Russia and Italy were greatly reduced; one reached the entire audience, and nothing was lost, neither gesture nor mimicry. I received an ovation, even the congratulations of Renaud himself. As for Ginsburg, he became like an excited child, radiating happiness. He was a wonderful impresario; he gave out so much in encouragement, in compliments, even when one well knew a performance had been slightly below par. Maybe he thought differently, but certainly he never showed it. He was to me a natural man of the theatre, he had the tools of it under perfect control, and could size up so quickly all effects, and even defects.

I had my quarrels with him too, and sometimes we never exchanged a word for weeks at a time, yet I never stopped liking the man, and he always respected me. Like myself, he had his flaws, but always I was ready to forgive, as he put so much real heart into his work. I remember having a dreadful row with him, that almost ended in a duel, though it was more ridiculous than frightening.

Ginsburg "with God's help", as he used to say, even wrote an opera entitled *Ivan the Terrible*, and into it he piled everything, including the gas-stove. We had in it a fire, a hunt, a bacchanalia in a church, the most mad dances and frenzied battles. Ivan himself rang the bells, played chess, danced and died. He crammed in all the better known Russian words, like Izba, Boyarin, Zakuska, Steppe, Vodka. A work of monumental ignorance and daring, but Ginsburg was firmly convinced that he had written a master-piece, and kept on repeating: "This is a remarkable piece. There isn't a better opera anywhere. All will fade and be forgotten, and only Mozart and I, who stand before you now, will remain. Even if the public doesn't understand this opera now, it will be understood in a thousand years."

I really lost my temper with him, and told this aspiring genius he was a cocksure little fool. How angry he got, with a face as red as the turkey cock, as he declared: "Chaliapin, for words like that, in France, swords are called for."

I willingly agreed, and suggested that his weapon should be more lethal than my own. I also suggested that the duel be postponed until after the first performance of the work, as should I be killed, there would be nobody to play Ivan.

Maddened even further by my jokes, he rushed off at once to arrange about seconds. I waited, but they never came. The quarrel fizzled out. We kept clear of each other's company for a fortnight, but after the production, the *Terrible* production, we made it up. Yet in spite of the fact that Ginsburg's musical effort was sheer hotch-potch, almost entirely the borrowings from other works, and notwithstanding the sheer absurdity of the plot, the performance itself was well produced and acted.

A real theatrical event in the shortest and broadest sense, where the artists were given absolute freedom, and even made an instructive spectacle out of sheer nonsense, it seemed apt that this extravaganza should have closed the season.

It was time to return to red-tape-ridden Russia, where everything is forbidden, and where everybody is so fond of issuing commands. I was soon involved in an unpleasant incident. We were doing *Russalka*, and the conductor was—shall we say—a certain Slav, a former choir-master, who had probably been appointed conductor on the same basis by which a police inspector was appointed to the post of professor in Kharkov University by the Emperor Nicholas the First.

As I knew my part, and in fact the whole work, inside and out, I was not very attentive at rehearsals. Imagine my horror, therefore, when during the actual performance I discovered the first act to be monstrously mutilated by this conductor. The tempi were changed, rhythm itself seemed entirely eradicated. It was so blatantly done that I could only accept it as deliberately calculated. It tied me hand and foot.

The conductor stared down at the score as though he had never seen it before, whilst the audience had quickly noticed that something was wrong, though they sat through it with the patience of those who can get used to anything, since life at home was probably even more tedious than the theatre. But I was furious, and in the interval asked this conductor what he thought he was doing.

Raising his voice, he informed me that he wished to have nothing to do with me, and that if I had any protest to make, then I must do so at the office of the administration. This only made me more angry. I at once went to my dressing-room, changed, and left the theatre, determined never to return. But on the way home I calmed down somewhat, and reflected. An official was after me hotfoot. I went back and completed the performance. Lucky for me, too, was the fact that the performance was not held up by my absence, and the audience remained unaware of the incident. Such incidents are purely the concern of the theatre, and have nothing whatever to do with the public, but as usual it leaked out, and the headlines in the papers the next day boldly declared: "Another Chaliapin scandal."

"Well," I thought, "I have to perpetrate a great many more scandals like this, and many will be to no purpose. One cannot heat the sea with an awl, no matter how hot one may make it."

One truly beautiful day I had a visit from Diaghilev, who asked me if I would come to Paris with him, where he was planning to organize a number of symphony concerts, in order to acquaint the French public with Russian music and its historical development. I agreed to take part in them since I knew how interested Europe was in Russian works. I was most enthusiastic about his idea. This for me was a new adventure, and I looked forward to it very much.

When we reached Paris I took up residence in the same hotel as Diaghilev. I soon understood that what we had embarked upon was work of the greatest importance, and everybody concerned was throwing heart and soul into the task. I will say this, that there was more life humming round Diaghilev than in all the streets of Paris. He told me that there was such an enormous interest in the forthcoming concerts that even the Grand Opera House would not hold the thousands who were already clamouring for tickets. He said that Rimsky-Korsakov, Rachmaninov, Scriabin, and many other composers would be taking part in the concerts, and that Rimsky-Korsakov, Blumenfeld, and Nikish were to conduct.

We began the first concert with the first act from *Russlan and Ludmilla*, and it was very well received. I myself sang excerpts from *Sadko*, *Prince Igor*, and *Boris Godunov*, as well as a number of ballads with pianoforte accompaniment. The French are erroneously considered to be frivolous, but they were very much drawn to us, liking particularly the Mussorgsky music, and spoke of this composer with great enthusiasm. The concerts were so successful that it gave us the idea of bringing Russian opera to France the following season. And this we did.

The mere announcement that Diaghilev was putting on *Boris Godunov* was sufficient news for the Parisians to acclaim it as a gala season. I shall never forget what feeling, what electrifying energy, the chorus and orchestra of the Grand Opera put into their work. It was simply wonderful. We produced the work in full, something quite impossible in Russia owing to the censorship. The work was most impressive, and in all my twenty-five years in the theatre I have never witnessed such a magnificent production.

At the dress rehearsal we invited a select Parisian audience—painters, men of letters, and of course many journalists. Korovin and Golovin were already working on the *décor*, but unfortunately neither it nor the costumes were ready. The rehearsal could not be postponed, and we were all apprehensive about the impression we were creating, walking about the stage in our ordinary clothes. My own costumes were ready, but I would not wear them, nor use make-up, since it would have spoiled the general effect.

The opera began. I do not think the French had ever heard such a chorus before, but I have always thought Russian choirs to be superior, since all, or nearly all, of its members sing in churches from childhood, and they sing with those exceptional nuances, demanded of our liturgical work. I only regretted that the actual atmosphere was missing, though all artists are capable of creating the required illusion. I remember when I came to the hallucination scene, many people in the audience turned apprehensively to where I was gazing, and some even jumped in their seats. Rewarded with stormy applause for this scene, I felt as happy as a child.

The first night passed off as magnificently as the dress rehearsal, and everybody—artists, chorus, orchestra, designers—rose to the occasion; all were worthy of Mussorgsky's music. The enthusiasm for this work registered itself throughout the Parisian Press, the death scene creating a tremendous impression. We were overwhelmed by the excitement of the French public.

Looking back on my life, I can say this—that much of it was hard, but much of it was good. I have lived through moments of great happiness, thanks to the art I love. Love is always happiness, no matter what we love, but love of art is the greatest of all.

I only regretted that in *Boris* the inn scene could not be included, due solely to the fact that no singers of stature were available—and that in spite of all the talent to be found in Russia. In my youth I often sang both Boris and Varlaam in the same performance, but I didn't dare do it here. For me this production was a test of Russian originality, and Russian maturity in art. We were at last face to face with Europe, and Europe admitted that we had passed that test.

Boris Godunov was given ten performances, following which I had a visit from the new director of La Scala, who suggested that the Mussorgsky work should be put on in Italy. Already acquainted with the tastes of the Italian public, I could not see *Boris Godunov* going down very well there, and pointed this out to him.

"But I'm an Italian, and this work enthralls me. How can you be so sure that other Italians will not like it?"

I loved Milan and its sensitive theatre-going public, and indeed I very much wanted to go back there to sing, but there was one big drawback. In Paris we had sung the opera in Russian, whereas the La Scala director wished the work to be sung in Italian, with Italian artists and chorus. This meant that I would have to sing in Italian, and there was no translation of Boris in that language. The director declared that, if I agreed to sing, he would send off the opera immediately to an expert linguist, who in principle had already agreed to do the translation. I consented, though with some misgivings, half expecting the administration in Milan to say: "Oh no, we cannot present this barbarian opera."

On my return home to Russia I learned that the administration of La Scala had already commissioned Golovin to do the sets for them, and not long after this I received the score of the translated work—a very poor job indeed. There were actual changes in the music itself, whole passages were added, others deleted. It seemed unthinkable to me. So I decided to approach the conductor of the Petersburg ballet, Drigo, with a request: help me with a translation. This he kindly agreed to do, and between us we managed a new and fairly good translation of *Boris*.

Before very long I was back in Italy. Almost one of the first people to greet me was my old friend, the La Scala porter, Giovannino. The dear old man embraced me, talking nineteen to the dozen, full of my Paris success, and saying how passionately he had been interested in the production of the opera, *Boris Naganov*, which was the title he had given it.

"Ah, Signor Chaliapin, through your lips Russia will speak to us. She will say her word to the world, just as we Italians do."

Thus an Italian porter! These Italians never ceased to amaze me. The rehearsals began very soon. The opera was conducted by Vitali, a man of about thirty, an excellent musician, and a fine conductor. He invited me to the rehearsal room and requested me to demonstrate some of the tempi, and started to play the piano. I was astonished how well and how deeply he understood Mussorgsky's music. He kept on repeating his admiration for the work, the beauty of it, and the originality shown in the chord groupings. This man was already deeply imbued, and it made me very happy.

Naturally it fell to my lot to play the part of producer at these rehearsals, and much that I had to show to both singers and chorus was entirely foreign to them. They listened with great attention, and I very soon saw that Russian art was attracting these very impressionable people. There were some amusing incidents: I was asked how Russian Jesuits dressed. Police officers wore uniforms as designed in correct period but ordinary constables appeared on stage looking like present-day Russian policemen. The boyars themselves looked like highwaymen. All, or nearly all, might well have been copied from some cheap and popular prints. The *décor* too was weak, and oleographic, as it often is abroad. But the orchestra played magnificently and seemed like wax in the hands of the talented conductor, who, quite inspired, moulded it to his will. I was greatly impressed by their attention and utter devotion to their conductor. The chorus, too, were splendid, though they could not emulate their Russian confrères. In any case Italian chorus singers off-stage are mainly working people, tailors, drapers, glove-makers, small shopkeepers. They love singing, they have naturally placed voices, and a finely developed ear. Many of them dream of an artist's career. Their voices are brilliant, and when they have to sing with full voice they do so inspired, superbly. But I found they could not achieve a quiet, tender type of singing in a minor key. In *Boris Godunov*, in order to achieve the necessary effect of prayer in Pimen's cell, the choir had to be placed a long way back-stage, and the conducting was done with the aid of an electric bulb which the conductor could switch on from his desk. This effect came off well.

The orchestra opened with the first few chords. I stood listening back-stage, feeling more dead than alive. The action continued, the singers sang well, the conductor lived up to expectations, and yet the theatre seemed to sway like a ship before a storm. The first scene ended, and the applause was vigorous. I calmed down somewhat, and as the action developed, so did the success of the work progress. The Italians were seeing an opera-drama for the first time. They were amazed and thrilled.

They heard the entire performance with rapt attention, and I felt wildly happy. I rushed about embracing my colleagues, who were like delighted children. Everybody was united, artists, muscians, producer, stage-hands— a satisfying manifestation of artistic unity. As for my dear old porter, Giovannino, he behaved as though he had written the work himself. I appeared in this work eight times before eventually leaving for Monte Carlo, from where I twice returned to Milan on insistent public demand. I knew then that Italy had fallen in love with Mussorgsky's opera.

It is a curious fact that the easier one's acting seems to the onlooker, the more difficult it is to answer the questions asked about it. This apparent facility of mine created some odd misunderstandings. The questions often amused me, as, for instance: "How do you manage to hold yourself so simply on stage? You don't seem to have any gestures or poses prepared in advance, and each time you seem to act a scene in a new way, entirely different from the first."

I explained as best I could, but it did not always clear up the misunderstandings. I remember how Cirino, who had a beautiful voice and sang Pimen, would watch me closely on the stage, perhaps more intently than the other artists. He loved the part, and thought I did Boris very well. But this singer would suddenly say to somebody: "What a pity that Chaliapin's voice is not as good as mine. For instance, I could take not only top G, but even an A flat. If I had played Boris, I might have done it better. The acting is not all that complicated, and I would have sung better."

This singer did not conceal his opinions from me. Very tactfully he would ask my permission to watch me make up. He thought the make up the most complicated part of it all. I would explain to him minutely, as I proceeded.

"Yes," he commented, "all that is not difficult, but in Italy we have no such paints, nor have we any good wigs, beards, and moustaches."

My final performance over, I approached Cirino and, handing him a wig, beard and moustache, said, "Here is the make-up for Boris. I would gladly leave you my head, but I require it myself."

He was touched, and thanked me warmly. But a year later when I was back in Milan I bumped into Cirino in the streets, and watched him flying towards me, making horses stop in their tracks, colliding with every kind of traffic. Much to the astonishment of passers-by he warmly embraced me.

"Bon giorno, amico Chaliapin," he said.

"Why this exaltation?"

"Because now I have understood what an artist you are. I played *Boris* myself, and was an utter flop. I acted shockingly. Everything looked so easy when you did it. Why, all that make-up is nonsense. It is you, you only."

I tried to calm Cirino. "Quiet, quiet. People are staring," I said.

"To hell with them. I must confess to you, Chaliapin, that I did not know your worth. I love your art, and I kiss your hand."

This was a little too much, but Italians are like that, and I was moved by this demonstration of a fellow artist.

I can recall another occasion of real Italian warmth of heart. I was rehearsing Gounod's *Faust*, and I noticed that the splendid singer who was playing Marguerite had no idea how to comport herself on stage. Indeed, she acted abominably. I chose a convenient moment and used great tact in broaching this to her. She sadly agreed with me and said she felt she could not act, but would I help her? I was only too delighted to do so, and after rehearsal I went over some scenes with her, sang her aria. She was very grateful for my help, and I was glad to note the changed opinion of the Press on the following day. The singer brought me armfuls of flowers that day, expressing her thanks. I can say here, and without boasting, that abroad the artists I worked with never objected to any advice I offered, and sometimes learned from me. That pleased me much. In Russia, unfortunately, things were very different.

We happened to be doing *Boris Godunov* at the Imperial Theatre, and at once I saw that the artists were quite indifferent to their roles, a real "couldn't-care-less" attitude. The part of Shuisky was played by a very well-known tenor, a young man with a good voice. He sang beautifully, but was utterly out of character. He didn't sing Shuisky; he just sang. I pointed this out to him, and he replied casually that he just hadn't thought about the matter. I then offered to go through the part with him. He agreed, and after some study the position was much improved. This little scene was observed by the other artists. Immediately they called a meeting in the foyer and protested that I was not the producer, but just a singer like the rest of them, and had no right to throw my weight around. They decided to inform me of this to discourage my monopolizing the prerogatives of the producer. But for some reason they said nothing. Their behaviour had the effect of a cold shower, and when I told the administration of the incident, and how much I disapproved of the present attitude to opera production, they replied simply: "Well, then, try and produce it yourself."

"If you give me a free hand, I will," I replied. But there the conversation terminated. I would never have allowed the curtain to rise on anything less than a perfect production.

It was the same devil-take-it attitude when we decided to put on *Khovanshchina*. The first rehearsal was shocking. They warbled it, in much the same manner as they warble their way through *Madame Butterfly* or *Rigoletto*. In effect they were saying that they liked operas best that could be sung without words, with nothing required but the usual tra-la-la. The costumes were pretty, and you sang well enough. What more was required? Certainly story content and dramatic interpretation were not important. In opera singing was all. Unfortunately this attitude towards a work like *Khovanshchina* just would not do, and I got intensely irritated by the careless way it was approached. I saw the utter ruin of the performance. People came out dressed in period costume, though even that was not necessarily correct, and sang their tra-la-la's, whilst the chorus boomed. This could be very gay, very well done, or it could be frightfully boring, but it had nothing to do with Mussorgsky's opera.

I was quite unable to contain my intense irritation, and told my fellow artists bluntly that if they continued to sing in this way then the work was

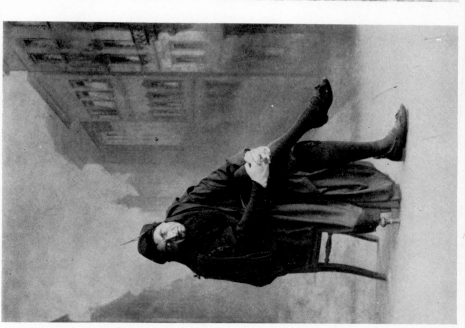

42. *Chaliapin as Mephistopheles in Gounod's opera* Faust *(Russian Private Opera, Moscow), 1897.*

43. *Chaliapin as Mephistopheles in Gounod's opera* Faust *(Mariinsky Theatre, St. Petersburg), 1895.*

45. Sketch by A. Golovin for Chaliapin in Boïto's Mefistofele, at La Scala, Milan, 1901.

44. Sketch by V. Polenov for Chaliapin's costume for Mephistopheles in Gounod's opera Faust.

Opera, Paris), 1912.

Moscow), 1906.

Left 48. Chaliapin as Mephistopheles in Gounod's opera Faust
(Bolshoy Theatre, Moscow), 1916.

Below 49. Chaliapin in the title role of Boito's Mefistofele
(Metropolitan Opera, New York), 1921

ruined before it had even begun. I foresaw an audience plunged into gloom, and finally into sleep. I then proceeded to sing all the parts as I felt they should be sung, to which my colleagues listened attentively enough, and even the chorus agreed that I was right. The rehearsal was then concluded with enormous aplomb, especially the projection of the splendidly written character-part of Martha. Everything went well at the dress rehearsal, and the work was not only well received by the public, but turned out a great success. This sealed my feeling of bliss. I recall making some kind of speech, and then going off to the Kazan Cathedral to sing a requiem for Mussorgsky. The whole choir came with me, and sang beautifully. After which I laid wreaths on the graves of both Mussorgsky and Stassov.

This success of *Khovanshchina* in St. Petersburg made me want to put it on in Moscow, but when I arrived there it was to discover the artists in a state of great agitation, expecting me to impose on them impossible demands. I invited the conductor to my house and asked him to go through the score with me, to which he agreed most amiably. I felt that in the interests of greater dramatization certain parts should be altered, here a few bars slowed down, there a speeding-up. But the conductor kept pointing out to me the composer's instructions, allegro, moderato, etc., saying he could not deviate from the score. Yet he finally saw my point of view. Let me say that, in general, I always strictly observe the composer's instructions, and in the case of this work, particular deviations were in no sense drastic, and no undue licence was taken. Sometimes the extra spark may be struck from the anvil.

But at the rehearsal I began to notice that the conductor was waving about his baton with the utmost indifference, with the result that the dawn music acquired only a very bleak and unpolished character. I drew the attention of the director of the Musical Academy to this point. He agreed that things were going badly. The chorus arrived, and started singing apathetically, even raggedly. I asked them to follow the orchestra carefully, whereupon the conductor said that if the chorus failed to sing with the orchestra it was because the singers were trying to act, more than to sing. The word "act" was obviously emphasized, and I then realized that my desire to make the mass scenes come more alive were not to the conductor's taste. The only reply I could make to this was to point out to him that the chorus were not too busy acting, but that he himself was paying no attention to them.

"Ah! So that's it. You don't like the way I conduct," exclaimed the maestro.

Upon which he put down his baton and strode off, leaving the orchestra without a head. His action was greeted with applause by some of the artists, and there were one or two "boos" in my direction. The rehearsal came to an abrupt end.

I, too, might have gone home, but then the whole work would have been sabotaged. I asked myself whether I shouldn't conduct myself, since I knew this opera from beginning to end, but the orchestra would surely sympathize with the conductor. I foresaw "another Chaliapin scandal" which, if reported, would do the cause no good.

I decided to telephone to St. Petersburg and ask for another conductor, a very talented young man I knew. He was in Moscow the very next morning, and at midday we had the dress rehearsal. All went well; the singing was good, everybody was attentive, and things passed smoothly. But already the newspapers carried reports about my despotism, bad manners, and general rudeness. The publicity was badly timed, and the public became hostile to me.

When I came on the stage the audience sat in angry silence. I had to find some way of breaking through this mood, which, in my opinion, is part of an artist's duties. By the time I had sung my final phrase, accompanied by the sonorous tolling of a bell, the audience had quite forgotten its earlier mood, and I was rewarded with tremendous applause. I ran off the stage, shut myself up in my room, and burst into tears.

I have often wept alone. The public knew me only from the newspapers, and heard, moreover, of "my debaucheries". I am in no way excusing myself, knowing how useless it is, but life can be unbearable at times. Believe me, when one lives the part of a king, a devil, or a miller, it isn't easy, or pleasant, to be aware of malicious gossip, and horrible and inconsiderate red-tape attitude to one's most sacred beliefs.

Singing for me has never been a trifling amusement; it is the sacred duty of my life. The public so often tend to regard the artist—if I may be forgiven the comparison—in the same way as did the cabby who once drove me along a Moscow street.

"What do you do for a living?" he asked.

"I sing," I replied.

"No. I don't mean that," he said. "I mean what work do you do? We all sing. I sing myself if I have a drink, or sometimes just to relieve boredom. No, I'm asking you what do you work at?"

I then informed him that I sold cabbage and firewood, and that I had a coffin shop and supplied all kinds of funereal trimmings, on demand. This wise and serious cabman expressed in my view the opinion of a vast proportion of the public, for whom art is not a serious business, but just one of those pleasant diversions for filling up spare time, and sometimes dispelling boredom.

13

My performances in Italy and Monte Carlo helped to make my name, and before long I had received an invitation to sing in New York. I had long been interested in the New World, a country in which people made fortunes faster than we in Russia make bast sandals, and where they fearlessly build towers of Babylon anything up to sixty stories high. Having concluded a contract to sing *Mefistofele, Faust, The Barber of Seville* and *Don Giovanni*, I boarded a boat and six days later found myself in New York harbour. The thought of appearing in this stern land of businessmen, of whom I had heard so many fantastic stories, so agitated me that I was hardly aware of the ocean-crossing.

The first thing I saw was the Statue of Liberty, the noble and symbolic gift of France which America had transformed into a lamp post. I expressed aloud my admiration for this grandiose monument, its simplicity and dignity. A Frenchman who pulled my leg during the voyage drew my attention to the sad face of Liberty herself, the way she stood with her back to the New World, gazing longingly across to France. His words were of little interest to me. I was far more interested in the way that emigrants were received into God's own country.

How roughly the poor people were undressed by officials, their pockets turned inside out, and the women asked where their husbands were, girls asked if they *were* girls, and how much money each had brought with him. Only when these formalities were over were the fortunate or unfortunate people allowed to go ashore, and some sent back to where they came from. This sorting of the sheep from the goats took place right under the Statue of Liberty.

At the harbour I was met by some "businessmen", very efficient-looking gentlemen, theatrical agents, and reporters. The latter were a tough bunch indeed, and had about them a no-nonsense air. All terribly clean-shaven. I was asked if I had had a good journey, where I was born, whether married or single, did I get on well with my wife, had I ever been in gaol for political reasons, and what I thought of the past, present, and future of Russia and America.

I was not only surprised, but quite touched by their interest in me, and honestly recounted to them all the details of my birth, marriage, tastes. I informed them that I had not been in gaol, but quoted to them the Russian proverb which advises people not to be too sure that they will never go begging or to prison.

"All right," they exclaimed, and went about their "business".

The next day I was informed that the press had printed incredible things concerning me. I was an atheist, I hunted the bear, alone, despised politics, could not abide beggars, and hoped that on my return to Russia I would be put into gaol. It further transpired that the kind consideration of these charming people had cost a pretty penny, for each of the "business" men presented me with a small bill for expenses in connection with my reception. Every town has its own character, I thought, but I refused to pay the bills. Ten hands dipped into one pocket is a little too much.

The hotel at which I was staying was rather a magnificent affair, oozing luxury and had the appearance of an expensive furniture shop. I still remember the lunch there. I had some shellfish, crabs, crayfish that looked as if it had been rubbed through a sieve, almost pre-chewed to save the diner the trouble. After this I went off to look at millionaire property on Fifth Avenue, but the particular buildings I was looking for turned out to be in the city.

New York made a great impression on me. Everything alive moved with great speed, in all directions, as though fleeing from some impending catastrophe—on the ground and under the ground, and even in the air, as the lifts shot up to storey after storey. The whole was accompanied by deafening noises and the continuing hooting of motor horns. The overhead trains were entirely new, and from time to time I pulled my hat over my ears, expecting something to drop on me at any moment.

I thought of Italy, the serenade under the window. Heaven help the serenader here, guitar and all, with his beloved somewhere on the 49th floor. The noise was truly infernal, so that the impression conveyed to me was that another city was being built right inside the present one. In this boiling, humming, and sizzling melting-pot I felt terribly alone, insignificant, unwanted.

I never saw anybody relaxed, or strolling casually; everybody rushed, tearing newspapers from the vendors' hands as they shot past, reading them in flight, then dropping them under their feet, and as they went on, and inevitably on, pushed other people out of the way without even an apology for lack of time. Meanwhile these desperate people puffed at pipe and cigar and cigarette, sending up enough smoke to screen off the sunlight. I saw the sun endeavouring to get through, and it almost had a hurt look, as though it were saying, "Sorry. Not needed here." Oddly enough, there wasn't a single sparrow anywhere to be seen, and it is the bravest bird in the world.

For some six days before rehearsals began, I wandered about this city, looking round, and looking in wherever I was permitted. I visited museums full of incredible treasures, which, of course, had all come from Europe. Finally, I found my way to the Metropolitan Opera House. I must confess that at first I thought it was a shop, one of those expensive exteriors that catch the eye on Fifth Avenue. Inside it was a sheer riot of raspberry-coloured velvet upholstery, whilst the corridors seemed filled with pale, clean-shaven people, all terribly busy about something, and completely uninterested in theatre.

The rehearsing of *Mefistofele* revealed that this was going to be a production on stock lines, safe lines. But even in their supposed thoroughness there was yet a hint of the haphazard, a feeling of sheer caricature. I kept on getting angry with these people; I tried to show them how wrong it was, but nobody appeared to understand. One of the artists confided in me: "Subtlety is not required here. So long as it's good and loud—that is all that is necessary."

The only real support I got came from the impresario. He himself was paralysed, and brought to rehearsals in a wheel chair. Seeing how tormented I was, he shouted to the producer: "Please listen to Mr. Chaliapin, and do what he says."

After this some concessions were made, though it did not help very much. My nerves were on edge, and on the first night, feeling really ill, I sent in a note to the administration informing them that I was unable to appear. The reply to this note was startling.

In my room I was suddenly confronted by a long, bony lady wearing spectacles, with frowning eyebrows, and a turned-down mouth. Pointing her finger at me, she said something in English. I gathered she wanted to know if I was Chaliapin and I replied in the affirmative, apologizing in my best Russian for appearing in a dressing-gown. With eloquent gestures she then bade me to lie down on the bed. I did so, and to my horror saw her removing instruments from her doctor's bag.

She ordered me to go to bed, and then to my further alarm I saw that I was to have a colonic *lavage*. This scared me and I yelled for the valet, who spoke French. He explained that the lady was a doctor who would cure me within twenty-four hours. I asked him to convey my respects to her, but that I was not requiring her services. In spite of this she insisted that I should go to bed. The instrument for *lavage* hung in the air; I pleaded with her to go away.

"I will sing. I will sing! Just go away. Please." And she went. The scene made me laugh, and in fact calmed me down a little. Although that night I was feeling exhausted, I sang well.

Apparently the press had put me over in a big way, and the public had been told that I was a phenomenal wall-crushing bass. Besides, they said, who doesn't know what Russian basses are like! They knew there were no tenors in Russia, but, to make up for this, the basses were powerful enough to send whole belfries crashing down by singing three notes. Evidently they were not interested in tenors, only Russian basses. I daresay the audience expected me to rush in, let out a roar, and knock the occupants of the first six rows right out of their seats. However, I failed to maim a single American music-lover, and the following day the newspapers wrote something like this:

"What kind of a Russian bass is this? His voice is of a baritone timbre, and quite soft. . . ."

On the whole, however, the reviewers were indulgent to me, although they summed up tersely enough with: "Chaliapin is not an artist for America." There was no mention of my acting or my interpretation.

There was one other incident during my American stay. I had a sore throat and had to see a throat specialist. Judging from the look of his waiting-room, this man had a very prosperous practice. The surgery was magnificent with strange, shining apparatus, and all the machinery electrically operated. He practically oozed his scientific ability. The doctor himself appeared to be a considerate, decent and charming person, and after I had paid for my visit I offered him a box at the opera. He then asked what I was singing. "Mephistopheles," I replied, at which his eyebrows went up. Would I please tell him what it was all about? I thought he was joking, but in fact he had never heard of *Faust*, and certainly never read Goethe.

The performances succeeded one another. With the arrival of the celebrated conductor, Mahler, we began rehearsals of *Don Giovanni*. Poor Mahler. At the very first rehearsal he was plunged into deep despair, for he had not seen anywhere about him the enthusiasm and love which he himself invariably put into his work. Everything was rushed, things were got through anyhow; it didn't much matter, since the public was so indifferent. The audience at the Metropolitan Opera House only came to hear "voices" and nothing else. The Italian artists endeavoured to improve things, but everything broke down, cooled off under the walls of this raspberry-filled theatre.

We did *The Barber of Seville*, and I think I had quite a success in this work. I was therefore considerably astonished when two days later I received an anonymous letter in which was enclosed a number of newspaper cuttings. These flayed me, and through them all ran the same theme, the same complaint, which was briefly something like this: "It is painful and degrading to see this Siberian savage portraying a priest and profaning religion."

A fat lot they understood. Nothing could be further from my mind than the profanation of anything when I played the part of Don Basilio.

I moved from my first-class hotel to another one, also quite luxurious, though I must confess a gloom lay over the whole establishment, as though each room contained its own corpse. Everything appeared extraordinarily quiet, people talked in undertones, and sinister-looking old ladies paraded the corridors. I merely slept in this morgue, spending my days roaming about the town and visiting various places of entertainment.

In New York City with each step one takes one is confronted by a garish sign announcing, "MUSIC HALL". These are small places wherein artists sing, declaim, and dance, and where acrobats perform. There are also eccentric comedians and jugglers; the programme is always varied, and often amusing. The public roars with laughter.

But I wanted to visit the serious theatre, I wanted to hear Shakespeare spoken in his own language. Then I learned that there was no such theatre in existence, and that Shakespeare was only performed by visiting foreigners like Salvini. This surprised me, though a journalist explained that America looked upon the theatre in quite a different way from Europe.

"In this country," he said, "people work so much and so hard that they have no real desire left for watching drama and tragedies. Life for them is dramatic enough. In the evening one should relax, watch something gay and unusual."

This explanation intensified in me a curious feeling of oppression. Life became tedious, and I just dreamed the days away, longing for my return to Europe.

Once, whilst walking about town, I found myself at the docks, and saw a Russian ship, the *Smolensk*, berthing. I went aboard and asked if I could look round the ship. An officer enquired who I was, and when I told him he was overjoyed, and I was at once introduced to captain and crew. The moment these sailors gathered about me, I felt myself back on the Volga. I had a delightful meal with them, eating cabbage soup, and drinking vodka. I was pleased to hear the Russian tongue once more, and the accented "o's". As there were some singers among the crew we soon had a gay Russian party going. It was my happiest day in America.

I was well paid for my New York performances, receiving 8,000 francs per performance. I was advised not to keep all this money on me, but to place some of it in the bank. This I did, depositing the money in a branch of the bank set up in the opera house itself. A few days before I sailed for Europe, I was told that the bank had failed. So much for my money.

On the eve of my departure I was visited by journalists anxious to gather my impressions of their city. I showed them newspaper cuttings berating me for profaning religion, and told them frankly that, where art was concerned, they were decidedly lacking in sensibility. I recalled that *The Barber of Seville* was written by a Frenchman, the opera itself by an Italian, and I, a Russian, was singing the part of a Spanish priest. I said they would understand little until an American Beaumarchais and Rossini appeared on their horizon. They did not like this, I'm afraid. After my departure a Jewish friend wrote telling me of the amount of space taken up in the press dealing with my ingratitude, uncouthness, and other sins. Much later I received several invitations to return to New York, and always declined, and only in 1914 did I sign a contract for a tour of American cities with a Russian company. But the war put an end to that contract.

I was soon invited to go to South America. I didn't want to go, but my old friend, the impresario, Cecchi, insisted that I should, and wouldn't take no for an answer. So in May of that year I set out for Buenos Aires. It was a wonderful, peaceful, and enjoyable journey. For eighteen days the sea remained pond-like. There was the special Neptune ceremony on crossing the Equator. I have no desire to compete with Goncharov, who has described so superbly this amusing English pastime, but I can say that it was terribly funny.

Rio de Janeiro absolutely delighted me, with its picturesqueness and its air of brilliant festivity. The people even seemed to play at working. Life was easy and gay. Everything reminded me so much of Europe. Their outlook on the arts was European, the performances in theatre and opera house well done.

On July 14th, the French national holiday, I had a deputation from the French residents asking me to sing the "Marseillaise" in the theatre. I agreed, and sang this magnificent hymn with a choir—very solemn and grand, followed by deafening applause. Representatives of all nations had turned up, fired by a love of France, the first beauty of the world. The French colony had a medal struck in my honour. It was the best award I have ever received.

My return journey was made in an English ship which stopped at St. Vincent and Madeira. I was fascinated by the island of St. Vincent, austere, absolutely bare and burnt-looking, like a great stone fallen from the skies. I was informed that only one tree grew on the island, which the natives considered sacred. They were as naked as their land, and extremely beautiful, like statues cast out of bronze by ancient Greeks, magicians of the plastic arts. They rowed out to the ship in primitive little boats, shouting in ringing voices, asking for coins to be flung into the water, like the urchins of the Bay of Naples. In Madeira we drank the strong juice of that blessed land. I went riding about the stone-paved streets, not on wheels, but on runners—not due to too much Madeira, but because it is an old custom there. In parts of the Vyatka Province of my native land people also drive in sleighs, winter and summer. It was pleasant to recall this, although in Vyatka this is due not to the stone paving but to the abundance of marshlands.

An old French actor, a friend of mine who came with me as companion and secretary, had a misfortune just before leaving Buenos Aires. Saying goodbye to some friends on the wharf, he suddenly cried out that he had been robbed. It turned out that he kept all his money, the savings of a lifetime, some 14,000 francs, in the hip pocket of his trousers. As he paid for me wherever we went, the thieves had been observant, and were presumably hoping to steal my money. The poor old man was utterly crushed by this loss, and I was afraid he might do something desperate against himself. I gave him 14,000 francs myself, and he returned to normal again.

"Why do you carry all that money on you?" I asked him.

He then explained that he was living with a woman to whom he was not married. He was not young, and if the money were deposited in a bank, in the event of his death the woman would be unable to inherit it. As it was, she would simply take it, and that was all. I was touched by this regard for his "wife". On the way I made another discovery. I found out that in Buenos Aires my friend had paid the claque some fifty pesetas for each performance, which amounted to twenty-five roubles.

"What on earth for?" I asked furiously.

The Frenchman answered: "I know that for you this was not necessary, but for them it was absolutely essential. Those poor people, mostly Neapolitans, looked like gangsters, and were starving. Of course they could not affect your success in any way, but what was to prevent them coughing and sneezing throughout the performance? It was to stop them doing that, that I paid them."

What on earth was I to do with this naïve being? Thanks to him, the claquers received money from me, the one and only time in my career.

14

My success as a singer had at last aroused interest in England, and I had several invitations to sing at Covent Garden, but for one reason or another the trip was always being postponed. Then one summer's day when I was in the country, peacefully fishing, and planning to go to Orange in a fortnight's time, where my old friend Ginsburg was planning an open-air production in the ruins of a Roman theatre, I received a telegram from a seemingly eccentric American lady, then living in London. She invited me to come to London for one evening to sing some songs in her drawing-room. Not knowing my address, she had sent off telegrams in every direction, and I first got one from the Imperial Theatre Administration, then one from a friend, and then yet another. This American proposal surprised me, in rather an unpleasant way. There was something eccentric about it, smacking of New York. Not wishing to go, I replied, setting forth impossible terms, but to my utter dismay she immediately wired back her consent, and against my will I was forced to go.

On arrival I put up at an hotel. I remember I had a tiny bedroom that had an oval window. It was hot and stuffy. I took off my clothes, pushed my table against the window, climbed up, and began a survey of this gigantic city. The part of it now revealed to me was fantastically majestic. I could see Westminster Abbey, the Tower, a bridge across the Thames, and rows of houses that appeared to have been hewn out of granite, and an impression of power, of sheer indestructibility, was sharply conveyed to me. It created an illusion of an extraordinary and sombre strength, I found this most stimulating.

The following day I called on the American lady. She lived in a palatial mansion, in a magnificent park—a venerable person with a youthful face beneath white hair. She reminded me of Catherine the Great. There were three other ladies already in her drawing-room. I was offered tea, and we chatted in French. I suddenly noticed that the main preoccupation of the American lady was whether or not I justified the fee I was getting from her. She kept repeating that she would like to hear me that very day—at once, if possible. To put her out of her misery, I sat down at the piano and accompanied myself. The moment I started singing she seemed well satisfied.

The next day, the accompanist and I presented ourselves at the house, and were met by a butler in brightly-coloured livery, knee-breeches and stockings, and aglets. He led us into a small room, the window of which opened onto the garden. Through the hum of voices I could hear the song of a nightingale. The trees were thickly hung with multi-coloured Chinese lanterns. Under the trees I discerned some gentlemen seated, together with elegantly attired ladies. The gentlemen appeared to favour a parting of the hair in the middle of the head, and this stretched from the bridge of the nose to the nape of the neck. There was the buzz of conversation, clouds of smoke, glitter of lights reflected in monocles and marble-hard shirt-fronts. Above all this soared the song of the nightingale. I was quite unable to make out where this wonderful bird came from, besides which it seemed all wrong that he should be singing in the middle of the summer. Could it be that in England nightingales were differently brought up?

When the butler served us tea, I enquired about this bird. Was it a caged bird, I asked. This important personage, in almost carefully distorted French, explained to me that the bird was simply sitting on the tree.

"Strictly speaking," he said, "it isn't a bird at all, but a gentleman who knows how to whistle, taking the part of the bird. He is just an ordinary man, but paid like any artist. He will get ten pounds for tonight."

"And he is now sitting in the tree?" I asked.

"Oh yes," replied the servant, "and very comfortably."

"I hope they won't ask me to climb a tree," I thought anxiously. But everything went well. I sang some Russian songs, and made the desired impression. I was asked for encore after encore.

I remember there were sitting in the front row some rather thin ladies wedged into corsets, and when they applauded they seemed to rattle inside them, like pestles in a mortar. The guests liked me, and after the recital the hostess invited me to dinner. The atmosphere was relaxing, free and easy. It was a buffet dinner, some sat, some stood, everybody chatted gaily, and all were charming and friendly to me. Involuntarily it recalled to me a certain concert in St. Petersburg, in an aristocratic house. There, when the concert was over, the host shoved fifty roubles into my hand, as though paying the doctor, and saw me to the door.

During that evening I met Lady Grey, the wife of Sir Edward Grey. She asked me to her house, and when I went, she invited me to sing at Covent Garden. I had my own reasons for declining her flattering suggestion. She then told me that the Queen wished to hear me, that she had already spoken to her about this, and that in a few days I would be invited to Windsor.

The day for this concert was fixed, but I couldn't go, since a message turned up suddenly from Orange, informing me that my non-arrival there was holding up rehearsals. I made my apologies to Lady Grey, and set off for Paris, and from there, together with the celebrated Edouard Colourne, I went on to Orange. There I met Paul Mounet. Mounet was a giant, highly intelligent, with a wonderful wit, and I took to him at once. He invited me to lunch, and we went off to a restaurant. I recalled that Mounet had once written an excellent thesis on the dangers of alcohol, but during the lunch he began ordering one bottle of wine after another. Feeling that this was beginning to have a devastating effect on me, though Mounet himself seemed to be none the worse for it, I made a protest.

"You'll have to get used to it," he said. "Get into training. Wine is essential for life, and for an artist it is the nectar that brings the inspiration."

"But what of your thesis on the dangers of alcohol?"

"Ah! I was young then, my thesis all theory. But life is life, and it devours all theories, as Saturn devoured his children. I assure you I wouldn't, and couldn't, write anything on wine except to praise its virtues."

I often watched Mounet on stage, and he was as wonderful there as in real life.

The performance at Orange has remained in my memory. It was a beautiful southern night, the bright stars burned in the darkest of blue skies, and on the stone steps of the ancient amphitheatre sat a multitude of people in rows of multi-coloured spots brightly lit by electricity. I, as Mephistopheles, stood high up in the niche of a half-ruined wall. I climbed up there by way of a very wobbly, hastily constructed stairway, and from there by rope, and not without risk of breaking my neck. The atmosphere itself was eerie. Strange, hoarse sounds, like angry sighs, seemed to come through the cracks of the Cyclopean masonry from time to time. Night birds, disturbed, flapped their wings against the stones.

The orchestra opened. A cold beam from the spotlight fell on me. I sang, "Ave, Signor." From somewhere came a strong current of air that wafted my cry away from the audience. I changed my pose, and continued singing, much stimulated by the unusual surroundings. All this may not have been very artistic, but at least it had the merit of imagination, and it greatly appealed to the public. With the ending of the Prologue the applause was frenzied. I went down the rope, then down the steps to the arena. Bowing to the audience, I felt myself back in the theatre again.

At long last came the opportunity to appear in London. I was going there with a mixture of excitement and anxiety. I had the feeling that Russian music would hardly be understood by the English people. In spite of the fact that I had already been in London and received impressions of the city and its aristocratic people, many were telling me that the English were haughty, uninterested in anything except themselves, and looked upon the Russians as barbarians. This made me apprehensive about the fate of the Russian concerts, though at the same time it fired me with a desire to conquer this English scepticism towards anything foreign. Whilst not having a great deal of confidence in myself and my abilities, I was yet unshakeably convinced of the power of Russian music to enchant, and this conviction has remained with me always.

I arrived in London with Diaghilev's troup. Rehearsing, sight-seeing, wandering about the town, I was convinced that to do justice to its riches would take no less than three years. I was greatly impressed with the British Museum. This sublime temple housed amazing treasures of world culture. London itself, from the docks to Westminster Abbey, shattered me by its grandeur. I was equally shattered by the composure and confidence of its people, their faith in their own abilities. And watching them, I was again disturbed. Would such people understand and appreciate the quality of our music? I was very soon to learn.

When, after the first scene from *Boris Godunov*, there came deafening applause, and ecstatic shouts of "Bravo" from the audience, I was beside myself with happiness. The last act of that opera was for me the supreme triumph of Russian art. In expressing their delight the English behaved every bit as expansively as the Italians; hanging over the sides of their boxes, quite perilously, they shouted equally loudly, and their intelligent, all-seeing eyes seemed to me sparkling with enthusiasm.

But more triumphant still was our final performance. The audience, as one man, applauded and thanked everyone, beginning with the sponsor of that Russian season, Sir Joseph Beecham, and his son, a superb musician and conductor. They called for the artists, the conductor, producer, chorus, all in turn. Somebody in the audience made a wonderful speech, and my colleagues asked me to reply. I thanked London for its most marvellous reception. All this was wonderful, quite unforgettable, it was so sincere, and it put paid once and for all to that nonsense about the cold-bloodedness of the British people. I can still look back with delight upon that ecstatic audience.

After this I became the favourite with the London public, and I am proud to say was equally well received both by the charming society ladies and the simple working people. I have had occasions to visit the drawing-room of the Prime Minister, the homes of orchestral musicians. I have drunk champagne in embassies and stout with the stage carpenters.

Believe me when I say this, it is not to boost Chaliapin, who from a cobbler's workshop in Kazan, climbed into the aristocratic drawing-rooms of London. That is not the point, and it never was. The fact is that I am a man from an oppressed and tormented country—a country which, in spite of its unbearably hard life, has created a great art, needed by all, and comprehensible to the world. I cannot adequately express what I feel, except that it is something good, and I am talking not about Chaliapin the singer, but about the Russian people whom I love. True, there is much bitterness in this love. Like everything in the world, love can be unjust, and no one needs it more than we Russians.

My life has not been without its embarrassing experiences, and naturally they had to come my way in London. I used to receive many letters, but not understanding English, I, of course, never read them. Once, however, I happened to pull out from under a chest of drawers a letter written on beautiful notepaper, and I handed it over to a man who knew English. It turned out to be from the Prime Minister's wife (Mrs. Asquith) asking me to lunch. Unfortunately, I had missed this invitation by five days! What then was I to do? Politeness decreed that I should apologize. I asked various ladies, friends of Mrs. Asquith, for help. In all difficulties women are the best help. They so managed to arrange things for me that my negligence was forgiven, and I was invited to lunch after all.

I had received so much hospitality that I felt I had to give a dinner. Having consulted some English friends about this, and been promised their help, I booked the whole floor of a restaurant and a venerable lady took upon herself the responsibility of the dinner arrangements, whilst I did the other half, arranging the music, dancing, and general entertainment.

The dinner date arrived, and so did the guests. The meal itself opened rather solemnly, and decorously. Among my guests were many members of the English aristocracy, foreign diplomats, etc. The toasts to art were many. In my capacity as host I, too, had to make a speech, and was continually pressed to do so by my lady organizer. This was a dreadful ordeal. In the voice of one already condemned to twenty years' hard labour, I began a speech in which I said that art was wonderful, England was wonderful, everything was wonderful, but especially the women, without whom there would be no art, and no life. In brief, of what use the sun, stars, earth, without a beloved woman. Such were my sentiments, and my guests agreed with me wholeheartedly.

The dinner over, Chuprynnikov's Quartet sang, and my friend, Artur Rubinstein, played. The quartet especially appealed to the guests. A young English girl from a very aristocratic family danced a Russian dance. I found it all perfectly charming. Here splendidly and simply displayed was a truly civilized people.

I carried the spell of London with me when I left. I had met some extraordinary people, and I was left with the impression that these island people, for all their businesslike seriousness and great respect for work, had yet a sunnier side to their nature—a charm, even a childlike gaiety.

Within a year I was back again in this great city. We now extended our repertoire, Diaghilev adding *Khovanshchina* and *Prince Igor*, in which works I played the roles of Konchak and Prince Vladimir Galitsky. Now the King himself became interested in our work, and he applauded as warmly as anybody after a production of *Boris Godunov*. I remember, after the hallucination scene, I was told that His Majesty wished to see me. So, in full costume and make-up, I had to go through the auditorium to the Royal Box. The people rose in their seats to stare at Czar Boris, all fresh from his bouts of madness.

When I entered the box the King rose to receive me, saying not a word, and I found these seconds of silence most disconcerting. Then it suddenly occurred to me that His Majesty might be shy, and I, although etiquette precludes this, decided to speak to the King. I told him how inexpressibly happy I was to play in the presence of the King of such magnificent people as the English. He expressed his pleasure at this wonderful opera, and commented on the simplicity with which I played my part. Smiling goodnaturedly, he said he hoped it was not the last season of Russian opera in London. Later I heard that the King had been delighted by the performance and had asked for his thanks to be conveyed to the whole company.

Looking back, I can remember a slight hitch arising just before that memorable production. The King was unable to be present at the theatre on the appointed day, and the English impresario had asked the company to remain in London for an extra day. The artists agreed willingly enough, but the chorus did not, requesting from the impresario a further ten pounds each for the performance. Considering we were carrying a chorus of seventy, no wonder the impresario was upset.

Prior to this I myself had been involved in an incident that was rather shocking. For some reason the whole troup appeared to be jumpy, and uncertain about some arrangement with Diaghilev. This had begun on our way from Russia to Paris. The chorus maintained that they were being underpaid, and this unhappy atmosphere became even more heightened in London, with the result that the relations between them and the management went from bad to worse.

One evening, during a performance of *Boris Godunov*, I heard the orchestra playing "Glory to the Czar" before the appearance of Boris on stage, but the chorus remained silent. I peered out from the wings. The supers were all in their places, but there was no sign of the chorus. I'm quite unable to describe my reactions to this. It seemed fairly obvious to me that the performance was being sabotaged, and the situation was deplorable. Here we were, abroad, in a country whose people were taking us seriously, and extending to us the greatest kindness, whilst we for our part were carrying out a cultural task, the presentation of Russian art to London. I was in a quandary, I just did not know what to do. And I had to go on stage. The orchestra continued to play. I came out alone, I sang my phrases, crossed to the other side of the stage, and asked in a whisper:

"What is the matter? Where is the chorus?"

"I don't know. Something disgraceful is going on. The chorus is paying Diaghilev back, but for what I don't know."

I was furious. I considered it intolerable to start dragging out personal grudges before the audience. Cursing the chorus and everyone on stage, I went back to my dressing-room. I was followed immediately by one of the artists, who declared that the chorus considered Diaghilev and myself to be the chief conspirators, and the chief cause of their discontent. In fact he had just heard one of the chorus singers calling me various names. This enraged me, and hardly realizing what I was doing, without even delving into the cause of the commotion, and obsessed by a single conviction—that the performance was being killed stone dead—I rushed backstage, found the man who had been cursing me, and demanded an explanation. This gentleman folded his arms on his chest, and said with perfect composure: "And I shall continue to call you names."

I hit him. Upon which, the whole chorus, armed with the staves they used in the performance, rushed at me. The battle was on.

I am quite certain that, but for the actresses who rushed to my aid, I might well have been maimed. Backing away from the attackers, I pressed against a pile of boxes. They started swaying, and I jumped quickly to one side, and saw to my horror a pit many feet deep. These demented people came on, crying out, "Kill him. For God's sake, kill him."

Somehow, and thanks to the protection of the English stage hands, I managed to get back to my room. One of these men, through an interpreter, told me not to worry and to continue the performance, and that he was authorized to tell me that the stage hands would beat up this chorus if there was any more interference. So I decided to continue. I am not so spoiled by life as to be put off by such things. I had had all this before; it was nothing new. I had been beaten, and I had beaten others. Obviously Russians cannot live without a fight.

However, the performance ended well, and the chorus achieved its aim. Fortunately the audience had noticed nothing of this ugly scene, since it took place during an interval when the curtain was down.

When the opera ended, I was told that the man I had hit had been unconscious for some minutes, but he came round. I went to his room, and found several members of the chorus there. I said how sorry I was, and asked him to forgive me. He, too, repented of his violent temper. We all wept and embraced, then went off to a restaurant to dine, trampling the incident into oblivion in the approved Sukonnaya Sloboda style. We carry Sukonnaya Sloboda with us wherever we go.

In some way the English people did hear of this scandal, yet so far as I know the English press did not devote a single line to it. For them, it was just "our affair", and not for public discussion. Telegrams, however, had already been sent to Russia, describing "the Chaliapin scandal". I had to read many Russian newspapers both reproaching and moralizing about me. The general tone was, "We send a Russian representative to Europe, and just look at what he does."

A plague on all gentleman moralizers. If only you could live inside my skin, carry it about for one whole year. The surroundings in which you live have nothing in common with mine, but I suppose if a man is set on the propagation of morality, then it seems best to let him have his head. Otherwise it's a case of still more fault finding, and, perhaps later, something quite vicious.

Upon my return to Russia, Diaghilev never even bothered to acquaint the public with the precise cause of the English incident, nor indeed my part in it. In Russia we are not particular about slander, even though it may be directed against a friend.

When I next returned to London it was for a rehearsal with an orchestra. When I went on stage and approached the footlights, the conductor introduced me to the musicians. I was greeted with applause. As in all theatres the musicians here worked a certain number of hours daily. We happened to be rehearsing *The Maid of Pskov*. Something went wrong—either the *décor* hadn't arrived or someone was having an argument—but the rehearsal became prolonged. It was now four o'clock in the afternoon, and time for the orchestra to leave. Cooper, the conductor, turned to me and said that he was letting the musicians go, and suggested that I sing the opera without a rehearsal. I was not put out, since I already knew the work, and was actually rehearsing for the benefit of others.

55. *Chaliapin as Boris Godunov (Bolshoy Theatre, Moscow), 1913.*

54. *Chaliapin as Boris Godunov (Bolshoy Theatre, Moscow), 1911.*

56. Chaliapin as Boris Godunov (Drury Lane Theatre, London), 1913.

As we were speaking Russian nobody in the orchestra understood a word we were saying, but they were watching us. At the moment of dismissal one of them, a venerable, grey-haired violinist, rose to his feet and spoke to Mr. Cooper. They had guessed what the trouble was, and now suggested that Mr. Chaliapin carry on with the rehearsal. I thought this most touching. At home, we Russians are not used to such consideration, nor indeed to a devotion to one's work, and the understanding of its importance.

This warm, modest people grew closer to my heart. With some of them I became very friendly, and in my free moments would ask them home to tea, and once one of them invited me to his own home. Cooper and I went together. The musician lived in a modest little street, in a cosy house. It was poor, but it was also warm, comfortable, and pleasant. A few other musicians followed us, and there they played for me Tchaikovsky's Quartette, and something of Borodin's. They played well, and with real feeling. I remember we drank tea, and ate sandwiches, smoked and talked in an atmosphere of equals.

On leaving that nice house where I had heard such fine execution of my countrymen's music, I could not help but recall another evening in Moscow. Artists and musicians had gathered in a restaurant to do honour to César Cui. We were seated at dinner, and everything was going along fine, until near the end, when some who had had more to drink than was wise, and drawing inspiration from their befuddled state, began speechifying. In reply to a toast proposed in my honour, one of the musicians suddenly said:

"Of course, Chaliapin is a celebrity. People are always drinking his health, and he himself, most of all. But we have gathered here today not to fête such a bogus personality as Chaliapin. If we drink at all, it shall be to the health of César Cui. And all the time. I have finished."

"Better if he'd never even begun," I thought to myself.

This created a very unpleasant atmosphere, and had I not taken control of myself, the consequences might have been even worse. Such is my misfortune. It has always been like that. Whenever I was in any gathering, whether it was painters, or writers, or musicians, the reunion invariably ended with some totally unexpected insults, and ridiculous incidents. Is it my fault? Perhaps it is, but it was not always so. The envy which I arouse in people is the real culprit more often than not. Now I try to avoid these so-called "friendly gatherings", since I see no reason on earth why I should too often have the epithet "conceited" hurled at me. No, I had not become conceited, but it so happens that in my country we often have to defend our dignity by ways and means, which, in any other country, would seem unthinkable. No one, of course, thinks or knows that I, loving company and people, suffer much from having to miss such evenings, that under normal healthy conditions could be gayer and more agreeable.

During my second stay in London I was again invited out to dinners and lunches, and once more decided to organize a "five o'clock tea" for my English friends. I remember inviting some of the chorus, the 'cellist, and the accompanist, Pokhitonov. They helped to make it quite an elegant and pleasant evening. There were artists, journalists, writers, one of the Dukes, with his wife, our own Ambassador, Mrs. Asquith, the Duchess of Rutland, Lady Grey, Mrs. Walker, and Rosa Newmarsh.

The choir was magnificent. They knew what they were presenting, they lived their Russian folk songs, and the canticles they sang most beautifully. This church music appealed greatly to our English guests, and was warmly received.

I also sang, both solo and with the choir. At first we did some melancholy airs, but later, having got into our stride, we sang some gay songs, and it changed the whole tone of the evening, the mood lightened, and everybody became more relaxed, simpler.

My English guests were lavish in their thanks, and the next day followed it up with many charming letters. I remember the director of the London Conservatoire writing ecstatically, saying that in many years of experiencing such things, he could not recall one as memorable as that of the previous evening. I have a great collection of such letters, many of them from the most illustrious people in the world, and for me they add up to a sincere salute to Russian art.

One day as I was walking down the street, I suddenly heard music. An orchestra was playing the Marseillaise. A great crowd of women wearing rosettes, and carrying baskets of flowers, were marching along. The procession was flanked by policemen, some smoking pipes, and looking comically dignified. From time to time one of the women would cry out, and the whole company then chorused, quite drowning the music. Above the heads of the crowd waved flags and banners. Everything was colourful and bright. At the head of the procession was a pretty girl beating a drum. I was transfixed by this sight, my mouth open wide. The girl with the drum suddenly rushed up to me, pretending at first to push the drum-stick into my mouth, began laughing, and then planted a flower in my buttonhole. She did it quickly, lightly, and charmingly. It was a procession of suffragettes.

At night, when the city lay bare, the rich people hid in their houses, and London streets, like the streets of cities the world over, showed up a strange sad solitude, a human grief. Here were the silent, hollow-cheeked women with babies in arms, and a shilling put into the hand of one of them was immediately carried to the nearest pub. There are many alcoholics in London. Quite invisible in daylight, they stick out like rotten stumps the moment darkness falls.

How different from the great British Museum, my visit to which I have never forgotten. I think of it in terms of a simple, wise and good book about the world's culture.

England did something for me, for I left London feeling not only stronger, but younger.

15

In Monte Carlo one afternoon Raoul Ginsburg informed us that we had been invited to give some performances in Berlin, and that I would have to sing *Mefistofele*, *Don Carlos* and *The Barber of Seville*.

In a good mood one can play even in hell. I had never sung in Germany, and was looking forward to my visit with avid curiosity. We travelled in a train reserved specially for us by Raoul. We might well have dispensed with this luxury, but then Ginsburg always had a tendency towards Muscovite lavishness, from which I, not without pride, recognized some aspects of Russian culture in this very international gentleman. The journey was interesting, and very well organized. We stopped at stations to discover that lunches and dinners were laid on, ordered in advance by telegram. Often the people from the near-by villages came in to watch us eat, drink, sing, and even dance. During the journey, and in each carriage, "branch offices" of the Monte Carlo Casino were formed, and we all played cards, particularly a game called "Noses", in which the loser was struck on the nose with as many cards as he had lost. Highly educational.

Germany, begging your pardon, is also an interesting and cultured country, though one soon senses a certain woodiness, a heaviness of expression that I never noticed either in England or France. Perhaps it was a too-conscious seriousness. I found the laconic sign "Verboten" too often repeated like another one as commonly seen, the word "Abort", often in lettering a foot high. I knew that "Verboten" meant "forbidden", but "Abort" having but a single connotation for me, had me flummoxed. Could it possibly mean *that* . . . in such a well organized state?

From my very first day in this country, and unlike neighbouring countries, I could see that the conception of freedom was purely a philosophical one, entirely subservient to their conception of order. I was informed by a rather droll fellow that in Germany people had the right to be born only on October 13th, and to die on dates set in advance by the government. This is not true. The Germans, like people everywhere, die at any old time.

In Berlin, where we began rehearsals almost at once, I was to discover the word "Verboten" rearing its head in a very determined manner. We were rehearsing *Mefistofele*. As usual I was in a state of nervous excitement, and just before the performance lit a cigarette in my dressing-room. Immediately, I was confronted by a huge, stony fireman, who came up and announced: "Verboten."

With my finger pointing to head, heart, and other parts of my anatomy, I tried to convince him that it was essential for me to smoke. He didn't believe me but insisted on making a long speech, and I could only understand the one word, "Strafe," fine, or penalty.

"All right. Let's have the strafe then. But I'll smoke all the same."

He went off in a huff, and I thought I would be arrested. Fortunately the impresario appeared, and I begged him to get me permission to smoke. The almighty Ginsburg somehow managed to arrange it. But my stony fireman put in another appearance, this time armed with two buckets of water, which he placed one on either side of me, probably in case I set fire to myself. He explained that water has the property of extinguishing fire, to which I replied, "Jawohl." This seemed to pacify him, and he left my room, though he remained on sentry outside the door throughout the performance. I longed for him to go into action, but lacked sufficient knowledge of the language to bring this desire fully home.

Our production went down well with the public, and even the Kaiser liked it. *Mefistofele* amazed the German dramatic artists, with the exception of Barnay, whom I had known as the producer at the Royal Dramatic Theatre. Many of them visited me in the dressing-room, and were always surprised that I acted opera as a drama. I had a number of what I might call heavyweight compliments paid me. As for the Emperor himself, he was present at every performance, his uninhibited guffaws of laughter reverberated through the theatre. He would hang over the barrier of the Royal Box and behave like any good-humoured German. On the last evening we presented extracts from various operas. I sang in *The Barber of Seville*, and during the interval the Kaiser invited the French artist, Renaud, who had also sung Mefistofele, the conductor Cooper, the producer, and myself into his box. When we arrived there, I saw Wilhelm standing with his weight on the right foot, and his hand on the pommel of his sword, the habitual stance. He was no longer young, and there were deep lines beneath his dashingly twirled moustaches. His hair was grey. The piercing, greyish-blue eyes, and his whole figure suggested energy and determination.

"You are a Russian artist?" he asked, in French.

"Yes. I am an artist of the Imperial Theatre."

"I am delighted to see you here, and admire your original talent. I would like to present you with something as a souvenir of our country and our theatre. Do you sing Wagner?"

"Only at recitals. I have not tried any of his operas."

"What does your country think of this composer?"

I told him that he was revered and admired.

From a tall man wearing a frock-coat, who stood behind him, he now took a case, and from it the Gold Cross of the Prussian Eagle. He wished to pin it on my chest, but unfortunately nobody present had a pin, although there were ladies in his party, including the Empress. He smiled, and handed me the Order.

I felt awkward standing in front of him in the costume of Don Basilio, with my grotesque nose and terrifying face, wearing the grease-spotted cassock of a Catholic priest. The dignified tone did not go well with my face and figure. I realized this as I watched him and his party smile, and was considerably relieved when the audience was over. Renaud, Cooper, and the producer also received Orders, and were very flattered. We decided to celebrate the occasion, and a big crowd of us set off for the Hotel Bristol, where I was staying. The waiters there, who until that moment had scarcely noticed us, now started bowing and scraping, eyeing with some awe the Orders we were wearing. The maître d'hôtel came up to inform us that his cellars contained excellent wines only served for rare occasions, and this was one. The usual thing followed, much drinking, silly speeches, and everybody being congratulated on reaching the heights of the Prussian nobility. It was all so funny that even some of the Germans laughed. I only regretted that on that night there were no respectable Russian citizens in the restaurant, known world-wide for their aversion to alcohol. A pity, they would have had another proof of my being a confirmed alcoholic. For like my friends on that night I did not restrain myself from the consumption of such splendid wines.

The restaurant was almost empty, the lights half-extinguished, when we decided to retire to bed. I remember the wine had seriously affected my legs, and I had to take careful aim when going through the doors. But my brain was clear and I remember my watch saying it was 4 a.m. Unfortunately, I had forgotten the number of my room. I daren't go downstairs to ask the porter, since this would only mean having to climb up again. Then I saw a door, and it certainly looked like the door of my room. I opened it and entered. It was quite dark, and suddenly an unseen man began speaking in coarse German. This puzzled me, and I enquired what he was doing there.

I hastened to explain to him that I was about to go to bed, and that there was nothing I required. The light was switched on, and from a wide bed I beheld a balding man, whose remaining hair curled about his temples. Stamping his bare feet, this gentleman, improperly dressed, and his face swollen with sleep, began yelling at me and clenching his fists, until he saw the Order, noble on my breast. He calmed down, and explained that it was not my room. I had made the mistake.

"Not my room?" I said. "In that case, goodbye."

Supporting my elbow, he led me out and deposited me in a long corridor that was swimming in doors, each one looking like its neighbour, and all of them looking like the door of my own room. I was quite bewildered, and suddenly realized that I would never find mine. I gave it up, walked as far as the staircase, sat down on the steps and fell peacefully asleep as any well-brought-up gentleman should. But I was soon awakened by men in green aprons, and armed with diabolical-looking machines. I asked them to leave me in peace. They couldn't understand me, and like everybody else in that hotel, stared amazedly at the Order on my coat. It was only then that I remembered losing my way. Collecting together all the German words I knew I said, "Nommer Mein Zimmer—— Phew! Forgot. You understand?

Zimmermann. Zalz—— Not restaurant, room—understand? Green devils, do you understand?"

They did, and they found my room. Installed, I slept the whole day through. Thus the effect of Orders and decorations.

Whilst on this subject I might mention that France awarded me the Legion d'Honneur, the Emir of Bokhara a Star, and the Russian Government the Order of St. Stanislaus of the fourteenth or sixteenth degree, normally given to the Ministry errand boys and, I think, night watchmen with more than twenty-five years of unblemished service to their credit.

Of course, and everybody knows it, I almost fell over myself in my zealous attempts to get Orders and decorations, but I never wear them since I consider I haven't got enough. Indeed, I wore them only once, and that was in Moscow, back in 1905, during the troubled days "before the constitution". Then, I was living in a dark and dreary Zachatyevsky Pereulok. The electricity didn't work, there was no water, there was nothing at all in fact, since we were in the middle of a general strike. The rumours were persistent that the Black Hundred would soon start exterminating decent people. I was very miserable, and remained at home in complete solitude, wearing a dressing-gown and slippers. I remember that to amuse myself I stuck on my dressing-gown all the Orders and medals I had so far received, wore my sash, hung a watch about my neck, and pinning other remaining gifts on the gown, paraded my room, singing the recruits' song, "The last Day of Freedom."

It was then that a painter friend, alarmed at the events, came to see me. I was delighted, rushed to greet him, forgetting my absurd get-up, and only his consternation brought me back to earth.

"What on earth's all this?" he asked.

I explained to him that I was privately celebrating the last days of bureaucracy, and resumed my song. The painter was highly offended.

"God only knows what's going on around us," he said. "They're putting special marks on all the houses, crosses, there's a charcoal cross on your own door, and there you stand, clowning. You can't play about with such things. If anybody, God forbid, sees you dressed up like that, they'll shoot you. And they'll be right."

He turned on his heel and vanished, leaving me to my solitude and boredom. Just that once in my lifetime did I make use of Orders and decorations that brought me neither pleasure nor profit. When I come to make my will, I shall stipulate that, when my death-throes begin, I shall want people from the funeral parlour to arrive wearing top hats, place upon cushions my Orders and medals, and carry them ceremoniously to the cemetery, where at the edge of the grave they are to wait for me for four days and nights, totally disregarding the weather. Such is my will and testament. Won't that be a beautiful piece of self-advertisement?

When I arrived in Kharkov in 1904, a workers' deputation turned up with a request that I might sing something for them at the "Workers' House", which they had created with their own means. Immediately I agreed, and indeed with gladness—for I had long wanted to sing to ordinary simple people, the people from whom I came. But this desire, so hard to realize in our way of life, came and went in the hurly-burly of living. Now, I had no time for the workers' concert, as I was due to sing opera that evening, and on the following morning was leaving for Kiev. It was therefore decided to hold the workers' concert in the daytime. It happened to be a holiday, it was autumn, and it got dark rather early. The hall of this "Workers' House" was not very big, and there were tens of thousands of workers. The vast majority would never get into the hall. Consequently those who had to remain out in the street cut the electric wires, as if to say, "If we can't see him, then you shan't either." But the public gathered nevertheless, and found a way out of the difficulty by producing candles from heaven knows where. It created a curious effect. It felt more like a religious service in a dark cave than a concert.

Each time I came out on stage I was flanked by two workers, each holding two candles, providing direct lighting for me. Another group similarly obliged for the accompanist. I didn't see the audience at all, but a kind of Egyptian darkness spread out before me, and in this darkness I felt something alive, huge, unbreathing, attentive, frightening, yet enormously exciting. Never did I have a more responsive and attentive audience than those workers. At first there had been terrible noise, laughter and shouts, and it seemed no power on earth would quench it. Yet they had their own discipline, and soon exacted it, something that might be envied by the more conventional concert-going public. It was enough for me to appear on that stage surrounded by candles, and the entire hall was still, with a silence that in the darkness almost suggested the hall was empty. It was this that induced in me the feeling of fright, of awe.

Before this black and silent void I sang song after song, between which I would say a few words about the composers, explaining to them what it was meant to express in music. And following each rendering came the cry, "More. More. More, Feodor Ivanovich."

It was inspiring. I had begun singing at four in the afternoon, and without noticing the time, or even feeling tired, went on singing until the impresario was suddenly on stage beside me, pleading with me to hurry to the theatre where another kind of public was waiting and clamouring for my appearance. I hated leaving that hall, the wonderful atmosphere, and splendid audience, but the concert had to end. Before I left, I asked the workers to join in with me. First we sang "Down the Volga", but somehow it didn't fit in with the mood, and I then suggested "Dubinushka", which they did with enormous enthusiasm. Meanwhile, the candles had burned down, and though we were virtually in darkness I continued to conduct with one hand. I remember feeling the impresario's tug at the tails of my coat. I had to end it, but with curiously mixed feelings. I felt happiness within me, and yet I also felt an emptiness. The workers raised me up and carried me into the street.

"Thank you," they shouted, and I replied, "Thank you, dear comrades."
Everyone present rejoiced, all but one person, and he sat somewhere back-

stage, trembling. This man was Isai Dvorishchin. I had known him a long time. As I travelled through towns, I often noticed this quick-witted and jolly youth of eighteen among the choristers. At rehearsals and during performances this inexhaustibly volatile little figure was always able to amuse both artists and public, always ready with something funny whenever artist or audience needed cheering up. He was incredibly sensitive to atmosphere, and being a comedian by nature, introduced his wit and humour into an occasion with the greatest of ease. I thought him talented, and was often delighted by his quips. I felt a warm sympathy for him, and we became great friends.

Isai was a Jew, much frightened by life, for more than once he had suffered cruel jokes, though I must say it had neither destroyed his own sense of dignity, nor his sensitivity to everything that was beautiful. Whenever I had cause for doubt over the interpretation of some role or other, I often turned to him for his apt comment. He was perhaps a little fond of wearing the jester's coat, but actually it was his armour and self-preservation against the hard knocks that life dealt out to him. Few could have guessed that under that coat there existed a pure soul, and the sharp mind of one who had suffered much. He knew the value of life and people.

I recall that the act he most successfully put on was one that manifested the fear of authority, beginning with the most ordinary of policemen, and progressing upwards to the mighty, of limitless power. He did this superbly, and gave the impression that he really was panic-stricken in the face of authority. This fear is no stranger in Russia, and for the Jews it is a compulsory one. So this same Isai, immediately we had finished singing "Dubinushka", began pleading with me.

"Feodor Ivanovich," he said, "please, for God's sake, leave this place."

"Why?"

"Why? Don't you know that the authorities might send cannons here and shoot everybody. You, the public, me."

"But what for?"

"What was the song you were singing, eh?"

"You're talking nonsense," I said.

"Nonsense. If the authorities take it into their heads to take exception to 'Isaiah, Rejoice', then they'll shoot you for 'Isaiah, Rejoice'. Do you understand me?"

But there were no cannons, and everything passed off safely.

"Until the next time," Isai predicted gloomily.

The rumours of this concert for the Kharkov workers had immediately spread to Kiev, and when I arrived there, I was met by a workers' deputation asking me to arrange a concert for them. I knew by chance that the Kiev Circus was free, and that it would hold some four thousand or more people. Having talked it over with the workers, I went to the authorities to ask for permission to hold a concert in the Circus.

At that time the Governor-General of Kiev was Sukhomlinov, whom I had met more than once at Dragomirov's, a man of great wit and overwhelming generosity. Sukhomlinov appeared to me to be a very modest person. He kept his distance, and was not talkative. But for some reason I did not dare to go direct to him, but instead saw Savich, the Governor. Having heard my request, Savich replied with emphasis: "Impossible."

I did my very best to persuade him, pointing out how very seldom I had the opportunity to sing to ordinary people, and how vital it was that they should make some acquaintance with art. In reply to my pleading Savich conducted me to his study, where he showed me a curious document, a report from the Security Department, marked "Secret".

The document stated that, according to the available evidence before the Security Department, Chaliapin gave concerts in aid of revolutionary organizations, and that such activity must be discouraged at all costs.

This was absurd, besides there wasn't a grain of truth in it. I am by nature a democrat, I love my people, and I fully understand their need for political freedom. I can see how much they are oppressed economically, but I have never engaged in the activities which the Secret Police attributed to me. Savich evidently believed in my sincerity and gave his permission for the concert to be held, on condition that I gave him my word of honour that it would not be turned into a political demonstration. I gave him that assurance, and offered to chop off my hands, feet, and even head if anything untoward occurred at this concert. I was certain, too, that the workers were more intelligent and better disciplined than the Administration gave them credit for. These were not hooligans or the scum of the street. I said I would be personally responsible for maintaining order, but only on condition that there were no police present. This, however, was not agreed to for some time, but at long last I got the permission, and joyfully communicated it to the workers, who were waiting for me at my hotel.

On the eve of the concert the workers invited me to their village, and here once again I was looking upon the forgotten life of Sukonnaya Sloboda—the self-same hovels, the same dire poverty, the same cockroach-infested and bug-ridden atmosphere. The only difference was that this time there were no drunkards, and nobody swore. The people, it seemed, were in a festive mood. Their clothes were clean, they smiled pleasantly, and looked at me with affection, as though I were an old friend. They kept inviting me into their huts, and whenever I did go in, I would be treated to tea and wine. It was all so homely, so simple.

The time of the concert was approaching, and I must confess I was still apprehensive lest at the very last moment the police should forbid the performance. It was here that my friend Isai came to my help. He rushed around, visiting the police-stations, telling the police anecdotes about me, giving impersonations of me. He could tell stories about me in a very funny manner. All this rushing around the police stations of Kiev was a great help to us. Nevertheless, on the very day of the concert, when I was sitting in my bath, Isai burst in, and in an alarming whisper announced: "The police inspector's coming."

"What on earth for?"

At this moment I heard the well-known and dread sound, the jingling of spurs. Somebody had entered the next room. Isai then explained:

"I'm sorry. I invited him myself. He's a nice man, and we ought to give him a little hospitality and be kind to him. He is really very nice, though, who knows, he may do us some harm."

Putting on the air of an utter débauché, I asked the inspector into the bathroom, apologized for appearing naked before him, and invited him to join me in a little refreshment, explaining to him that one of the greatest pleasures of my life was drinking vodka in the bath. So Zakuska[1] was hastily organized, and served on the bathroom stool. The inspector sat on another stool, and sipping our drinks, we discoursed upon the vagaries of life in general, and the policeman's lot in particular. I found it disgusting, though pretended that it was a perfectly natural and agreeable occupation for me, whilst the inspector, calling me the "Russian Minstrel", tried to prove to me that the policeman's lot was not an easy one. He was not only not offended, but kept on repeating delightedly, "This is devilish original. I've been around, and to many kinds of receptions, but this is the very first time I have drunk vodka with my host sitting in his bath. What a pity the tub is so small, otherwise I should have climbed in. We could sit facing each other, a bottle in each hand. Wouldn't that be fine?"

Isai was delighted with this idea, sympathized with the uneasy lot of policemen, and kept on making the point that, whatever else, our concert could not possibly give the police the least anxiety.

"Chaliapin won't let you down. Don't worry."

The inspector then left. We parted friends, and I had no wish to let anybody down, the police or anybody else. Unfortunately we forgot to take into consideration one very important factor. There were tens of thousands of workers in Kiev, and the Circus at most could hold but six to seven thousand.

From four o'clock in the morning, on the day of that concert, there were great movements of people in the streets of Kiev. The trams stopped running because a vast crowd had filled the main street, and in front of the Circus incredible scenes were taking place. The place was alive with people, pressed together like caviare. The earth itself hummed. Isai came running in, and having described all this to me, also reported that with his own ears he had heard a man selling postcards outside the Circus, and saying to somebody who wanted to buy my picture: "If you ask me once more for a picture of this Yid, Chaliapin, there'll be damn all left of your mug."

"Feodor Ivanovich," exclaimed little Isai. "People are saying that you are a Jew. I swear. And I swear they will beat you up. Let's run away now, and to hell with the concert."

"Stop talking nonsense, Isai," I said.

"Please. Let's run away. They say the troops have been called out."

Past the windows of my hotel I saw an infantry detachment file by,

[1] Hors-d'oeuvre.

followed shortly afterwards by a detachment of cavalry, dispersing the people. I was now certain that the concert would be banned, and my one hope was that the police would not be able to fight their way through the vast crowd before the concert started.

As for us, the participants in the concert, we found ourselves in the curious position of being unable to get into the Circus. However much Isai pleaded with the crowd to let me pass, with the best will in the world it simply could not do so. The crowd swallowed up Isai, and for some time I heard his voice crying out: "Stop! Let me through. I am taking part in this concert, devils——."

Since it was quite impossible to enter the Circus in the normal way, I suggested that we climb out of the hotel window on to the roof of the Circus, which of course my courageous colleagues, violinist Averino, and pianist Koreshchenko, did. We got out, crawled along the cornice to the guttering, slid down the pipe and lowered ourselves to the roof of the circus. To me this presented no difficulties, having been used to this sort of escapade from childhood, but podgy little Averino, and delicate Koreshchenko, as spoilt as a Turkish Pasha, found it very difficult indeed. Looked at from the outside this must have appeared a very comical episode, but we ourselves were not laughing. Helping my friends, I somehow managed to lead them across the roof to the stable window, lowered them through it, until we finally found ourselves in the arena, at the bottom of an enormous bowl, the sides of which were literally encrusted with thousands of people making the most incredible noise. We were greeted with a deafening Hurrah!

A man who had had too much to drink climbed into the arena and, waving his arms about, informed me that there were no bourgeois people there. He was immediately removed by the workers, and the concert opened.

Without boasting, I can say that I never sang better than I did that night. I was uplifted, exalted. After each song the applause was like thunder, which made the Circus itself shake, and seemed indeed to split the air. I sang much, not wishing to stop, though it was nearing midnight. The audience then demanded that I should sing "Dubinushka". I said that I would if they all joined in.

"All right. Begin," replied hundreds of voices.

I have sung that many times, with big choirs, and magnificent orchestras, but never have I heard such singing as on that night, when a choir some six thousand strong roared out: "Hey Dubinushka. . . ."

And not only we, the concert party and workers, were swept away on a wave of emotion; even policemen, disguised as civilians, sang with tears in their eyes.

I knew of their presence of course, and of members of the Secret Police, for the workers themselves had quickly recognized these disguised guardians of law and order. The concert ended wonderfully. The workers dispersed in complete order, and Kiev remained standing. Russia had suffered no harm, and I had lived through one of the best days of my life.

I wanted very much to give one or two annual concerts for the workers, but I must say that these were projects fraught with the greatest difficulties, apart from involving enormous effort.

During the Lent of 1915 I wanted to give a concert for the workers in the Petrograd People's Home. I thought it necessary. The year was a hard one, the mood of the people was one of despondency, and I desired to bring some brightness into the dark and difficult life of the working people. My friends helped me distribute the tickets for this concert, in factories and foundries, and various other plants. Everything was going along smoothly, till just a day or two before the concert we met with disaster. One of the workshops in a gunpowder factory had blown up, and there were many casualties. The official communiqué concerning it was of course delayed, and this only intensified the feeling of anxiety. The administration of the Home then announced that the time was inappropriate for holding such a concert. I, on the other hand, considering that this grievous accident, itself only a kind of herald of another disaster relentlessly approaching us, was determined that the concert should go on since I felt the dark days should be lightened, and I carried on.

On the evening of the event I received a telephone call from the Governor, who suggested that the concert be cancelled, since, according to information supplied him, somebody was planning a disturbance at it. He repeated his conviction that the concert would be sabotaged, and that I myself would be accused of being the instigator. In discussing the matter, he began talking about the disaster at the gunpowder factory and said that the concert would be bound to have a bad impression on the workers. He concluded by saying it would be banned and two hours later sent me an official notice to that effect, but the very wording of it suggested that it was not being banned by the Administration at all, but cancelled by me.

This conversation took place at two o'clock in the morning, the newspapers were going to press, and the notice of cancellation had to go to them immediately. We were all very upset by this, especially Isai. He said: "Feodor Ivanovich, when you die the government will thank you from the bottom of its heart."

I then repeatedly informed the Governor that I was in disagreement with his conclusions, and that if he was not going to take upon himself the initiative for this, I was in no way willing to cancel it. We ended on that note. It was now 6 a.m. and the concert was due to start at two in the afternoon.

Nerve-racked by this, and by a sleepless night, I was convinced that my first appearance before the workers would not come off in the way I wished. Yet everything went off not only smoothly, but splendidly. Before the concert I could see that all my friends, particularly Isai, were endeavouring to look brave, but these friends, let it be said to their honour, were bad actors, and it was clear to me that they expected something to happen, and were afraid for me. My nerves by this time were almost deadened to all feeling, and I concentrated upon one thing—the successful portrayal of Boris Godunov.

When I came on stage an audience of some four thousand greeted me in stony silence, but after the first scene there was a special short round of applause. It seemed to me then that but one single human being was doing this, yet it was the whole audience as one man, and I sensed this unanimity and discipline.

During the interval I experienced a sudden reaction after twenty-four hours of tension. I just wept. This helped, something broke, and for the rest of the concert I sang more freely, more enthusiastically, and the audience were generous in their approval. When it was over, a happy Isai informed me that the workers wanted me on stage without make-up. I came out and was greeted with great rounds of "Thank-yous".

Leaving the theatre I saw the workers standing in orderly rows, saluting me affectionately. With great consideration and delicacy which touched me, they made way for me to pass to the car. A trifle you may think, but to me it seemed a testimony of their respect for an artist. With the public I usually serve, this respect is not so highly developed. I am looked upon as its property, one who is paid for services rendered.

Though this concert was free, the workers were adamant about paying for the next one, and donating the proceeds to the University fund. This was done. An entrance fee was charged at the second concert, and some 3,000 roubles were raised.

I cannot foresee what the future will bring, but it is my ardent desire to give cheap concerts for the workers, even though this will involve the surmounting of many difficulties, not the least of them being official. Owing to some misunderstanding the authorities are against them. Artists find the idea quite alien and it is not easy for them to take part in such entertainments. The theatre belongs to the theatrical management, and the director who takes on the responsibility is not always willing to give away an evening cheaply. And the arrangement for such a concert requires time and effort. It is most difficult to overcome indifference, and what is even worse, antagonism. Even so, I shall continue to give such concerts. They bring me joy, and are, I hope, not entirely fruitless to the people by whose labour our country lives.

Touring the country I once arrived in Samara, where the public welcomed me most kindly, with a touching warmth and hospitality, whilst I was still on board, in advance, so to speak. On the following morning I went to the cemetery where my mother, who had died from overwork and exhaustion, was buried. She died in the District Hospital, and I wished to know where she was laid to rest, and to see that at least a cross stood above her grave. But no one, not even the cemetery watchman or the local priest, could tell me where the local poor were buried from the hospital during the year she died. Another priest led me into a corner of the cemetery overgrown with weeds, and said, "I think somewhere here."

I took a handful of earth, which I've kept to this day. I had the Requiem sung, mourned and wept for my mother, and in the evening, wearing a frock-coat, triumphantly sang at the concert. I suppose all this is as it should be.

My father survived my mother. In 1896, when I was singing in Nizhni-Novgorod, he came to visit me with my brother, who was then about ten years old. Father was thin, gloomy and silent, and somehow distrustful of anything that had to do with me. I don't believe that he even accepted the existence of the very chair on which I was seated. My salary appeared incredible to him. He didn't believe this either, but I was not long in convincing him that the youth whom he had tried so hard to force into a night watchman's job was really earning fabulous money. He started attending the theatre whenever I appeared, but uttered never a word to me about his impressions. Only having seen me in *Russalka* and *A Life for the Czar*, one day at dinner, he gave me a quizzical look, and said: "Can't make it out. There's gentry and such-like sitting all around, and you are showing them a moujik in bast sandals. Not bad."

On another occasion when he was sitting in the theatre, and the audience was calling for me, he turned to the General sitting next to him, and in his sober and most respectful manner said, "Your Excellency."

The General raised his eyebrows, and looked coldly at his strange neighbour, who was clad in a bottle-green frock-coat, a soft crumpled shirt, and a string necktie. "What is it, my man?"

"Can you hear, your Excellency. They are shouting Chaliapin's name."

"Well, yes, they are indeed calling for him."

"That's my name, too, your Excellency."

"As I understand it, they are not calling for you, but for the artist Chaliapin."

"That's my son."

The General stared in silence, but in the interval he made enquiries, discovered that I was his son, and after that indulged in amicable conversation with my father.

My father did not enjoy staying with me. Once, when drunk, he told me quite frankly that life with me was hellishly dull. He said my singing wasn't bad, and that I portrayed the moujiks fairly well too, but that I lived so uncouthly, with no vodka in the house, no fun of any kind; in brief he considered that my life was not up to much.

Often he asked me for money, and on receiving it, would immediately disappear. He made friends with all the local cobblers and tailors, and spent his time sitting in public-houses with them. From these places he would send off gentlemen, none too steady on their feet, to ask me for money. These visits became far too frequent, and fearing for his health, I refused him money. After this I was told that he had stopped a well-dressed man in the street, and said to him, "Please, kind sir, I am the father of Chaliapin that sings in the theatres. The miser won't give me the price of a drink. Please give Chaliapin's father enough money to buy half a bottle."

I went out into the street and brought him home. When I reproached him for what he was doing, he sulked in silence.

Often I caught him on the streets, drunk, and begging. Always there was trouble when I insisted on taking him home. Once, during the winter, I locked him up in his room, and took away his boots to prevent him going out in my absence. He banged on the door for quite a while, swearing, and begging to be let out, and then grew suddenly silent. I thought he'd fallen asleep, and was appalled when I opened the door to find the room empty. He had got out through the skylight, like an acrobat, and in spite of the snow and the bitter cold, had gone off barefoot to a tavern. All my efforts to make him refrain from drinking, or to drink only at home, were without result. I saw the uselessness of persuasion. When drunk he became gregarious, and had to go to a pub. Finally he said that he could not stand the life of Moscow, he hated the place, and everything in it, and only wanted to get back to the village. I agreed that he would be better off in the country, and, keeping my brother with me, sent father to Vyatka.

Later I heard that, on reaching Kazan, he had spent the whole of his money on drink, sold his clothes, bought a soldier's coat, and then gone on to Vyatka on foot. For some odd reason my father was fond of soldiers' coats. I remember, whilst still a child, this passion for soldiers' coats, and his telling me how he had walked from Vyatka to Kazan wearing one. There was much misery in Russia, and tramping the length and breadth of the land in such a coat aroused the people's sympathy, who knew more about misery than anybody else on earth. That was why, perhaps, the sight of this coat roused generous feelings in the villagers.

On his arrival in the village my father wrote me, saying that he wished to build himself a hut, and would I send him some money. I did so, but the hut was never built, and to the end of his days he lived in a dilapidated little hovel which he rented from one of the villagers. Just before I set off for Milan to sing in Boito's opera for the first time, I received a letter from him in which he said he was very ill, and wished to see me before he died. I at once gathered a few things together and set off by boat from Kazan to Vyatka, and then a hundred versts further on to Medvedki on horseback. I rode over dismal fields, past a sparse forest, and arrived at the tiny village of Syrtsevo, set among bare fields. Meeting a woman, I asked her if she knew where Ivan Chaliapin was living. She replied with the question, "Who might you be?"

"I'm his son."

"Oh, then it's that hut over there."

There was a horrible stench in the hovel. Clouds of flies hummed in the air, cockroaches ran amok, and these the hens chased, in an unsuccessful endeavour to exterminate them. Light scarcely penetrated through the window panes, which were fly-spotted and covered with dirt. In a corner, on a wooden bench, on a dirty heap of rags, lay my father, skeleton-thin, sharp-nosed, with sunken chin, the cheek bones protruding. There was a sluttish-looking woman in the hut, whose pathetic eyes set in a blank and wooden face I well remember. The moment she left the room, father spoke in a whisper, and with great effort.

"She is robbing me, Feodor. While I was well, it was all right, but now things are bad."

I could see how impossible it was to live in such an atmosphere. Even a healthy man would rot there. Immediately I made my way to the village hospital, some eight versts away. I got there just on visiting time. There was a long queue of women with children, old men and women. A rough-looking drunken man with a bandage on his cheek appeared from nowhere, and looking at me with bleary, shifty eyes, asked truculently: "What the hell do you want here? A healthy bull like you has no business in a hospital."

"I've come about my father."

"What father? Ah. Chaliapin. Ivan? I know. He's sick. Now I'll have nobody to drink with. And what are you to him?"

"He's my father."

"Then you must be his son. Well, I never."

The drunkard spoke in a low voice, and from the questions asked by the peasants around us, I gathered that father had boosted me as a singer. Then someone asked me if it was true that in Moscow they actually had green "litricity" which ran up and down wires, and made the wagons move. I spent two hours there, waiting to be received by the doctor. Talking to my fellow-countrymen I had obviously made a hit, for the man with the bandaged cheek said thoughtfully: "Look at him. He comes from these parts. Yet just look at him."

The doctor received me quite coldly, and in a tired voice asked what I required. I told him. He said he would come and look at father the next day. He did come, gave him one look, and said his condition was serious, and it seemed hardly worth while taking him to hospital. Father kept

57. *Chaliapin as Don Quixote, sculpture by Kavaleridze (Bolshoy Theatre Museum).*

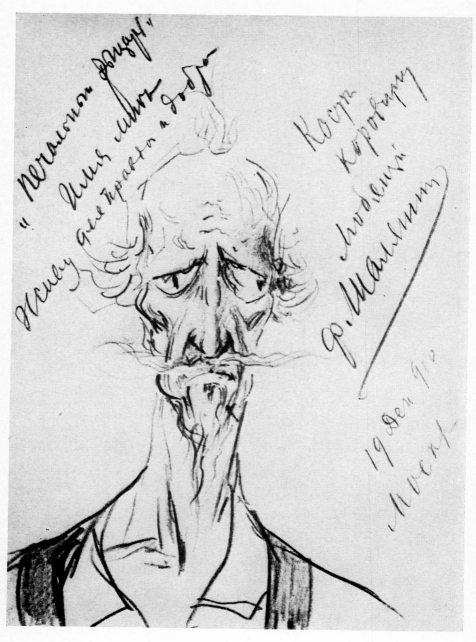

58. *Chaliapin's sketch of himself in the part of Don Quixote, inscribed: "To Kostya Korovin, affectionately F. Chaliapin. Moscow, December 19, 1910."*

59. Chaliapin as Don Quixote (Bolshoy Theatre, Moscow), 1910.

Right 60. *Chaliapin as Don Quixote, 1910.*

Below 61. *Scene from Chaliapin's production of Massenet's opera* Don Quixote *(Bolshoy Theatre, Moscow), 1910.*

struggling for breath, and retching. Finally it was decided that he should go to hospital. There he was given a separate room, clean and pleasant. Having given instructions for the patient to be given a bath, the doctor invited me to a cup of tea, during which he told me father's condition was not as serious as at first thought, and that he might even pull through.

I had to set off for Milan, and so I took leave of my father and went. The moment I arrived in Moscow I received a telegram from the doctor saying that father had died the day I left. My brother told me that he had died peacefully, speaking to him up to the final moment, when he turned over on his side and fell asleep.

From Italy I travelled to London, and then on to Paris, intending to go to Karlsbad later for a rest cure. It was July 25th, the streets were crowded with people anxiously reading the latest bulletins displayed in the shop windows. Everyone was talking of war. On that day, lunching with a prominent banker, I asked him how seriously he took these rumours, to which he replied with confidence: "There will be no war."

According to popular opinion, international politics are run by bankers, and these gentlemen should know whether or not people will fight. His statement pacified me, and that evening I bought tickets for Karlsbad.

Only some three hours later the train was stopped, passengers were ordered to alight, and we heard that war had been declared and the train was proceeding no further. Nor were there any trains for Paris. In addition, all horses had been requisitioned, and I was left with my suitcases at a little station among crowds of anxious and excited Frenchmen. To make my return to Paris easier, I opened my cases and started giving away most of their contents to poor people, leaving myself with the barest essentials. All currency of small denomination vanished from sight, right out of circulation. I had only 100-franc and 50-franc notes in my pockets and nobody would change them. I remember being asked in a restaurant: "What sort of money have you got?"

"French francs," I said.

"Sorry, we can give no change."

As I was very hungry, I said, "Give me a piece of meat, and a bottle of wine, and take fifty francs."

All the way back to Paris I had to resort to this expensive way of eating, and slowly I made progress, now by horse, now on foot. After a while I found this method of eating rather idiotic, and I began inviting people from the streets, especially the poorly dressed ones who looked in need of a square meal. They would join me at lunches and dinners. I would make friends with them, discuss the news, the war, and then invite them to a restaurant. In a small French town one can have an ample meal for at least ten people with a hundred-franc note. Often I would invite along the friends and acquaintances of such people, with the result that the un-negotiable banknote vanished in a trice.

Conversations I had revealed to me another side of the French nature. They were truly gay and frivolous, but they were also realistic, being only too well aware of the horrors of war. They spoke on this subject with a detachment and composure enriched by experience. No easy victory was foreseen. They sensed that the war would be long, and would exact great effort from the whole country. Eventually I reached Paris.

Here the atmosphere was one of alarm and extreme tension. The streets were perpetually crowded with violently gesticulating people. Yet the moment the first German aeroplane dropped both bombs and leaflets demanding the surrender of the city, these people received both the leaflets and the bombs with jeers and laughter.

"The great German army is at the gates of Paris," proclaimed the leaflets.

The French reply was very simple:

"Come in."

There was little I could do in Paris, and for the first time in my life, I found myself longing for my native land. So from Paris I moved to Brittany, to a little place on the coast called La Baule. From here I made up my mind to get across the Channel to England.

Reaching Calais I proceeded to the office of the British organization there, and applied for tickets. On informing them of my nationality, I was told that it was impossible for them to oblige me. Apparently all transport-space was being made available for British subjects only. It was now impossible for me to get back to Paris. The only route now open, from Dieppe, might be closed at any moment. On enquiring from the British Consul there, I received the same answer. They were sorry but they couldn't help me. It was understandable, the interests of their own nationals came first, but, they said, as soon as that difficulty was passed, they would endeavour to help me. I remember thinking then how wonderful it was to be a subject of a country whose nationals were so well looked after.

It was only through the intercession of the British envoy that I managed to persuade the Calais consul to give me a permit for Dieppe, via Paris. I took the last available train. Before we set out the railway officials had visited each compartment, advising passengers to lie on the floor in case of an attack. I had with me my Chinese servant, who incidentally had been an interpreter during the Russo-Japanese War. He found everything of passionate interest, and I recall him running in and out continuously, staring up at the sky, peering across the fields, dying to see a German aeroplane or a patrol. I had with me two revolvers, and he took one of them, saying, "Levolvels velly good."

We finally reached Dieppe. The port was crowded with people. They lay about in the streets, on heaps of goods, all over the place. At the station I met a Belgian soldier. I remember his drinking some wine given him by a Frenchman, and his vain endeavours to cheer everybody up, though his eyes were full of bewilderment and sadness. He had come straight from the trenches, in tatters, and created an extraordinary impression by his laughter. Looking at this man I realized the terrible tragedy that was going to be played out, and what agony he had suffered, whose whole country had been seized and occupied.

Meanwhile the orders at the port were strict. No one was allowed aboard ship at night. The following morning I discovered the English sailors lined up in a double row along the jetty, letting people through. Each person showed his passport, and from time to time came the voice: "British subjects first."

If a foreigner tried to forge ahead, he was stopped, taken from his place in the queue and sent to the end of the line again. I am sure many Europeans looked on disgruntled as they beheld Negroes being given precedence, but they were British subjects, and were the first to embark. I was lost in admiration at the way Britain treated her subjects.

In England I received a warm welcome. My arrival coincided with the Russian retreat from East Prussia. I remember being asked anxiously on all sides, "Who is Samsonov?" Alas, I didn't know who he was, not having had time to read the newspapers. I wasn't even aware of our defeat. I felt the anxiety behind these questions, but understood nothing. Instead I imagined the most dreadful things to have happened, and now wanted to get home more than ever. My English friends wished me to remain in England, pointing out to me the dangers of the journey. I appreciated this, but I had decided to go home, and so telegraphed for some money.

When this came through, an official of the bank asked me if I would like it in gold.

"Would I like it in gold?"

I was staggered. No gold had been seen in France for quite a long time.

"Yes, please, a little in gold," I said.

"You can have it all in gold."

My draft was for some 2,500 roubles. I remember his taking up a little shovel, and filling it with coins, weighing it, then handing it to me. When I made to count it, the official smiled, and said, "Not necessary. Don't worry. It won't be a drachma short." It wasn't.

I passed through Newhaven, London, and Glasgow. I was greatly struck by the work of the Boy Scouts. These bright, intelligent boys appeared in every railway carriage, offering foreigners efficient help. I remember their touching solicitations for a Jewish family. The Scouts milled round the passengers like ants, being helpful. They tended crying babies, calmed the bewildered adults, joking and laughing, and nothing being too much of a trouble, even to tying up luggage and carrying it to wherever required. It was all done so quietly, so speedily, and there was such kindness in it that I was near moved to tears. How close this brought the terror of wars. I was lost in admiration. "What a remarkable people the British are," I thought.

I arrived in Glasgow early the next morning, and embarked on the ship

Sirius, an old Norwegian vessel of around 1,000 tons displacement, long and narrow like a yacht. Every approach to the ship was jammed by crowds, among whom was spreading the rumour that she would capsize and drown us all. There was a noticeable lessening of the density after this, and I finally managed to get aboard her. I even managed to get a separate berth, though this seemed impregnated by an everlasting stench. And so we sailed.

It was the end of September, and we ran into heavy fog. Then another rumour ran rife, this time that a ship from America had recently gone aground on this route. However we were soon pitching and rolling so violently that sea-sickness proved the best killer of the fear aboard. After three days and nights we reached Bergen. I was glad to be out of my cabin, which had grown even dirtier during the voyage. I found myself a place in the bows, and didn't mind in the least about the waves that were breaking over. My waterproof coat was immediately water-logged, but it didn't prevent me from enjoying the experience. I might have been back on the Volga.

Here was Bergen lying at the foot of steep, bare, and frowning cliffs. The Norwegian stevedores, with enormous, sinewy arms, worked away in spite of the rain. They worked so calmly that one imagined there to be no trouble in the world at all. The next day I was in Christiania[1], a much more beautiful city than Bergen, and far more animated. I went off to inspect the theatre there, a handsome edifice erected in honour of Ibsen and Björnsen, whose statues stood in a near-by garden. I couldn't help thinking then: "Hardly dead, and yet here are monuments erected in their memory."

The Norwegians are a calm, even a phlegmatic people, yet they knew how to do honour to their great men. We Russians are a restless lot, and to this day we have not a single monument to Turgenev, Dostoievsky, Tolstoy, Nekrasov. We have not even found time to do honour to Pushkin and Lermontov.

I went off to the industrial exhibition. There was something morbid about the contours of these buildings, but I was greatly struck by the presentation of the various exhibits. Without understanding a single one of the inscriptions, I yet knew quite well the smallest detail about their fishing and forestry, not only in the modern methods applied to them, but also to their gradual development. Here one could see the culture of a country at a single glance.

Stockholm was gayer than Christiania, the people more lively, the colours brighter. There was music in the parks, and young people went about singing songs. On the wharves and at the railway station aid to home-coming Russians was splendidly organized.

Women and young girls were everywhere, carrying placards with the information in Russian as to where the Russian Embassy and consulate were situated. They informed you which ships were going to Finland, which trains to Torneo. Both soldiers and civilians behaved as though their main

[1] Renamed Oslo in 1925.

preoccupation in life was rendering aid to the Russians. They gave it unstintingly.

In Torneo a gay Finnish girl caught my attention. She was serving tea at an inn, smiling all the time, and quietly singing some strange little song in which the word "Aurinka" kept repeating itself. I asked her its meaning.

"The sun," she said.

The day was dull, the sky heavily overcast, yet here was a pretty girl singing about the sun. It delighted me, and it was in this mood that I returned to my country, the mood in which I eventually reached St. Petersburg, that already had been renamed Petrograd.

CORRESPONDENCE AND NOTES

In the correspondence sections, notes to references in the text will be found in the *Editor's Note* at the end of the relevant letter.

Letters from Chaliapin to his Family

FROM CHALIAPIN TO HIS DAUGHTER IRINA (London, June 19 [July 2], 1913).[1]

My sweet, darling Irina—Rosmarina,

I'm aghast at the time that has elapsed without my having written you a single line. But allow me to explain. Imagine this.

I arrive in Paris, and at once I am swamped with rehearsals, meeting people, paying visits, having lunches and dinners, performances, interviews, seeing the press. All this takes up such a tremendous amount of time, that sometimes I think I'm done for. And add to this my disgusting habit of getting up late, after sleeping too long, and you will realize the reason for my tardiness.

But today, I fooled them all—oh, I am so sick of them—so I said I was ill, and thus was able to spend a whole day locked up in my room, without even showing my nose outside.

So now, at last, I can get down to some letter-writing, and you would hardly believe how many letters I have to write. Truth to tell, I've written to no-one. Just a few scrappy lines to Mummy and that is all. You see how things are, my dearest. Well now, I'll tell you about Paris and London.

Although I was in this city seven years ago, it was a fugitive affair, since all I did was to sing in the drawing-room of a very rich American lady. This time it is so different.

Our Russian Opera Company has given three performances in a big theatre called Drury Lane. The success has been enormous, and this in spite of the fact that, as in Paris, they don't know a word of Russian. Considering this, I can only call it a triumph. The English go mad, shout "bravo" to exhaustion, and the enthusiastic calling upon the artists, yes, and even more so than in Moscow or St. Petersburg.

The newspapers glow with the reports of our work, articles about us, about Russian music, about me, in which they express regret that I haven't been asked to sing in London before.

When I hear all this (the reviews are translated for me, since I cannot read English), I am positively delighted, both for myself and my splendid colleagues, in brief, we feel very proud.

Also, it makes me reflect that perhaps, after all, things artistic are not so bad in Russia as many foreigners imagine. There are things that are good, and some that are very good indeed.

You see how it is, my little one.

Paris went off very well. We gave twelve performances. But neither I, nor the opera seemed a novelty to that city. We've been there on several occasions, but here in London, it is for the first time.

I live in a very attractive furnished flat at No. 11, King St., St. James's (my address incidentally), and I am very happy. But when I first arrived here I had the greatest difficulty in finding a room.

In England, this is the busy season. The city swarms with people, and the hotels are full. Wherever I went, it was only to receive the same answer. Full up. "Regrettons infiniment, tout est occupé". I managed to find a miserable little room, and there I spent one night. The following morning I started off on my dreary round of the London hotels. No luck. I found nothing.

In utter despair, and feeling almost resigned to this awful hotel, I chanced to meet a French actress, who plays in comedy and operette. A happy accident, since she brought me here, and showed me the charming flat. You cannot imagine my delight.

I pay £12 a week for it, which amounts to about 120 roubles. The English pound is valued at nine roubles, and fifty kopecks. It isn't cheap, of course, but then neither is it exorbitant. It is a really nice flat, and the furnishings are chic.

I shall remain here until the 5th or 6th, after which a fortnight's break, then I go to Deauville for more performances. I've planned to go down to Capri to spend some days with Gorky.

Dear, darling Irina, let me have some news, about all of you, and talk it over with Mamma. I would love to buy you something over here, dearest, just tell me what you'd like. If you think of something, send me the measurements. In London clothes are good, and comparatively cheap, and I so want to buy presents for you all.

Well, darling, I think I've been long-winded enough, so it's time to stop and get this letter off to you.

I kiss you, my sweet, and love you so very very much.

Your Daddy.

Editor's Note: [1] Wherever applicable, dates are given in accordance with the Gregorian calendar (in current use in Russia up to the time of the Revolution) with their modern counterparts in square brackets.

FROM CHALIAPIN TO HIS DAUGHTER IRINA (June 29 [July 12], 1913).

11 King St., St. James's, S.W.

My dearest little one,

I cannot tell you how much joy your letters bring to me. I try to imagine your life, and am overwhelmed with sadness at being parted from you.

I am having a tremendous success in London, and in a few days I shall be signing a very advantageous contract for next year, again for May and June. I shall make certain not to put pen to paper if it should prevent me from spending July and August with you.

The way of life here is strange, I am not accustomed to it, and sometimes I find it wearying. I meet a great many English people here. I am invited to lunches, teas, dinners, and suppers. This means my getting up early to reply to letters, paying calls on one and another. My knowledge of English is practically nil, and although all the people I know speak French . . . I still feel hampered. So I've decided to start learning English, and this is something I would advise you all to do. To me it's a most important language, and I do want you and Lida, Tanya, Fedya and Boris to begin to study it. Tell this to your sisters and brothers.

I'm delighted you are enjoying good weather, and able to do a lot of swimming. Glad, too, that you are finding that bulldog good company.

We had meant to close our season on July 17th, but yesterday the King of England, at present in the north of the country, telegraphed to say that he wished to hear me in *Boris Godunov*. He is unable to get to London on the 17th, and has asked for a special performance on the 27th. I shall have to be in London for that.

Here, they have splendid museums and art galleries. When you grow up, and have learnt English, I'll bring you here. Won't that be fun?

Give my love and kisses to everybody, especially Mummy. I am planning a little surprise for her when I return home.

A big hug and kiss for you, my little swallow. I love you so dearly.

Your Daddy.

P.S. Note the address at the top of the first page of my letter, since I find you write "Aing", when it should be "King".

FROM CHALIAPIN TO HIS DAUGHTER IRINA (Deauville, August 6, 1913)

My sweet, my darling little Ririkuka,

I've just this moment got your letter, and almost died laughing, visualizing you trying to launch that boat. It must have been great fun, and oh, I wish I had been there to enjoy it with you. My God! If only I could tell you how tired I am of all this traipsing round the world, singing, singing.

I am impatient, I am longing for August 27th, when my commitments will have ended, and I shall be back with you all.

After leaving London I spent some time in Switzerland, travelling both by train and car. I enjoyed it, I relaxed, and had a real good rest. I feel so well, and could have quite a nice time, but I miss you all so desperately. The weather is excellent, and of course the place is crowded with people. Tomorrow I think I'll have a dip in the ocean, and when I am swimming, I shall be thinking of you. Remember Rimini?

The King of England was delighted with my Boris Godunov. He invited me to his box, and paid me no end of compliments. After which, I was invited to the Palace by Queen Alexandra, the sister of our old Czarina. I sang them some ballads. They were very kind, and I had tea there. Afterwards, they presented me with their signed photographs.

I am really thrilled with London. I had such a marvellous reception from the audience. I'll tell you the whole story when I get home.

Can you manage all right on those bicycles? There aren't that many good roads.

I was sorry to hear about poor Vera Dmitriyevna. Alas, what can one do? We are all mortal.

I have now signed the new London contract, for next spring. I shall try to earn as much money as possible. Independence is a trump card in life, and I am thinking of that.

I look forward so much to the 27th, when I can return to Moscow. I can hardly wait for the day to arrive.

Lots of kisses, my darling little daughter, whom I shall see so very soon. My greetings to Lelya and Mademoiselle. Kiss Mummy for me, and all my pot-bellied brood.

Your adoring father.

EXTRACT FROM A LETTER FROM CHALIAPIN TO HIS DAUGHTER IRINA (May 26 [June 8], 1916. On board Goncharov's boat sailing from Samara to Saratov.)

My sweet darling Irina,

I too, feel bitterly disappointed, and sorry that I have been unable to send you a single line. But let me tell you what happened. I kept telling myself that as soon as my season ends on the 17th May, I'd dash over to Yalta. Alas, circumstances decreed otherwise. Maxim Gorky has suddenly fallen ill, thrombosis in his leg. It is both a painful and long-lasting trouble, and as I must remain with him—it is absolutely essential since we are working together—I am now, so to speak, nailed to the ground.

I didn't wish to go to the Crimea without him, since it would have meant twiddling my thumbs, doing nothing for nearly two weeks. I have to go to Essentuki in any case.

I decided on this watering place, as I would like to be done with my treatment, whilst Mamma and the babies go on to Yalta. Unfortunately I have no means of letting her know of my decision, and it is a sheer impossibility to get a telephone call through to Moscow. One really cannot talk about such things in a letter, or on the telephone, with real satisfaction, they are so personal.

That is why I waited till I got back to Moscow. Having discussed everything with Mamma, I sent you the telegram about what we have decided to do.

. . . I miss you terribly, and I know how you miss me, but cheer up, we shan't have long to wait now.

Gorky and I live where we can be quiet and undisturbed. I will be coming to Yalta often, or wherever you happen to be. Our work will occupy no more than three weeks, during which we shall live incognito in some one-eyed little hole. Three weeks in Essentuki, and three weeks' work with Gorky, takes us into July. This means I shall be back with you all by the fifteenth of the month. . . .

Editor's Note: From personal collection of Irina Chaliapin.

EXTRACT FROM A LETTER FROM CHALIAPIN TO HIS DAUGHTER IRINA (Kislovodsk, September 7 [20], 1917)

My darling Irina,

Your letter arrived the day before yesterday, and I was overjoyed to hear that for the time being you are managing, and all right for food. I was, and am, terribly concerned about this side of your life. Anything else is more or less bearable to me, but it would be dreadful if you had to starve.

God forbid that it should ever happen, but if it does, then there is nothing for it but for you to come here to the Caucasus. Things are all right here, at least so far as food is concerned. There is plenty of everything, and quite often we have white bread.

I am happy to say I feel fine at the moment. I had a most satisfying concert on the 27th of August, the returns being in the neighbourhood of 14,500 roubles. After expenses were covered, I received about 10,000 roubles. Needless to say, the newspapers turned on the poison, and I was called a thief and marauder, and anything else that happened to creep into their minds. However, the tickets were sold out within three hours. . . .

FROM CHALIAPIN TO HIS DAUGHTER IRINA (Riga, October 20, 1921)

My darling little Irina,

At last, I am aboard ship and on my way. So now I can get this letter off to you, and one or two other important ones that I could not get done in London. There, I never had a spare moment.

For someone like myself, life in a city like London resembles the cinema, where one is always in the limelight. Everything on the screen vibrates, dazzles the eyes. Not one peaceful moment, my little girl. Your letter came, and one from Mamma. My grief is endless. I cried, but it did not help, it never does. Sweet little Irina, my heart aches for you. The moment I get back to Moscow, end of December or early January, I shall act at once, indeed I will move heaven and earth. You simply must be allowed to go abroad for treatment. Absolutely essential.

My own affairs flourish brilliantly, so far at least. I gave five concerts in England, two in London, one in Birmingham, one in Sheffield, and one in Liverpool.

The enthusiasm was tumultuous, so that I honestly cannot help bragging. Yes, I strutted about, relishing my triumph.

It is a sad fact that amidst the waves of triumph, there were a number of exploiters around, and it appears that I have been grossly cheated. Nevertheless, I did manage to collect some funds for famine relief in Russia.

The sum from England alone will be considerable, above one thousand pounds, I believe. Of course for the poor victims of this terrible disaster it is a mere drop in the ocean. All the same, I feel glad that I have had some sort of moral influence on the English, which can be turned to advantage for the starving. I received many sympathetic letters. Only words, it is true, nevertheless, when one is unhappy a kind word gladdens the heart, as a toy can soothe a child.

But America is something wholly different. Yes indeed. The Washington department of Immigration made me sign a document, in which I had to state that I would not ask for contributions to any cause. It amazed me to learn that my own contracts forbid me to give any concerts that would help these poor starving people at home. I was given all this information by my agent, or manager. Only after my arrival in New York can I hope to sort things out. There is dirty work going on somewhere, and I have very strong feelings about it.

Oh my Irina, if only you knew the rascals and swindlers one comes across in Europe and America. They shelter under the respectable title of "business men". If one of them grabs something, he calls it "business", a splendid term. It doesn't sound as bad as plain robbery, though charmingly retains the same meaning.

By this time you must have received the newspaper cuttings I sent you, so you will know how well I have been received here. Except, of course, by my Russian compatriots who abandoned their country at the worst possible time. Like rogue camels they expel torrents from the mucous membranes of their noses, left, right, and centre. I felt sorry for these miserable creatures. Never have they so blatantly demonstrated their own insignificance. Russia has lost nothing by their departure, so many stuffed dummies with tiny heads and enormous stomachs. I know of course that they cannot all be like that, yet the good ones are not much in evidence. Somewhere, perhaps, the good and the modest are quietly starving. All the same, I feel sorry for them.

Darling, I am writing this letter today, the 20th, but will be unable to post it until the 27th or 28th, when we berth in New York.

The shores of Europe we have left behind us, and today the sea is peaceful and majestic. You scarcely notice the rolling of the ship. Though the weather is overcast and dull, it is yet warm and good. Oh, how quickly you would get better if you were here with me now. They eat splendidly aboard this ship, and around five meals a day is the thing, with oysters and prawns, lobsters, meat and ham on the menu, and most important of all, as much white bread and fruit as one can wish.

One of my co-passengers is the writer H. G. Wells, who visited me in

Petrograd last winter. Another is the well-known composer, Richard Strauss. We have a pleasant time sitting in the bar, where we sip whiskies. How pleasant it is with a whisky and soda in front of you, and the conversation flowing so smoothly and gaily. They are delightful, and I enjoy being with such extremely intelligent people.

My little one, all my love, and a big kiss. And I beg of you not to take amiss some of my "vulgar" expressions. You know I would never say things like that to anybody I didn't love, and I love you so dearly. Sometimes, out of sheer distress and longing, I tend to shout out stupid things.

Your loving father.

EXTRACT FROM A LETTER FROM CHALIAPIN TO HIS SON BORIS (Cleveland, U.S.A., January 2, 1922)

Dearest Boris,

It seems ages since I last wrote to you, but then, you know how I hate writing. You wrote to me, and at long last I am replying to it. My dearest boy, you ask me to bring you various wood sculpting instruments. Of course I'll bring you anything you want, provided it's possible to do so. Indeed I'd bring you all kinds of things, but I'm afraid of anything untoward happening on the way. You do realise the sort of time we are living in. Every item that I bring with me, and there are bound to be many, will have to be taken over several countries. Every country has its Customs, every Customs House its collection of crooks. (Naturally I exclude my country from such allegations, because I do want to believe that ours has fewer crooks.) One never knows when they may choose to grab something and then one will have one's work cut out to find redress.

Never mind, I shall certainly try. I'll bring you some shoes and socks, shirts and pants. This itself is a problem, for I don't know your sizes, but I shall make every effort to bring you the paints and canvas you want, and every kind of instrument all the way down to fretsaws.

I seem to have got stuck in America. I should really be on my way home, but that blasted illness delayed me. I can't leave for London before the end of the month, and that's a nine-day trip. After a stay of eight to nine days in London, I will set course for Russia[1], nipping in to Berlin on the way, if I can, so I can have a couple of days with Lida.[2]

America, my boy, has been quite a strain. So far I have given ten performances, two at the Metropolitan Opera House, and eight concerts in various towns. This is what I find tiring, it knocks the stuffing out of me. I find their trains poor, at least compared with our own. Things like sleeping berths are arranged well enough, but unfortunately they are arranged for people of medium height. For me they are all too short, and I must sleep in a bent position.

Yesterday, New Year's Day, I sang in Chicago. I was there last month, but I felt ill, and the concert was cancelled. You can imagine the distances

I have to cover; from New York to Chicago it is no less than 1500 versts. Now I have completely recovered from my illness, thank God, and I'm glad to say the concerts were a success.

I was ill for a full five weeks, and think of it, never earned a penny in that time, besides which I had to pay damages for seven cancelled concerts. There was a time when I thought I might be compelled to travel by Shanks's pony. However, I'm recovered, and have been able to earn enough to pay my fares in style. The moment I get back to New York I shall send you each fifty dollars. How are you all? It's a whole month since I've had news of you. And what of my darling Irina? How is she? I do hope she's not still ill. It breaks my heart to think of it. What times, what times. Never mind, I shan't allow myself to get depressed, and I don't want you to do so either. With God's help we shall overcome everything and somehow, manage.

Don't be despondent, my darlingest, bear up just a little longer. When I come home I shall tell you so much about all the countries I visited. Until then, I embrace you all, and you, my darling Boris, I embrace with all my heart.

Your ever loving father.

Editor's Note: [1] Chaliapin came back to Russia early in 1922. In the autumn of the same year, with the permission of the Soviet Government, he went abroad, never to return to his native land.

[2] Chaliapin's daughter.

Chaliapin's son, Boris, is a distinguished portrait painter. His portrait of Rachmaninov hangs in the Moscow Conservatoire, a gift of the artist. He also painted Toscanini, Kussevitsky, Heifetz, and nearer our own time, Ulanova and Theodore Dreiser. He made many portraits of his famous father; reproductions of two are included in this book.

FROM CHALIAPIN TO HIS DAUGHTER IRINA (dated Cleveland, Ohio, U.S.A., January 2, 1922)

My Irina, my darling baby.

How are you? Where are you? What are you doing? Are you ill? My God, my God! May these lines from my heart bring you recovery, and give you strength. It has to be a short letter this time, because I have already written to Boris in great detail, and there seems no point in repeating it all.

I sent you a telegram on December 31st, from Chicago. I don't know if you ever received it. I saw the New Year in in my hotel room with our celebrated ballerina, Anna Pavlova, and a few friends. We stayed up till two o'clock, then I had to go to bed, because of a concert I had the following day, which, praise to the gods, went off brilliantly.

I am well now, and singing like a nightingale. On the 9th December I sang Boris for the first time at the Metropolitan Opera House. They gave

62. Chaliapin—sculptor, working on a self-portrait, Moscow, 1912.

63. Self-portrait, a sculpture by Chaliapin.

64. *Gorky and Chaliapin on the stage of The People's Theatre, Nizhni-Novgorod, 1903.*

I. E. Repin painting Chaliapin's portrait. (Repin was not satisfied with the portrait and used the canvas for another painting. This photograph is the only record of the portrait.)

66. *Gorky and Chaliapin on the banks of the Volga, a sculpture by Kavaleridze.*

me Caruso's dressing-room. He was a marvellous fellow, and a great friend of mine. And there, on the wall, as a memento, I wrote a little poem, in Russian. Here it is, just to amuse you. You know that I am a poet at heart.

> Today, with trepidation in my heart,
> I entered your theatrical abode,
> My dear and distant friend.
> But you, minstrel from a Southern land,
> Smitten by cold death, are lying in
> the earth—you are not here.
> I weep, and in response to my
> memories of Caruso, your muse is
> softly weeping, too.

Well, and what do you think of that, my little one? A bit like Pushkin, eh? Ha ha. That'll show you.

Goodbye, my darling. A big hug and kiss to you.

Your loving father.

FROM CHALIAPIN TO HIS DAUGHTER IRINA (Edinburgh, October 14, 1922)

My darling Irina,

I write you this letter whilst waiting for the train that will take me to London. Whether it will ever reach you, I hardly know. It is being said that out of spite against the Bolsheviks post office workers are not forwarding on the letters. Let us hope that in this case their wrath will be tempered with charity. . . .

Naturally, I'm disconsolate at not having been able to meet Mummy.[1] This was due to the unexpected Scandinavian concerts. And I could kick myself for missing my little Tanya! Here I am now, off to America for another six months. It's a long time. I know that. God, the curse of having to make money. . . .

. . . Life without Russia, without her art, by which I've lived, how dull and repugnant it is. Money of course is fine, but where is my beloved Russia? Where are all the marvellous opportunities? When will Russian artists give up being politicians, and apply themselves to their real métier, and do it honourably. When, oh when? There is something cruel about being driven to America in my old age. And how boring I find these charming "purple devils". They remain raw fledgelings, they understand so little, and they are so rich and full of good intentions.

Still no news from Mummy in Italy. She must be in Milan, and I'm so anxious that she might run out of money. I did send her something from Scandinavia, but it wasn't enough. I must send her more. The trouble is I don't even know her address. I don't want to send money through the bank, since it is far better to send it to her in English pounds.

I do hope that next year I shall manage something for you. I want you to come to Europe, if only for a little while.

How splendid it would be if I could manage to get Pavel[2] into some Soviet Mission. Next year, let us hope, the Soviet Government will be recognized both by Europe and America, after which we may be able to live as we should. Otherwise—no matter where you go over here, the mere sight of a Soviet passport makes them shy off, like the devil from a whiff of incense. Civil servants. Idiots. What on earth can one do with these people?

Well, my little one, what else can I tell you? To date everything is taking its course, and nothing extraordinary is happening. I don't smoke, but must say that I imbibe whisky and soda with great delight, a splendid drink.

When the spring comes (if I haven't dashed off to Australia, and they are begging me to do so), I shall bring a couple of cases of whisky to Moscow and Petrograd, and to you and Pavel I shall bring many presents.

Your loving father.

Editor's Note: [1]Chaliapin's wife Iola was at that time visiting Italy.
[2]Irena's husband, P. P. Pashkov.

FROM CHALIAPIN TO HIS DAUGHTER IRINA (Philadelphia, November 22, 1922)

My darling Irina,

My greetings and kisses to you from Philadelphia. A large and rather dull town, it is about two and a half hours drive from New York. Strange, but in spite of all their boasted liberty, there seems little sign of it here. So much is prohibited. All one can do is gape at the strictness and absurdity of their laws. They have of course got the dollar. It makes up for a lot, I dare say. With that currency you can buy practically everything, wholesale and retail.

Love and lots of kisses,
Your loving father.

EXTRACT FROM A LETTER FROM CHALIAPIN TO HIS DAUGHTER IRINA (Chicago, January 22, 1924)

My darling Irina,

Thank you for your letter, which I received in New York a week ago but have had no time to reply. My sweet one, it grieves me to hear that your career in the theatre is not progressing smoothly.

Of course, it might be quite fun to travel in Siberia (to see something of its natural beauty and the life of the people), but, on the whole, this is neither a serious nor a happy occupation. How sad it is that conditions are so hard for the theatre in Russia. But, let us hope that soon, when we get stronger and the foreigners will stop interfering, we shall work well in the theatres as well.

To tell you the truth I did not expect America to take such a tough line against recognising our government. Never mind, I think it is a matter of time. And when they recognise us, I think our life will be better—all will work as one and the engine will go at full speed. Patience!

I was in a delicatessen shop the other day, and I gave a ticket for my *Mefistofele* to one of the counter girls. After the performance I found her waiting for me outside the stage door. She was embarrassingly grateful, and told me it was the first time in her life she had visited an opera house. She must have been twenty-five if she was a day. "But why, I asked her, why only for the first time?"

Her answer. Oh, she didn't know—"just somehow," she exclaimed.

Yes, it is very dull, very unsatisfying, but of course they do pay me in gold. Ah well, perhaps after the next season I shall be able to work at home. Until that happens I must strengthen myself in the material sense, for I am not as young as I was.

I had a letter from Lida a few days ago. Of course, it is fine that she is enjoying success, but I don't like the theatre she is working in and generally don't approve the line pursued by such theatres.[1]

I also heard from Mummy, everything seems all right. About Usatova,[2] I shall send you 200 dollars, please as a favour to me, send her 15 or 20 dollars a month. I am terribly sorry to be so behind, but I swear I just have no time to transfer money. And it is difficult to do it from here.

All my love dearest, and many kisses.

Your loving father.

Editor's Note: [1] Lidya Chaliapin left Russia at the end of 1921. She worked in the Theatre Miniature "Cage d'Or" in Berlin.

[2] M. P. Usatova, the wife of D. A. Usatov, Chaliapin's only teacher.

EXTRACT FROM A LETTER FROM CHALIAPIN TO HIS DAUGHTER IRINA (Baden Baden, July 16, 1925)

. . . I'm stagnating here, getting rid of sugar, and fortifying myself for the next bout of hard labour in America. Next summer I shall probably go to Australia. How dearly I would love to come home, but alas, no luck so far, since I could reach no agreement with theatrical managers. Now it looks as though I shan't get home until 1927 or thereabouts. . . .

(Los Angeles, U.S.A., January 14, 1926)

What can I do my darling Irina: I've just had the news that Mummy has arrived in Paris, and now lives there with Boris, Lida and Fedya. I haven't the faintest idea what they intend to do there, now, or in the future, though Mamma apparently is planning to go to Moscow.

Did you get that two hundred dollars I sent you for the holidays? I know it's not exactly a fortune; still I hope it comes in useful for something.

Provided my health remains good, and I can manage to get two more seasons like the coming one, I shall have around 70 concerts at 3,000 dollars each. Then I really shall send you a better present.

The one awful thing for me is that I'm beginning to age, and my ability to work is diminishing. I get ill from time to time, my throat bothers me, rheumatism pesters me. In brief, I look as old as the devil, and my mug is becoming as wrinkled as an empty purse. Small wonder. On the first of February I shall be fifty-three. Dying time, as they say, "he was fifty-three-four-five-six etc.", on the gravestones.

Ah, to hell with such melancholy. I shall spend another ten years fooling the public. They can listen until they're sick. Then I'll retire to some cosy little cellar, and sip wine to my heart's content.

Well, my darling, I will see you in 1927, probably the Spring. Then I hope you will spend the whole summer with me.

All my kisses. . . .

Letters to Chaliapin from his Friends and Contemporaries

FROM CÉSAR CUI TO CHALIAPIN (September 7 [19], 1899)

My dear Feodor Ivanovich,

Would you please do me a tremendous favour? Would you collect the score of my opera *Saracen* from Jurgenson, and study the part of Count Savoisi, and should you decide on a tour in St. Petersburg, please include the *Saracen* in your repertoire.

I discussed this matter with the new director, Prince Volkonsky. He has no objections, since the role is extremely suitable for you.

Your efforts will by no means be wasted, since I have Telyakovsky's official promise that the opera will be included in the Moscow season, and naturally with you in the part.

Please do this for me. It would be such a comfort.

Yours,
C. Cui.

Editor's Note: César Antonovich Cui, 1835–1918, Russian composer, who, with Balakirev founded the Nationalistic group known as the "Mighty Handful"—Borodin, Mussorgsky and Rimsky-Korsakov making up the five. Cui wrote six operas, and completed the score of Mussorgsky's *Sorochinsky Fair*.

LETTER TO CHALIAPIN FROM THE AUTHOR OF *MEFISTOFELE*, ARRIGO BOITO, FOLLOWING THE FIRST NIGHT OF *BORIS GODUNOV* AT LA SCALA, MILAN (undated, but possibly March 17, 1901)

My dear Chaliapin,

Please accept the expression of my sincerest admiration of your wonderful portrayal of Boris.

Last night you reached the very heights of artistic expression, retaining simplicity and austerity.

Bravo!

Je vous serre la main bien fort.

Affectionately yours,
Arrigo Boito.

Editor's Note: This letter is reprinted from the periodical *Footlights and Life*, No. 26, 1918.

FROM A. T. GRECHANINOV TO CHALIAPIN (1901).

Dear Feodor Ivanovich,

To-day I am sending you a copy of my song, "Parting of the Ways".

In a few days' time my opera goes to the printer, and I wondered if you would be kind enough to look at the part of *Dobrynya Nikitich*. I would much like that. I have practically given up hope of ever seeing you at my place, so could you see your way to making an appointment with me for an hour or two this week, for this purpose. Suppose I came to you, say about six p.m. on Wednesday?

Yours,

A. Grechaninov.

Editor's Note: From Chaliapin family archives, and dated according to re-construction of events. The song mentioned by Grechaninov was duly passed by the Censor on October 24, 1901. His opera *Dobrynya Nikitich* opened at the Bolshoy Theatre on October 14, 1903, with Chaliapin in the lead.

FROM V. I. NEMIROVICH-DANCHENKO TO CHALIAPIN (end of 1901)

Dear Feodor Ivanovich,

Both last year and this year you promised to sing for me in aid of our poor pupils. I know full well how difficult this is for you, which is why I am making the following proposition.

On Sunday, December 1st, at 1 o'clock in the afternoon, Gorky will be reading his *The Lower-Depths* in the foyer of our theatre. Only about fifty tickets will be sold and the price will be 25 roubles (though many are paying more). Thus we shall have a very intimate matinée. I am taking it upon myself to promise these forty or fifty people that you will be in the theatre to hear the play, and that later you will sing something informally, in whatever you happen to be wearing, even a frock coat.

In a word, what I am trying to say is this. I thought of say two or three songs in the foyer; I don't want to fatigue you. The whole affair will be over by about half-past four.

I would like to ask Rachmaninov to accompany you. Would you please, when you write me, tell me that you are agreeable to the above. Would you let me have Rachmaninov's address?

Do forgive me for not coming along and requesting this personally. I know how very busy you are, and perhaps you'll find it easier to receive a letter than a visit.

V. I. Nemirovich-Danchenko.

Editor's Note: Dated according to contents. Chaliapin archives.

FROM A. I. SILOTI TO CHALIAPIN (July 20 [August 2], 1902)

My dear Fedya,

I have received a letter from Moscow, from which I learn that Safonov is busy preparing Schumann's *Manfred*. Perhaps this report is incorrect, perhaps it isn't. If the latter is the case, then Safonov, knowing that you will be doing *Manfred* for me, will obviously not want to cast anyone else. It seems to me there is only one way out. He will try and wangle things so that you would repeat *Manfred* at his function in aid of his fund.

When he asks you, you will inform him that my arrangement with you precludes him from having your services without my permission. He might also say that he, Safonov, would agree to my conducting the work, but I must warn you that my name, and that of Safonov cannot possibly appear on the same bill.

I write you this letter, just in case. I have just read the first volume of Skitalets's poems. Magnificent.

Our version of *Manfred* will be printed by Jurgenson with a Russian text.

My love to your wife, and a hearty embrace from your affectionate friend.

A. Siloti.

FROM A. I. SILOTI TO CHALIAPIN (December 28, 1903 [January 10, 1904].)

My dear dear Fedya,

I have two enormous requests.

Firstly: On Sunday April 4th (end of Easter week) there will be a concert in Petersburg, and on Saturday the 10th, in Moscow. I am organising both concerts for the composer Edvard Grieg, who will himself conduct. Do you think you could possibly take part, and sing a few of his compositions, the composer himself conducting? For each concert I promise you (and will actually pay!) 1,000 roubles. According to contract, I believe you are free to sing after Holy Week. So the decision depends entirely on you.

Secondly: So far as I know, you are free to give two concerts in Petersburg. How would you like to give a blessing to my concerts, and sing for me next November the solo part in Rachmaninov's Cantata, *The Spring*, and perhaps one other number with orchestra? I can offer you a maximum of 800 roubles. My prices are not high, but the expenses, because of the opera choir and orchestra, are monumental.

I need hardly say how delighted I would be if you found yourself able to agree to this.

Don't write me, simply cable "April-November agreed." That would be the best possible message.

Yours,
A. Siloti.

FROM A. K. GLAZUNOV TO CHALIAPIN (December 6, 1905)

Dear Feodor Ivanovich,

First of all, allow me on behalf of Rimsky-Korsakov and myself to express our deepest gratitude at your readiness to help me with my undertaking.

Immediately on receiving your letter I went and saw Monakhov at the Mariinsky Theatre, from whom I made enquiries concerning your engagements there from the week 5th to 9th of December. Apparently Wednesday the 7th is a ballet night, so I immediately decided on this date. Until I have your reply, I have left in abeyance the question of other artists. In any case, how would you take to other singers participating? I had in mind an instrumentalist or two, somebody like Siloti, and the young violinist Zimbalist.

They won't let us have The Noblemen's Assembly Hall, and I feel it my duty to inform you of this. Owing to this refusal, we began negotiations with Prince Tsereteli concerning the Concert Hall of the Conservatoire, and have received a favourable answer.

The only obstacle now is Telyakovsky's permission. I went to see him this morning.

He keeps on insisting that your contract with the Management of Imperial Theatres provides that for every appearance not sponsored by them, you must pay the sum of 3,000 roubles for breach of contract.

I tried to bargain with him, and he seemed generally agreeable, but in this particular matter he refuses to budge, in spite of the fact that I quoted him your letter.

A sum like 3,000 roubles is going to be difficult to raise, I am therefore asking you, pleading with you, to do anything you can to talk Telyakovsky around, somehow, anyhow.

It would be helpful if you could let me have your reply before you arrive in St. Petersburg. Somebody on my behalf will call on you for a reply.

As Prince Tsereteli is letting us have the Conservatoire Hall and the orchestra, I wonder whether you wouldn't like to sing with it. I shall not give up hope that Telyakovsky will accede, especially if you exert your influence. Even if it necessitates having to pay for your breach of contract, I shall not forgo the pleasure and honour of having you participate in a concert I am organizing.

My renewed apologies for all the trouble.

Yours,
A. K. Glazunov.

Editor's Note: From the Chaliapin family archives. Dated according to contents. This letter is a reply to Chaliapin's of November 23, 1905: see page 227

FROM DONALD BAYLIS TO CHALIAPIN (April 2, 1914)

Dear Mr. Chaliapin,

I propose setting up a concert for you on the 14th June, at the Albert Hall. These concerts have become popular, and are an excellent advertisement for the Opera Season. Only the most celebrated artists are engaged to take part in these concerts.

I should be glad if you would telegraph me signifying your willingness to sing, and perhaps you'd be kind enough to let me know the fee you would expect.

The concert will be an afternoon one, in which I propose to give an entirely Russian programme; possibly several items will be accompanied by a choir or sung with other soloists.

I look forward to your return, and can assure you that this time the success will be greater than last year.

Yours sincerely,
Donald Baylis.

P.S.—Sir Joseph and Thomas Beecham send their kindest regards.

Editor's Note: Chaliapin family archives. This letter was written before the second season of Russian Opera in London.

FROM K. S. STANISLAVSKY TO CHALIAPIN (April 19, 1922)

My dear Feodor Ivanovich,

Through the kindness of Iola Ignatyevna, to whom I send my warmest regards and thanks (please kiss her for me), I have received the £25 you sent me. Allow me to be the temporary guardian of this until better days.

I am most touched by your thoughtfulness, your kindness and affection. Now we value the impulses of the heart, a hundred times more. Thank you for them.

You, in your turn, must not deny me the pleasure of sending you a small memento of your first visit to my studio.[1] It is a small hand harmonium copied from an eighteenth century original, and the only one in Moscow.

During my peregrinations in Europe I met a singer in a railway carriage who used to accompany himself twice a day on a similar instrument. Perhaps this toy may prove useful to you on your many journeys. The thought that this little trifle may serve to remind you of your constant and ardent admirer gives me great happiness. Don't deny me this.

Yours sincerely and gratefully,
K. S. Stanislavsky.

Editor's Note: [1] Stanislavsky's Music Studio, founded in 1921.

Chaliapin family archives.

Letters from Chaliapin to his Friends and Contemporaries

FROM CHALIAPIN TO ANTON CHEKHOV (December 9, 1902)

My dear Anton Pavlovich,

I am as furious as hell that I have missed the pleasure of spending a few more hours with you. But this blasted benefit performance takes up practically every moment of my time. It is a pity, a great pity, but there it is, and not a thing can be done about it.

My warmest thanks to you for sending me your photograph. I am thrilled to have it, and will treasure it.

I, in turn, send you one of mine, in which I look like a bandore. Sorry I had nothing better to send you.

My best wishes for your health and happiness. Believe well that I love you with all my heart, and embrace you as warmly as I love you.

Yours,

Feodor Chaliapin.

Editor's Note: Lenin State Library archives.

FROM CHALIAPIN TO V. A. SEROV (January 19 [February 1], 1904)

My dear Valentin,

Dr. Troyanovsky has just informed me that you would like to hear me in *The Demon.* My dear friend, if you only knew how happy this has made me.

Praise to the gods that you are well.

Please go to the Grand Circle, Box 5, on the left-hand side. There you will find Nemirovich-Danchenko, and Maxim Gorky, together with their wives, and a certain Pyatnitsky. They will be told of your coming, and I am sure will be delighted to have you with them, so do go, my dear friend.

I embrace you good and strong, the way I love you.

Yours,

Feodor Chaliapin.

Editor's Note: State Tretyakov Gallery Collection, from V. A. Serov's Archives X-IX-172.

FROM CHALIAPIN TO V. A. SEROV (October–December, 1905)

My dear Anton,

Here I am, sitting like an owl in an ivy bush, blinking and staring. I couldn't even scrape together five roubles, let alone send a hundred to you. I am left penniless because of the strikes. I applied to the Administration for an advance. Hopeless, just left high and dry. To add to this, the banks are closed. I really feel ready to howl. Never mind, to-morrow morning I'll go round the town and endeavour to rustle up some money, and naturally I'll manage to squeeze out a hundred roubles for you, perhaps more. Who knows? How about joining me this evening at Maxim's. I'll call for you in an hour and a half.

Your Feodor.

Editor's Note: Dated according to context, and the mention of strikes. "Joining me at Maxim's" refers to Maxim Gorky.

FROM CHALIAPIN TO A. K. GLAZUNOV AND N. A. RIMSKY-KORSAKOV (Moscow, November 23 [December 6], 1905)

My dear Alexander Konstantinovich and Nikolai Andreyevich,

Need I tell you how delighted I am to take part in your splendid concert. With all my heart I am happy to do anything to help those poor people who are, in one way and another, fighting for our precious freedom. I only regret being unable to fix the date of the concert, since I am not yet certain what my commitments will be at the Mariinsky Theatre.

Alexander Konstantinovich, could you do something to find out, even approximately, how I am fixed for December, and then arrange the concert to take place according to what free days I have, having first got permission from Telyakovsky for me to appear. Tell him that I am whole-heartedly in favour of the idea.

I hope to be in St. Petersburg on December 1st. We can then work out the programme for the concert.

Yours,
F. Chaliapin.

Editor's Note: From the archives of V. N. Rimsky-Korsakov.

FROM CHALIAPIN TO M. F. VOLKENSTEIN (The Ganeshin Sanatorium, Kislovodsk, August 9 [22], 1915)

Dear Misha,

I was unable to telegraph you, and for this reason: Aksarin offered me the chance to sing in *A Life for the Czar* on the 30th August. A charity performance, I think. Now all this would be very fine, but there happens to be the appalling circumstance of us Russian people, and the terrible times through which we are passing. When one looks seriously at our life, and perceives the dreadful terrors to which meaningless traditions and stupidity has brought us, it can only strike one as absurd that *I* should be asked to sing in *A Life for the Czar*. Here we are on the very brink of disaster, with thousands of our people dying, and why? Because our czars and their pathetic hangers-on have imposed the traditions to suit only them. I repeat, how absurd, on 30th August, to indulge in paeans like *A Life for the Czar*.

This, to me, fits perfectly in line with all those prayers for victory. Don't you agree?

Aksarin informed me that the prince expressed his desire: "it would be nice, if, on the 30th of August, Chaliapin were to sing *A Life for the Czar*".

You know my attitude to these things. To me that opera is a magnificent composition, and I sing the part of Susanin with great enthusiasm, since I consider the character has epic qualities. But—when all this is being pushed at me solely to boost "the landlord", the owner of the patrimony which is called Russia, then quite honestly I feel sick, and that splendid part, the wonderful music, is dimmed in a moment. No. Enough of hypocrisy.

I could sing almost anything on the 30th, but simply, and with no fists flailing the air, otherwise we are all of us brought down to the level of clowns in a circus. Now you will understand why I did not telegraph you. I just didn't want Aksarin to know that I was disinclined to sing *A Life for the Czar*. At the same time, if the prince stipulated that it must be *A Life for the Czar*, then he won't be able to put on any other opera. Tell him I am full of engagements, that I won't be in St. Petersburg. Meanwhile, I embrace you fondly, and wish you all good health.

Please forgive the tone of irritation in this letter, but you cannot imagine how much I suffer for my country.

This place is ideal for convalescing. The place isn't bad, and the waters are splendid. Yet, with things as they are, one's nerves ache, and there is no rest.

What is to be done? If anything happens, send me a telegram. I shall be here until the 20th, after which I go to the Crimea for two days, then back to Moscow.

Editor's Note: From the Central State Archives of Literature and Art, Moscow. Glinka's opera, *A Life for the Czar*, was duly performed on August 30, 1915, presented by Aksarin, with A. I. Mozhukhin singing the part of Ivan Susanin.

TO THE CIVIL SERVANTS IN CHARGE OF THE SALE AND AUCTION OF TICKETS FOR THE PERFORMANCE OF *MEFISTO-FELE* ON NOVEMBER 18TH, IN AID OF THE PATRIOTIC ASSOCIATION (September 16 [29], 1903)

I, Chaliapin, have twice sent my servant round with my card, on which I humbly requested the sale of two tickets to me anywhere between the first and fifth row, for the above performance, in which I am to take part. My request has been refused.

I am making this third and final request for the tickets, and I would like them immediately, otherwise, I may be forced to offer you, gentlemen of the Civil Service, the opportunity of singing the opera yourselves. I myself would have the fun of watching you from the wings, to see what would come of it.

Artist Feodor Chaliapin.

Editor's Note: Archives of the Bakhrushin Museum. Among material kept at the Leningrad State History Archives, there is evidence of correspondence between the Administration of the Imperial Theatres and the Moscow police, which lays down the procedure for selling tickets for Chaliapin's performances. The reason given is the desire of the authorities to prevent profiteering, in reality they were afraid of some spontaneous demonstration. The police therefore decided to stop open sale of tickets and they could only be obtained by applying to the box office in writing in advance.

TO HIS WORSHIP

The Director of Administration of the Moscow Imperial Theatres
from
the Soloist of His Imperial Majesty
Feodor Ivanovich Chaliapin
November 12 (25), 1913

APPLICATION

Having served in the Imperial Theatres in Moscow and Petersburg for more than fifteen years, I have, with great patience, observed the bestowal of medals, orders, and other regalia, upon such people as ushers and box-keepers. Decorations have been handed out to all and sundry, but, owing to some miserable intrigues within the administration, and indeed amongst those in charge of such matters, I have been deprived of any such recognition.

I am quite unable to understand the reasons for being so ignored, and humbly request Your Worship to recommend me instantly for an award of some kind, any little order indeed, that will carry the administration office number and stamp.

Soloist of His Imperial Majesty
F. Chaliapin.

Editor's Note: Archives of the Bolshoy Theatre.

Telyakovsky's[1] diary records that it was Chaliapin's friendship with Maxim Gorky which prevented his being promoted to the status of "Soloist of His Imperial Majesty" for so many years. He also records that after the revolutionary events of 1905, when Chaliapin sang "Dubinushka" on the stage of the Bolshoy Theatre, Nicholas II demanded that "this hooligan" be chased out of the Imperial Theatres.

On February 6, 1905, the newspaper *Russkoye Vedomosti* received and printed an open letter signed by many leading Russian musicians and artists, which included the names of Chaliapin, Taneyev, Rachmaninov, among others, in which they affirmed that:

"When there is neither freedom of thought nor conscience in a country, when there is no freedom of speech or press, when all creative activity is stifled and hampered, the title of free artist becomes a mockery. We are not free artists, but merely the victims of abnormal social and legalistic institutions, deprived of the rights of ordinary Russian citizens."

This, quite obviously, had had an effect on Chaliapin's artistic life and career in the Imperial Theatres, although the authorities did not dare dismiss him, partly out of fear of a public scandal, and partly from practical considerations, since Chaliapin's appearances invariably led to "House Full" notices outside the theatre.

A. V. Lunacharsky, Commissar for Education, at one of the concerts organised in the Mariinsky Theatre after the revolution, introduced Chaliapin as the First People's Artist of the R.S.F.S.R., which the singer said was the honour and title he prized most of all.

Editor's Note: [1] Vladimir Arkadyevich Telyakovsky (1861–1924); from 1899 director of the Moscow Office (Administration) of the Imperial Theatres.

TELEGRAM TO L. N. TOLSTOY (Moscow, September 6, 1902)

It is highly unlikely that in the life of a man, an occasion like today can be repeated, when a message of greeting can be so genuinely permeated by the most profound gratitude. Today, we want to say to you that we love you as a mature person can love the best and dearest dreams of his youth. We venerate you as a man who works constantly and unceasingly to awaken both our thought and conscience. We are proud of you and of the century during which one of the greatest men lived and worked, and whose spirit will continue to influence human thought for centuries to come.

Artists of the Moscow Art Theatre.
Nemirovich-Danchenko
Alekseyev
Maxim Gorky
Eugene Chirikov
Feodor Chaliapin
Leonid Andreyev

Editor's Note: This telegram was sent to mark the 50th jubilee of Tolstoy's literary activity. The original is kept in the archives of the Tolstoy State Museum (Manuscript Department).

Gorky Letters

EXTRACT FROM LETTER FROM GORKY TO ANTON CHEKHOV
(Nizhni-Novgorod, between October 1–7 [14–20], 1900)

I have just returned from Moscow, where I spent a whole week rushing around and feasting my soul on such marvels as *The Snow Maiden,* and Vasnetzov, *Death of Ivan the Terrible,* and Chaliapin.

Chaliapin is a simple fellow, enormous and clumsy, with a roughly hewn, intelligent face. Everything in him proclaims the artist. I spent no more than half an hour with him. . . .

Editor's Note: Text taken from Gorky's complete works in 30 volumes, State Publishing House, 1952. Vols 28 and 29.

All Gorky letters, unless otherwise stated, are from the Gorky Literary Archives.

FROM GORKY TO CHALIAPIN (Nizhni-Novgorod, September 14–15 [27–28], 1901)

My dear, my good Feodor,

Thanks for the telegrams and do shake the Baron's hand for me. Forgive me for opening with a request, the writer, Veritskaya has asked me to try and persuade you to give a concert in aid of Moscow women students. As you probably know, there is a society for aiding these students and it has two hostels for them in the city, and three canteens. To keep up this good work requires some 6,000 roubles a year, and they have no income beyond that supplied by membership fees. In addition to this the society makes grants of some five roubles a month to about two hundred girl students out of 500 applicants. So, if you can, please help them.

Yesterday I received a notification from the police. I am forbidden to live in Nizhni-Novgorod, and this means a move to some other part of the district in the very near future. So much for my Moscow hopes. I shall try to get permission to go to the Crimea. You can die of cold and other inconveniences in a provincial town during the winter. It won't help the children either. Do try and get something moving for me so that I can travel to the Crimea. I was thinking of writing to Prince Svyatopolk-Mirsky about this.

To return to this concert idea. Please think about it. As you know

Veritskaya is in Moscow, her address is: c/o Rittig, Granatny Pereulok. Please let her know.

The society offers you five hundred roubles for your performance at this concert.

Well, my dear friend, the last query. When do we see each other?

A. Peshkov.

Editor's Note: Gorky's son, Maxim, was then four years old, and Ekaterina just born. On April 17, 1901, Gorky was arrested and put into prison at Nizhni-Novgorod, accused of anti-government propaganda amongst the workers. But a deterioration in his health led to his being released in May of that year, thanks to the help of his friends, including Tolstoy. Nevertheless, the Ministry of Internal Affairs forbade Gorky to live in Nizhni-Novgorod, and he was ordered to move to Arzamas, a railway junction between Moscow and Kazan.

EXTRACT OF LETTER FROM GORKY TO K. P. PYATNITSKY[1]
(Nizhni-Novgorod, September 13 [26], 1901)

. . . All this time I have been engrossed, enthralled by Chaliapin, and now I am at full steam with my own play. Chaliapin is something tremendous, astonishing, and oh, how Russian. Defenceless and vulnerable, a semi-literate cobbler and turner, he has passed through the thorny path of every conceivable humiliation. He has reached the top of the hill, is crowned with glory, yet withal, he has remained a good, sincere, and simple person. This to me is magnificent. What a personality! He gave a concert here in aid of the People's Theatre, and we got around 2,500 roubles from the proceeds, from which sum I have already frittered away around 600 roubles. Dreadful. Never mind, I'll scrape through somehow.

Generally speaking, life on this earth is of amazing interest. Chaliapin feels the same way. He is endeavouring to get me a permit to come to Moscow in October, where I dearly hope to be for the production of my play.

Editor's Note: [1] Konstantin Petrovich Pyatnitsky (1864–1938), head of the Znaniye Publishing House.

FROM E. P. PESHKOVA [GORKY'S WIFE] TO CHALIAPIN
(September 13 [26], 1900 or 1901)

If you decide to write to Aleksei, please send the letter care of myself, because letters and telegrams addressed to him go though the police department and arrive here opened. This is what happened with your telegram.

It is unpleasant to receive letters in this way, and if it happened to be a letter from yourself, someone so near and dear to him, he would find it particularly distressing. It is quite possible that my own letters are being opened and read, but they are at least brought to me here direct from the Post Office, and appear to be unopened.

Left 67. *Chaliapin as Holofernes in Serov's opera Judith (Russian Private Opera, Moscow), 1898.*

Above 68. *Sketch for Chaliapin's costume and make-up in the part of Holofernes, in Serov's opera Judith, by the painter V. A. Serov, the composer's son.*

69. *Chaliapin as Holofernes in Serov's opera* Judith *(Zimin's Opera, Moscow), 1915.*

70. Chaliapin as the Miller in Dargomyzhsky's opera Russalka (*Mariinsky Theatre, St. Petersburg*), *1916.*

Chaliapin as Eremka in Serov's The Power of Evil (above) and as Salieri in Mozart and Salieri (below)

We still exist in the golden glow you created for us. You are a constant topic in our conversation. The day after you left, Aleksei started work on his play. He wants to finish it by October, after which we may get the chance to go to Moscow. It would be a good thing if you could persuade him to go to Yalta. He is coughing again, and working at high pressure. I only hope he doesn't collapse. However, this is not the time for mentioning such things. We hope to see you soon, and thank you once again. We did enjoy our stay with you.

Editor's Note: Chaliapin family archives, dated according to contents.

FROM GORKY TO CHALIAPIN (end September [beginning October], 1901)

Dear friend Feodor,

I sent off the music and the photographs which you left behind you. Now, listen to me. Please don't bother about finding some money for me. Not necessary. The big fact is that I am being exiled from Nizhni-Novgorod to Arzamas, though for what reason I do not know as yet. I sent in an application for permission to go to the Crimea, so if there is anything at all that you can do, do please try. Another thing, d'you think you could manage to send me 1,000 roubles, say before the 1st of the month? If so, please send, and I'll repay you in the Spring.

For the time being I shan't do anything, there is no time, my head feels heavy.

I am sending you some books for the Baron, c/o yourself, not knowing his address.

I shall never forget the days spent with you. What a splendid person you are, Feodor.

Keep well. You know there are rumours in the town that I am being banned from here because of the concert, and its programme. The idiots! The devils!

A. Peshkov.

Editor's Note: Gorky refers to Chaliapin's concert, which took place in September 1901, the proceeds from which were paid into the fund for the construction of the People's Theatre in Nizhni-Novgorod.

TELEGRAM FROM CHALIAPIN TO GORKY (October 26, 1901)

Dear Leksa,

Yesterday received letter from Svyatopolk-Mirsky granting you permission to go Yalta delighted this news will be Petersburg December and will make all efforts for future embrace you as strongly as I love you. Kiss my dear Katerina's hands for me. Greetings to all.

Your Feodor Chaliapin.

FROM GORKY TO CHALIAPIN (Nizhni-Novgorod, between October 13–21 [October 26–November 8], 1901)

My dear dear friend,

Thank you for all the trouble you have taken on my behalf. Don't forget the photographs for me.

I watch the newspapers like a hawk, reading about you. I feel proud, I rejoice at your success. How I should have loved to have seen you in *The Maid of Pskov*. I feel frustrated. If they do really allow me to go to Yalta, I shall use all endeavours, fair or foul, to stay in Moscow, if only for a single day, just to see you. I do so want to.

I am being heavily pressed by the police. But that's a mere trifle.

Incidentally the money will be paid back to you direct from the Arts Theatre, that is as soon as the censor passes my play.

Au revoir for now. I'll let you know the date of my departure from Nizhni. Dare I hope that you will be in Yalta over Lent? All my family and friends send their greetings.

A. Peshkov.

P.S. Let me have the details of Svyatopolk-Mirsky's letter.

Editor's Note: Gorky's play, *Meshchane*, "The Philistines", had its first night at the Moscow Arts Theatre on March 26, 1902, whilst the company were on tour in St. Petersburg.

FROM GORKY TO CHALIAPIN (Nizhni-Novgorod, end October [beginning November], 1901)

My dear friend,

I have now received permission to go to the Crimea, and will set out about November 10th. I shall, of course, go via Moscow. It is essential for me to stay there for a week or two, is there anything you can do to help get me the permission to do so? Please try.

Your Alexei.

Editor's Note: Gorky's hope of a week's stay in Moscow was not realized. The police, dreading any political demonstration, had stopped the writer en route, at a small station not far from the city. They transferred him to Podolsk, from where he was taken by train to the Crimea. On hearing this, his friends, Leonid Andreyev, Alexander Bunin, Teleshov, Pyatnitsky and Scholz (German translator of Gorky's works) all went to Podolsk. In his reminiscences, Teleshov writes: "I and Chaliapin came to see Gorky at Podolsk station. Whilst tea was being prepared, and the table got ready for supper, a rumour spread through the town that Gorky had arrived with other writers, accompanied by Chaliapin. Upon which long queues of people began to stretch towards the station. Meanwhile the following incident took place in the first-class restaurant: "We had just settled down behind a curtain and begun talking, when we heard the sound of approaching footsteps, complete with tinkling spurs. They went by. Our German became anxious, and asked what was happening. His anxiety getting the better of him, he went outside to look. In a terrified voice, he announced: 'They are rummaging in our coats.' We quietly explained to him that this was a common occurrence, and that he should not allow himself to be upset by such trifles. A few moments later a very embarrassed landlord appeared, the hotel register in his hands. He put this on the table and demanded that we all sign it, stating who we were, where we came from, where we lived, and our full names. Suddenly, and with all seriousness, Chaliapin announced: 'I am the only traveller here, these gentlemen are my guests, and there is no law that requires their registration. Hand me that book. I shall do the necessary signing.'

"With some trepidation the landlord watched him writing in the register. And finally, when he saw that his tormentor was an artist of the Imperial Theatres, he sighed with relief."—N. Teleshov. *A Writer's Note-book*. Published by *Soviet Writer*, Moscow, 1950, pp. 99-100.

FROM GORKY TO CHALIAPIN (Arzamas, June 13–16 [26–29], 1902)

Dear friend Feodor Ivanovich,

There's a rumour you may be coming to sing at the Fair, do please tell me if this is true. If so, when, please. If I know this, then by the time you arrive I shall try to wangle permission from the authorities to visit Nizhni-Novgorod, and hear you, the Nightingale sent into the world.

Life remains fair to middling, though my health is cracking up. Spitting blood. As sure as sure is, I shall go down if I have to remain here until the winter.

A. Peshkov.

GORKY TO CHALIAPIN (Moscow, December 30–31, 1902 [January 12–13, 1903])

My dear friend Feodor Ivanovich

I would be happy and delighted to see the New Year in. Please come, and of course bring Iola Ignatyevna, to the Arts, they all long to see you. So now, for the time being, I excuse (embrace) you warmly. Don't know how "excuse" crept in, it had no business there. Let me hear from you my dear friend, and don't forget to ask Iola Ignatyevna.

Yours, Alexei.

Editor's Note: Iola Ignatyevna—Chaliapin's first wife. "Come to the Arts" refers to the Moscow Arts Theatre, where Gorky's play, *The Lower Depths*, was presented on December 18, 1902.

There is an interesting entry in Telyakovsky's diary dated December 20, 1902: "Very interesting evening at my place. At eleven o'clock read through

Gorky's new play, *The Lower Depths*. Chaliapin had arrived earlier in the day, and when he learned about the reading, offered to read it himself. He did, and read superbly, like the true artist he is. He obviously knew it to the bone. The reading continued until 3 a.m."

In Vladimir Karenin's book, *Vladimir Stassov* (page 681, 1927 Edition), there is Stassov's own account of Chaliapin's readings from the works of Gorky.

EXTRACTS FROM LETTERS FROM GORKY TO HIS WIFE, E. T. PESHKOVA (Staraya Russa, July 15–16 [28–29], 1904)

. . . As I already told you, I saw both Alexin and Chaliapin in Moscow. Chaliapin has grown fat, and talks a great deal about himself. Not a good sign. He should leave that sort of thing to other people. Nevertheless, he is a sweet person, though success does sometimes rather spoil him.

(St. Petersburg, September, 1904)

. . . That's a great blow about the girl, but I'm sorrier still for you. You've wasted the whole summer. Chaliapin is here, and he tells me that his daughter had exactly the same trouble, and has had four operations already. His wife is expecting another child in September. I'm disgusted about this, since it's quite obvious to me that the eldest girl has T.B., suffering as she does from a bad stomach and high temperatures. Igor[1] died from malnutrition. Why have children in such circumstances?

As ever, Chaliapin sings like a god, and acts like the great artist he is. He's sending the kids to Yalta, and you'll probably meet him there.

Editor's Note: [1]Igor—Chaliapin's eldest son (1899–1903)—died from acute appendicitis.

EXTRACT FROM A LETTER FROM GORKY TO HIS WIFE, E. T. PESHKOVA (St. Petersburg, July 11–12 [24–25], 1904)

. . . We have just buried Anton Chekhov, my dear.

We expected speeches at the graveside. Alas, there were practically none. The people present began demanding that I should speak. Whenever Chaliapin and I appeared we became objects of curiosity. They stared, they sort of fingered us. Still not a word, not a single sound about Chekhov. Who were all these people? I haven't the faintest idea. They climbed trees and laughed, broke the cemetery crosses, swore and squabbled for ringside places. In loud voices they kept on asking "which one is the wife? And the sister?" "Oo! Just look. They're crying." "Have you heard? He hasn't left a penny. Everything goes to Marx." "Poor Knipper." "Oh, no need to pity her. She is getting at least 10,000 roubles in the theatre," and so on, and so on.

All this slime crawled into our ears. It forced its way in, intrusively, impudently. One didn't want to hear any of this. No. One just longed for a single sincere and sorrowful word. Alas, it remained unspoken. The whole thing was unbearably painful. Chaliapin burst into tears, then began swearing, "and for this sort of scum *he*'d lived and worked".

I led him away from the cemetery.

The mob surrounded us as we were getting into the carriage. They grinned, and they stared. That's all. . . . Then suddenly somebody, one voice from the thousands, shouted, "Ladies and gentlemen, leave them. This is indecent."

But they did not leave.

Editor's Note: Chekhov was buried in Moscow on July 9 [22], 1904.

FROM GORKY TO CHALIAPIN (Capri, September, 1909)

My dear Feodor,

Konstantin Petrovich[1] is here, and has told me of your desire to write and publish your autobiography. Allow me to say that this piece of news alarmed and disturbed me. So I hasten to write to you, my friend, and say just one thing.

You are starting something big, important, and of universal significance; something of interest, not only to us Russians, but to the entire civilized and, particularly so, the artistic world. Do you understand this?

It requires much thought, and certainly cannot be slapped together any old how. I implore you, and you must trust me, not to say anything about this to a living soul, in brief, do nothing, until you have spoken to me.

It would be sad indeed if this splendid material fell into the claws of some small-minded creature who wouldn't understand the whole national importance of your life, a life symbolic in a sense, for it must bear witness to the might and power of our country, yes, and of the living sources of blood that flood its heart, that today lies heavy under the yoke of its Tartar overlords. Watch out, Feodor, don't fling your soul into the lap of the word merchants.

And believe well, I am not pursuing a single personal advantage in guarding you from what might well turn out to be a disaster. I say this, my friend, bearing in mind your headlong kindnesses, even a somewhat endearing inconsistency. No. It could be a mistake.

Now here is what I offer you. Either come here for a month and a half, and *I myself shall write your life as you dictate it,*[2] or invite me to some place, outside Russia, and I shall come to you and we shall work on your autobiography, for perhaps three or four hours a day. I shall not cramp your style. I shall just point out what should be emphasised, and what should be left in the shadow. I shall even supply the language should you wish it, and if not, then make whatever changes you like.

My feeling is this. Whatever has to be written must be excellently written. I am not pushing myself forward, far from it. All that is required is that you yourself should talk about yourself.

Tell nobody of this letter, show it to none, and I really mean this. Ah, the devil take you, but honestly I'm so terrified at the thought that you might underestimate the national, the Russian significance of your auto-biography. My dear friend, close your eyes for an hour, and think. Look carefully about you, and in a vast grey desert you will behold a giant figure, a genius of a moujik. How can I tell you what I feel, or what, with burning claws, is tearing at my own heart. Ask Konstantin Petrovich, the best and most honourable of men I have ever met; ask him how important and dear to me is the very thought now so near to you. He will tell you. So, as a friend, I beg you not to rush into anything, move warily, begin nothing prematurely, at least not before talking with me. And I promise you I will not spoil a thing, I want to help you in so many ways, and be very sure of that. If you can't write, then telegraph your reply. And once more, not a word about it, to a single soul. That is my most earnest plea.

Alexei.

P.S. Dear Konstantin Petrovich sends greetings to you, and to Maria Valentinovna.[3] So do I.

Editor's Note: [1] Pyatnitsky, K.P.

[2] This was done in the summer of 1916.

[3] Chaliapin's second wife.

FROM GORKY TO CHALIAPIN (Capri, between July 2 and 15, 1911)

My dear Feodor Ivanovich,

I have received your letter, and I have thought hard about it, astonished as I am by its simplicity and brevity.

I should have thought that our relationship, and the very virtue of it, would have induced you to write me long before this, if only to acquaint me with how you yourself look upon the wild idiocies perpetrated by you, not only to your great shame, but to the sorrow of all honest people in Russia.

You write to me, but not one single word is mentioned about the very matter, which as you know, as you must know, cannot but torment me, and which will never be forgotten, and never forgiven in Russia, however much of a genius you are. The rabble which normally surrounds you will regard it in a very different fashion. Yes, they will even justify your actions, try to bring you closer to themselves. But is your place in their ranks? Truly? I am sorry for you, Feodor, you cannot imagine the despicable nature of your action, I feel that. If you yourself feel no shame, it is better that we don't meet. So don't come to see me.

This letter is just between you and me, and very obviously so. I will not stand in the company of those who consider you a lick-spittle—I know this is wrong, I know this is not true, as I also know that your self-appointed judges are no better than you.

If only you could understand how appalled I am, how terrified I feel for a country where the best people are devoid of fastidiousness even of the simple kind known to animals. If only you could realize how bitter and shameful it is to imagine you, a genius, on your very knees before the most loathsome villain, yes indeed, the most abominable of all the villains in Europe.

A. Peshkov.

FROM CHALIAPIN TO GORKY (Vichy, July 18 [31], 1911)

... I can find no words, Alexei Maximovich, to describe the sadness your letter has caused me. Oh—I can't tell you how much it hurts me to read it, yes, and read it, and reread it. For several days now I have felt completely crushed. Especially as you are right. I should never have written you such a short, irrelevant little letter. Quite right.

But I swear to you that I was intentionally avoiding the subject of my "misdeed", hoping to tell you about it personally. The times that I have tried to write you in detail, and each time I felt so disturbed that I simply could not put my letter into a clear enough form, at least not the way I can talk to you in words. Nor do I suppose I shall succeed even now, because in addition to the turmoil I experience within myself, I also lack the ability to put down simply and clearly what goes on in my soul. Now that the possibility of talking this over personally with you has vanished, to my great grief, I shall try to do the best I can. Please listen.

I had put in a great deal of hard work into my dream project, this new production of *Boris Godunov*, on the stage of the Imperial Theatres. At long last my dream became real, and I, happy, inspired, and excited about this marvellous new production, with the décor by Golovin, went off to play in my favourite opera.

The performance began, and I, after my first scene, was loafing about backstage, upset by the indifference of the public, for there was no applause, not even as a joke, and this despite the fact that the artists, the chorus, and the orchestra were doing their work with devotion and care. So that when I came out to do my big scene with Shuisky, and the hallucinations, I was in a rage.

They say that when I am angry I play with greater inspiration, I don't know, perhaps I do, but by the end of this scene the audience had really come to life, and there were shouts and bursts of applause. Scarcely able to breathe through strain and fatigue—feeling like some broken-winded horse—I, at a sign from the conductor, went on stage to take the usual bow. The curtain rose and fell, and I bowed again. In brief, everything seemed to be as usual, and I was on the point of returning to my dressing-room to have tea and wet my parched throat, when suddenly behind me I heard a voice say: "Where do you think you're going? What are you doing?" I turned round, and there was the producer. He appeared to be frightened by the extraordinary goings on, which took almost everybody by surprise. All around me stood the members of the chorus, bewildered, almost demented, and the artists who had taken part in the performance. They were actually fighting and crashing their way through the only door that led to the stage, provided in this set, Czar Boris's chamber. There was something frantic, rather mad about it. Then all at once they fell on their knees and started to sing the national anthem.

Not understanding the meaning of this I tried to get clear of the stage, but I could not, there existed no physical way of removing myself. The place was seething with people, so that I was forced to remain on stage. I just stood and looked about me. There was certainly something afoot, something very peculiar, and from time to time there were a series of what I can only describe as indeterminate exclamations of, "Feodor Ivanovich, Feodor Ivanovich, you won't go away—you don't want to—don't go—don't leave —", or something of that nature, and through it all the singing went on, so that I could not hear properly. I was rooted there, dumbfounded. The thought flashed through my mind that this had been organised on purpose, to get me into some sort of trouble (I have become so inured to this that I am every moment expecting it), and I stood and stared. Was this a cleverly arranged intrigue against me? Will a scandal break out now, this very moment? My imagination ran riot, and I was struck dumb. Nor could I get away from the stage. I was perplexed, and scared. I lost all capacity to think clearly, and went down on my knees by an armchair which stood near me, upstage.

Thus I became the unwilling participant in that foul and obscene demonstration, and when, a moment later, I understood its real meaning, it was too late. Yes, I was really "in the soup" as they say.

Shaken, terribly upset, I managed to get to my dressing-room.

Immediately several members of the chorus came to see me, and with tears in their eyes asked me to go to their dressing-room. Wishing to get to the bottom of this extraordinary scene I went with them, and listened to the expressions of "profound gratitude", and "cheers" in my honour, for my support of their hardships. "Only you, Feodor Ivanovich, and the Czar, can save us from the oppressions of the administration."

This upset me, and without bothering to ask them for details of their oppressions, I left. To this very day I do not know what prompted them to go down on their knees. It seemed to me the prelude to the presentation of some petition or other to his imperial majesty.

In the interval I sent for the director, Telyakovsky, and I told him quite straight that I was outraged by the appearance of the chorus on stage during my scene, it had no right to be there, that I should have been warned about it, that I disliked such surprises and did not want them—but the excited and embarrassed director replied that he knew nothing about it, that what had happened was as much a surprise to him as it was to me. Moreover, he expressed his anxiety about the affair, and of how the authorities might feel about this demonstration.

A day later I left Petersburg for Monte Carlo, with a sad and heavy heart, and I felt that nothing less than a mountain of filth pressed upon it. And as usual it was news, the papers had it, within hours. I read that the chorus and orchestra of the Mariinsky Theatre, headed by Chaliapin, had staged a solemn manifestation, by singing the anthem on their knees. Some papers, greedy for sensation, even had drawings of me, in which I was depicted with hands together, standing in front of the chorus, zealously opening my mouth and proclaiming "God save the Czar".

That was only the beginning. From then on they really did exercise their talents. The papers even printed statements allegedly made by me, in the course of alleged interviews. In these I was supposed to have passionately declared that I was just a simple moujik, that I cannot help going down on my knees before the Czar, that if I even see him at a distance I crash down flat on my face at once, as befits an observer of true Russian customs, etc., etc. In a word, the wheels were set in motion, well and truly.

For quite some time I kept my silence, and felt profoundly hurt by it all. The affair went on rising, higher and higher, and automatically inflating itself. From Petersburg a letter was forwarded to me from Amfiteatrov (he sent it to me in Petersburg, so naturally there was some delay). There was an occasion when I went to Nice and ran into a group of Russians, and they organised a demonstration for my benefit at the railway station. I pretended not to notice their antics, but they arrived in Villefranche by the same train, obviously intent on beating me up. In the end I did have to fight with them and, greatly distressed, alone, not knowing what to do, whom to consult, I asked Maria Valentinovna to write to Konstantin Petrovich and ask him to come to Monte Carlo. He promised, but did not turn up, perhaps prevented by his own affairs. Then, bombarded from all sides with anonymous letters, I decided to write a letter to the newspaper, and did. It was a stupid letter, if only because I was its author. I did not know which way to turn, I lost my presence of mind. Then I began writing a reply to Amfiteatrov. From Moscow and Petersburg I heard that he had sent copies of his letter to me to various people as well as to newspapers, and that it was having the widest circulation.

This struck me as odd on his part, and malicious into the bargain. It also became quite clear to me that he wrote me, not because he "loved me so much", as he had stated in the letter, but for reasons of his own. I then decided not to write to him.

All this astonished and frightened me, and involuntarily I was beginning to fear your opinion of me. Several times I tried to write you, and nothing came of it. Somehow, each day I was tearing up a letter. Maria Valentinovna, seeing my doubts and anxieties, wrote off to Konstantin Petrovich, asking him to find out if I could come to see you, so, about a month ago, when I arrived in Milan, she gave me the reply that you had no objections and that my arrival would not embarrass you. I was overjoyed, and all ready to start, and then I had this swelling of my leg and arm, so that instead of going to Capri, I was forced to go for a cure, about which I wrote you a

CHALIAPIN

short note. And that is all that happened. Please permit me to tell you that neither my heart nor my soul took any part in what happened and I am guilty only because firstly I lost my head, and secondly because I happen to work for an establishment, where, unfortunately, the surprising incident of finding oneself on all fours cannot be ruled out.

I was beginning to think that I should not return, I mean not only to the Imperial Theatres, but not return to Russia at all, but maybe this is not such a good idea.

I sing, of course, all over Europe, but what kind of Italian or French artist do I make? If I left Russia for good, that would be the end of my art.

It is good to come to Paris or Milan, give five or six concerts, but I get almost no real artistic satisfaction from it. In Russia I dreamed of a theatre of my own, but it is impossible for me. For that one requires administrative talents, which I lack and with life in Russia as it is at present, they can only think of the best ways of blackmailing me. It's enough to make one perish altogether, yes, and lose one's health and voice. Sing in private theatres? That's worse still. They go in for all sorts of tricks, and modern stylistics. It would make me more than sick to sing there. So the only way out is to work for the Imperial Theatres, there at least there is a twice yearly chance of a good production, one's heart lifts, for there is a good deal of real art to be seen. So life goes on.

You say, "The rabble which normally surrounds you will, of course, try to justify your actions."

I have not been anywhere for two years, and most of the time I try to be alone. I have chased away many, the result being that former acquaintances now trumpet out as one man the same refrain: "He got too big for his boots, the son of a bitch," and this on every suitable occasion. They blackmail me when it strikes their fancy, it has become an almost routine thing in my life. Just imagine how they jubilate when they see me in this trouble. My God! How they rejoice, with what delight they kick me, a boundless happiness possessing them.

Dear Alexei Maximovich, never before have I told or written what I have said to you now, and I don't suppose anybody has told you my side of the story, as it really was.

I feel bowed down by the thought of having caused you pain. I repeat once again, all that foulness and obscenity has no place in my heart, and what happened, oh, the devil alone knows what and why. It just happened.

There! To conclude, even though I have been packed into filth as thoroughly as a corpse is put into a coffin, I nevertheless reserve the right, in spite of anything and everything, to love and respect you as I have always loved and respected you.

Feodor Chaliapin.

Editor's Note: A. V. Amfiteatrov sent Chaliapin a rude letter (January 26, 1911) in which he congratulated him on the "monarch's pleasure", accused him of "allegiance to the throne", and said that he was breaking off his friendship with the singer.

FROM CHALIAPIN TO GORKY (Vichy, early July, 1911)

My dear Alexei,

Never in my life have I been visited by so much bad luck as at this time. I was on the point of coming to you, and the very thought of it thrilled me, and then alas, my foot swelled up (the after effects of a badly set dislocation, and sprained tendons due to an awkward fall on stage[1]). Result, I am unable to walk. I detest the idea of arriving in Capri on crutches, which I am forced to use at the moment, and on top of that my doctor has just ordered me back to Vichy, because in addition to this dislocation, he also found some pretty hefty symptoms of gout. I shall have to follow a course of treatment for the next three weeks.

Believe well that the moment I am clear of Vichy, I'll rush to you. So please let me know whether you'll be at home at that time, that is to say, end of July approximately, or beginning of August (our calendar).

I need to talk to you about so many things. But first of all, a big question. Have you a piano in your new home? If not, d'you think you could get one in time for my arrival (and see that it is properly tuned)? I have an inordinate desire to sing to you, and I am thinking of bringing a good pianist with me. Write to me at Vichy, poste restante.

Greetings to Maria Feodorovna, and my love and a big hug to you.

Feodor Chaliapin.

Waiting to hear from you. See you soon.

Editor's Note: [1] At a performance of *The Maid of Pskov*, in Milan, Chaliapin was thrown by a horse, finished the opera with a badly sprained foot, and hurt it again in Paris, in *Don Quixote*, on some badly secured scenery.

FROM GORKY TO CHALIAPIN (Capri, between July 20, and August 1 [August 1–14], 1911)

And I love and respect you not less than I have always done, for I know that in your heart of hearts you are an honest man, incapable of servility and sucking up, but you are an absurd Russian none the less, and I have told you this time and again. You don't really know your own worth, yes, your true and great worth.

I suffer unbearable pain for you, even to tears, and I think of you a great deal especially of how best to help you. But how? Do what? I feel powerless, I see no way.

It really was unwise that you did not, immediately after this whole business, come to me and explain the circumstances, for, getting it from your own lips, and trusting you as I do, I might, I could have managed something to stop the mouths of your judges.

Now we shall just have to bide time. I should love you to come here, very much so, but this place is full of Russians. Moreover, I am on bad terms with them, and they would not miss the chance of a scandal, if only as a pin-prick to me. In addition to the locals, we have the weekly crowds of tourists from Russia, they arrive in herds, fifty at a time, a wild and vulgar lot.

Yet we must meet. Hold on for a while, and I'll write you about how and where we can meet without noise and publicity. To do so now would revive the scandal all over again. How they would enjoy using you as the stick to beat me with, and then me as a stick to hit you. They live for show, an exhibitionism; they are all so keen to show their honesty, a very sure sign of the reverse.

Till we meet again, my dear Feodor Ivanovich, keep well and don't let things get you down too much. It will sort itself out.

A. Peshkov.

TELEGRAM FROM CHALIAPIN TO GORKY (August 3 [16], 1911)

Thank you dear Alexei Maximovich for your letter. It revived me. Will write you in a few days' time, giving you my address. Greetings to you and Maria Feodorovna.

Feodor.

FROM CHALIAPIN TO GORKY (Switzerland mid-August, 1911)

I was very very happy to receive your letter, dear Alexei Maximovich. It revived me, for believe me I was beginning to think I'd reached the end. My thanks, too, to dear Maria Feodorovna, whose few lines came to me like a silent pressure of the hand, and moved me to tears.

At the moment I am roaming about Switzerland. Very boring, in spite of the fact that everything is so splendidly organised. You feel as though you're just walking in some giant "luna park" (like the one on Coney Island). There are all sorts of attractions, the funicular railway, the blue water, vast mountains and so on. And all of it looks as if made out of papier-mâché. The people are silent, quiet, helpful.

We are surrounded, on the one hand, with bored "Swiss" maîtres-d'hôtel, and on the other, with equally bored herds of tourists, in constant search of amusement. I feel a bit vexed at thus being sandwiched in their midst.

All these sunrises and sunsets, and mists and Mont Blanc. Beautiful, yet I want desperately to get away from it all. The many Russians here love the place, and I recall that we have a place back home in Kazan, a range of hillocks called "Russian Switzerland" and a "German Switzerland", yet here am I, Kazan born and bred, and I don't like it.

And then I stop to think of what is awaiting me on my return to Russia. I get a spasm of the heart and long to creep away into some ravine.

Yes, dear Maximovich, I really have landed inside the frame of public opinion. And how.

Our trusting, and in its majority, stupid public does, on the one hand, love me very much, or perhaps I should say loved, and on the other, judges me entirely on the contents of the theatre and music columns of the newspapers, where, and especially these last few years, they have been painting my mug in such colours that I have failed to recognise myself. Various "friends" of mine added a few deft strokes to complete the portrait, and, as I said above, I'm now well and truly "framed".

This frame does not fit, it presses upon me painfully, and sometimes I don't know whether I have the right to scream with pain. Perhaps I am guilty of something. God, wouldn't I love to know the answer to that one.

Invariably people are inclined to think the best of themselves. Perhaps all that I think of myself is just nonsense, I don't know. But I would love to talk about it with some real honest man. I look about me, I see so very few honest people. Now only you stand out before me. And I want to listen only to you.

I realise the embarrassment of coming to you. Perhaps we can arrange a meeting somewhere, unknown to anybody.

Given our sort of conditions, there are few honest newspapers. The devil knows what they may invent, and what buckets of filth may pour out from them, this time, on you also. The public is one big fool and will believe anything.

Please, write, my dear Maximovich, if it is possible without embarrassing you, for that is my one concern. And don't stand on ceremony with me. Please. If it can't be done, it can't, and I'll just have to wait for the possible occasion.

I shall have to go to Petersburg at the beginning of September, so if we find no possibility of a meeting now, we shall have to wait until next year.

Now I am off to Lugano to see the children, and will remain there until I hear from you. My address is:

Lanzo d'Intelvi, Gr. Hotel Bella Vista,
F. Chaliapin

Maria Valentinovna thanks you for your kind wishes, and in turn, sends hers to you and Maria Feodorovna. God send you good health.

Yours,
Feodor Ch.

FROM GORKY TO AMFITEATROV (Capri. August 28 [September 3], 1911)

Dear Alexander Valentovich,

I have Feodor staying with me, and it would be a very good thing if you could meet each other. He will be here until the twelfth, since on the nineteenth he is due to sing *Boris* in Petersburg.

My opinion is that this man should not be pushed to places to which he has no desire to go, for he is a person for whom one can and should fight, a

245

symbolic Russian, good and bad, though there is really more good than bad in him. Anyhow I should like to think the best possible of him, and to meet and talk with you about it. He is worth the trouble, isn't he?

Your letter made him most unhappy, of course, but he does not deny his "guilt", and that letter need not prevent our meeting, and yours with him. He is having a difficult and unpleasant time. He looks like a lion, bound and ready to be flung to the pigs and torn to shreds.

A country where Pavel Milyukov, who declared himself to be "the opposition of his majesty", got away with it without being howled down and judged, should not condemn Chaliapin without appeal, for he is worth more than six hundred Milyukovs.

Looking forward to hearing from you soon.

A. Peshkov.

Editor's Note: Chaliapin stayed with Gorky in Capri from August 27 to September 11, 1911. In spite of Gorky's personal request, Amfiteatrov did not come to Capri, nor did he resume his friendship with the singer.

FROM GORKY TO N. E. BURENIN (Capri, September 2–11 [15–24], 1911)

This, Evgenyich, is a letter to you concerning Feodor's "crime". So if they start attacking and baiting him I want you to defend him as best you can. Buy yourself a copy of *Le Gaulois* June 15th, 1911 (No. 12297) and on the first page you will find an article: "CHALIAPIN. By FOURCAUD." This article is interesting, quite apart from its relationship to Chaliapin, for we have here a European's view of Russian art. It would be good to have it translated and printed, wherever possible.

We sit here of an evening, all four of us, and often think of you. Sometimes Feodor feels like singing, but alas, "Evgenyich is not here", says he, and pokes his fingers into all the piano keys at once.

Editor's Note: This letter accompanied the one which follows and which Gorky intended to publish in the Russian press under the title: "A Letter to a Friend". (A copy of "A Letter to a Friend" was also sent to A. N. Tikhonov, the editor of *Letopis*.)

Burenin did not carry out Gorky's instructions. On the contrary, he advised Chaliapin against writing any letter to the press.

Chaliapin soon began to feel the heavy consequences of his silence. Knowing that the suitable moment for explanation was lost, he almost hoped for some demonstration against himself, to have an opportunity for making his statement. This, alas, never presented itself.

The negative attitude of the democratic circles towards Chaliapin manifested itself in numerous protests against the publication of his autobiography in *Letopis*. It is in reply to these protests that Gorky wrote his foreword to the autobiography, on Chaliapin's behalf.

The story of Chaliapin's part in the "kneeling incident" had been exaggerated out of all proportion, even in the works of certain Soviet critics, who should have known better. They had at their disposal Gorky's archives, including his correspondence with Chaliapin and his letters to Peshkova, Burenin and others, in which Gorky himself cut the incident to size.

FROM GORKY TO BURENIN (Capri, date as above)

Dear friend,

I don't understand all this noise which is being raised against Chaliapin, but listening carefully I can detect a great many pharisaically-minded notes, we are none of us such sinners as this publican. Now what has happened? Feodor Chaliapin, a natural born artist, a man of genius, he who made all Europe sit up and take notice, made them realize that the Russian people, the Russian moujik, is not the wild savage that Europe hears almost too much about. No. Chaliapin, who has rendered Russian art the great and unforgettable service, went down on his knees before Czar Nicholas II. So the collective sinner of all Russia went mad with delight at this highly convenient opportunity for self justification. It started roaring, "Down with Chaliapin. Trample him into the filth."

How did this happen? To what extent was Chaliapin's gesture premeditated? Was he really a lick-spittle, at that moment, or did he simply lose his head? To that no one gave a thought, and never even bothered to try. No, all were so ready to condemn him. And why? Because condemning this artist is a really profitable business. The small time, cowardly, insignificant little sinner will always try to interpret the stupid action of a great man as despicable, bringing him down to his own level, drag him far down, among the dregs, where he will be lost amongst the host of those motley little souls whose main function in life would seem to be rummaging around, and nothing more than that. And the parrot cry, "See, he's no different to us."

It has long been more than a suspicion with me that the Russian moralists require large-scale sinners, large-scale criminals, for in the very depths of their souls they feel themselves to be criminals against the Russian people, against the beliefs of yesterday, that are now rejected, betrayed. For a long time, and you must see this, they have grovelled on their knees amidst the foulness, invested as they were by every kind of boot-licking tendency.

Just think of Pavel Milyukov's resounding announcement, so grandly echoing, across all Europe: "We are His Majesty's opposition." And the confident voice of Gershenzon, advocating the use of bayonets in order to instil in the Russian people the proper respect for statesmanship. Of these deeds there is a whole series. These people were not condemned as severely as they should have been, although, from the social-pedagogical point of view, their deeds cannot be compared to that of Chaliapin. They, and a whole multitude like them, were far too frightened, far too corrupted by dirty political intrigues. They escaped censure. To what do they owe this escape? Only to the fact that those who sat in judgment were no better than themselves. And they knew it.

Now, sobered up somewhat, they realize their mistakes, and each hopes to whitewash himself by accusing his neighbour. Oh, no. They won't succeed. To clear ourselves in the eyes of each other, we need, not courts and judgments, and not lynch-law, but a great concentrated effort of self-education, in the spirit of reason and honour, in brief, real work of social education. The fact that they can hurl the dirt at this great artist, or anyone else for that matter, will not make them any cleaner. On the contrary it will make them even more pathetic and miserable.

F. Chaliapin, a symbolic figure, yes and an astonishingly integral image of democratic Russia, this huge personality embodies in himself all the best and most talented that is in our people, and it does not exclude the bad or the weakness that lies in us all. He reminds us all of how powerful, beautiful and talented is the Russian people. He is flesh of its flesh, a man torn through the thorns and great hustle of life, yes, and he proudly takes his place amongst the best in the world, for he sings to all about Russia, to reveal that she, in her innermost depths is big, and talented, and enchanting. Russia should be loved, she deserves it, for she is rich in great forces, and in her own bewitching beauty. And that is what Chaliapin is always singing about; it is what he lives for, and we in turn should bow to him in gratitude, in friendship, and not spend our time magnifying his mistakes, trying to degrade him.

Such people should be loved and cherished, for they are more precious to us, than those who yesterday were playing fanatics, and today are nihilists. Chaliapin will always remain what he is, blindingly bright, a joyous cry across the world. Here is Russia, and this is what her people is like. Make way. Give it freedom.

A. Peshkov.

FROM GORKY TO BURENIN (Capri, mid-September, 1911)

My dear Evgenyich,

Feodor will be arriving in Petersburg within the next few days, and I would like you to see him at once. It is possible that he might have to write an open letter to the press, in which, he firstly will admit his faults in losing his head, so committing a stupid act; secondly will recognise the indignation of decent people as being natural and proper; thirdly, he will tell how all those vulgar interviews and telegrams for which he is being blamed originated.

This letter must be simply written, clear, and sufficiently convincing. I should be grateful if you would introduce Feodor to Stassov, and then ask Stassov on my behalf to help him write the letter.

73. *Chaliapin, a portrait by N. V. Kharitonov, 1916.*

74. Chaliapin and Rachmaninov, 1916.

75. *Chaliapin and his friend, Moskvin, an actor in the Moscow Arts Theatre.*

. Chaliapin and V. L. Nemirovich-Danchenko (the successful Imperial Theatre dramatist, who, together with anislavsky, founded the Moscow Arts Theatre) with a group of actors from the M.A.T. Second Studio, 1916. On haliapin's left, Alla Tarasova, who joined the M.A.T. that year. She was last seen in London in 1964 in The Cherry Orchard.

77. Chaliapin, a portrait by Yakovlev (detail), 1917 (Irina Chaliapina's collection).

This idiotic muddle must be unravelled, the truth separated from the lies, from this awful malice. Last but not least, we must all of us do our utmost to guard and protect this remarkable and exceptionally talented man.

Act, I beg of you.

Be well and happy.

A. Peshkov.

EXTRACT FROM LETTER FROM GORKY TO N. E. BURENIN (Capri, October, 1911)

. . . Were you right in persuading Feodor against a public explanation? I think not; the public can harbour resentments, and for a long time carry a stone in its bosom, especially long if it is given the right to throw the stone at a sinner.

FROM CHALIAPIN TO GORKY (Petersburg, November 15 [28], 1911)

My dear Alexei Maximovich,

It seems centuries since we parted, and save for a few unimportant telegrams, I haven't written you a line. It's rotten, really, but please don't reproach me.

Today I have locked myself at home, and none will be allowed in whilst I write this letter to you. Now, about my stay in Petersburg.

First, I went to see D. V. Stassov, and I told him that in the event of any scandal I would have to write to the papers. His reply was that it would do no good at all, not in the present circumstances with the air rife with blackmailing tactics. He had meant to write you himself if anything had happened. But, fortunately, nothing happened, and my first performance was in *Boris* with a full house, a great success, about which I sent you off that telegram.

I saw Evgenyich[1] several times, he, poor man, had to go into some sanatorium, though he is better now.

Kuprin came to see me (sober). We spent whole days together, and then, on the insistence of some writer called Manych (I am ignorant about who Manych is), we were photographed, and the result sent off to various newspapers. I thought that Kuprin wanted this, but no, it turned out that that fellow Manych wanted it. He was brought to my house, so that he, Manych, could make a little money from these papers. Well! What can you do?

I am very sorry for Kuprin, and cannot understand why he drinks the way he does, and persistently associates with circus acrobats and clowns.

Not long ago, Leonid Andreyev came to see me. There was an absurd incident in Khodotov's house, when Andreyev was nearly strangled, though whether by Kuprin or Skitalets, I wouldn't know. Quite a brawl. I, too, was invited that evening, but bitter experience being my teacher, I declined it. Thank God.

A few days ago, a small schoolboy, ten or eleven years old, the son of our colleague, the artist Sharonov, gave me some food for thought. When I asked him if his father ever sang at home, I was informed that he did not know, and did not wish to know, because he considered his father's a disgraceful occupation. Music and singing, said the boy, when the world outside is working on inventions like aeroplanes for the armies, was something to be ashamed of. This is the kind of youngsters we are getting these days. Heaven preserve my young ones from "fighting" games.

Now, a few words about *Khovanshchina*. Dear Maximovich, what a pity you were not here. What a marvellous work it is, and how we in the theatre rejoiced. I saw many people that took part in it cry. I can never sing this opera calmly. How much of our people has gone into it, what truth, despite the absence of historically correct truth, and a certain amount of muddle in the libretto. I hardly need to tell you that with this work Mussorgsky began something really splendid, and only his illness, and then his death, prevented him from completing it. The greatest pity, for I feel I know what Stassov and he had in mind. What astonishing seeds did Mussorgsky plant, yes, and think of him surrounded by poisonous vermin that tried to prevent their growth. If you have not read his letters to Stassov, then I will send them to you. This little volume appeared only a month ago. What wonderful letters they are, and what a splendid picture we have of this man of genius.

At the dress rehearsal I addressed a few words to the company, and suggested that we have a mass for Stassov, Mussorgsky and Rimsky-Korsakov. They agreed, and we all went off to the Cathedral of Our Lady of Kazan to sing the requiem. Alas, some sort of dean there refused to let us sing, the devil knows why, perhaps a whim, I don't know, though I'm aware that the clergy don't like me very much. How foolish we were made to look amongst the multitudes, some five to six thousand people gathered there.

Send me a list of books, dear Maximovich, as you promised. Now, just one more thing, and please don't mind my saying it, but I wish, I beg you to accept a little money from me—I shall have some in December. I'll send it with pleasure, whatever I can manage. And I hope you will take a little trip somewhere, and have a rest.

God willing, next spring I shall introduce you to a certain M. I. Tereshchenko, he is Telyakovsky's assistant at the moment, and a very rich man. Who knows, perhaps he will agree to do something you have always been dreaming of, you remember, that journal? I don't want to talk to him myself, in case I ruin it. I am trying to persuade him to come to Capri with me, he has all but promised.

Goodbye my dear friend, I love you dearly, and send you all the good wishes that you can expect from

Your loving **Feodor Chaliapin.**

Editor's Note: [1] N. E. Burenin.

FROM CHALIAPIN TO GORKY (Monte Carlo, January 19 [February 1], 1912)

I wanted to write you immediately, dear Maximovich, but I went down with a cold on my arrival here, which I must have picked up en route. If I have not written you from Russia for so long it was because I was induced to a certain caution. A lady called Isakova came specially to Petersburg to see me about it. From her I gathered that some gentleman who had been in prison with her husband has now been released, and is accusing me of singing at concerts to raise funds for the 1905 revolt, and mentioning particularly a concert given at the Fidler school. She says I must be careful, on the alert for anything, including possible searches. I was also told that letters were being opened at the post offices, nothing terrible in that, nevertheless it's unpleasant to send a letter knowing some other person may be reading it. The general position seems to be that Russia is squaring accounts with all so-called "free-thinkers", and with a vengeance. You probably know that Korolenko[1] has been arrested. The Government has again taken the mace into its hands and is swinging it right, left, and centre. How I long to know what the truth is, where it is.

My Russian winter season is over, and I left the country in a slight haze. The point is really this. Society was undoubtedly full of indignation concerning the stupid incident I was involved in, in January last year. Needless to say all the blame was laid at my door, the newspapers played it up to the limit. Believe it or not, and begging your pardon, I felt I was being driven into a privy from which there was no way out. Yet the whole season passed uneventfully, save for a trick played by some ruffian at one of my performances in Moscow. When I appeared on stage on horseback, as Ivan the Terrible, this hooligan blew a police whistle. What puzzles me is why society did not make some demonstration against me.[2] Had they assumed I was not guilty? The only attempt I made at justifying myself was one rather vulgar letter in *Le Matin*.

Do they think I'm not worth demonstrating against, or are they all heroes when it comes down to words, and less brave when the time arrives for action? What is it? Quite honestly, I can't say that such a gesture towards me fills me with joy. After all, if you decide to call someone "swine", then why bother to shake his hand? This time, and especially in Moscow, I have witnessed much malice, and much more cowardice.

Never mind, what's past is past, and what is, *is*. Let's change the subject, this one must lie quiet since I would much prefer to talk to you in person.

I was indescribably glad to read in your letter that you trust Pyatnitsky, and consider him a worthy, honourable man. It could not be otherwise. I don't know everything that is happening to him, but whatever it is it cannot affect him to the extent that it would send him downhill. Or is my reasoning faulty? Is there some other cause? One thing I do know. He is devoted to you.

M. I. Tereshchenko is staying at Cannes at the moment. I want to bring him with me to Capri. Would you like me to? I could speak to him in advance. Perhaps you would let me know what kind of journal you have in mind. Will it be the continuation of *Znaniye*, or a new magazine or newspaper? To tell you the truth, I'm a little afraid to talk to him myself for fear of spoiling something—I can be pretty dumb, as you know, especially in matters outside my competence. Anyway, just write and tell me. He offered to build me a theatre, but I resisted the temptation.

Perhaps it might be all right to talk to him about a newspaper. As you know journals spring up in Russia almost daily, nothing serious of course, mostly gutter-press type. The papers must be furious with me.

On December 26th I gave a concert in aid of the famine victims, and the profits, some 16,500 roubles I divided between six provinces Ufa, Simbir, Saratov, Samara, Kazan, and Vyatka. I wrote a letter to the editor of *Russkoye Slovo*, thanking the various people who had helped to organize the concert, and accounting for all the expenses. I requested of other papers, "Please copy". Not a squeak out of them, not a single one. Ah, but when it comes to reporting that I've lost my voice, or that someone called me a "cad" in the theatre, which they jump at daily—that makes news. Anyhow, do let me know if you want me to broach the subject with Tereshchenko.

That's all the news for now. Things jog along, the public says "charmant", and that they find this "musique sauvage de *Boris Godunov*", to their liking.

My greetings to all that know and remember me. I embrace you and love you dearly.

Feodor Chaliapin.

Editor's Note: [1] Vladimir Korolenko (1853–1921), Russian writer, close associate of Gorky's "Wednesday" literary circle. Died during the 1921 famine. Stories include "Makar's Dream" and "The Blind Musician". In 1912 Korolenko was sentenced to two weeks' imprisonment for publishing S. Y. Yelpatkevsky's article, "People of our Circle" in the periodical *Russkoye Bogatstvo*. But the sentence was evidently suspended since he was not imprisoned.

[2] In 1966 I met a very old lady in Moscow who described to me how she, with a whole group of revolutionary-minded students, went to the performance of *The Maid of Pskov*, to which Chaliapin refers in the above letter. They certainly planned a "demonstration" and came armed with cabbage heads, rotten fruit and other such-like ammunition. The first sight of Chaliapin charging on to the stage on his steed was enough to disarm them. They sat spellbound and forgot all about the demonstration. The magic worked.

N. F.

FROM CHALIAPIN TO GORKY (Monte Carlo, March 5, 1912)

Dear Maximovich,

You probably know that there is an excellent pianist, indeed he is a famous one, by name of Raoul Pugno, a charming young man and a great admirer of my work. When I saw him a week ago (he had been at one of my performances) he conveyed to me, with some enthusiasm, his great desire to write an opera for me. He asked me if there was any particular play, or part that I would like to play. Taking into consideration his being French, I can see his almost insurmountable difficulty in composing music for a Russian theme. However, I invited him for a meal, and we talked. When he left I had already promised to think it over. And I did. Suddenly into my mind came Oedipus Rex, for believe me it is one of my dearest dreams to play this great part. But now there comes the question of a libretto. That is difficult to do. Who shall write it?

I recalled how, some six years ago, when I was not yet the swine that I am now, I talked to Amfiteatrov about this matter. Without knowing how sincere he was, I was yet struck by his enthusiastic response, for he began work and even wrote part of a libretto. I think my memory serves me right. The time passed, and there was no composer to hand. I myself remained silent. Now there is a composer, but I have lost the librettist.

Amfiteatrov may despise me as a man, and even refuse to shake my hand, that is a matter for his own conscience, but he can scarcely despise me as an artist. Such is the line of my somewhat confused thoughts.

There is also the difficulty of approach on this matter of a libretto. Is it possible to find one, or would he rather write one himself for the opera for me? Perhaps he wouldn't even reply.

Then again, any such move on my part may lead him to suppose that it's a trick, that I am only trying to creep back into his good books. That I wouldn't like at all, so I repeat, the matter must be left entirely to his conscience. I can look him straight in the eye, for there's nothing inside me that could make me blush.

This is why I want your advice. What should I do? Could you possibly arrange something, perhaps in an oblique manner, without saying anything about me? Perhaps he could write the libretto, and hand it over to Pugno. Then, when the opera is ready, he might not object to my playing Oedipus. Tell me what you think about it.

Perhaps I'm wrong, I just cannot make up my mind, perhaps it wouldn't be the honest approach, perhaps even better to forget the whole thing. Or should I look for another librettist? Do let me know what you think about it.

And at this point I want to stress that Amfiteatrov, the rascal, really does know the stage, and, as I remember it, his opening work on the libretto was very good. Yes, I'll admit it, he's an expert, and it would be a pity if he didn't write it. One goes on beating one's head against a brick wall. What's to be done? Aleksa, my dear friend, for God's sake give me some advice, I shall be on tenterhooks waiting for your answer. No, perhaps it wouldn't be honest, I'll forget the whole thing. Or look for another librettist. What do you think?

Maria still hasn't given birth . . . I am struggling with the translation of

The Maid of Pskov into Italian (i.e. only my part of Ivan the Terrible) and continue to shiver for the reception this opera will have in Milan. I am dreaming of being with you in Capri at the end of May and also of seeing you in Milan, but I fear that my dreams cannot come true and you won't manage it. Early in May, after the Milan season, I shall be singing Borto's *Mefistofele* at the Grand Opéra in Paris. This is another cause for trembling, I don't know if they'll like it. I have not been satisfied with my Mefistofele of late; I feel I ought to re-think him, but there just isn't the time.

Keep well, dear friend. A big hug to you and my greetings to Maria Feodorovna.

Yours affectionately,
Feodor Chaliapin.

P.S. I am waiting, waiting, waiting for your reply.

Editor's Note: Gorky did write to Amfiteatrov about his libretto for *Oedipus Rex*, and Amfiteatrov, in a letter dated March 13th, same year, replied that he did the libretto for *Oedipus*, for Chaliapin, and would hand it over to any composer, although naturally, he would have preferred a Russian. He goes on: "Raoul Pugno is an excellent pianist, an intelligent musician, and there seems no reason why he should not write a good Oedipus, or why I shouldn't send him the libretto. Chaliapin knows the text, in parts, so that the rest is a mere business transaction. I can polish up and complete the work in three or four weeks from the moment I receive the commission. That's all." This opera never materialized. In 1927 Stravinsky's opera, *Oedipus Rex*, with a libretto by Cocteau, was produced in Paris.

FROM CHALIAPIN TO GORKY (extract, Milan, March 25, 1912)

. . . . I am delighted with *Buslayev*, oh, what a work. Can't tell you how much I long to see this done. Thank you, my dear Maximovich, for this marvellous thing.

I am feverishly casting about in my mind for a composer, the right one. I don't think Glazunov will take it on, and Rachmaninov's guts are not right for this, he couldn't tackle Buslayev. But there is a young composer here, son of the late artist, Stravinsky. This talented young man has already written one or two things, including a ballet called *Petrushka*, presented in Paris last year, and with great success. I'm thinking of bringing him over to see you, though, naturally, I shall first do some prospecting over the ground, just to find out how qualified this young man is to take on a subject like *Buslayev*.

He's in Monte Carlo at the moment, but I'll drop him a line, and ask him to come to Milan. . . .

Editor's Note: Gorky wrote the libretto of an opera, *Vasily Buslayev*—a Novgorod legendary hero, a character that had always attracted him. In

Vol. 5 of his works, 1950 edition, p. 417, Gorky says that he read the work to Chekhov. In the early thirties he tried to persuade the composer, Y. A. Shaporin, to write an opera based on *Buslayev*, and even promised to collaborate on the libretto.

Stravinsky's ballet, *Petrushka*, was produced by Fokine during Diaghilev's season of Russian Ballet in Paris, in 1911, with Vaslav Nijinsky, and Tamara Karsavina in the leading roles.

FROM CHALIAPIN TO GORKY (extract, Milan, March 30 [April 12], 1912)

". . . . And so it came to pass"—to use a favourite gambit of our reporters to mark an event. Yesterday, March 29th, (Russian style) *The Maid of Pskov* was successfully presented at La Scala, Milan. The opera house was filled to overflowing, the applause tumultuous, they seemed never to stop applauding. Particularly popular was the Ancient Assembly scene, and the choir, although it left a lot to be desired. No matter, they did try, and accomplished this very difficult act with great enthusiasm. But what was most marvellous was the music itself, and the orchestra. Serafin, the conductor, is outstanding, I wish we had people like him in Russia. He really loves music, and always identifies himself with the composer s intention, not like some of our own, who will, for an agreed fee, dutifully swing the baton to mark the time, stifling the occasional yawn, and stealing the odd glance at the watch, as if to say, "must get it over, quickly".

My dear Maximovich, my dear, dear friend! What happiness danced in my heart last night. Just think: fifteen years ago Mamontov himself was in doubt, and didn't want to put the work on; who could have supposed that this truly splendid work (though difficult to understand, even for a Russian audience) should be put on by Italians, and be so much admired! A sweet and glorious miracle.

I am a little chagrined to-day. That dear old sow, the critics, didn't understand a damn thing, and the pages of the local papers significantly, and many-wordedly, drooled out their own illiteracy. But that's of no importance. I'm sending you the papers, read for yourself.

They seem to be talking always in terms of "race". The Latin race, the Slav race, and the old chestnut, "*l'âme slave*" (the Slav soul). Have you ever heard anything like it? As if this "âme" can be dressed up to order, now in the uniform of a titular counsellor,[1] now in the cassock of a Catholic priest. The stupid devils got it all mixed up, forgetting that the soul does not wear galoshes.

Dear Maximushka, why don't you come over here and hear it? I am ready to guarantee your incognito—I'll arrange things so that no one will ever know you're here.

Feodor.

Editor's Note: [1] Lowest civil service rank in czarist Russia.

GORKY TO CHALIAPIN (Capri, March 1 [14], 1913)

My dear friend,

I received your letter from Berlin. Thank you. I meant to reply the same day, and here I am, writing eight days later. Just been seeing off Lyatsky and Tikhonov, and, as usual, got buried in paper. Please write to me, or ask Maria Valentinovna to write, about your affairs. You know what I'm asking about, and what troubles me.

Let me say at once what I have said to you on many occasions, and am bound to say to you many times more, remember who you are in Russia. Don't put yourself on the level with scum, and don't allow trivialities to upset and enslave you. You are a greater aristocrat than any prince of the blood and all those boors and lackeys should recognize this. You are first in the sphere of Russian music, just as Tolstoy is first in the written word. And this is said to you by no flatterer, but by a Russian who really loves you, a man for whom you are a symbol of Russian might and talent. Whenever I look at you, I gratefully pray to some Russian god and say, "Thank you, God, for showing us, in the person of Chaliapin, to what heights our down-trodden, tortured, grief-racked land can rise. Thank you. I know what force there is in it. What beautiful force."

Nor am I alone in thinking this, believe me. Perhaps you'll say to yourself, "It's hard on me." But all big men have found it so in Russia. Pushkin felt the same things as you do, and so do dozens of the best people, in whose ranks your place is rightfully assured, because in Russian art, Chaliapin, like Pushkin, is an epoch.

We are not very good at valuing ourselves, and we have such a poor knowledge of our own terrible and barren history. We don't clearly understand our services to our country. I dearly want, and would love you to realize your role, your significance in Russian life.

These are words from the heart, and they well up each time I think of you, my friend. Sometimes I feel like yelling at those who fail to understand you, and what you mean in our life.

My regards to Maria Valentinovna. I like her, she is simple, direct, and strong, and so loyal to you.

Alexei.

Editor's Note: Here, Gorky expresses his anxiety concerning the singer's answer to the demand of the administration of the Imperial Theatres, regarding his taking part in a concert to mark the tercentenary of the House of Romanov. Chaliapin did not sing, pleading ill-health.

FROM CHALIAPIN TO GORKY (Moscow, April 19 [May 2], 1913)

My dear Alexei,

Such is my fate, but it seems that every letter I write you must begin with an apology for a long silence. Forgive me. Day after day I've put off writing you, and gradually the opportunities to do so have got smaller and smaller. To-day I have ordered the whole household to tell visitors to go to hell, and that no-one knows when the hell I'll be back. So here it is, at long last. I can really write something to you, my friend. I seem almost incapable of organising my life, with the result that I get so little time to myself. And somehow, there always seems to be a crowd here, and so often the discussions seems worthless, and yet, how can I get out of them?

I had decided to write you during Lent, but my eyes got sore, so badly that I had to wear bandages. Malignant abscess, like styes on the eyelids. I felt worn out by this, even grumbling at the Deity. However, it passed, and I am perfectly well again.

Now I shall tell you about everything that has happened since we parted, and in the right order, I hope.

You probably know I was ill in Berlin. This upset the Director, and as is laid down, I was thoroughly picked to pieces by those "true Russian patriots", and promoted at least to the socialist-revolutionaries. The concert was in no way remarkable, and the celebrations passed off modestly enough, that is if you dismiss the "defilé" (last scene from *Life for the Czar*), with Sobinov portraying Czar Mikail Feodorovich, Figner, carrying the crown of Mononmakh, and other distinguished artists masquerading as various personages of the era. That's all.

However, there was an announcement in yesterday's papers, that many, if not all the participants of the Romanov celebrations have received various awards, orders, medals, and promotions to the status of soloists of his Imperial Majesty. So there is nothing left for me but to bite my nails in envy, for I was awarded—nothing this time. I'm wondering if I should write to Telyakovsky and demand that they send me the order of Andrey Pervozvanny, or make me the iron chancellor, or something. Otherwise it is embarrassing.

It's really amusing to see their joyous faces, framed in all that cheap glitter. It seems to be that happiness is all things to all men. However I got a satisfaction of a different order.

For the past two weeks I have been singing at the People's, so-called, Nicholas II Theatre—five concerts in aid of the Lomonosov Society for the propagation of literacy among poor orphans. The clear profit, after all expenses were paid, came to over twenty-two thousand roubles, and I made about ten thousand. I'm glad that the poor kids will get something out of it (there's enough to pay the milkman), first and foremost. And once more I was able to see for myself how eager people are to come to my concerts, especially the young.

They have a tradition in the People's Theatre, whereby a whole tier of seats, part balcony and part gallery is given free of charge, about eight hundred seats. To get to this concert the young people spent two and even three days queueing outside the theatre in rain and snow. Isn't that happiness? It was a real honour to me, Alexei, yes, a real honour, and most moving.

I asked the Administration to allow them into the building for two or three hours each night, for it made my heart ache, witnessing such patience, devotion and enthusiasm. What a pity indeed that the bureaucratic and somewhat peculiar organisation of the so-called People's Theatre should give so little opportunity to the good, ordinary, simple people to go there. The working-man enters such a place with caution, and I think he's right, for the sleuths are always active.

What a reflection upon us all. What can we do? Such is our Russian life. I doubt if there is anyone living in or passing through the town who is not watched. Great frightful eyes, watching, always watching. If the eye should light upon any place where a strike is pending, then it must surely bulge.

Tikhonov and Lyatsky came to see me on several occasions in Petersburg, and we talked a great deal. The latter is interested in our composers, and wants to awaken a new interest in Russian folk tales and legends, but alas, our composer resources would appear to be rather meagre at the moment. There are two or three capable of treating Russian subjects effectively: one is a drunkard, the second is lazy, and the third is prevented by his multitudinous family. Just imagine trying to create in such circumstances.

With this letter I am sending you some biographical data concerning Stepan Razin, perhaps it might be of some use to you. The information was collected by a friend, at my request. It's not easy to read, there is something wanting, and what I send is in some disorder. Perhaps something will come out of it.

I was in Zvenigorod some days ago. I went to the monastery there and heard the Easter service. I spent two days climbing up into the belfry, ringing all the bells. It was marvellous relaxation for me, and I derived real pleasure from it. I found the monks most hospitable, and they treated me to smoked sausage and vodka. They even showed me a siskin in a cage that also partook of the same repast. They tried their best to convince me that it really was a siskin, though I had my doubts. I think it was nothing more than a common sparrow, dyed green on purpose. Anyhow, I had my laugh.

The theatrical world is daily afflicted by "quests", and this is all very well, but there are so few talented people about that these "quests" remain theoretical, and do nothing except induce a certain despondency. Diaghilev decided that we are living in an age of "Alexandrian culture", and doing so, we must propagate Eros. More, he avows that if art can be achieved in our time then it can only do so in the world of ballet, because, and I quote, "plastic art is all". It is not given to me to fathom such things, neither do I, know whether or not I should feel sorry about it. Still, he is no fool, and notwithstanding the "Alexandrian culture", he has organised and presented splendid opera in Paris and London. I shall be going to Paris from Petersburg on May 1st (our calendar).

I shall be in Petersburg the day after to-morrow, as on April 26th I am due at a concert at the Noblemen's Assembly, then on May 9th, I am off to Paris for the first production of *Boris Godunov*.

Dear Alexei, if you can manage it, and I implore you, come and hear it. I promise you it will be good. Yes, we shall be showing real art, with not a thought about any "quests".

There will be another theatre open in Moscow next year, to be called "Free Theatre". There is a lot of money behind it, and believe it or not, nearly a thousand artists have been auditioned. Their choice has been made, and they plan to give everything: opera, operette, comedies, drama, tragedies. More power to their elbow. And yet there is something that sounds just a little too good about this fanfare, and I am somewhat sceptical. I know that it takes no special genius to initiate it, but without a school of some kind the thing presents difficulties. There are now many schools, of all kinds, and yet the real kind, the kind that's needed, simply does not exist. There is much muddle.

They teach them how to put on a tail coat, how to adjust a necktie, but, seated at a banquet table strewn with flowers, as rightly becomes "Alexandrian culture" they yet use two fingers to blow their noses. This happens all over the place. Oh, if only I could describe it all, I don't know how to begin, and I wish I did.

I would love to start a school, something I've been dreaming about, something I tell myself I might even manage to get off the ground. Perhaps M. I. Tereshchenko would agree to sponsor it. (It will require a great deal of money.) To tell the truth, I have already spoken to him about it.

I just bought from K. F. Yuon a number of sketches for his décor for *Boris Godunov*. He did them in Paris. Daily my eyes feast on them. Beautiful, except perhaps the Inn scene. I paid him one and a half thousand, and from them got one hundred thousands' worth of pleasure. Beautiful, lovely things. What a talent he has, the devil take him.

You will really see something when you come to Paris, because I got your portrait out of Pyatnitsky, the one that was painted in Kuokkala by Grinman, or some such name. What a source of joy. You hang so nicely in my room, opposite Mussorgsky (a portrait in oils done in 1881, not very well, and probably from a photograph, by a gentleman named Maximov). It was given me by Figner, and I thought it very kind of him.

Now something about my bourgeois life: kids all over the place. Four in Petersburg, and five in Moscow. It's true to say that only two of the Petersburg children are mine. But how I love the imps, mine and not mine. My Maria walks about like some stately Juno, a delight to behold, and although she shouldn't try to teach her grandmother to suck eggs, she does attempt to give me a lesson here and there. Ah well! She loves you as much as I do myself, which makes me adore her all the more. She's lazy though, just like me, and that's bad. Never mind. Let her be. . . .

The children are all lovely, and give me great pleasure. Have I by this time written you into boredom, my dear Alexeyushko? Don't grumble, you know how positively incapable I am of half measures. If I keep mum, I keep mum, and if I write, I write.

See you soon. I shall expect to see you in Paris, and just you remember that.

Your loving Feodor.

Editor's Note: During 1913–15 the Russian press often reported that Gorky was contemplating writing a libretto for an opera on "Stenka Razin", on Chaliapin's request. *Birzheviye Vedomosti*, in an evening edition of July 12, 1915, wrote: "Gorky is particularly attracted to the subject. . . . When the libretto is finished Glazunov has promised to do the music. Thus we shall have an interesting triumvirate: Gorky-Glazunov-Chaliapin". Glazunov wrote a symphonic poem, "Stenka Razin", in 1885. During the 1905 revolution, N. A. Rimsky-Korsakov was considering writing an opera on the same subject.

EXTRACT FROM A LETTER FROM GORKY TO I. P. LADY-ZHNIKOV (Baidary, July 16 [29], 1916)

. . . . There is no one to whom I could write about my work on the biography. This place teems with foreigners of all kinds, peacocks, pythons, antelopes, borzoi dogs. As for the Russians, they are practically illiterate; their attitude to the printed word is like that of the devil towards incense. Besides which, they are drunk from morning till night, with much song singing. Neither Feodor nor Maria Valentinovna wrote to anyone. My own feeling is that all these "miracles in St. Petersburg" are being performed by the miracle worker Isai.

The work grows both in scope and depth, and I greatly fear that we shan't be able to finish it. Five hundred pages have already been typed, and we have only got as far as his first trip to Italy. I am doing everything to hasten it, but alas, there exists one almost unsurmountable technical difficulty. The young lady here cannot take down shorthand notes for longer than two hours. The rest of the time, until the evening, is spent endeavouring to decipher them. Naturally, I don't always catch up on the editing.

At times Feodor tells his story in a flat, dull, and verbose manner, then again there are moments when he amazes me. The main work on this MS will be done in Petersburg. This is quite clear to me now. When will it be finished? Well, I still hope by the twentieth or twenty-second.

For myself I feel fine, and my leg has ceased aching, but I neither swim nor sunbathe. I take Feodor down to the sea, a couple of miles generally. He dives into the water and swims ashore like a walrus. I walk very little —there is no time.

. . . To tell you the honest truth I believe we have chosen a bad time to start all this business of the biography. Still, having started, it has to be finished.

FROM CHALIAPIN TO GORKY (Sydney, September 7, 1926)

Dear Alexei Maximovich,

Today I read in the papers that somebody has published my memoirs. I would not have believed it had I not read an extract from it, precisely the part which has never yet been printed. You are well aware of the Russian attitude towards matters of copyright, which means I shall probably be unable to sell them in America as I had planned to do. Publishers will simply refuse to buy, they will do an English translation and publish when and where they like.

I simply cannot imagine how this has happened. My own copy is in my possession, in a strong box in Paris. Did you by chance have a second copy anywhere? Perhaps, if you left it in Russia, someone might have stolen it from your library and organised the whole thing. It grieves me for two reasons. First, because I have been waiting for the psychological moment to sell it to a publisher for a high price, as high as possible, and secondly, there are some things in it that I wish to alter before it gets into print. Last year in New York I was delighted with an offer made to me, of which I informed you at our last meeting in Naples. This sale would have brought enough money, and you, with your precarious position, and any number of literary difficulties, might have got some relief; I myself neither wanted to take any money, nor had the right to do so. This unpleasantness has upset me, more on your behalf than mine. What bad luck! What can be done?

I have read your *Artamonovs*[1] (as I do anything written by you) with the greatest delight, and I look with the same sort of bitterness on the generations. Oh, I love you, my great giant, and I consider it a great happiness to be living in the same period as yourself, and far more, that I have the privilege of being your friend. Dear Alexei Maximovich, I am so proud of this, not loudly and not in any base way, but tenderly and delicately. Life has been kind to me, it has been given to me to see and hear a little more than others. I see you, hear you, and feel you deeply, and my soul, whenever I have a chance of touching yours, is filled with an inexpressible happiness. Everyone reads Pushkin, but not everyone is aware of the relation of light to shade (please forgive technicalities). And the same with you. Multitudes read you, but they can feel "the young birch stands, exiled from the forest". I am being a bore. I cannot help shedding at least one tear of joy. Especially here in Australia, where it's baseball and football and cricket, and boxing, and other physical pastimes, which I sometimes think makes English hearts and brains harder and harder. Life with them, even at a distance, is dull, off-putting. They are rich, they know nothing, they are interested in nothing, except sport. They consider us Russians savages, as they do our music. It requires a great deal of spiritual concentration, and I don't mind adding, ability, to make them listen to Russian music, in Russian. Things may improve in the future, but alas! "I shall not be there."

I sang in three Australian towns, Melbourne, Sydney and Adelaide, ten concerts, then eight concerts, and three concerts, respectively. On Friday I am off to New Zealand, then back to America, so that I shall only get back to Paris ("home", with your permission) about the end of April.

Next year I shall have comparatively little to do, and very much hope to see you, and to live somewhere near you for a while. My Maria and the children are all well, and they send you their greetings. I embrace you, with much love.

Yours ever,
F. Chaliapin.

My address: Chaliapin, c/o Hurok, Universal Artists Bureau, 1440 Broadway, New York.

P.S. Maria just reminded me that you said you had a second copy of the MS in Russia—that's where they must have "pinched" it.

Editor's Note: [1] Gorky's novel, *The Artamonov Affair*, published in Russian, in Berlin, 1925, was dedicated to Romain Rolland.

The first half of Chaliapin's autobiography, written for him by Gorky in 1916, was published by *Priboy* (*The Surf*) under the title "Pages from my Life."

FROM CHALIAPIN TO GORKY (Paris, July 19, 1927)

Dear Alexei Maximych,[1]

Rumours which reached you that said you had sold the book to *Priboy*, and that I had alleged this, are absolutely untrue. I said no such thing. May I suggest that such information has been passed on to you by a person of no uncertain complexion. When last winter I saw the announcement in *Priboy* that they intended to print two more sections of the work, I sent telegrams both to the editor, and to Lunacharsky, protesting, and informed you of this. In reply to my protest *Priboy's* editor sent me a letter of apology, offered me a fee, and said that further instalments of the book will be stopped until such time as I gave my consent.

I said nothing at all regarding the fee, as I don't intend to accept any from them. This will only show you that if I had meant to fling this particular insult at you, I should have been in no position to do so.

I well remember how much was printed in *Letopis*, and from what *Priboy* put out, and from the announcement made, I definitely established the fact that they had printed more than *Letopis*.[2]

I received from Tikhonov, and you will remember this better than I, a fee of some six hundred roubles, and that only on your insistence, because I thought then as I think now, that it was unbecoming of me to accept money for the book. It never interested me. On several occasions Tikhonov informed me that he owed me some money, but I never received anything further, nor did I ever remind him of it.

A few days ago Miss Wright wrote me from America, informing me that she had a clear profit from the sale of the book of some five thousand dollars, and I at once sent her a telegram instructing her to forward you two thousand five hundred dollars.

The tone of your letter has hurt me. If I appear to have been pre-occupied with the money side of the book, then it was only to make sure that you got a few thousand dollars, which I presumed would not be unwelcome to you. When the book eventually appears in America this winter you will see what a difference there is between what you did, and what Miss Wright did.

To enable you to get some money from this book I have agreed to allow the later reminiscences, after 1914, to be published too. I do realize that everything that has been written now, without your help, is very feeble, but what can I do?

Not a single publisher would entertain the idea of doing the book where it ended in 1914, and yet, if I did not hurry on this matter, I know very well that the material would have been used both in Russia and abroad, probably in bad editions, with the profits going into other people's pockets.

I am certain that you know me only too well: I have many faults, but there is no meanness nor nastiness of spirit in me, and I always love and respect you.

I leave for Vichy to-day. I hope you will send me a line or two. What's to be done?

My address: Pavillon Sévigné, Vichy.

F. Chaliapin.

Editor's Note: [1]A familiar form of Gorky's patronymic—Maximovich.

[2]Chaliapin is mistaken here when he says that *Priboy* printed more of his material than was printed in *Letopis*; the first and second editions of his autobiography (*Priboy*, 1926–7) included only the text which was published in *Letopis* in 1917. See issues Nos. 1–12, *Commentaries to F. I. Chaliapin*, by E. A. Grosheva, and Irina Feodorovna Chaliapina, published by Iskusstvo State Publishing House, Moscow, 1957.

FROM CHALIAPIN TO GORKY (Barcelona, December 25, 1929)

My dear Aleksei Maximovich,

I had a letter from my daughter Tanya a few days ago, telling me she had been to see you, and sending me your greetings. This reminds me that I never acknowledged the present you sent me. Disgusting of me. I imagined that you had gone to Russia, after which the thing went right out of my head. From either indolence or pre-occupation with other matters, I somehow failed to get the letter off. Please don't take this omission to heart.

I am reading *Samgin* with sheer delight, and as usual see everyone and everything as though I'd lived through it all. Your books remain close to my heart.

Until the New Year I shall be working in Barcelona, where I have several performances to fulfil. Maria and I live on a high mountain, well away from the town. I find it dull, redeemed only by the sea and the bright sun. This compensates for the boredom.

We are planning to go into the Swiss mountains. I long to see snow again, and feel homesick for a real winter.

Yours ever,
Feodor Chaliapin.

FROM GORKY TO CHALIAPIN (Sorrento, Italy, August 9, 1930)

For the second time I am writing to you, Feodor Ivanovich. Perhaps my previous letter did not reach you, since this can be the only explanation for your silence.

I wrote to you of the absurdity, of the disgrace, in your bringing this suit against the Soviet Government, and whatever some worthless wretches may say, it is still the Government of the more enlightened workers and peasants, who strive passionately and successfully to lead the working masses towards the building of a new kind of State.

I am perfectly convinced that you yourself did not think up this disgusting business. Rather was it prodded into you by the parasites by whom you are surrounded. Surely they started all this in order to make certain that the door of return to your native land should be slammed shut forever.

You know full well that I have always tried to defend you, both as a man and an artist, from the attempts of various swindlers who set out to compromise you in one way or another. Nor is this confined to the case of the writer, Nagrodskaya, whom, if you remember, I chased out of your house on Perm Street. Believe me, Feodor, the only desire that motivates me now, is that you shouldn't disgrace yourself.

I don't know on what grounds your lawyer built his case, but allow me to remind you, that I, too, have had something to do with your memoirs. They came into being on my initiative, and I persuaded you to dictate them to my stenographer, Yevdokiya Petrovna. In all you dictated for nine hours. No more than that. The transcript was re-written and edited by me, the manuscript was written out in my hand. I am sure, too, that you haven't forgotten that the memoirs were first published in the journal *Letopis*. For this you were paid at the rate of 500 roubles per quire.

Another thing I remember is that, in 1926, you sent me 2,500 dollars from the American edition. I am sorry I ever took the money, but out of that sum I paid back to you my debt of 1,200 dollars.

I bring all this up just to remind you that three-quarters of your memoirs is my work. If you had been led to believe that you have a legal right to assume them your property, then allow me to say this: I don't consider you to have any moral right to dispose of this "property" in such an unscrupulous manner.

78. *A group photograph taken on the occasion of a special jubilee production of Glinka's opera* Russlan and Ludmilla, *November 27, 1917, to mark the 75th anniversary of its first production at the Mariinsky Theatre. Standing in the back row, on the left, Chaliapin in the part of Farlaf.*

79. *Chaliapin as Philip II in Verdi's opera* Don Carlos (*Bolshoy Theatre, Moscow*), *1917.*

80. Chaliapin as Philip II in Verdi's opera Don Carlos; *drawing by Yakovlev, 1917.*

81. Chaliapin as Yashka the Turk, in a dramatisation of Turgenev's story The Singers (The People's Theatre, Petrograd), *1919.*

As an old friend, my advice to you is—do not bring shame upon yourself. The suit against the Government will always remain the stain in the people's memory of you.

Believe me, it will not be just Russians who will criticise you over your greed for money. This passion to amass wealth has done you great harm as an artist, and this latest manifestation of it is, perhaps, the most infamous of all. Please do not allow every kind of rascal to treat you as a mere pawn. You are such a great, such a wonderful artist. How can you behave yourself in such a disgraceful manner?

A. Peshkov.

Editor's Note: Letter is typewritten, with corrections in ink and blue pencil. In the right-hand corner on the first page, in red pencil in Gorky's handwriting, the word "Copy". The signature and date are in blue pencil.

FROM GORKY TO CHALIAPIN (Sorrento, January 17, 1933)

In your book, *Mask and Soul,* you write:

> "They have taken away from me everything that could be taken away, and which, in one way or another, could not be hidden. They have taken my house, my money in the bank, my car."

That is a lie. You know very well that the circumstances of your departure are known to me, in all details. You cannot deny that all the valuables you kept in the safe were handed back to you. I know this, because you yourself told me about it, with touching expressions of gratitude to the Soviet Government. You have never before mentioned this matter: "They have confiscated the money in my bank." You used to say that 140,000 roubles were confiscated in Yalta. At that time they were probably worth no more than 1,400 roubles.

As to your house in Moscow which brought in no income; this was not confiscated, indeed, your wife Iola Ignatyevna lives in it to this day. Nor was your Leningrad house, which did bring in some income, confiscated either. Your part of the house is being looked after by Isai Dvorishchev [*sic*].[1] You were allowed two railway coaches for the transportation of your belongings from Moscow and Leningrad.

Among the valuables which you took out of Russia were the Gobelins bought for 100,000 roubles. You even boasted that you were offered two million francs for them.

Why do you lie and persist in saying that you "left Russia a pauper"? Don't I know what valuables you have bought at bargain prices?

I have the feeling that you are lying, not of your own free will, but because of a basic weakness in your own character, and because you are surrounded by people who stand best to gain by this lying. It is these people, taking advantage of your greed for money, your semi-literacy, and your utter ignorance of social problems, that force you into this quite ignominious lying.

And why do they do that? To live on you, batten on your blood, like the parasites they are. One of them, the biggest, may speak for all, when he came out with the weighty phrase: "Feodor will return to the Bolsheviks only over my dead body."

Just look at what they are doing to you. Look at the things in your memoirs, the memoirs of a great world artist, sprinkled with such howlers as:

"Pulse 280." "The anthem is a lofty and precious thing, the representative sound of a nation." "The blood of Ivan and Boris will out."—What? In *your* veins? Shame on you.

The people who published your book didn't even bother to edit it, probably on purpose—let the reader see for himself what idiotic nonsense Chaliapin writes. They haven't an ounce of respect for your past. If they had, they wouldn't have left in that series of disgraceful, illiterate and stupid bloomers.

That scene with Kuklin was invented by you. Nothing of the kind ever took place, and it couldn't have taken place, since, though you have a measure of belligerence, you are a coward. Whereas Kuklin knows what he is worth. If you had only touched him, he would have reduced you to pulp. You have also invented the meeting with Lenin in my Moscow flat. Lenin was not in Moscow in 1905. I, myself, only met him in 1907. Why on earth did you have to concoct this? Oh, Chaliapin, what a sad end this is for you.

Editor's Note: [1] Gorky obviously meant Isai Dvorishchin (1876–1942), singer, actor, producer of the State Academy Theatre and Ballet (formerly Mariinsky), Honoured Artist of the R.S.F.S.R., Chaliapin's secretary.

In June 1930, Chaliapin's lawyer, D. Pechorin, sued the Soviet Government in the French court in Paris, accusing Soviet departments of unauthorised publishing and sale of Chaliapin's memoirs, of illegal importation of the book into France, and of selling it in Paris. The damages claimed amounted to two million francs.

When the court heard the case, the Soviet Trade Representative read out Chaliapin's correspondence (letters which passed between him and the *Priboy* publishing house) from which it was evident that back in 1926 Chaliapin had waived all claims against the publishers. Further, he disproved the allegation that the *Priboy* publishing house had made use of the Chaliapin manuscript without his knowledge or permission. What in fact really happened was that *Priboy* merely reprinted, without any alterations whatsoever, the text of Chaliapin's autobiography, published in 1917 by the periodical *Letopis*. As to the plaintiff's claim that, as a result of the memoirs being published and certain information concerning Chaliapin's private life being released, the singer had suffered moral damages, the court was shown a copy of the American edition of the memoirs, which in the main consisted of a straight translation of the autobiography issued in 1917. In this American edition, published with the consent of the author, are reproduced all the facts against the publication of which Chaliapin was protesting. The court dismissed the case and the singer lost his suit.

Of great importance in the establishing of the facts of the writing, creation and publication of the memoirs, were Gorky's letters to V. S. Dovgalevsky, the Soviet Ambassador in France, and to the editors of *Pravda* and *Izvestia*. Here are the texts of these letters, taken from the *Complete Works of Maxim Gorky* (30 vols.), Goslitizdat, Moscow, 1952, pp. 28 and 29.

GORKY'S LETTER TO V. S. DOVGALEVSKY (Undated, but published in *Pravda* on December 20, 1930)

Dear Comrade Dovgalevsky,

I hear that Feodor Ivanovich Chaliapin is suing the Soviet Government for the publication of his manuscript.

I feel it my duty to acquaint you with the following facts concerning the background and the history of how this manuscript came into existence. In the course of several years I have been vainly trying to persuade Chaliapin to write his autobiography. Finally, in 1915 I succeeded in bringing this about in the following manner. I went to Foros, in the Crimea, where Chaliapin was living, and I sent for a stenographer, Yevdokiya Petrovna Silversan, who was later employed in the Vsemirnaya Literatura Publishing House. Over a period of time Chaliapin talked with her, an hour or so a day, telling her about his life. I then edited and worked on what she produced, myself adding various details that I had had from Chaliapin personally at various times. Therefore, Chaliapin's "Memoirs" are written in my hand.

Later, in the winter of '15–16, the "Memoirs" were published in the periodical *Letopis*, for which Chaliapin received 500 roubles per printer's page.[1] This of course was not a high fee, but bear in mind my labour. Besides the periodical was not rich.

All this is well known to the former editor of the journal, Alexander Nikolayevich Tikhonov, who now works in Moscow, in the Federatsia Publishing House, "Herzen's House", Tverskoy Boulevard, 25. Y. P. Silversan lives in Finland and I do not know her address.

One thing I must add. The fact that Chaliapin's memoirs appeared in *Letopis* deprives the author of the right, so it would seem, of receiving remuneration for any translated editions of the memoir. However, about four years ago, Chaliapin published these memoirs in America and offered me 2,500 dollars for my work. I needed the money. Some time before this I borrowed $1,200 from Chaliapin and I repaid this sum out of the $2,500. I hope all this may prove to be not without interest and perhaps even useful to you.

Editor's Note: [1] 40,000 typographical units.

The dates are incorrectly given, since the autobiography was written in 1916, and published the following year.

GORKY'S LETTERS TO THE EDITORS OF *PRAVDA* AND *IZVESTIA* (December 20, 1930)

In a report in one of the white emigré papers concerning the law suit brought by Feodor Chaliapin against the Soviet Government claiming two million francs for the publication of his memoirs, it is alleged that the *Priboy* publishing house "printed a part of his, Chaliapin's, 'intimate diary', which he had handed to Gorky for editing and correction".

This is not true. Chaliapin never handed to me for "editing and correction", either the whole or any part of his intimate diary. Moreover, I maintain that before his departure from Russia he never kept any diary. *Priboy* publishing house reprinted the memoirs published in 1917[1] in the periodical *Letopis*.

These memoirs came into existence on my initiative, and with my direct participation. In 1916 I persuaded Chaliapin to tell me about his life in the presence of a stenographer, one Yevdokiya Petrovna Silversan. This he did over a period of several sessions, taking in all not more than ten hours for telling his story. After these chaotic stories had been deciphered by the stenographer, I gave them coherence, re-wrote parts, and added everything which I knew from Chaliapin previously. In 1916 he gave permission for their publication in *Letopis*, for which he was paid 6,500 roubles.

M. Gorky.

Editor's Note: [1] In the original the date is erroneously given as 1915 (N.F.).

Chaliapin's Obituary Note on Maxim Gorky

(Published in an unidentified French newspaper, July, 1936. Gorky died on June 19, 1936. The text quoted is taken from *Gorky Readings*, Moscow, 1955.)

On the way from New York to Le Havre on the *S.S. Normandie*, there came to me with my breakfast coffee a newspaper, on the front page of which I read these three words. GORKY EST MORT.

I cannot find words to describe the force of that terrible blow. I got up to take the coffee, but seeing these headlines I fell back on my bed. I closed my eyes, and immediately there rose before me a figure in a black jacket, his magnificent head of hair brushed back, the kind grey eyes. Maxim Gorky. I saw him sitting on the windowsill in the foyer of a theatre at the Nizhni-Novgorod Fair. His hands were clasped between his knees, a young but already stooping man, who seemed in a moment to be saying to me, "I'm glad to meet you, Chaliapin, because, as I said to you yesterday after the performance, you are one of us."

I remembered the previous evening, just after the performance of *A Life for The Czar*, how this same man walked into my dressing-room, announced that his name was Gorky, in a strong Nizhni-Novgorod accent, an accent he never lost, and said to me: "How marvellously you play a Russian moujik. Although I'm no admirer of such Russo–Germanic subjects, nevertheless, when you, as Susanin, weep, remembering your children, I love you."

"Yes, I always try to give a true portrayal, even of parts which may not be entirely true. . . ."

This was my first meeting with Gorky, and that evening began our long, lasting, warm and true friendship.

What sort of man was he? In a black jacket I suppose that any man looks more or less all right. But you have to see a man naked in the baths to know him really. Gorky and I often went to the baths together. It was there that I realized that his stoop wasn't due to a hump. It was as though "the wings" on his back stuck out somewhat unduly. His chest was sunken, and he had prominent veins on his legs. Looking closer I noticed that he was marked with scars and callouses.

"What are you stooping and straining your veins for?" I asked him. To the end of my days I shall remember his answer. "Oh, Feodor, life is a bit easier now, but you see this here," and he pointed to a scar near the heart.

"I did that out of stupidity. Perhaps because life had then driven me to despair. I tried to shoot myself with a self-loading pistol." "What do you mean?" I asked. "Why?"

The reply was prompt. "I saw no sense in continuing my existence. I was surrounded by misery and falsehood. They rushed me off to hospital, and some of my friends came to see me. One of them said reproachfully, 'You blockhead. And you want to be a writer. Going about trying to shoot yourself. You should have tried to hang yourself'. You know, Feodor, I wanted to live as never before, so I suppose my wings as you call them, and my veins and all the rest of it were just meant to be there. This is where I tried to shoot myself, here is where my ribs were broken."

I tried to make light of it. "You're a fine one, first you try to kill yourself, then you break your ribs."

"I didn't break my ribs. They were broken for me. I'll tell you about it. By chance I witnessed a scene in a village. There was a naked woman, her hair streaming down, harnessed into a cart, just like a little horse, and the men, several of them, were seated in it and beating her with whips. Apparently she had been unfaithful to her husband. And a little to one side of this stood a priest, silently, approvingly. You can well understand my reaction to that. I went up to them there and then. 'Have you gone out of your minds?' I asked, 'you sons of bitches. What the hell are you doing?'

"The priest came up. 'Who do you think you are?' he asked. 'What are you interfering for?'

"I let him have one. Later I came to in a ditch. Luckily, and only because it started to rain; the cold water streaming through the ditch brought me round. I crawled down to the infirmary on all fours. That accounts for the ribs."

I cannot help feeling that those same marks sank deep into the man. That woman being tortured, the terrible exhausting labour, the homeless existence on the Volga, and not only his own, but that of millions, the almost brutal despair, the dark and helpless people, the great doubts about life, the sense and truth of it—it is this that provided the charge for Gorky's home-made pistol.

Whatever one may think about him, whatever may be said of him, I myself am profoundly convinced, indeed I know without the slightest shadow of doubt that all his thoughts and feelings, his achievements, his very mistakes, had one root only, the Volga, that great wandering, groaning Russian river.

I have heard people talking about his cupidity, his life of luxury in the villas of Capri and Sorrento, his riches. I burn with shame for such people. I can truthfully say, for this is something I know too well, that Gorky was one of those people who would forever be penniless, and this no matter how much he earned or amassed. He didn't spend it on himself. He did not like money, was absolutely indifferent about it. He simply wasn't interested. I remember lending him some on one occasion, this happened from time to time. Perhaps later, I would ask him if he needed any more. I got the characteristic reply.

"Don't bother, Feodor. There'll never be enough rubbish to fill our dump."

Nor was he ever able to collect enough for the causes for which he himself gave so generously, and so freely.

No. It was not cupidity, it never once motivated Gorky. I have mentioned his everlasting ache for people, and now I shall mention his other abiding passion, his love of Russia. I remember this very matter arising between us many years later.

The great storm that burst upon our country flung Gorky and me into different parts of the world. I was living in Paris at the time, and Gorky arrived from Sorrento in Rome, on the way to Moscow. I remember his sympathy when I was leaving Russia, his saying to me in so many words, "This is no place for you, my friend."

We did not meet again until 1928, in Rome, and he told me that much had changed at home, and that in his opinion, it was possible for me to work in Russia. He urged me to return.

This is not the place to go into why I refused to yield to Gorky's persuasions. And to this very day I don't honestly know which of us was right. All the same, when he spoke, it was in the voice of love, for me, and for Russia. He was motivated by a profound consciousness that we all of us belong to our native land, to our people, and that we belong to them, not just morally, about which I used to fool myself, but also physically, with all our scars, and callouses and humps.

*　　　*　　　*　　　*

Editor's Note: The need for roots—Chaliapin returns to this subject again and again, though he always maintained that the spiritual force by which the Western world lived was equally dear and close to the heart of the Russian artist:

We all drink from the same source of creation and beauty. I adore Russian music, and I've expressed this love in speech and writing. It does not imply that Western music is any the less beautiful. All things are beautiful in their different ways. To me, Western music lacks the Russian complexity, a certain intimate ruggedness, but it has not less admirable qualities. Even the great works of the Western world differ in their beauties, if we consider only the works of Mozart or Wagner. By what objective instrument can we measure the comparative greatness of either of them? Personally, I would define my own reactions to them in a slightly paradoxical form.

I imagine myself, a young musical enthusiast, with an album of autographs of my favourite composers. I'll give my soul for an autograph of either of these great men. So I pluck up my courage, and go in search of the giants.

I find Wagner's home. An enormous building, great granite blocks, an over-imposing and monumental entrance, with heavy oak doors, and austere carvings. I knock timidly, and after a while the door is opened to me by a

271

butler in a rich livery. He looks me up and down in a rather haughty manner, the cold grey eyes beneath bushy eyebrows piercing me, and then he speaks.

"Was wollen Sie?"

"I should like to see Herr Wagner."

Away he goes, leaving me trembling with fear. They are bound to throw me out. But no, he is back again, and I am invited to come in. Dark halls lined with grey marble, majestic, Olympian, cold. Suits of armour mounted on pedestals like skeletons. The entrance to an inner door is guarded on both sides by stone centaurs.

I enter Wagner's study. At once I am oppressed by its loftiness, its vastness, dominated by its statues of gods and knights. I am immediately aware of my own insignificance. An act of impertinence to come here at all. The master enters. What eyes, what a brow. He gestures me to an armchair. This looks like a throne.

"Was wollen Sie?"

With some trepidation, indeed almost with tears, I announce, "This is my album of autographs."

He smiles, like a ray of the sun piercing a dark cloud. Then he takes my album and signs his name.

"Who are you?" he asks.

"A musician."

A sympathy grows, and in no time at all an impressive-looking manservant arrives with coffee. The master talks about music, and I will never forget it. But when finally that massive door closes behind me, and I see once again the sky, the ordinary people, I am unaccountably happy. A great weight has been lifted from my soul. The oppression has vanished.

So now I go in search of Mozart's house. A small house, with a little front garden. I knock, and a young man opens the door.

"I would like to see Herr Mozart." "That's me. Do come in. Sit down. Here's a chair. Make yourself comfortable. Oh, I see. An autograph. Certainly. Not that it's worth much. Come through to the kitchen. We can have a chat whilst the coffee is brewing. My old lady's out. Gone to church. How very young you are. Are you in love? Let me play for you my latest trifle."

The hours pass. It's really time to go, but somehow I can't, no, I am too enchanted by all this, as I am bewitched by Mozart's pan pipe singing to the spring sun, in a forest clearing.

Wagner's battle of centaurs was grandiose, full of a strange, superhuman force. But I shall never be lured to the spears that must pierce the heart to draw the sacred blood.

To my heart, which loves Rimsky-Korsakov, the Pan pipes in a forest clearing seem nearer.

One has only to remember that the right of personal predilection to one type of beauty and grandeur, does not necessarily shut out one's admiration of another.

Nor can the European theatre ever be foreign to a Russian. I shall never forget an evening in Moscow, and this was thirty years ago, when for the first time in my life I saw upon the stage at the Maly Theatre, a great European actor, Thomaso Salvini. I was so moved by this that I ran into a corridor and wept. Since that time I have experienced many thrills in the theatre, and these I owe to the great European actors and actresses, Duse, Sarah Bernhardt, Paul Mounet, Novello, and Farabella, that incomparable Italian comedienne.

Extraordinary, and I can't think why, but I have never had the opportunity of seeing any of the famous German artists, but the Meiningen, the Lessing, and Reinhardt theatres, and the Vienna Burg theatre have entered into the history of European theatre, en bloc, like great constellations. I think of Keinz and Ludwig Barnai, Albert Bassermann and Pallenberg.

And America. A young country that is now revealing its own individuality, and has already given us some great actors. I need only mention the Barrymore family, and the amazing Charles Chaplin who belongs to both hemispheres. This brings me back to England. Irving, Ellen Terry, Sybil Thorndike. Whenever I find myself in London, it is with reverence and awe that I take off my hat, bow my head and stand before the monument to Irving, and feel that in his person I salute all the actors of the world.

To see a monument to an actor in a public place. What an incredible joy. So often, especially at home, do the memorials to great actors have to be searched for in those long-forgotten cemeteries.

I remember a very pleasurable occasion in London when I met several distinguished actresses of the English theatre. This was at a lunch given by George Bernard Shaw, who on this day had decided to gather about his table only his contemporaries.

He questioned me about some distinguished members of the Russian theatre. Strangely enough, every time a name was mentioned, I had to announce that they were all dead.

The irrepressible Shaw replied with a grave air, "How splendidly you've got things organised. He lived, and worked, and died, she lived, and worked, and died. Just look at us."

With a sweeping gesture he embraced the old guard of English theatre, now beginning to lay down their arms but refusing to die, and I recall half a dozen admonishing fingers rising into the air, rebuking this celebrated wit.

Western actors seem to me to have one invaluable quality, and it sometimes eludes the Russians. It is this tremendous feeling of measure, a great plastic freedom. But as they say, every quality has its drawbacks, and every drawback its qualities.

How I envied these Europeans, their lightness, their freedom of gesture. The Russian may possess a soul freer than the wind, his brain may teem with eagles, and the nightingales sing in his heart. But let him enter a drawing-room, and like as not he'll knock over a chair, spill his tea, trip over something. Invite him to speak at a banquet and he will be embarrassed, mumble a few ill-chosen words, and then dry up. Why is this?

Perhaps due to the very fact that for far too long the Russian has spent his days under the fierce eye of the Czars, Boyars and land-owners. He has been a slave. Told too often to "shut up", and "nobody's asked you to speak".

Out of this very shyness, one of the great Russian magicians of sound, Rimsky-Korsakov, so often made a hash of the composition he was conducting. He would make his appearance, his figure awkward at any angle, then raise his baton in a sheepish, disconcerted manner, wave it about in a half-hearted way, timidly, as though he were apologising for his very existence. And yet this same man astonishes by his aristocratic artistry, his great lyrical sense, a noble restraint in expressing emotion. It is these things, this very quality, that give such a delicate charm to all his work.

On the other hand, I think that Russian actors are endowed with a greater spontaneity, and with far more striking temperaments.

One thing I must regretfully admit, and that is that real operatic artists were as rare abroad as they were in Russia. There are good, even superb singers, but, in the full sense of the word, real operatic artists are difficult to find.

No matter how effective an aria, it will always be cold, almost official, if the intonation of the phrase is not right, if the sound itself is not clothed in the essential hues and tints of emotion.

This fault constitutes the cruellest sentence to the whole body of operatic art. It isn't exactly a revelation, for I myself was tortured by this back in Russia for many years.

For instance, I might be playing Holofernes in Serov's opera *Judith*, trying to re-create something reminiscent of the epoch, but what about those other people around me, the Assyrians, the Babylonians, the Judeans? What did they do? Painted their faces brown, stuck on a black beard, and put on whatever costume happened to be around. Accepted. But it never allowed one to forget that just before the performance all these people had been partaking of Russian cabbage soup. When I look back over the years, I am aware of the great number of parts I have played, both serious and comic, in many of the world's theatres. There was never such a thing as my theatre, anywhere, ever.

If we are to approach perfection, in say Korsakov's opera *Salieri*, then we must make certain it is endowed with a good Mozart. To take another case, say *Don Quixote*, it is wholly impossible to carry a production and call it perfect if we have a superb Sancho Panza, and a poor Don Quixote.

Orchestrally speaking, every member of it participates in the performance, to say nothing of the conductor's role.

I have sometimes plumbed the depths of despair in my own art, considering it unyielding, fruitless. Fame never consoled me, since I knew what fame meant. I have experienced it, and it was at times the uncracked nut, of which one can test the texture with one's teeth, but can never taste the flavour. What real joy is there in fame, except the material advantages, and occasionally the satisfaction of ordinary everyday ambitions? So often I felt I had half buried the very talents so generously recognised by my contemporaries, that God had given me much, but I have done little. I sang well, but where was my theatre?

Once, when I was obsessed by these doubts I happened by chance to meet the poet Gabriele D'Annunzio, who at that time was writing *The Passion of St. Sebastian* for Ida Rubenstein. I went to the Chatelet Theatre to watch the performance. It was then that I realized what an original and interesting talent he possessed.

At our next meeting I resolved to share with him my dreams of a theatre, from which all routine, all triteness would be ruthlessly banished, a theatre where all the arts could be fused into a marvellous harmony. Naturally, I was thrilled at his response, at the warm sympathy he expressed towards my idea.

"Let us meet next year," he said, "and we'll try to make our dreams come true."

That was in May 1914. But in August of the same year that winged spirit boarded a real aeroplane and went off to Fiume, in the very reverse direction, and far from our peaceful dreams.

For a long time I have cherished this idea of founding a centre in Russia, not just theatre, but for the arts generally. How often I have visualized that secluded haven, where, surrounded by gifted and serious young people, I could pass on to them my experience and passion for this noble cause of Theatre. I wanted to gather into one group singers, musicians, actors, artists, and together with them work in quietness and peace, and to surround them with the beauties of nature, and the joys of a guaranteed prosperity.

There lies in Suuk-Su, in the Crimea, a rock that runs down to the sea. It bears the name of Pushkin. And there I wanted to build my own castle of Art, and I mean castle. I'd say to myself, "Well, the kings and knights had their castles, so why shouldn't artists?" The embrasures of our castle would not be intended for any death-dealing weapons. No. A finer weapon would be at hand, a shining torch. So I bought the rock, and commissioned an architect to draw up plans for a castle. I bought Gobelins for its walls. My broken dream remained in Russia.

From time to time you hear people exclaiming, "Oh, some noble patron of art will come along one day and create your theatre." And always, like a kind of joke I would reply, "But where will we find the Pushkin rock?"

None of this is a joking matter, for my dream is indissolubly linked with my country, with Russian talent, with sensitive youth. The very idea of such a castle, say in Ohio, or on the Rhine, holds no lure for me. As to those "noble patrons", I shall never cease being amazed at one single, paradoxical fact. There are people in America who spend hundreds of thousands of dollars a year on Opera, from which one is expected to assume that they are sincerely and deeply in love with theatre. Rubbish. Their art is the cheapest kind of "ersatz". Season after season, year after year, this year and last, everything about it is hackneyed and lifeless. It will probably go on for years and years. Traviata is Traviata is Traviata. False actors, false reputations, false decor, false notes, a cent's worth of giftlessness.

These same people will spend fortunes to acquire a genuine Rembrandt. With the most fastidious grimace they turn their backs upon all that is not genuine, not first class. It's a great puzzle. A gallery must have an original, and it must be a masterpiece. And in the theatre that costs a lot of money they put up with imitations, the third rate. Can it possibly be that painting, as distinct from theatre, represents not only a form of art, but also a very good investment? This always makes me think of Mamontov, a man who spent fortunes on the theatre, and died a bankrupt. But what nobility of thought, what fabulous enlightenment, what passionate devotion to art, in a single person. Yet he lived in a "barbarian" country, and was of Tartar descent.

A Visit to Tolstoy with Sergei Rachmaninov

Chaliapin's friendship with Rachmaninov was life-long. Rachmaninov stimulated and encouraged him, and ever afterwards the singer acknowledged the debt. He took the greatest pains to awaken his interest in Mussorgsky and Rimsky-Korsakov. Later it was Chaliapin himself who was to be the real discoverer of Mussorgsky, not only for Russia, but for the world. Thanks to him, *Boris Godunov* circles the earth. One of the great regrets of Chaliapin's life was that he never met this most Russian of Russian composers. As he himself says: "He died before I ever reached Petersburg. That was my grief and my loss. It is like being late for the train of destiny. One rushes to the station but the train departs before one's eyes, into the distance forever."

He knew most of the composers of that time, and accepted their friendship and interest as great gifts. Many long evenings he spent with Stassov or Rimsky-Korsakov. He was struck by their modesty and recalls an evening at the latter's flat in Zagorodny Prospect.

"The furnishings were very simple. Russian musicians and writers do not live so well as we singers. Such a small sitting-room, just a few chairs, and a grand piano, and the dining-room itself just as simple. Around the narrow dining table we would sit shoulder to shoulder, eating shashlyk that was as closely packed as the guests themselves. There we discussed the contemporary works, the hope of productions, and often we sang together. More often than not the choir consisted of Rimsky-Korsakov, César Cui, Blumenthal and myself."

To return to Rachmaninov. He recalls a day in January 1900, when the composer and he went off to visit Tolstoy, who was then living in Khamovniki.

"I remember us climbing the wooden staircase to the second floor of a charming, cosy, modest, and as I recall it, half-timbered house. We were warmly welcomed by Sophia Andreyevna[1], and by her sons Mikhail, Andrei and Sergei. As usual, we were offered tea, though I myself was far too excited to think of eating and drinking. Imagine it. For the first time in my life I was to see Tolstoy face to face, a man whose thoughts and words had already touched the world. Hitherto I had only seen him in photographs, and now here he was in person, standing near the chess

[1] Countess Leo Tolstoy.

table talking to young Goldenweiser[1]. My first surprise was to realize that he was shorter than medium height. In the photographs he had seemed so tall. And now my blasted aural sense had begun to work (always a professional hazard), even in that so significant moment, and I was recording the fact that he spoke with a jarring voice, and that some words were pronounced with a mixture of lisp and whistle. It may have been due to the absence of a few teeth. I noticed all this in spite of my own fear, and that feeling of awe as I walked up to the great writer.

"How simply and charmingly he took my hand, how ordinary the questions he asked me. How long had I been in the theatre? How boyish I looked.

"Rachmaninov was a little braver than I, and yet he too was excited, and his hands were quite cold. He whispered in my ear, 'If they ask me to play I don't honestly know if I'll be able to. My hands are like ice.'

"And Tolstoy did ask him to play. I can't recall what he played, I only know of my own one worrying thought. 'Suppose he asks me to sing.' My heart went further into my boots, when Tolstoy looked Rachmaninov straight in the eye and asked 'Tell me, does anyone want this type of music?'

"Later, he asked me to sing. I remember I sang him the ballad, 'Fate', which Rachmaninov had recently written on the theme of Beethoven's Fifth Symphony, with the words by Apukhtin, the composer accompanying. We both did our best, but whether Tolstoy liked it was another matter. In any case we never found out. Indeed, he said nothing, except to repeat the former question about music, adding, 'What kind of music do people need, more folk music, or the cerebral, clever scientific offerings?'

"I sang some more songs, including Dargomyzhsky's 'The Old Corporal', with the writer sitting directly opposite me, his hands tucked into the belt of his tunic. I glanced at him from time to time, noticing with what interest he was watching my face, eyes, and mouth. When the last words of the soldier came, I was not the only one to feel the emotion, for I saw his hand leap from the belt, his finger flick the tears which rolled down his face.

"Recalling this, I feel a certain amount of embarrassment, as if my singing had caused such emotion to well up in his soul. All I had done was to convey the real feelings of an old soldier. Having finished, they applauded, and all kinds of flattering things were said to me. But Tolstoy remained silent.

"Later his wife spoke to me. 'For heaven's sake,' she said, 'don't let on that you noticed his tears. He can be strange at times. He says one thing, but in his very soul, in addition to cold reasoning, there is also a fiery feeling.'

"'Do you think he liked my interpretation of "The Old Corporal"?'

"'I'm sure of that,' she replied.

"And now I began to feel both the inner warmth and kindness of the stern apostle, and I was happy. At that moment his sons, of the same age as

[1] Boris Solomonovich Goldenweiser (b. 1875), pianist, composer, Professor of Moscow Conservatoire, People's Artist of the U.S.S.R.

myself, dragged me off into another room, exclaiming, 'You can't stay here any longer. You'll get bored. Let's go to Yar. The gypsies are there, we'll sing and have fun.'

"Whether or not I'd have been bored, I don't know, but certainly I felt tense and uncomfortable in front of the great writer. I dreaded his suddenly asking me a question, and I being unable to answer, whereas, being what I am, I am never stuck for an answer to a gypsy girl, whatever she may ask.

"Of this experience I have my agonising moments. How much I let slip by, like the indifference with which a Muscovite passes the Kremlin, and the Parisian ignores the Louvre.

"I think of my life. I think of what I have missed. Perhaps I might have come closer to Tolstoy, might have spent more time with the bespectacled Rimsky-Korsakov. But what a deeper, richer, sigh I might give at the thought of our own dear Anton Pavlovich Chekhov, listening to his little stories being read by Moskvin, and watching him cough into little pieces of paper twisted into cornet bags. Yes, I saw it all, but I didn't sigh deeply enough.

"I shall remember Rachmaninov's cold hands, I shall remember him accompanying me. The singer has no reason whatever for anxiety. When he plays for me I can truly say, not that 'I'm singing', but 'we are singing'.

"I remember that. And I owe him much."

Letter to the Editor of *Novoye Vremya* from Angelo Masini (March 15, 1901)

I am writing to you, still under the spell of Chaliapin's performance of *Mefistofele*. As you will know, the audience at La Scala is particularly demanding and severe towards young and untried singers. But this evening has been an unqualified triumph for the Russian artist, a performance that evoked a tremendous enthusiasm and ended with an unprecedented ovation. The deep impression made by him is quite understandable. Not only a splendid singer but a superlative actor. And in addition to this, he possesses a positively Dantesque pronunciation. This is an incredible manifestation in an artist who does not own to Italian as his mother tongue.

Listening to him, my enjoyment was twofold, because Chaliapin comes from Russia, a country I have grown to know and love.

82. *Stars of La Scala, Milan, in a production of Rossini's opera* The Barber of Seville: *Almaviva—Tito Schipa; Figaro—Benvenuto Franci; Bartolo—Salvatore Baccaloni; Don Basilio—Chaliapin; Rosina—Toti Dal Monte.*

83. *The Italian tenor Tito Schipa, speaking at the unveiling of a memorial plaque outside the house in Moscow (25 Tchaikovsky Street), in which Chaliapin lived and worked from 1910 to 1922. The ceremony took place on August 9, 1957.*

85. *Chaliapin at a fair; a portrait by Kustodiyev,*
1922. The painter chose this setting for his monumental
portrait because Chaliapin was first "scorched by the
theatre" at just such a fair. Immortalised at Chaliapin's
feet is his bulldog Kharlashka. Also in the painting, just
below the figure of Chaliapin, are two of his daughters
and his secretary, one-time actor and producer of the
Mariinsky Theatre, Isai Dvorishchin.

Below 84. *Chaliapin, 1928.*

CHALIAPINE

avec le concours des

CHŒURS DE LA CATHÉDRALE RUSSE À PARIS

sous la direction de Nicolas AFONSKY.

PROGRAMME

I

1. a) Psaume 67 ... ... Bortniansky
   b) Chant des Pâques (De voskresnet Bog) ... ... N. Kedroff.
   c) Cantiques Eucharistiques ... ... A. Gretchaninoff.
   d) Credo. — Solo Madame G. PAVLENKO ... ... A. Gretchaninoff.
   e) Hymne des Cherubins N° 7 ... ... D. Bortniansky.

   Les Chœurs de la Cathédrale Russe à Paris,
   sous la Direction de Nicolas AFONSKI.

2. **FEODOR CHALIAPINE (*)**

II

3. a) Credo (du "Liturge domestica") "Sougoubaya Ektenia" ... A. Gretchaninoff.
   b) Légende des douze brigands ... ... A. Rubinstein.
   c) Chanson Persane ... ...

   FEODOR CHALIAPINE avec les Chœurs de la Cathédrale Russe
   à Paris, sous la Direction de Nicolas AFONSKY.

4. a) Chœurs de l'Opéra "Sadko" ... ... N. Rimsky-Korsakoff.
   b) Étude. — Solo Mademoiselle A. ZAKHAROVA ... ... Chopin.
   c) Tchikou-Tchikou, chanson ukrainienne populaire, arr. ... G. Davidovsky.

   Les Chœurs de la Cathédrale Russe à Paris,
   sous la Direction de Nicolas AFONSKY.

5. **FEODOR CHALIAPINE (*)**

Au Piano Maria KALAMKARIAN

(*) Avant chaque chanson, Feodor Chaliapine annoncera son numéro d'après le texte du programme.

Above 87. *Poster of the last concert given by Chaliapin on June 18, 1937, at the Salle Pleyel, Paris.*

Left 86. *Chaliapin at a concert, 1934.*

89. *Chaliapin, a portrait by his son, Boris Feodorovich, 1932.*

88. *Chaliapin, a portrait by his son, Boris Feodorovich, 1928.*

V. I. Nemirovich-Danchenko on Chaliapin

(i) AN EXTRACT FROM HIS BOOK, *FROM THE PAST*. Published by Iskusstvo, Moscow, 1952.

Those were years of outward calm and complete prosperity, yet from the very depths of a one hundred and sixty million strong human ocean, wave upon wave disturbed. There, on the one hand was St. Petersburg, the Imperial Court, the Guards regiments, Grand Dukes, High Society and the Demi-Monde, the Mariinsky Theatre, the Opera, the Ballet, the long processions, parades, balls, the "Novoye Vremya", the civil servant spirit, Paris, London, the glitter of civilization. But distinctly those unseen waves carried with them a great smell of sweat and burning, the cruel chill of outright mercilessness.

Between these opposing worlds, the one visible and carefree and idle, the other concealed and lost in the immensity of its own tragedy, there lay a boundary zone. And each living breath of this ocean but served to widen it, and from its depths there rose up new hope, new forces, new beliefs, a new courage. It carried to the surface men like Gorky and Chaliapin, and they served to strengthen a new faith at work in the creative force of the people through art. It was once said that when God created Chaliapin he was in a good and generous mood, for he made this man to bring joy to all.

(ii) AN EXTRACT FROM HIS BOOK *THEATRICAL HERITAGE*, Vol. 1. Published by Iskusstvo, Moscow, 1952.

. . . Whenever I came away from one of Chaliapin's performances . . . the first truly finished singer and actor with our trend of thought, I would try to recall some feature of his performance. I was never able to say where the source of his enchantment lay. Was it the way he moved, or sang, or the way he wiped cold sweat with a red silk handkerchief? Was it his silences, his very pauses that seemed to hold within them the ultimate of expression?

Look at a photograph of him as Don Quixote, note the eyes that seem to have renounced reality, the emaciated figure of radiant fighter, the pauper knight carrying war to windmills, and you will see both the inspired and the ridiculous. It is truly an artistic portrait. Take a look through the other galleries, the celebrated singers of Aidas, Delilahs, Hermans, Raouls, Marguerites, Snow Maidens, Onegins and others. A gallery of mummers.

Vladimir Stassov on Chaliapin

This article, "Boundless Joy", first appeared in February, 1898, in the *Birzheviye Novosti*, and later in 1949, in a volume of his criticisms.

As does Sabinin in Glinka's Opera, so I, too, exclaim, "Boundless joy". A fortune had descended from heaven, and a great new talent is born. All who were at the Conservatoire Hall yesterday, the 23rd of February, will probably never forget that evening, nor indeed the horizons opened up to us. For the first time, and this after an appallingly long period of censorship and wilful ignorance, one of the best of all Russian operas, *The Maid of Pskov*, by Rimsky-Korsakov, was performed.

This opera is so outstanding, reveals such a richness of talent and is so original, that it is not to be wondered at that its absence from our stage has been long, and we, duty bound to ignore it, prefer a great profusion of rubbish.

Only the private Moscow Opera, recently arrived for a short tour, has a different outlook on music. Indeed it allows us glimpses of the many miracles that are being so carefully and so thoroughly concealed from us. And as a consequence of the habits that have been grafted on us, we tend to be hesitant in our approach to some of the Russian masterpieces. Last evening one such stood out before our eyes, yet the hall itself was half empty.

Twenty-seven years ago, in 1871, I remember writing an article in the *St. Petersburg News* on February the 13th, in which I said, "As from this moment we have one more great work of art—the statue of Ivan the Terrible, by the sculptor Antokolsky." So, a quarter of a century later I can repeat with the same confidence, "As from this moment we are richer by one more great artist."

Chaliapin is the seed and the light. And he has created something astounding in the Russian theatre. Like Antokolsky, he is a very young man. The character of Ivan the Terrible, as created by him, is something that has never been seen before on any operatic stage. Nor is it the first time that I have seen and heard him. As a mere youngster, some four years ago, he appeared in the role of Prince Galitsky in Borodin's *Prince Igor*. An entirely unknown young man. The talents of this youngster amazed and thrilled us.

Everything in the role demanded by its author, dissipation, rowdiness, force, independence, the wild nature of a mediaeval prince, was portrayed by him with a mastery and forcefulness rare indeed on an operatic stage.

The impact was tremendous. The singer's most unusual gifts, the very originality of the opera, was something we all felt, and it won the admiration of the public.

All the same, this very fact did not prevent Chaliapin becoming superfluous for the Mariinsky stage (obviously we have such embarras de talents). He was forced to leave Petersburg and go to a private theatre in Moscow. And not a single effort was made to retain this bright star. One can hear it all being said. "What on earth for? Who needs him anyhow?"

Shortly after, rumours began to filter through. News of further conquests, greater achievements, Chaliapin's mastery of so many dissimilar parts. And not least, his growing popularity with the public.

And something else. In January last I attended the first performance of Rimsky-Korsakov's opera, *Sadko*. This work, too, reveals unusual talent and originality, indeed it plays a significant part in the history of Russian music. Naturally enough, it was doomed to be rejected by the Mariinsky Theatre. They have so many better, more important works there. And here lies the whole unhappy state of the most important of the Russian operas. Think of Dargomyzhsky, Mussorgsky, Cui, Borodin, Rimsky-Korsakov. Which one of these composers has not experienced it? Have they ever heard anything other than, "we don't want it", and "we don't need you", "we can manage very well without you".

So there I was, seated in the Mamontov Theatre, pondering upon the precarious state of Russian art, when suddenly, in the third scene of *Sadko*, an ancient Viking giant appeared on stage singing the Varangian song, one of Rimsky-Korsakov's great inspirations. The very melodies, powerful, austere, conjured up the visions of rock itself, upon which broke the waves in one long incessant roar. And out of this very atmosphere arose the Varangian himself. There he was, one whose bones might have been forged out of the very rocks.

He stood there, enormous, leaning on a huge poleaxe, a steel helmet on his head, bare armed. Strong features with drooping moustaches, the powerful chest encased in chain mail. The legs swathed in strips of leather. What do I remember?

A gigantic voice, the movement of body and arms as though some enormous sculpture had come to life. There he stood, staring at us from under thick, bushy eyebrows. . . . It was so novel, so powerful, so profoundly true that I could only ask myself the astonished question. Who can this be? Who is this actor? Where in all Moscow do they find men like this? The answer came in the interval, a reply to breathless questionings. The programme and the bills outside proclaimed only the name of an unknown actor, whose part, at a moment's notice, had been taken by Chaliapin. I was delighted, I was lost in admiration.

The incredible versatility. To have created such diametrically opposed human beings. And yet the parts of Prince Galitsky and the ancient Viking paled before that portrait of Ivan the Terrible. The living pulse of a whole period beat passionately, with a terrible inevitability, under that strange robe.

Chaliapin creates not just individual scenes, separate characters and figures, but whole parts, great parts, human beings in all their variety, moment and situation fused in an unforgettable magic, as though by some strange compulsion we are carried into another dimension. That evening I witnessed Ivan the Terrible in the many vivid and dreadful moments of his life. The whole thing was to me the conjurings up of the miraculous. What mastery of situation, of moment, of crisis, of weakness and strength. How obediently, how brilliantly his voice changed, level upon level, portraying these endless, varying expressions of the Russian soul. What triumph, what fluidity in all his movements, each pose crying out for immortality, some permanent sculptural identity, and thus ensuring to us all, everything new, everything exciting, everything extraordinary. How splendid that the whole thing was achieved so naturally, with such astonishing simplicity. Nothing "inventive" here, nothing theatrical, the whole refusing the very echo of what we call theatrical routine. An incredible talent in a young man of just twenty-five years of age.

Stanislavsky on Chaliapin

The following extracts are taken from Stanislavsky's books *My Life in Art* and *The Actor's Workshop*, published by Soviet Theatre, 1936.

. . . . I have noticed that many great artists, among them Duse, Ermolova, Fedotova, Savina, Salvini, Chaliapin, Rossi, and many of the most talented of the Moscow Arts Theatre actors, have something in common, a kindred, an inherent quality that formed a bond between them. For a long time I could not even guess what it was. To begin with, I only noticed that in a creative mood an important part is played by freedom of the body, by the absence of all muscular tension, and by the complete subordination of the whole physical apparatus to the artist's will. Only by such discipline can one achieve properly organized creative work, which allows the artist freely to express with the body what is felt in the soul.

The opera singer has to contend not with one, but with three arts at once —vocal, musical and theatrical. In this reside both the difficulty and the advantages of his creative work. The problem lies in the varied processes of mastering the three arts, though this done the singer has the greater and more variable ability to act upon the audience, than do we dramatic actors.

These three arts the singer must fuse into one, and direct it to a common aim. If, however, one of these arts exercised an influence on the audience, and another impeded it, we would get a highly undesirable result, since one art would be destroying what the other was creating. This is a simple truth, yet the majority of opera singers appear ignorant of it. Many indeed are not seriously interested in the musical side of their profession, and so far as acting goes, they not only do not bother to learn, but frequently enough actually disdain it, so proud are they to proclaim that they are singers, and not just common or garden actors. To me, Chaliapin is an outstanding example of how the three forms of art can be fused. Synthesis in art, especially in the theatre, is rarely achieved, and I have cited Chaliapin, though even he had not attained it in all his parts.

He is a great master of recitation. Though not aware of all the laws and rules, he nevertheless achieves the intonation of a born genius, and almost invariably finds the right expressions. . . .

There is prevalent a fixed idea about facing an audience, yet there are times when the reverse view can be more expressive and more telling than the features, and I would like to cite an example from the Bolshoy Theatre.

Sancho Panza is delivering his aria in *Don Quixote*. To make certain that he is noticed by all, he rushes about the proscenium. Upstage, with his back to the audience, so as not to interfere, sits Chaliapin. He is smiling. I cannot see his face, yet I know he is smiling. Suddenly he begins to write something, stops for a moment's reflection, searching perhaps for a rhyme, then begins writing again. The entire audience is riveted on Chaliapin, caring deeply about whether or not he finds that rhyme. Sancho Panza was trying so hard, yet getting nowhere.

Let us take a scene from *Khovanshchina*:

Enter Dositheus. He reaches deeper and deeper into his capacious priest's pocket. Then, suddenly, he is distracted by something. He forgets he is looking for a handkerchief. He starts to listen. No. All is well. Once again he dives a hand into that depthless pocket. In the whole of that vast scene he was endeavouring to get out his handkerchief, yet never managed it. It was quite remarkable.

Take a look at Chaliapin's hands. You would never recognize his wrists. He varies the make-up of his hands so richly that at one moment it is a beautiful elegant hand, yet in the next it is nothing more than a rough claw.

Again, Chaliapin never looks at the gesture he makes, instead he feels it in every movement. If gestures are logical, then there is no need to emphasize anything. Do exactly what you need to do. Anything you have to try for is superfluous.

Whenever I think of the need to "devour" knowledge, I always remember him. Particularly well do I remember a certain evening party I attended. I was sitting next to Mamontov, and we were watching the young Chaliapin standing in a circle of several great masters, among them Repin, Serov and others. He listened avidly, not missing a single word. Mamontov nudged me and remarked, "Look, Konstantin, see how he gobbles up knowledge."

Consonants should be sung and savoured. Both Chaliapin and Battistini sang every consonant to the end. Without consonants there is no bel canto. Chaliapin sings every letter, and it is this that distinguishes him from all other singers.

I recall a talk I had with him in America, in which he maintained that any word of a phrase can be stressed without losing the essential rhythmical emphasis in singing. His power lay in the word, in diction—mother-of-pearl vowels in the golden setting of consonants.

Chaliapin: A Reminiscence, by Lev Nikulin

It was the spring of 1917, and Russia was experiencing its third month without a Czar. Millions were on the move. In the villages the peasants were demanding division of the land, and many factories were strike-bound. The front was still holding, and the railway stations were crammed with soldiers, little bundles on their backs, sullenly waiting for the trains that would take them East.

We stood in the shadow of great events, though even then those who called themselves the "Provisional Government of Russia" were making the pathetic and most desperate attempts at appearing active.

It was at this time that a group of well-known Russian film actors (among them Maksimov and Polonsky) were busy filming in the Crimea, and I was a student and budding writer. It was not the first time I had tried my hand at film scenarios, and I was invited to go to the Crimea, and there and then think up some local stories for films, set amid the beauty of Crimean parks and villas.

In those days a film script consisted of some sixty or seventy small scenes, all of which could easily be contained within the pages of a school exercise book. Yet it was not easy to write them, as, by order of the Production Company, Biofilm, one was restricted to the eternal triangle of husband, wife, and lover. Within such limitations one was forced to invent the usual love intrigue, with either a tragic or lyrical ending, under the pale light of the moon, or by the sea, or on a road lined with majestic cypresses.

We arrived late at night at our destination, a place called Gurzuf. The park was still save for the rustling of leaves and the distant rumble from the sea.

We reached a building bearing the proud title of "The Fifth Hotel", and found its occupants fast asleep. The slippered night porter showed my companion and myself to our room. On the table stood a vase of magnolia in full blossom. It filled the room with its sweet, intoxicating scent.

Through the open window I glimpsed the gently swaying top of a cypress tree. A warm rain fell during the night, and the morning revealed the freshly washed cypresses glistening in the sun. The sea was a pale, tender blue. The peak of Ayu-Dag towering in a spring sky, looked deceptively close. For a while we stood on the balcony admiring the scene, so beautiful, so different indeed from Moscow's own anaemic season.

Suddenly I heard a voice, an extraordinary voice, and because of this, oddly familiar.

"I say, what is the time?"

I turned and gasped. There, leaning on the balcony, wearing a brightly-patterned dressing-gown, and exposing a great expanse of chest, stood Chaliapin. It was enough just to recognize the magnificent line and strength of his neck. The folds of the gown fell picturesquely from his shoulders.

I regained my breath.

"It's just after ten," I said.

"What a morning," and he took a deep breath.

He stretched, making wide circles with his arms, then clasped his hands at the back of his head.

"I had no idea we had such an illustrious neighbour," remarked my room mate.

"I've been here a whole week," said Chaliapin. "Was it you arriving late last night?"

He turned suddenly to the French windows behind him, called out, "Who's there," and vanished from sight.

For a while we just stared incredulously at the empty balcony. And then I remembered. Somebody from the Moscow Literary and Art circle had mentioned that the singer was staying at Gurzuf.

We saw him day after day, for some three weeks. It was tremendously exciting to watch him, like a rare, extravagant creation of nature herself.

Until now we had only seen him on stage, from "the gods".

On this splendid May morning in Gurzuf I sweated over the routine agonies of a Nina and George, precisely let it be said, at the time when these and their prototypes, "heroes", for want of a better word, were just about living their last care-free days.

Nevertheless work had to be done. After all, I hadn't arrived at Gurzuf just to sit around, for I was receiving a fee that promised a fairly prosperous existence for the coming three months. So there I was, in the middle of a perfectly idiotic story, with the poetic title of "The Moonlight Magnolia". I suffered agonies working on the plot, whilst all the time the heavy scent of real flowers was making my head go round and the usual pangs of labour, this time about Tamara and Valerian, when again I heard the familiar voice.

"Still writing, poet. Rather nice having a poet for a neighbour."

Who but Chaliapin could have pronounced the words in just that way? What other voice but his sound so magical on a still May morning?

"Why not come over to my place, neighbour. You should do something about distracting a poor lonely artist."

I flung my notebook into a drawer and went next door.

Chaliapin's balcony was submerged in flowers. His female admirers were quite evidently not neglecting that "poor, lonely artist". "Help yourself," he said. "Some wine over there. It's a light, Crimean wine. There's a glass on the terrace."

The hospitality lavished upon me, a quite unknown young man, I found as surprising as it was delightful. Later I was to learn the reason for it.

"Your father and I are old friends. He came here to see me from Sebasto-pol. Talked me into singing for the sailors. There! A souvenir of the occasion."

A sailor's cap lay on the sofa, the St. George's ribbon round its crown, and the ship's name, "Panteleimon", in gold lettering.

"The artists like your father, yet we theatre folk don't often like people. He has a kind nature, though I can't say the same about myself."

Chaliapin showed the most charming manner towards his guests, even to his way of addressing them. He talked simply, kindly, quite unaffectedly. One might be an old friend. But then his guest came from an old theatrical family, it might be just that. I was no personality myself, in fact I was nothing, and it would have been a sheer waste of time for Chaliapin to impress me with his greatness. All the same, the beautiful morning and the long rest he had enjoyed put him into a good humour.

He took up the sailor's cap, and put it on, in the most correct manner, its badge resting just over the bridge of his nose. There, indeed, was a handsome sailor, a real swashbuckling blue jacket, fit to join any ship's crew.

"That's how I looked when I sang at Sebastopol. I did the whole thing, complete uniform, it pleased them. And I actually arrived here, still wearing it. Friends nearly fainted, seeing me. A sailor, they seemed to say. Perhaps he has come to search the Grand Duke's palace."

He threw off the cap and sat down, and for the first time I was seeing Chaliapin's face at very close range. It was the pleasant, attractive Russian face in the prime of life. His chin was round and smooth, and there was some-thing strikingly youthful about the nose, with its large, nervous, sensitively dilating nostrils. He had a clear intelligent forehead, a lock of hair falling over it. The eyes were large, with fair eyelashes.

He was dressed entirely in white, and this, with his enormous height, made him look even taller than he was. The large handsome hand dangled a Russian cigarette. And there he sat, smoking and discoursing, three feet away from me in a rattan armchair.

"I heard your lot arguing yesterday," he said. "Here it's so quiet in the evenings, I can hear every word. Well? What do you think? How long d'you suppose it'll last? And when on earth will all these meetings be over? Talking, talking, catching up on three hundred years of lost time. Don't get the idea that I'm against it. I myself called in on the St. Petersburg Soviet, I was one of the first to do so after the Czar was overthrown. What the devil do I want a Czar for? I am a peasant's son, and have done all the bowing and scraping that I ever wish to do. So, whoever else may want him, I don't. Besides which, I never liked the police. To tell you the honest truth, they scared me stiff. Yes. There was I, Chaliapin, the whole world knew me, yet a drunken police officer could insult me, even kill me, so help me God. As if there were no such cases. That's why I like living abroad so much. Never mind. They're overthrown, and it's all to the good." He paused.

"But there's no order," he said, a certain irritation in the voice. "Not a vestige of it. Nothing on earth but speechifying. At the Mariinsky Theatre you cannot get anybody to listen to anything. Absolute chaos. The shows are put on any old how, with every Tom, Dick, and Harry only too ready to taunt, 'The times have changed. Enough!'

"To whom are they saying this? To me. I took a lot, yes, but by God, how I've given. I, too, say enough! And until this is all over, I shall remain here and refuse to budge. There's one thing wrong with this place. It will soon be hot. But how glorious are the autumns here. Let's hope that things are normal by that time."

I have never forgotten that conversation. There was in Chaliapin's tone of voice a mixture of Russian complacency and the spark of craftiness. Gorky himself so often pin-pointed this as a trait of character. Chaliapin was talking politics to a Moscow student with a secret thought: students are always mixed up with politics, and perhaps better than anybody else they understand what is going on. For this reason he often invited my companion and myself for walks in the mountains, or by the sea. Often enough we heard his grave, unhurried speech, studded with lively observations, and often fair and to the point, about the past and present, about life in general.

In a rather severe tone he once asked me if I ever wrote for the newspapers.

"Seldom," I replied, "and then only verse."

"It's good that you write verse, otherwise you might take it into your head to commit to print all I've been saying to you. But I speak as a friend, off the record you might say. Now let me tell you something. People say that I'm rude—but who says it? Newspapermen, of course. I've asked Telyakovsky to add a clause to my contract providing for a guard of two soldiers to be posted outside my dressing-room, with permanently unsheathed sabres, to keep out the reporters. I am an artist. And not the scraping of the barrel either. They should respect me, damn them. How do they write about me? Any son of a bitch from the *Petersburg Gazette* can write about me, in letters a foot high, 'Chaliapin is a brawler', or go into screaming headlines—'Another "achievement" of the famous bass'. The devil take the lot of them. I am a man, a father, I have growing children and these scribblers dare write such stuff about me. Disgraceful. And some people actually call it publicity. Thank you very much for your publicity. They can keep it."

Chaliapin's eyes flashed with anger, and I had a sudden vision of him in an uncontrollable rage.

"I have lived abroad. They of course have their newspapermen too. An absolute plague. But a mere Frenchman is no match at all for our lot, like Ivan Pozdnyshev or Kugulsky."

Many years have passed since that talk. Now I am glancing through the pages of an old illustrated magazine, *Iskra*, a supplement to the daily, *Russkoye Slovo*. I find in it a full-page photograph of Chaliapin making a recording in London. He is without a coat, the left hand tucked into the armhole of his waistcoat, a long Russian cigarette in the right hand. The head is thrown back, the eyes half closed. Chaliapin is singing, inspiration is written on his face, and he carefully avoids looking at the microphone.

A second photograph shows him listening to a play-back of his own records. Here all is tense concentration, for he is his own most severe judge. And, finally, I look at one of him in the street, attired in a loose-fitting overcoat and grey topper. His bearing proclaims both dignity and greatness, a fine Russian artist on a visit abroad. Yet the caption beneath this trio of photographs read as follows:

"Before leaving for Moscow for the Autumn season, Chaliapin dropped into London, at the invitation of some rich Americans, and made recordings of both Russian and Italian songs. The sum pocketed by Chaliapin for this performance is not disclosed but, according to popular rumours, the fee was colossal, in the American style."

This impertinent and malicious tone (the reactionary writer Burenin accused him of a certain lack of elegance on stage) was only part of the whole pattern; a vulgar, sniping attitude towards the singer was popular in the press of that time.

This great bass had come up from "the lower deck", and this became the subject of countless trivia, rather flat jokes, platitudinous feuilletons and banal cartoons. He would be portrayed wearing a Russian shirt, home-made bast sandals, a balalaika in his hands. Below, one found the sneering caption "Glinka's knight-errant". Or he would be shown as a gormless schoolboy, with Gorky portrayed as the village schoolteacher. To cut short a long and rather sad story, what should have been a matter of real pride, the talent of a man of the people, was held up to ridicule; it amused the vulgar, it provided food for every reactionary scribbler of the gutter press.

And this triviality dogged him, forever followed him. Cheap publicity flanked with real tribute to well-deserved fame. Feuilletons in prose and verse, "news items", couplets and satirical ditties were performed in the cafés-chantants. One music-hall singer, Ubeiko by name, included one in his repertoire, and it ran something like this:

"If I were Chaliapin, I'd growl like a bear,
    And slap the girls' bottoms if I'd any time to spare."

But what else could one expect from such rags as *Ranneye Utro,* or *Vecherneye Vremya*?

Enterprising spivs advertised "malt-extract sweets with diastase guaranteed to ease cough, hoarseness, and difficulty of expectorating" which concoctions went under the name sometimes of "Pushkin caramels", sometimes "Chaliapin caramels", according to how the spirit moved them.

Thousands of lines have been written about Chaliapin, much of it scurrilous nonsense, featuring the Chaliapin scandals, Chaliapin fees, Chaliapin eccentricities. Of his significance as a Russian artist of world-wide fame much less was said.

That it should have irritated and angered the singer goes without question. He always accorded high status to an artist, and loathed disparagement. The ignorant remarks of people who knew little or nothing about art, he cut with a knife.

It is true he did have disagreements with the public, especially if the audience presumed to take too much for granted. At a concert in Rostov-on-Don, a voice was heard calling upon him to sing "The Song of the Flea". He refused with a characteristic comment.

"I have many faults," he said, "but perhaps the worst is that I am prone to caprices and I sing what I like."

Following this incident a controversy flared up in the papers. Was it permissible for an artist to indulge in polemics with his audience? It was hotly argued.

For Chaliapin there was an air of offensiveness in these "demands", and he explained that a desire to sing this or that song arose in the singer as a result of extremely complex associations.

"I felt like singing 'Two Giants', and I was all keyed up for this, when somebody demands 'The Flea'. This meant breaking up my mood, my feeling, re-tuning myself as it were. And that's not easy."

When *A Life for The Czar* was given at the Olympia Theatre in 1904, the public demanded an encore of the Sabinin aria, sung on that occasion by Klementyev. Chaliapin gestured to the audience to be quiet, and called out in a loud voice, "A little more respect for Glinka." This brought forth protests and booing.

Every one of these "incidents" became the material and property of the gossip writers. Pompously they took upon themselves the right to moralize, to propound "thoughtful" comments on the subject.

Nor was it to be wondered at that the leading part in all this should be played by the newspaper with an unprecedented circulation, *Russkoye Slovo*.

Doroshevich, the king-pin of pre-revolutionary journalism, wrote lengthily and regularly about Chaliapin, and with obnoxious familiarity, something he had cultivated in the last few years of his journalistic activity. If we consider this, we can understand the singer's demand to Telyakovsky that two soldiers with unsheathed sabres should assume duty outside his dressing-room.

There may have been a slight suggestion of "pose" here, and, had the newspapers suddenly ceased talking about him, no doubt Chaliapin would have worried and found his own inimitable ways and means of making them talk. He was very susceptible to publicity, loved being photographed, and sitting for famous painters. There is a magnificent portrait of him as Boris Godunov, painted by Golovin in 1912,[1] that now hangs in the Russian State Museum. Chaliapin loved anything that increased his fame, and quarrelled with people before whom he had to assert himself as an artist. Unfortunately when fame did come, it brought in its wake much gossip, scandal-mongering and the vulgar scribblings of semi-literate critics and gutter reporters.

However, one cannot entirely blame those simple penny-a-line writers of the yellow press, when even serious newspapers such as *The Russian Musical Gazette*, in an article dealing with the revival of *Russlan and Ludmilla*

[1] See frontispiece.

at the Mariinsky Theatre, in 1904, commented thus on the Chaliapin performance:

"Mr. Chaliapin made more than a fool of Farlaf, he turned him into a hideous caricature of cowardice. Nor for a single moment would we imagine such a shady individual being received at Svetozar's Court—he overdid it, to the great joy of the 'gods'."

The "gods" in those days were normally occupied by young audiences, an essentially democratically-minded public. It is worth noting that the "expert" from *The Russian Musical Gazette* was in all seriousness pondering over the Chaliapin Farlaf, and even taking quite seriously the fact of a fairy-tale ruler Svetozar being an historical figure. There is hardly any need to add that the Chaliapin characterization was an outstanding achievement, and the Farlaf image remains untarnished in the history of operatic art.

At this Crimean resort Chaliapin was bored, and consequently in a sociable and talkative mood. And then one day the subject of conversation was films. Now this was not a very pleasant subject for him, for in those far-off days, at the dawn of Russian cinema, he had made an attempt to film the life story of Ivan the Terrible, with himself in the title role. He was apt to be furious every time the subject came up, and he certainly had reason to be.

Cautious by nature, and inclined to approach people with a certain suspicion, Chaliapin, invariably, became the victim of the tactics of shady characters, always provided they were capable of insinuating themselves into his confidence.

"I knew a regular bandit once. Even his name sounded like a highwayman's—Ivanov-Gai. He could talk nineteen to the dozen, a real live wire, and an absolute crook if ever there was one. I met him at a baths. Funny really, but even there, where people are naked, you can't always see into their hearts. I don't know what it was about this man, but I liked him. 'Feodor Ivanovich,' he said, 'you ought to make a film. Millions of people are dreaming of seeing you, just to see you would give them happiness. And what a splendid Ivan the Terrible you would make.'

"Imagine it. He talked me into it, the scoundrel. Result? A shocking disgrace. I arrived on location, and what did I see? Some extras standing around, the seediest-looking bunch of individuals I've ever laid eyes on. There they were, balancing precariously on pensioned-off police horses. Who on earth were these people? The Czar's falconers, if you please. They had to be seen to be believed, sitting there holding dummies in their hands—stuffed birds. They looked pretty stuffed themselves. And that was the Czar's falconry scene. I took just one look at them. Then that bandit Gai says to me, 'Don't get excited, Feodor Ivanovich, for goodness' sake. They may not look very presentable, but they are all right, students mostly, intellectuals.' 'What's their being students got to do with it? I'm not looking for a tutor. And what are those extraordinary rags they're wearing?'

"'The costumes,' quoted the bandit, 'are entirely in the style of the epoch. We hired them from Zimin, the costumier.'

"Well, I really don't know what made me do it, but I went on with it, dressed for the part, and put on make-up. I had a very definite idea of how to do Ivan, and I wanted him younger than he is in *The Maid of Pskov*. I thought the whole thing out very carefully. Emerging from my dressing-room I almost collided with the camera men, who concentrated on me. Little sticks stuck all over the place. 'What on earth are these for?' I asked, and what d'you suppose they replied? 'Please be so kind as to walk about from here to there, and not further than either of these lines—you've got six yards.'

'"Have you all gone mad?' I asked.

"'No, Feodor Ivanovich, we have not. This is necessary for technical, optical and other reasons.'

"I gave Gai such a look. He trembled, and blurted out, 'I swear to God, it's all for technical reasons, ask anybody you like.'

"'Listen,' I said, 'to hell with these sticks. I shall walk and act as I need, and let those two camera men chase after me and do their shooting.'

"'It cannot be done, Cinematographic art has not progressed that far.'

"I should have thrown them all out, finished the whole sorry business there and then. But no. That crook got round me again, talked me into it. And when we'd done the film, it was scandalous—there's not another word for it."

The whole of this conversation took place in front of our cameraman, a young man with a sense of humour. He almost died laughing as Chaliapin went over the experience.

But he was telling the truth. The cinema was in its infancy, and in those days, action and panorama shooting was still unknown to our cameramen.

"All very well for you to sit there laughing your head off," Chaliapin exclaimed. "But there was worse to come. How on earth can one act if all one is allowed to do is to take two steps forward and two steps back? I began a scene. The sun was shining, a light breeze blew. The setting: a little old church in a green field, on a hillock, all very real, not theatre props. I felt an enthusiasm rising within me. Perhaps Ivan the Terrible did come here with his falconers. But I was brought back to reality by the single shout of 'Cut'.

"'What's wrong?' I asked.

"'Sun's gone behind a cloud, can't continue filming.'

"My inspiration vanished. No. That kind of thing was not for me. What kind of art is it? Never again will I disgrace myself. Yet there are others who can do it, Mozhukhin perhaps, or Polonsky. Am I unlucky, or was the film? I don't know. But never again will I attempt a film."

One can imagine with what impatience his appearance on the screen was awaited by the cinema-going public. Chaliapin as Ivan the Terrible in *The Maid of Pskov*. It was even announced in advance that Chaliapin would write the shooting script; based on historical material. In October 1915 the film was released.

The criticisms were scathing. Speaking of Chaliapin's acting, the *Cinema Journal* commented:

"Not only does he stun us by his acting, he positively wears us out. By the end we are really exhausted. He rolls his eyes in a most awesome manner, bares his teeth, twists his mouth, wrinkles up his forehead, wriggles his eyebrows, screws his fingers into terrifying claws, writhes and contorts his whole body."

The Pegasus, organ of the Khanzhonkov Film Company, wrote as follows:

"F. I. Chaliapin's acting is reminiscent of the technique of the old-time tragedy actors, too much pose, over-emphasized mimicry, calculated slowness of gesture. One feels ashamed for him, as embarrassed as if one were watching a man dancing on stilts."

Chaliapin was inured to their severe and, almost always, unjust criticisms. His finest characterisations were slated; for instance, his Eremka in *The Power of the Enemy*, and Farlaf in *Russlan and Ludmilla*. Though one could disregard these attacks, he himself felt that there was a germ of truth in the articles questioning his merits as a film actor.

He was well aware that he had made a film without any knowledge of the medium. He could not help seeing that the falconers and the Boyars appeared as dressed-up clowns, and that the episode so well conceived by him, as for instance the symbolic finale with the fledgeling—Ivan carefully picks up the little bird that has fallen from the nest, and sets it free—these episodes did not look at all convincing on film. Ivan's general appearance, the bent neck, the old man's features, the walk, the mimicry, all these, so realistic and true in theatre, savoured only of crude, archaic melodrama, artificial and improbable. It was for this very reason that Chaliapin refused the lead in the *Boris Godunov* film. He reconsidered the cinema only when the great silent medium had been transformed by speech and sound. He made a film of *Don Quixote*, but it was not a success. Chaliapin was not fortunate in his film work.

I sat on my balcony one afternoon, ruminating, inventing touching emotions for a hero of one of my routine films. Behind the lowered awning of the next-door balcony I heard not only the rustle of newspapers, but some Chaliapin grunts of disapproval.

He often lowered the awning, and drew his curtains, in spite of the heat; passers by annoyed him. There was always the quest of the curious, trying to catch a glimpse of the famous singer.

Then I noticed a well-built young man, in military uniform, wearing the insignia of a volunteer. The elegant, perfectly fitting tailored tunic, trimmed with blue piping round collar and cuffs, proclaimed the Guardsman, as did the white top to his cap. He put a gloved hand to his cap in a salute and called out: "Feodor Ivanovich."

Chaliapin's chair gave a creak, he looked out, then with conspicuous politeness, and a touch of obsequiousness, greeted his visitor profusely. He invited him to come up.

They sat chatting on the balcony. The young Guardsman was strikingly handsome, perhaps too much so for the modest battle dress he was wearing. A friend of mine had dropped in to see me, and looking towards the balcony at once recognized the young man perched on the balcony railings.

"Do you know who that is?" he asked. "It's Felix Yusupov."

In those days the name Yusupov was almost a household word, not simply because the family were the richest magnates in all Russia, nor because Felix himself had married a Grand Duchess—an unprecedented occurrence in the Czar's family. This slightly effeminate and very elegant young man was known to all as one of a group of people who took part in the killing of Rasputin.

In the spring of 1917 the widow of Alexander III, and the former Grand Dukes and Duchesses, together with their families, were living in their Crimean palaces under house arrest. By order of the Provisional Government the local authorities treated them with courtesy, and it was only the sailors of Sebastopol that took the liberty of checking up on what the Romanovs and their entourage were up to on the shores of the Black Sea. . . .

Yusupov lived with his relatives, and taking advantage of the fact that he wore the uniform of a low-rank volunteer and was not under arrest (probably because he had killed Rasputin) he had come along to visit his old friend Chaliapin.

Chaliapin, a man of the people, with all the fame that had come to him, was nevertheless flattered by the attention paid him by the aristocracy. He was flattered by being asked to sing at the Yusupov house theatre, a little toy theatre on the Myoka, decorated chocolate-box style, and seating not more than a hundred people.

When we asked Chaliapin about the Yusupov visit he became slightly embarrassed. "Yes," he said, "I do know him. And I know the other one, Dimitri, too. I met quite a few of the Romanovs. They, of course, find it curious that Chaliapin, a moujik, has managed to become such a figure. I felt flattered at first, now it doesn't mean very much. But he is a handsome and cultured young man." He paused, then added abruptly, "The three of them murdered Rasputin together. Fell upon him as if he were a horse thief, all three of them. Rather disgusting really, three against one. I've met Rasputin, too. But then whom haven't I met in my lifetime? Once, at Gorky's place, I even played chocks and sticks with Azef [1]. Honest I did. Of course I didn't know who he was at the time. Nor did Gorky know the kind of bird he was. Only later he said to me, 'Now we know, Feodor, with whom you were playing, your partner was Azef.' " Chaliapin laughed over the reminscence.

Suddenly he was alert, staring into the distance. "There's little Vera," he said, waved his walking stick jauntily and set off to meet the little seamstress, an eighteen-year-old dresser at the theatre, who had come to Gurzuf with the film unit.

Society ladies, and the wives of Moscow millionaires, who had fled south from the alarming goings-on in the capital, were shocked, outraged, and positively scandalized by this little affair. How dare Chaliapin prefer this young, blue-eyed, fair-haired, pink-cheeked girl, a mere apprentice-wardrobe mistress, to their own company?

[1] A notorious agent-provocateur.

Here at Gurzuf Chaliapin looked like a lion in repose. People who met him casually marvelled: surely this could not be Chaliapin, that quarrelsome, changeable, insolent egotist, notorious for his sudden outbursts of unbridled rage.

What they really saw was the kind giant from a children's fairy-tale, a courteous, attentive, charming host, though one could fall too much for this simplicity and benevolence. In a relaxed moment the iron hand might shoot through the velvet glove.

He was a magnificent raconteur, and he loved a good listener. He sometimes tended to be repetitious, the same old story over and over again. One of his favourites told of an argument between a Russian and an English shopkeeper—of the who-can-drink-whom-under-the-table variety—and another of the drunken Moscow cabby who sang lustily all the way.

"I asked him why he was so chirpy, and he said he always sang when he was drunk. 'That's funny,' I said, 'when I'm drunk, Vlasov has to do the singing for me.' There is a bass of that name."

The Chaliapin passion for acquiring things astonished people. He bought up valuable paintings, land, houses. And he had sudden fits of greed about money. He would think nothing of a refusal to sing, say for a students' charity concert, demanding unheard of fees, and at the same time of singing all night to friends in a "cabinet particulier" of some expensive restaurant. He would make fishing trips with Gorky, and sing for him alone, with only the sea below and the sky above. Nobody around but Gorky.

He built a school at Malitovka, in Nizhni-Novgorod, and entrusted the care of it to Gorky. In those days it was the only school providing industrial training. He would sing to wounded soldiers at an infirmary he had built, and yet could, with equal ease, refuse the modest request for help to an old friend, with whom he had shared poverty in the old days.

He was calculating and extremely cautious in the drawing up of contracts even to the point of cunning, and would find fault with almost every word, though once he got carried away talking about motor-racing and signed a contract without even reading it.

There was the much publicized incident with Avranek, the conductor, in which he decided to tear up his contract with the Imperial Theatres. He invited several famous lawyers, all specialists in civil law, and discussed with them ways and means of breaking the contract without having to pay damages. When he was requested to show them a copy of it, he discovered he had lost it. Finally Chaliapin asked the lawyers to lunch, and quite forgot his original reason for inviting them. He had a veritable passion for litigation, though this tendency was more often comic than unpleasant, for he usually lost his cases.

There was a curious arbitration case between him and the painter Korovin, an old friend. The question raised was one of principle. Had a painter the right to sell a portrait without the permission of the sitter? Korovin painted Chaliapin and later sold the portrait to a collector. What the outcome of this case was is not known. He had many other conflicts with the painter. Having his country house built he spent hours arguing with the workers, who sensed in him one of their own kind, a curmudgeon, a cunning Russian moujik. Yet people who knew him intimately realized that for Chaliapin it was just a game. He took on landlordly aspects, and enjoyed acting the "niggardly miser". When Korovin and Serov laughed at him, he felt hurt.

But all the stories of Chaliapin are dimmed by the love of him, by the sheer power of his artistic enchantment. The contradictory traits of character, the very chasm separating artist and man, did not exist for us in that Crimean spring. Somehow, without even noticing it, we ourselves became his loyal suite, his fervent admirers, though there were among us artists who had already achieved world fame, and not only in films. Chaliapin enjoyed this adoration, so far away from the capital, disinterested, a genuine tribute to his great talents. Certainly he knew how to be gracious and charming to the young people surrounding him.

On the way from Gurzuf to Suuk-Su you could, until quite recently, see an iron fence and a garden gate. Beyond this fence not a sign of habitation. A lonely path led to a rock towering over a grotto. The land around belonged to a rich woman, Denisova by name, but that rock belonged to Chaliapin. From its great height there was a fine view of the sea and of Ayu-Dag, looking for all the world like a huge bear stretching its head avidly towards the water.

One evening a strange procession, carrying lanterns and candles under glass shades, was making its way towards Chaliapin's rock. They were artists invited by him, with guitar players, local fishermen, and cooks from the pier restaurant. It was already dark when they set out on their way. The park was deserted, there were no onlookers. The night was dark, the moon waning. Round a camp fire at the top of the rock stood four barrels of wine in symmetrical formation. The fire blazed gaily, fanned by a light breeze from the sea. There was a delicious smell of grilling shashlyk and the sound of sizzling fat. The owner of the rock reclined majestically on a carpet, and was in fine spirits. He told us a story of the Volga merchant who went abroad for the first time in his life. Having reached Hamburg the merchant got drunk at the station bar, and in his stupor clambered into a train that in due course landed him back in his native town. Asked what it was like abroad, he would invariably say, "They are awful drunkards in Hamburg, shocking." He himself was the only one drunk that day, in complete and splendid solitude.

We, of course, had heard it all before, but we never failed to laugh, he told it so well, disarmingly, comically, seriously.

I particularly remember a dramatic actress reading us some of Nekrasov's poetry, an extract from *The Russian Women*, with a moving warmth in her delivery.

The fire died down, and the barrels were empty. Guitars filled the air with music. It was quite dark now, with the moon hidden behind a mountain ridge. The candles burned down in their shades, but the stars were bright.

It was a balmy, warm, Crimean night. The cicadas sang their songs, the gentle splashing of waves just audible from the top of the rock. Then suddenly Chaliapin began to sing. He sang us a folk song, "The Little Taper", without accompaniment. How strange and magnificent that Russian song sounded on this southern night, high above the sea. From then it was song after song, he did not wait to be asked, just went on in blessed, joyful exaltation. He sang Glinka's "Doubt", and what bitterness and suffering lay in his rendering of the line, "No, no, I don't believe in these tales of calumny." Such moving melancholy, such reproach in the wonderful, unrepeatable voice that the women present stealthily wiped away their tears.

Even the old and hackneyed song, "Watching the rays of purple sunset", was given a kind of nobility. The rendering had the moan of despair, like a passionate reproach. The shapeless, colourless words of a "cruel" love song were poignant with sincere feeling.

Soon the sun began to rise over the mountain slopes, the stars grew paler, and the sea shimmered. Suddenly Chaliapin was on his feet, a lantern in his hand, now feebly flickering. He held it high above his head as he sang us one of Pushkin's stirring poems.

All this happened one day in May 1917, in Gurzuf, in the Crimea, on a rock that to this very day is still known as Chaliapin's rock.

Chaliapin's Repertoire

After the Tiflis opera season opened on September 28, 1893, presented by Forcatti, the paper *Tiflissky Listok* wrote:

". . . . Quite unexpectedly two newcomers to the opera, Agnivtsev (Amanasro) and Chaliapin (Ramfis), pupils of Usatov, both well known to us for their concert appearances, gave tolerable performances. Both sang and behaved themselves on the stage quite decently, although, of course, one could not expect them to have a thorough knowledge of the theatre nor demand of them a mastery of their vocal or histrionic means."

Chaliapin in his memoirs mentions that, soon after the opening of the opera season in Tiflis, "the whole of the bass repertoire fell on my shoulders." According to the advertisements printed both in *Tiflissky Listok* and *Kavkaz*, in the course of that season (from September 1893 to February 1894), Chaliapin appeared in sixty-two performances. Here are the dates and details:

September 28th—*Aida* (Ramfis)
September 29th—*Faust* (Mesphistopheles)
  October 1st—*The Demon* (Gudal)
  October 3rd—*Aida*
  October 8th—*The Demon*
  October 12th—*I Pagliacci* (Tonio) and the 2nd Act of *Les Huguenots* (Saint-Bris)
  October 15th—*I Pagliacci* and 3rd Act of *Russalka* (The Miller)
  October 16th—*Rigoletto* (Monterone)
  October 17th—*I Pagliacci*
  October 19th—*Rigoletto*
  October 20th—*I Pagliacci* and 3rd Act of *Aida*
  October 22nd—*Eugene Onegin* (Gremin)
  October 24th—*Faust*
  October 27th—*Eugene Onegin*
  October 29th—*Rigoletto*
  October 30th—*The Demon*
  November 3rd—*Aida*
  November 7th—*Rigoletto*
  November 9th—*I Pagliacci*
  November 14th—*I Pagliacci*
  November 17th—*Les Huguenots*
  November 21st—*Les Huguenots*
  November 23rd—*Mignon* (Lothario)

November 24th—*I Pagliacci*
November 29th—*I Pagliacci*
  December 3rd—*Les Huguenots*
  December 4th—*Faust*
  December 8th—*Aida*
December 10th—*Mignon*
December 12th—*I Pagliacci*
December 15th—*Mignon*
December 18th—A scene from *Mignon* and 2nd Act from *Carmen* (Zuniga)
December 19th—*Aida*
  December 21st—*Les Huguenots*
December 22nd—*I Pagliacci*
December 26th—Morning performance (*real* matinée) *The Demon*;
    evening—*Les Huguenots*
  December 27th—(Morning) *Faust*
  December 31st—*Mignon*
    January 9th—*Un Ballo in Maschera* (part unspecified)
    January 14th—*I Pagliacci*
    January 15th—*Aida*
    January 16th—*Rigoletto*
    January 28th—*I Pagliacci*
    January 29th—*Mignon*
  February 2nd—*Fra Diavolo* (Lord Rocburg)
  February 4th—*Faust* and *I Pagliacci* (Chaliapin's benefit performance)
  February 6th—*Russalka* (The Miller)
  February 8th—*Ballo in Maschera*
  February 9th—*Fra Diavolo*
February 11th—*The Queen of Spades* (again, part was not specified but
          Chaliapin probably sang Surin, as there was another
          bass on the programme, Sangursky, who probably
          sang Tomsky)
  February 13th—*The Barber of Seville* (Don Basilio)
  February 16th—*Rigoletto*
  February 18th—*Fra Diavolo*
  February 19th—*I Pagliacci*
  February 22nd—*The Demon*
  February 23rd—*Eugene Onegin*

These appearances did not remain unnoticed by the Tiflis press. On
October 13, 1893, *Tiflissky Listok* had this to say:

"Yesterday, October 12th, the State Theatre for the first time presented
the opera *I Pagliacci*. Chaliapin, who appeared as Tonio, managed his
difficult part quite successfully; we might even say that in the 'prologue'
and in the love scene with Nedda he was positively good—some of the rough
edges in his acting and singing will, no doubt, get smoothed out in the
performances to follow."

The same paper, on October 21, 1893, wrote:

"The second performance of *Rigoletto*, which took place on Tuesday, October 19, was incomparably better than the first . . . Chaliapin was good as Monterone. Apropos of this artist, one cannot help thinking that his constant participation in almost every opera must have an unfavourable effect both on his voice and on his future musical development. Such wasteful, extravagant frittering away of youthful and fresh artistic forces, and the haste and, therefore, inevitably, the carelessness in learning new parts and an insufficient attention paid to perfecting them, can have a very detrimental effect on a young artist only just entering his operatic and theatrical career."

Kavkaz, October 24, 1893: "Duvikler's great success (Ed: as Lensky) was shared by Chaliapin, as Gremin: the acting, manners, singing—all this was completely natural and relaxed, expressive and artistic and the audience responded with tumultuous applause."

Kavkaz, October 26, 1893: ". . . .Chaliapin, as usual, performed Mephistopheles with diabolical daring and, giving in to the insistence of the audience, gave an encore of the serenade from the 3rd Act, although his final laughter on *sol*, as usual left an unpleasant impression."

Tiflissky Listok, February 6, 1894: Reviewing Chaliapin's benefit performance on February 4, when he sang in two operas *I Pagliacci* and *Faust*, wrote: "Having sung these parts on many previous occasions, Chaliapin this time, too, demonstrated his musicality, the power of his voice and his skill in handling it. His acting, as always, was impeccable. The artist was in great form and on the public's insistence, he sang many encores."

At the closing of the opera season, the *Kavkaz* printed a long article by the critic V. Korganov, entitled "Our Opera", in which he gave an assessment of Chaliapin's work, which makes diverting reading:

". . . The appearance of these two young artists, Chaliapin and Agnivtsev, at first encountered prejudice. These singers, owing to their circumstances, have seen practically no real opera, and appearing every evening in different works had to create characters which have long since been created and are well known to the public. The fact that they enjoyed greater success in almost all their roles than other real [*Editor:* V. Korganov probably meant 'experienced'] artists, must be a tribute to their abilities. The first encore of the season was Chaliapin's rendering of the Mephistopheles serenade (second performance).

"Unfortunately, both these singers appear totally satisfied with their success. They merely thanked Mr. Usatov for the lessons he gave them and retired to rest on their laurels, without even a thought of perfecting their roles or of appearing in the theatres in Petersburg or Moscow, where we can find exemplary performances and where every true artist dreams to enter, as a soldier dreams of becoming a general. . . ."

Chaliapin's Opera Repertoire

The repertoire is listed in chronological order. Details of roles, dates and places of first appearances in a particular role in the Provinces, in the two Russian capitals and outside Russia are given in the tables.

Composer	Opera	Role	Date and place of first appearance	
Moniuszko	*Halka*	Stolnik	18.12.1890	Ufa: Semyonov-Samarsky
Verdi	*Il Trovatore*	Fernando	8.2.1891	Ufa: Semyonov-Samarsky
Verstovsky	*Askold's Tomb*	Stranger	3.3.1891	Ufa: Semyonov-Samarsky
			21.12.1897	Moscow: Russian Private Opera
Lysenko	*Natalka-Poltavka*	Pyotr	Summer 1892	Baku: Derkach's
Bellini	*Norma*	Oroveso	Summer 1893	Batum: Klyucharev's
Halévy	*La Juive*	The Cardinal	Summer 1893	Batum: Klyucharev's
Gounod	*Faust*	Valentin	1893	Kutaisi: Klyucharev's
			11.1.1905	Moscow: Bolshoy Theatre
Verdi	*Aida*	Ramfis	28.9.1893	Tiflis: Forcatti's
Gounod	*Faust*	Mephistopheles	29.9.1893	Tiflis: Forcatti's
			18.9.1894	Petersburg: Panayev's
			5.4.1895	(debut) Petersburg: Mariinsky Theatre
			18.5.1896	Nizhni-Novgorod: Russian Private Opera
			end Sept. 1896	Moscow: Russian Private Opera
			24.9.1899	Moscow: Bolshoy Theatre
			8.3.1904	Milan: La Scala
Rubinstein	*The Demon*	Gudal	1.10.1893	Tiflis: Forcatti's
			24.11.1894	Petersburg: Panayev's
			27.6.1896	Nizhni-Novgorod: Russian Private Opera
Leoncavallo	*I Pagliacci*	Tonio	12.10.1893	Tiflis: Forcatti's
			21.12.1905	Petersburg: Mariinsky Theatre
			1919	Moscow: "Hermitage" Hall of Mirrors
Verdi	*Rigoletto*	Monterone	16.10.1893	Tiflis: Forcatti's
Tchaikovsky	*Eugene Onegin*	Prince Gremin	22.10.1893	Tiflis: Forcatti's
			2.6.1896	Nizhni-Novgorod: Russian Private Opera
			1896/97 season	Moscow: Russian Private Opera
			29.1.1902	Moscow: Bolshoy Theatre
Meyerbeer	*Les Huguenots*	Saint-Bris	17.11.1893	Tiflis: Forcatti's
			11.1.1905	Moscow: Bolshoy Theatre
Thomas	*Mignon*	Lothario	23.11.1893	Tiflis: Forcatti's
			1896	Moscow: Russian Private Opera
Bizet	*Carmen*	Capt. Zuniga	18.12.1893	Tiflis: Forcatti's
			19.4.1895 (debut)	Petersburg: Mariinsky Theatre
Verdi	*Un Ballo in Maschera* [1]		9.1.1894	Tiflis: Forcatti's

[1] Chaliapin's name is listed among those taking part in the production, without specifying the part; he could have sung one of the two conspirators Sam or Tom, or the sailor Silvano.

Composer	Opera	Role	Date and place of first appearance	
Auber	*Fra Diavolo*	Lord Cockburn (Rocburg)	2.2.1894	Tiflis: Forcatti's
Dargomyzhsky	*Russalka*	The Miller	6.2.1893	Tiflis: Forcatti's
			30.4.1896	Petersburg: Mariinsky Theatre
			16.6.1896	Nizhni-Novgorod: Russian Private Opera
			29.9.1896	Moscow: Russian Private Opera
			12.9.1900	Moscow: Bolshoy Theatre
			25.3.1909	Monte Carlo
Tchaikovsky	*The Queen of Spades*	Tomsky	11.2.1894	Tiflis: Forcatti's
			26.10.1940	Moscow: Bolshoy Theatre
Rossini	*Il Barbiere di Siviglia*	Don Basilio	13.2.1894	Tiflis: Forcatti's
			13.4.1907	Berlin: Raoul Ginsburg's tour
			2.10.1912	Petersburg: Mariinsky Theatre
			18.10.1913	Moscow: Bolshoy Theatre La Scala, Milan
Offenbach	*The Tales of Hoffmann*	Dr. Miracle	24.7.1894	Petersburg: "Arcadia"
Meyerbeer	*Robert le Diable*	Bertram	17.10.1894	Petersburg: Panayev's
Glinka	*Russlan and Ludmilla*	Russlan	17.4.1895	Petersburg: Mariinsky Theatre
Cimarosa	*Il Matrimonio Segreto*	Robinson	17.9.1895	Petersburg: Mariinsky Theatre
Rimsky-Korsakov	*Christmas Eve*	Panas	1.12.1895	Petersburg: Mariinsky Theatre
Massenet	*Werther*	The Judge	5.4.1896	Petersburg: Mariinsky Theatre
Napravnik	*Dubrovsky*	Pr. Vereysky	1895/96 season	Petersburg: Mariinsky Theatre
Dargomyzhsky	*Russalka*	Match-maker	April 1896	Petersburg: Mariinsky Theatre
Napravnik	*Dubrovsky*	Andrey Dubrovsky	21.4.1896	Petersburg: Mariinsky Theatre
			18.10.1899	Moscow: Bolshoy Theatre
Borodin	*Prince Igor*	Galitsky	25.4.1896	Petersburg: Mariinsky Theatre
			15.11.1896	Moscow: Russian Private Opera
			5.11.1899	Moscow: Bolshoy Theatre
			9.5.1909	Paris: Chatelet (Diaghilev)
			8.6.1914	London: Drury Lane
Serov	*Rogneda*	Prince Vladimir	26.10.1896	Petersburg: Mariinsky Theatre
Glinka	*Ivan Susanin (A Life for the Czar)*	Susanin	14.5.1896	Nizhni-Novgorod: Russian Private Opera
			22.9.1896	Moscow: Russian Private Opera
			8.10.1899	Moscow: Bolshoy Theatre
			22.12.1899	Petersburg: Mariinsky Theatre
Saint-Saëns	*Samson et Dalila*	The Old Jew	30.6.1896	Nizhni-Novgorod: Russian Private Opera
			12.10.1897	Moscow: Russian Private Opera
Delibes	*Lakmé*	Nilakantha	5.11.1896	Moscow: Russian Private Opera
			9.11.1899	Moscow: Bolshoy Theatre
Serov	*Rogneda*	Wanderer	31.10.1896	Moscow: Russian Private Opera
			30.11.1899	Moscow: Bolshoy Theatre
Rimsky-Korsakov	*The Maid of Pskov*	Ivan the Terrible	12.12.1896	Moscow: Russian Private Opera

Composer	Opera	Role	Date and place of first appearance	
Rimsky-Korsakov	*The Maid of Pskov*	Ivan the Terrible	10.10.1901	Moscow: Bolshoy Theatre
			28.10.1903	Petersburg: Mariinsky Theatre
			25.5.1909	Paris: Chatelet (Diaghilev)
			8.7.1913	London: Drury Lane
Puccini	*La Bohème*	Colline	12.1.1897	Moscow: Russian Private Opera
Tchaikovsky	*The Oprichnik*	Prince Vyazminsky	23.1.1897	Moscow: Russian Private Opera
			21.10.1899	Moscow: Bolshoy Theatre
			18.1.1900	Petersburg: Mariinsky Theatre
Mussorgsky	*Khovanshchina*	Dositheus	12.11.1897	Moscow: Russian Private Opera
			7.11.1911	Petersburg: Mariinsky Theatre
			12.12.1912	Moscow: Bolshoy Theatre
			5.6.1913	Paris: Théâtre des Champs Elysées
			1.7.1913	London: Drury Lane
			18.4.1928	Philadelphia
Rimsky-Korsakov	*Sadko*	The Varangian Guest	30.12.1897	Moscow: Russian Private Opera
			27.10.1906	Moscow: Bolshoy Theatre
Rimsky-Korsakov	*A May Night*	The Headman	30.1.1898	Moscow: Russian Private Opera
			26.6.1914	London: Drury Lane
Serov	*Judith*	Holofernes	23.11.1898	Moscow: Russian Private Opera
			4.2.1900	Moscow: Bolshoy Theatre
			21.9.1907	Petersburg: Mariinsky Theatre
			7.6.1909	Paris: Châtelet (Diaghilev)
Rimsky-Korsakov	*Mozart and Salieri*	Salieri	25.11.1898	Moscow: Russian Private Opera
			11.11.1901	Moscow: Bolshoy Theatre
			21.12.1905	Petersburg: Mariinsky Theatre
Mussorgsky	*Boris Godunov*	Boris	7.12.1898	Moscow: Russian Private Opera
			13.4.1901	Moscow: Bolshoy Theatre
			9.11.1904	Petersburg: Mariinsky Theatre
			19.5.1908	Paris, Grand Opéra (Diaghilev)
			24.6.1913 (début)	London: Drury Lane
			1901 and 1904	Milan: La Scala
			1907	New York Metropolitan
Mussorgsky	*Boris Godunov*	Varlaam	13.2.1899	Moscow: Russian Private Opera
			2.2.1902	Moscow: Bolshoy Theatre
Serova, V.	*Ilya Muromets*	Ilya	22.2.1899	Moscow: Russian Private Opera
Rachmaninov	*Aleko*	Aleko	27.5.1899	Petersburg: Tavrichesky Palace[1]
			21.9.1903	Moscow: Bolshoy Theatre
Koreshchenko	*The Ice Palace*	Biron	7.11.1900	Moscow: Bolshoy Theatre
Cui	*Angelo*	Haleofa	4.1.1901	Moscow: Bolshoy Theatre
Glinka	*Russlan and Ludmilla*	Farlaf	30.1.1901	Moscow: Bolshoy Theatre
			10.12.1905	Petersburg: Mariinsky Theatre
			16.3.1901	Milan: La Scala
Boito	*Mefistofele*	Mefistofele	3.12.1902	Moscow: Bolshoy Theatre
			18.12.1902	Petersburg: Mariinsky Theatre

[1] Concert performance to mark 100th anniversary of Pushkin's birth.

Composer	Opera	Role	Date and place of first appearance	
Cui	*Feast in the Time of the Plague*	Priest	11.11.1901	Moscow: Bolshoy Theatre
Serov	*Power of the Enemy*	Eremka	24.9.1901	Moscow: Bolshoy Theatre
			7.11.1920	Petrograd: Mariinsky Theatre
Grechaninov	*Dobrynya Nikitich*	Dobrynya	14.10.1903	Moscow: Bolshoy Theatre
Rubinstein	*The Demon*	The Demon	16.1.1904	Moscow: Bolshoy Theatre
			30.12.1905	Petersburg: Mariinsky Theatre
			24.3.1906	Monte Carlo[1]
Plannquette	*Les Cloches de Corneville*	Gaspar	31.1.1904	Petersburg: Mariinsky Theatre
Verdi	*Don Carlos*	King Philip II	9.4.1907	Berlin (Ginsburg's tour)
			10.2.1917	Moscow: Bolshoy Theatre
			1917	Petrograd: People's Theatre
Mozart	*Don Giovanni*	Leporello	23.1.1908	New York Metropolitan
Ginsburg	*The Old Eagle*	Khan Asvab	26.6.1909	Monte Carlo (Ginsburg's)
Massenet	*Don Quixote*	Don Quixote	19.2.1910	Monte Carlo (Ginsburg's)
			12.11.1910	Moscow: Bolshoy Theatre
			1918–19 season	Petrograd: Mariinsky Theatre
Ginsburg	*Ivan the Terrible*	Ivan	2.3.1911	Monte Carlo (Ginsburg's)
Borodin	*Prince Igor*	Konchak	9.6.1914	London: Drury Lane

[1] In Monte Carlo the opera was sung in Italian with Sigrid Arnoldson, the Swedish soprano, as Tamara.

Bibliography

In addition to examining the original copy of the autobiography, written in Gorky's own hand, the following have been consulted and drawn upon:

Chaliapin (2 vols.), Iskusstvo, Moscow, 1957–8.

Chaliapin and Russian Artists, A. Raskin, Iskusstvo, 1963.

The Pride of Russia. Maxim Gorky and Feodor Chaliapin, Korn, Odessa, 1903.

The Diary of A. P. Ostroumov-Lebedev, MS., Saltykov-Shchedrin State Library, Folio 75, pp. 59–63.

Feodor Ivanovich Chaliapin, I. Yankovsky, *Muzgis*, 1951.

Chaliapin and Russian Operatic Culture, Yankovsky, Iskusstvo, 1947.

"About Art and Myself", F. I. Chaliapin, essay published in *Birzheviye Vedomosti*, St. Petersburg, December 16, 1913, No. 13909. (Lenin State Library, Moscow.)

"Chaliapin and the Volga Boatmen", Irina Chaliapina, published in *River Transport*, March 20, 1951.

"A Letter to Chaliapin", Irina Chaliapina, published in *Ogonyok*, No. 20, 1954.

"Hurok on Chaliapin", article in *Sovietskaya Muzyka*, No. 2, 1963. (Lenin State Library.)

The Memoirs of V. A. Telyakovsky, Academia, Leningrad, 1927.

The Near and the Distant, N. N. Khodotov, *Academia*, Leningrad, 1932.

"About Music and Musicians", G. O. Khubov, *Sovietskaya Muzyka*, 1950.

"The Fourth Don Quixote", N. K. Cherkasov, *Sovietsky Pisatel*, 1958.

Memoirs of L. L. Leonidov, Iskusstvo, 1960.

Reminiscences of I. I. Brodsky, Moscow edition, 1959.

Meetings and Impressions, A. Golovin, Iskusstvo, 1960.

Mussorgsky and Chaliapin, V. Karatygin, from the archives of the Kirov State Theatre of Opera and Ballet, Petrograd, 1–22.

Letters, Documents, Reminiscences, I. I. Levitan, Iskusstvo, 1956.

Articles on Chaliapin, V. V. Stassov, *Muzgis*, 1953.

Chaliapin Drawings, O. Eisenshtat, *Teatr*, 1955. (Bakhrushin Museum, Moscow.)

Chaliapin, Lev Nikulin, Iskusstvo, 1951.

"About Chaliapin", Ivan Bunin, *Don*, No. 10, 1957.

Gorky Readings, an anthology, 1949–59, published by the U.S.S.R. Academy of Sciences, 1954. (Central State Archives of Literature and Art, Moscow.)

"F. Chaliapin", E. Grosheva, *Sovietskaya Muzyka*, No. 8, 1948.

Reminiscences about Russian Artists, V. S. Mamontov, published by U.S.S.R. Arts Academy, 1950. (Lenin State Library.)

Letters to Artists, I. E. Repin, Iskusstvo, 1952.

Correspondence with Stassov, Repin, Iskusstvo, 1950.

F. I. Chaliapin, Life and Artistic Career, P. M. Sivkov, St. Petersburg, 1908. (Lenin Library.)

Chaliapin in Africa, N. A. Sokolov, Moscow, 1914. (Lenin Library.)

"Chaliapin Drawings", V. G. Solovyova, *Teatralnoye Nasledstvo*, published by Iskusstvo, Moscow, 1956.

"Chaliapin's Last Role", Lev Nikulin, *Ogonyok*, No. 39, September 30, 1945, (page 13).

F. I. Chaliapin, Mask and Soul, Russian edition, Iskusstvo, 1957.

Notes on Persons Mentioned

Andreyev, Leonid Nikolayevich (1871–1919). Writer, dramatist, theatre critic (pseudonym James Lynch), member of the writers' circle ("Wednesday") headed by Gorky, where he met and made friends with Chaliapin.

Andreyev, Vassily V. (1861–1918). Musician, balalaika virtuoso, organiser of the first orchestra of Russian national instruments, and a friend who helped Chaliapin a great deal in his work during his early career.

Bunin, Ivan Alexeyevich (1870–1953). Writer, poet, and translator of the literary circle ("Wednesday") founded by Gorky. Emigrated in 1917. He was elected fellow of the Russian Academy in 1909, was awarded the Pushkin Prize for his excellent translation of Longfellow's *Hiawatha*, and wrote short stories, essays, and verse. One of his best known works is *The Gentleman from San Francisco* (1915). He also wrote *Mitya's Love*, *The Village*, *The Life of Arsenyev*, and *Sukhodol*, a powerful picture of disintegrating gentry.

Chirikov, Evgeny Nikolayevich (1864–1932). Writer, dramatist, and member of the "Wednesday" literary circle.

Cooper, Emil Albertovich (1877–1960). Russian conductor: Odessa, Kiev, 1900; Zimin Opera, Moscow, 1904; Drury Lane, 1914; Russian Opera seasons, Paris and London; Chicago Opera, 1929–31; and New York Metropolitan, 1944–50, where he introduced *Peter Grimes* and *Khovanshchina*.

Dal Monte, Toti (b. Antonietta Meneghel, 1898). One of the last great Italian divas, soprano; engaged by Toscanini for La Scala in 1922 to sing Gilda in *Rigoletto*; and sang with Chaliapin at La Scala.

Dalsky (Neyelov), Mamont Victorovich (1865–1919). Actor, tragedian, and member of the Alexandrinsky Theatre company, 1890–1900. Played an important part in the young Chaliapin's artistic development.

Doroshevich, Vlas Mikhailovich (1864–1922). Reactionary journalist, theatre critic, writer, author of articles on Chaliapin, and editor of *Russkoye Slovo*.

Fedotova, Glikeriya Nikolayevna (1845–1925). Actress, from 1862 to 1905 with the Maly Theatre in Moscow. An outstanding stage personality.

Filippov, Tertiy Ivanovich (1826–99). Prominent official, writer and collector of Russian folk songs.

Franci, Benvenuto (b. 1891). Italian bass-baritone. Leading baritone in Rome Opera, 1928–49, and at La Scala from 1923; created Manuel in Boito's *Nero*; and sang with Chaliapin at La Scala in *The Barber of Seville*.

Golovin, Alexander Yakovlevich (1863–1930). Painter, theatrical decor artist, and friend of Chaliapin. Painted portraits of Chaliapin in the parts of Holofernes, the Demon, Boris Godunov, Mephistopheles, Mefistofele, and Farlaf.

Goncharov, Ivan Alexandrovich (1812–91). Russian writer, novelist. His works include *Frigate "Pallas"*, *A Common Story*, *The Precipice*, and the classic, *Oblomov*.

Grechaninov, Alexander Tikhonovich (1864–1956). Russian composer. He studied pianoforte with Safonov at Moscow Conservatoire and composition with Rimsky-Korsakov at St. Petersburg. After the revolution he went to the U.S.A. He has written much ecclesiastical music: two complete liturgies, three masses, several motets, and many songs. Very little of his work has been published.

Karamzin, Nikolai Mikhailovich (1766–1826). Russian writer and historian. His works include *Letters of a Russian Traveller, Poor Liza*, and *A History of the Russian State* in 12 volumes, a work of both great literary merit and scholarship.

Khodotov, Nikolai Nikolayevich (1878–1932). Actor of the Alexandrinsky Theatre, author of the book *The Near and the Distant*, and artist emeritus of the R.S.F.S.R.

Koreshchenko, Arseny Nikolayevich (1870–1921). Composer, pianist, conductor, and composer of the opera *The Ice Palace*.

Korganov, Vassily Davydovich (1865–1934). Music critic and historian, author of works on Beethoven and Mozart. He reviewed productions of the Tiflis Opera, including those in which Chaliapin took part.

Korovin, Konstantin Alexeyevich (1861–1939). Painter, friend of Chaliapin. Designed the decor for many of Chaliapin's operas, and for the Russian Private Opera, the Bolshoy Theatre, the Mariinsky Theatre, Grand Opera, etc. He painted many famous portraits of Chaliapin.

Lyubimov, Vladimir Nikolayevich (d. 1902). Chief director of the Tiflis Opera, 1892–4.

Mamonov, Yakov Ivanovich. A fair entertainer in Kazan during Chaliapin's childhood. He was Yashka the Clown.

Mamontov, Savva Ivanovich (1841–1919). Patron of the arts, dramatist, producer, sculptor, leading Russian industrialist, and founder (1885) of the Russian Private Opera. He played a vital part in Chaliapin's artistic development and career.

Masini, Angelo (1844–1926). Italian tenor, chosen by Verdi for the tenor role in the *Requiem*, which he sang in London, Paris, and Vienna, conducted by the composer. Appeared in St. Petersburg and Moscow. Verdi offered to write an extended aria for him if he would create the role of Fenton in *Falstaff*, but Masini refused.

Melnikov, Ivan Alexandrovich (1832–1906). Russian baritone, who made his debut in St. Petersburg in 1867. He created the title roles in *Boris Godunov, The Demon*, and *Prince Igor*; also created Don Juan in *The Stone Guest*, and Tokmakov in *Ivan the Terrible*. Retired in 1890.

Melnikov, Pyotr Ivanovich. Son of the above. Producer of Russian Private Opera, and, from 1909, at the Mariinsky Theatre.

Napravnik, Eduard Franzevich (1839–1916). Conductor and composer of Czech birth. He was Lyadov's assistant at the Imperial Theatres, and succeeded him as chief conductor in 1869. A brilliant musician and administrator, he greatly raised the standard of the Imperial Opera, and became famous for his attention to the skill and welfare of the orchestra. He conducted over 4,000 performances, and his first nights included *The Stone Guest, Boris Godunov*, and *The Maid of Pskov*, and three Tchaikovsky operas—*The Oprichnik* (*Life-guard* [of Ivan the Terrible]), *Vakula the Smith*, and *The Maid of Orleans*. Tchaikovsky dedicated the last named to Napravnik.

Nemirovich-Danchenko, Vladimir Ivanovich (1858–1943). Producer, dramatist, professor, and People's Artist of the U.S.S.R. With Stanislavsky he founded the Moscow Arts Theatre.

Nikish, Artur (1855–1922). Hungarian conductor. Originally a violinist, he played in the orchestra when Wagner conducted Beethoven's Ninth Symphony at the laying of Bayreuth's foundation stone. He was director of the Budapest Opera, 1893–5, and frequently appeared in Russia at the Bolshoy and Mariinsky Theatres. His pupils included Albert Coates.

Nikulin, Lev Veniaminovich (b. 1891). Soviet writer and author of the book *F. I. Chaliapin.*

Ostroukhov, Ilya Semyonovich (1858–1929). Landscape painter, and Chaliapin's friend.

Pchelnikov, Pavel Mikhailovich. Manager of the Moscow office of the Imperial Theatres.

Petrov, Osip Afanasyevich (1807–78). Bass, and a pupil of Glinka. From 1830 he was an artist of the St. Petersburg Opera. He was the first to sing the roles of Ivan Susanin, Farlaf, the Miller, Varlaam, etc.

Pokhitonov, Daniil Ilyich (b. 1878). Conductor at the Mariinsky Theatre, teacher, and People's Artist of the R.S.F.S.R.

Pugno, Raoul (1852–1914). French pianist, organist, composer, professor at the Paris Conservatoire, and friend of Chaliapin.

Renaud, Maurice (1861–1933). French baritone, Paris Opera, 1890–1902. In Paris he was the first Telramund and Chorèbe, and the first Méphistophélès in Berlioz's *La Damnation de Faust.* He was also with the Raoul Ginsburg company in Berlin.

Repin, Ilya Efimovich (1844–1930). Famous Russian painter. His portrait of Chaliapin remained unfinished—he painted a new picture over it—and the only record of that painting is the photograph reproduced in this book, No. 65.

Rossi, Ernesto (1829–96). Italian actor, tragedian, especially famous for his Shakespearean parts.

Safonov, Vasily Ilyich (1852–1918). Pianist, conductor, professor and director (1889–1905) of the Moscow Conservatoire.

Schipa, Tito (b. 1889). Italian tenor. He was chosen by Toscanini for the roles of Alfredo and Fenton during the 1915 season at Dal Verme, Milan. He created Ruggiero in Puccini's *La Rondine,* Monte Carlo, 1917. He appeared in opera in the U.S.A. and at La Scala until 1950, and was with Chaliapin in the La Scala production of *The Barber of Seville,* and in Buenos Aires in 1928.

Semyonov-Samarsky (Rosenberg), alias *Samarsky-Semyonov, Semyon Yakovlevich* (d. 1912). Singer, impresario, and Chaliapin's first employer in opera.

Serov, Alexander Nikolayevich (1820–71). Composer and critic. His opera *Judith,* after Wagner, was a great success and was followed by *Rogneda.* At his own request *The Power of Evil* was finished by Solovyev; and *Christmas Eve Revels* remained unfinished.

Serov, Valentin Alexandrovich (1865–1911). Son of A. N. Serov, painter, friend of Chaliapin. He painted Chaliapin many times.

Shaporin, Yury Alexandrovich (b. 1889). Russian composer of the opera *The Decembrists,* secretary of the Soviet Composers' Union, professor of the Moscow Conservatoire, and People's Artist of the U.S.S.R.

Sharonov, Vasily Semyonovich (d. 1929). Bass, from 1894 with the Mariinsky Theatre company.

Siloti, Alexander Ilyich (1863–1945). Rachmaninov's cousin, pianist, conductor, and organiser of symphony concerts in St. Petersburg. On his initiative and with the participation of Albert Coates, Chaliapin's "The Song of the Revolution" (1917) was orchestrated and arranged for a choir—and sung by Chaliapin at a concert-meeting of the Preobrazhensky Regiment at the Mariinsky Theatre.

Skitalets (Petrov), Stepan Gavrilovich (1868–1942). Writer, poet, member of the "Wednesday" literary circle, and closely associated with the Znaniye Publishing House.

Sobinov, Leonid Vitalyevich (1872–1934). Tenor. From 1897 with the Bolshoy Theatre. Sang with great success in St. Petersburg, after his debut in Moscow in 1894. He excelled as Lensky, Romeo, Lohengrin, and Orfeo.

Stassov, Dmitry Vasilyevich (1828–1918). Lawyer, one of the founders of the St. Petersburg Conservatoire and Russian Music Society, and brother of V. V. Stassov.

Stassov, Vladimir Vasilyevich (1824–1906). Russian art historian, theatre and music critic, archaeologist, and supporter of the "Mighty Handful". His influence on the development of Russian national opera was very great and his opinion was valued by all his contemporaries. He was the author of important studies of Glinka, Mussorgsky, Borodin, Cui, and Rimsky-Korsakov.

Svyatopolk-Mirsky, Prince Pyotr Dmitryevich (1857–1914). Statesman. Minister of the Interior, 1904–5.

Tamagno, Francesco (1850–1905). Italian tenor, at La Scala from 1877. He created the title role in Verdi's *Otello*. He was considered the greatest *tenore di forza* of his time, and appeared in Russia with great acclaim, as everywhere else. Retired in 1902.

Taneyev, Sergei Ivanovich (1856–1915). Composer, pianist, and director of the Moscow Conservatoire.

Tarasova, Alla Konstantinovna (b. 1898). Dramatic actress, from 1916 with the Moscow Arts Theatre. People's Artist of the U.S.S.R. She was seen in London in the last production of *The Cherry Orchard* by the Moscow Arts Theatre during the 1965 International Theatre Season at the Aldwych Theatre.

Teleshov, Nikolai Dmitryevich (1867–1957). Writer, organiser of the "Wednesday" literary circle, and, towards the end of his life, director of the Moscow Arts Theatre Museum.

Tereshchenko, Mikhail Ivanovich (b. 1888). Landowner and owner of sugar refineries. High official in the administration of the Imperial Theatres, 1911–12. In 1917, first minister of finance, then minister for foreign affairs in the Provisional Government. Emigrated after the revolution.

Tikhonov (Serebrov), Alexander Nikolayevich (1880–1956). Writer, editor of the journal *Letopis* (Chronicle), published by Gorky, and author of *Times and People*.

Truffi, Iosif Antonovich (1850–1925). Conductor. He worked with Chaliapin in Tiflis, then in the Paneyev Theatre in St. Petersburg, and, lastly, in Russian Private Opera.

Tsereteli, Prince A. A. Opera impresario. Emigrated after 1917.

Volkonsky, Prince Sergei Mikhailovich (b. 1860). Director of Imperial Theatres, 1899–1901.

Vrubel, Mikhail Alexandrovich (1856–1910). Painter. He worked a great deal for the Russian Private Opera, in particular on the decor of *Mozart and Salieri*, produced in 1898 with Chaliapin. His painting of the Demon greatly influenced Chaliapin's creation of the character in Rubenstein's opera of that name.

Yashka the Clown. See *Mamonov, Yakov Ivanovich.*

Yuon, Konstantin Feodorovich (1875–1958). Painter, stage designer, member of the U.S.S.R. Academy of Arts, and People's Artist of the U.S.S.R.

Zimbalist, Yefrem Alexandrovich (b. 1889). Russian violin virtuoso, living in the U.S.A.

Index